BCS GLOSSARY OF COMPU

Bangor Grammar School
Text Book Control

Student Name	Form Class	Academic year
Zak Martin		

BCS, THE CHARTERED INSTITUTE FOR IT

BCS, The Chartered Institute for IT champions the global IT profession and the interests of individuals engaged in that profession for the benefit of all. We promote wider social and economic progress through the advancement of information technology, science and practice. We bring together industry, academics, practitioners and government to share knowledge, promote new thinking, inform the design of new curricula, shape public policy and inform the public.

Our vision is to be a world-class organisation for IT. Our 70,000 strong membership includes practitioners, businesses, academics and students in the UK and internationally. We deliver a range of professional development tools for practitioners and employees. A leading IT qualification body, we offer a range of widely recognised qualifications.

Further Information

BCS, The Chartered Institute for IT,
First Floor, Block D,
North Star House, North Star Avenue,
Swindon, SN2 1FA, United Kingdom.
T +44 (0) 1793 417 424
F +44 (0) 1793 417 444
www.bcs.org/contact

http://shop.bcs.org/

BCS GLOSSARY OF COMPUTING
14th edition

Edited by the BCS Academy Glossary Working Party

Members of the Working Party
Arnold Burdett
Dan Bowen
Aline Cumming
David Fuller
Frank Hurvid
Adrian Jackson
Percy Mett
Thomas Ng
Marianne Scheer
Alfred Vella
John Woollard

Former members of the Working Party (whose work is included in this edition):
Diana Burkhardt, Diana Butler, Alan Hunter, Brian Jackson, John Jaworski,
Laurie Keller, Penny Patterson, Tim Reeve, Graham Rogers, Hazel Shaw, John
Southall

1st edition, BCS © 1977 BCS, reprinted 1978, 1978
2nd edition, BCS © 1979 BCS, reprinted 1980
3rd edition, BCS © 1982 BCS
4th edition, CUP & BISL © 1984 BISL, reprinted 1985, 1986
5th edition, CUP & BISL © BISL
6th edition, CUP & BISL © BISL
7th edition, Pitmans/Longmans © 1991 BISL, reprinted 1993, 1994
8th edition, Longmans © 1995 BISL, reprinted 1996, 1997
9th edition, Addison Wesley Longmans © 1998 BISL
10th edition, Pearson Education © 2002 BCS
11th edition, Pearson Education © 2005 BCS, reprinted 2005
12th edition, BCS © 2008 BCS
13th edition © 2013 BCS Learning and Development Limited
14th edition © 2016 BCS Learning and Development Limited

Published by BCS Learning and Development Limited, a wholly owned subsidiary of BCS, The Chartered Institute for IT, First Floor, Block D, North Star House, North Star Avenue, Swindon, SN2 1FA, UK.
www.bcs.org

ISBN: 978-1-78017-326-9
PDF ISBN: 978-1-78017-327-6
ePUB ISBN: 978-1-78017-328-3
Kindle ISBN: 978-1-78017-329-0

British Cataloguing in Publication Data.
A CIP catalogue record for this book is available at the British Library.

Disclaimer:
The views expressed in this book are of the author(s) and do not necessarily reflect the views of BCS Learning and Development Ltd except where explicitly stated as such.

Although every care has been taken by the authors and BCS Learning and Development Ltd in the preparation of the publication, no warranty is given by the authors or BCS Learning and Development Ltd as publisher as to the accuracy or completeness of the information contained within it and neither the authors nor BCS Learning and Development Ltd shall be responsible or liable for any loss or damage whatsoever arising by virtue of such information or any instructions or advice contained within this publication or by any of the aforementioned.

BCS books are available at special quantity discounts to use as premiums and sales promotions, or for use in corporate training programmes. Please visit our Contact Us page at www.bcs.org/contact

Typeset by Lapiz Digital Services, Chennai, India.

We dedicate this book to John Southall.

John was a member of the BCS staff and Registrar. He was instrumental in forming the Working Party of BCS Schools Committee members in the 1970s that started the small *Glossary*, which has evolved over the years into the current edition. John's wit, wide knowledge of computer terminology and of BCS, and his attention to detail, made him a strong support for those who follow on. He was working on the thirteenth edition when he died.

CONTENTS

FIGURES AND TABLES

INTRODUCTION

This *Glossary*, which contains over 3400 terms, provides not only a comprehensive definition of each term, but also sufficient additional material to enable the reader to understand the importance of the term, how to use it appropriately and its relation to other terms used in the same area of computing. To this end, terms are gathered into six parts, describing how computer systems are used, what they are made of, how they are developed and how computers work. A seventh part consists of reference material.

Who is the *Glossary* aimed at?

One of the principal aims of the *Glossary* is meeting the needs of pupils and students who follow courses leading to examinations in schools and colleges at a variety of levels. The authors attempt to ensure that the *Glossary* reflects developments in the National Curriculum for England and Wales, GCSE and A-level specifications, the Scottish Curriculum, the Northern Ireland system and related vocational qualifications.

It is a definitive reference source, mentioned in examination syllabuses. The content has increasingly found wide acceptance in universities and colleges for foundation courses and ESL students, as well as induction sessions and training courses. It is used in support of the European Computer Driving Licence (ECDL) and other training courses, within government departments and industry generally. The *Glossary* has also proved popular with home-based computer users.

How are the individual terms decided on?

BCS Glossary Working Party members continuously monitor relevant new terms and changes in usage. These are added when it is felt that they have become sufficiently established and widespread. Some terms that are no longer in common use are omitted.

The *Glossary* provides definitions that cover the use of terms in the context of very large computer systems as well as PCs and mobile devices. Although large computer systems may be outside the experience of many users, they are likely to encounter consequences of the use of such systems. It should be noted that some terms are included that have a different meaning in a computing environment to that in use in other subjects.

What are the origins of the Glossary?

The *Glossary* was first published over 40 years ago and has developed from a tiny listing to its current content. In 1974, the British Computer Society was invited by the Regional Examining Boards for the Certificate of Secondary Education to produce a standardised list of terms for use in computer studies courses, examination syllabuses and for their own reference. The Schools Committee of BCS set up a Working Party with a remit to produce a 'one-off' document containing about 100 terms. At the time, there was only one A-level computing examination and a small number of examinations for 16 year olds. Schools involved in computer studies relied on batch processing, preparing and sending their punched cards to university computing centres. Very few had access to an online terminal connecting to the local authority computer. Microcomputers were virtually unknown in schools. At this time almost all sources of computing expertise were inventing their own vocabulary.

Teachers soon requested that the *Glossary* be made available to pupils. At the end of 1974 work began on the first 'public' edition. This edition appeared in 1977, containing approximately 430 terms of which 260 were defined. Given that the target audience was the 14–16-year-old pupil, it was decided that, as far as possible without compromising technical accuracy, simple English should be used in the explanation of the term – an objective still retained wherever possible.

The popularity of the first BCS *Glossary* resulted in several reprints and the demand for further editions. These latter editions included new terms that were appearing almost daily. The publication was required to keep pace with the rapid development of technology and with the increasing use of computers in education. It has been the practice of BCS, The Chartered Institute for IT, to update the *Glossary* approximately every three years.

The Working Party has a changing membership drawing on a wide range of expertise from the computing community.

Development

Early editions of the *Glossary* were lists of defined terms and hence resembled a dictionary. Over many editions the Working Party steered the *Glossary* to its present themed and structured layout.

ACKNOWLEDGEMENTS

The Working Party has appreciated the help it has received from members of BCS and, in particular, Computing At School (part of the BCS Academy), for their comments and suggestions about material to include in this edition.

The Working Party also welcomes offers from teachers willing to involve their pupils in a review of this edition and would like to express its thanks to those who have already commented, criticised and made helpful suggestions.

Please send comments by post to: BCS, The Chartered Institute for IT, Publishing Department, First Floor, Block D, North Star House, North Star Avenue, Swindon, SN2 1FA, UK. www.bcs.org/contact   publishing@bcs.uk

Alternatively contact any member of the Working Party through BCS.

DISCLAIMER

Neither BCS, The Chartered Institute for IT, nor contributors to the *Glossary* shall have any responsibility for loss suffered as a result of reliance on the *Glossary*, and readers should take legal advice on the application of the terms covered particularly in Section B11, which is intended as an aid to understanding computer security. The *Glossary* is not a definitive statement of the meaning of terms.

HOW TO USE THIS GLOSSARY

The only place you will find a full alphabetical list of all the terms covered in the *Glossary* is in the index at the back of the book. The *Glossary* is not a dictionary and the definitions are not in general arranged alphabetically, even within the sections. Knowing how to use the index is crucial to deriving the maximum value from the *Glossary*.

For example, looking up *'virus checking'* in the index leads you to page 166. 'Virus checking' is not one of the main definitions on this page, but you will find it under *'antivirus software'*. Your eye should be led to it by the different appearance of the term you are searching for: **Virus checking**.

Antivirus software

also known as: vaccine utility
including: antivirus monitor, virus checking, disinfection, quarantine, computer hygiene
is used to detect and remove viruses.

Antivirus monitors are programs loaded permanently in memory continually monitoring the system for the tell-tale patterns indicating the presence of any of the thousands of viruses that have been identified. If any change is detected, the file is prevented from being run and a warning message is given. New data read into the computer is also screened for viruses and appropriate action taken.

Virus checking scans the files on a computer system to detect viruses.

Disinfection is the removal of viruses that have been detected.

Quarantine is the isolation of a file suspected of containing a virus. The file can then be investigated and the operation of the virus can be analysed.

Computer hygiene is the term used to describe the prevention and cure of problems caused by viruses.

An alternative way of finding the appropriate entry is to examine the lines immediately after the main entry: *'also known as'*, *'including'*. These provide a list of terms covered in that definition.

The *Glossary* is divided into seven parts as described in the Introduction. Each part is divided into sections defining terms on a particular topic and large sections are further subdivided. It is hoped that readers will take advantage of this structure to browse within sections; to assist in this, each section has a general introduction (see, for example, page 155 to page 156) providing additional information that puts the terms into context.

Within most definitions, you will find references to other terms (for example, *'virus'*) in the first line of the definition. You may wish to read these in conjunction with the definition you are examining.

There are, of course, other ways of using this glossary. Related terms occur together, and you may find it helpful to read through a complete section or subsection.

PART A: OVERVIEW

This section contains general terms that might be met by any computer user. Some sections in Part A are concerned with general issues and others with the design of computer systems. Some sections contain terms that might have been placed in other parts, but they have been kept with other related terms for completeness. Some terms have references to terms in other parts that will provide readers with pointers to other associated terms and concepts.

A1 GENERAL COMPUTING TERMS

When you approach computing for the first time you meet a range of terms that people involved in the industry take for granted. These terms are often vague generalisations and may mean different things to different people. They are also applied to a wide range of situations within computing and their precise meaning may vary between contexts.

Most jargon you meet when using a computer is related to the task you are doing. The **software** used to perform the task is called an **application**. Examples of applications include **word processing, computer art** and using a **database** program. However, there is some jargon that relates to running the computer itself, that is, how you control or operate a computer.

This section provides general definitions of some of the more common computing terms that are either used in a general context or apply across many areas of computing.

INFORMATION PROCESSING

Information processing

is the organisation, manipulation and distribution of information. As these activities are central to almost every use of computers, the term is in common use to mean almost the same as 'computing'. See also *data* and *information* page 255.

Information technology (IT)

including: ICT (information and communications technology)
is the application of technology to information processing. The current interest centres on computing, telecommunications and digital electronics.

In the UK schools sector, the preferred term is *ICT (information and communications technology)*.

Telecommunications

is a general term describing the communication of information over a distance. The method of communication is normally via a cable, either wire or *fibre optic* (see page 343) or electromagnetic radiation. See also *wireless communication*, page 342. Computer data uses the same network as telephone systems.

Computer

is a machine that processes data. It takes data, in digital form, which is processed automatically before being output in some way. It is programmable so that the rules used to process the data can be changed. It is an automatic, programmable, digital data processor. These ideas are expanded in the introduction to Section E1, page 287. The definition excludes the *analog computer* (page 288).

Computer system

including: configuration
is the complete collection of components (hardware, software, peripherals, power supplies, communications links) making up a single computer installation. The particular choice of components is known as the **configuration** – different systems may or may not have the same configuration.

Computing

is the use of a computer to manipulate data or control a process. It is also an umbrella term used in higher education to cover the multitude of subjects relating to computers that can be studied.

Embedded system

is the use of a computer system built into a machine of some sort, usually to provide a means of control. The computer system is generally small, often a single microprocessor with very limited functions. The user does not realise that instructions are being carried out by a computer but simply that there are controls to operate the machine. Examples are electronic washing machines, burglar alarms and car engine management systems.

Multimedia

is the presentation of information by a computer system using graphics, animation, sound and text.

Facilities management

also known as: managed services
is the contracting of an organisation's day-to-day operations to an outside company. The facilities management company employs the staff and runs the operation. Where it is computer operations to be managed, the equipment will usually be sited in the organisation's own premises, although it may be owned or leased by the facilities management company. The contract for this kind of service will specify what the computer system must provide for the price. This is distinct from *outsourcing* (see page 5), where a well-defined task will be contracted out.

Outsourcing

is the purchase of services from outside contractors rather than employing staff to do the tasks. This use of contractors for a well-defined task is distinct from *facilities management* (see page 4) where day-to-day operations are involved. Traditionally large computer organisations have employed many staff such as *systems analysts* and *developers* (see Section B9 Computer personnel). It may be more economic to contract another organisation to provide these services and not have the expense and complication of direct employment of staff. With the use of networking, it is possible to outsource anywhere in the world.

Some of these tasks may be provided by a *computer bureau* (see below).

Computer bureau

including: data processor
is an organisation that offers a range of computing services for hire (for example, data preparation, payroll processing). Bureaux usually offer two types of service:

- They provide computing facilities for organisations that do not have any of their own.

- They also offer specialist services covering vital common operations (for example, payroll) to organisations that do not have the appropriate piece of applications software.

Compare this with *facilities management* and *outsourcing*.

Data processor is the name used in the *Data Protection Act (1998)* (see page 157), for a computer bureau.

PARTS OF A COMPUTER SYSTEM

Hardware

is the physical part of a computer system – the processor(s), input and output devices, and storage. This is in contrast to the *software* (see page 6), which includes application packages, and the data in the storage.

Storage media

also known as: media
is the collective name for the different types of storage materials (such as compact disc, solid state, memory card, hard disk and even paper) used to hold data or programs. They are used either within the computer system or connected to it. See *peripherals* (see page 6) and Section E3.

Peripheral

also known as: device
including: input device, output device, input/output device (I/O device), storage device
is a piece of equipment (or hardware) that can be connected to the central processing unit. It is used to provide input, output and backing storage for the computer system. No particular peripheral is required by a computer but every computer must have some method of input and output (for example, a washing machine may simply have push buttons for input and *actuators*, page 118, for output). They are often referred to as follows:

Input device is a peripheral unit that can accept data, presented in the appropriate machine-readable form, decode it and transmit it as electrical pulses to the central processing unit.

Output device is a peripheral unit that translates signals from the computer into a human-readable form or into a form suitable for reprocessing by the computer at a later stage.

Input/output device (I/O device) is a peripheral unit that can be used both as an input device and as an output device. In some instances, 'input/output device' may be two separate devices housed in the same cabinet.

Storage device is a peripheral unit that allows the user to store data in an electronic form for a longer period of time and when the computer is switched off. The data can be read only by the computer and is not in human-readable form.

Software

including: applications program, application, applications package, generic software, productivity tool
consists of programs, routines and procedures (together with their associated documentation) that can be run on a computer system.

An **applications program**, frequently abbreviated to **application**, is software designed to carry out a task (such as keeping accounts, editing text) that would need to be carried out even if computers did not exist.

An **applications package** is a complete set of applications programs together with the associated documentation (see *user documentation*, page 425). Where the application is appropriate to many areas, it is usual to describe it as **generic software** or as a **productivity tool**. For example, *word processing* (see page 367) can be used in personal correspondence, the production of business 'form letters', academic research, compilation of glossaries, writing books etc.

See also Section B12 Systems software, *program* on page 212 and Section C4.

Integrated package

also known as: integrated program
is a single piece of software that provides a user with basic information processing functions. It usually includes word processing, spreadsheets and small databases

and may include additional facilities such as charts, a diary and communications. It is designed so that data can be simply moved between the various parts enabling complex tasks to be performed easily.

Tutorial

is a program that helps a user to learn about a new application. The tutorial will include a simple explanation of how to use the new system, diagrams and possibly examples the user can try while the tutorial program monitors the user's progress.

A2 USING A COMPUTER

Other related terms may be found in Section A1 General computing terms, and for fuller definitions see Section B12 Systems software.

There are important similarities between the way we use motor vehicles and the way we use computers. In both cases, the majority of users are completely unconcerned about the internal workings of the machine, but are nonetheless capable of becoming skilled in its use. Anyone using this *Glossary* is likely to be seeking an understanding of what goes on 'under the bonnet', but in this section we look at the terms and definitions that are to do with the general use of computers. The parallel with motorcars continues to be instructive: while most drivers are unaware of the technicalities of the car, they must be acquainted with some features that are not just to do with steering it in the direction they want to go – the need for petrol and oil, and the ways in which a flat battery may be avoided. The explanations in this section are the equivalent for the computer.

Computer tasks can be divided into two broad categories. There are those that have only been made necessary by the existence of the computer – the handling of printers, the storage of data on disks, and so forth. These tasks are performed by **systems software** and we would not need to undertake these tasks if computers did not exist. However, there is a much more important category of task. These are the things that we would want to do even if computers did not exist, and are generally known as **applications**, carried out by **applications software**. It is in this second category that we find word processing, where the computer enhances our ability to create, edit and lay out text. Letters were written and books published long before there were computers. Similarly with spreadsheets, where accountants tallied columns of figures and derived calculations from numeric data even before the mechanical calculator.

In operating a computer, users may find themselves performing the same types of actions in different applications, or even when interacting with systems software. These common operations are collected in this section. The subsection 'The size of things' may seem to be technical, but the terms **bit**, **byte** and **word**, described within it are often used to describe the size or capacity of a computer.

The power of the computer is so great that it is tempting to believe that it has created new applications – things we were unable to do before the computer. However, while the computer may have made some tasks practicable and feasible, in general a little reflection will reveal the possibility (if not the widespread practice) of most applications before the advent of the computer. It is worth remembering that photographers were retouching pictures before digital manipulation of images became commonplace, that librarians maintained card indexes before databases, that letters were sent before emails, and that musicians were creating electronic music before computers.

Perhaps the most likely candidate for a truly new application is in the use of the internet, and especially the World Wide Web. It is hard to see which human activity in pre-computer days parallels the creation of the personal statements of interests and activities that appear on web pages, much less the growth of ecommerce. That is, until we remember letters, newsletters, magazines and mail order catalogues!

SYSTEM SOFTWARE

Operating system (OS)

is the name given to the collection of systems software that manages the computer. It is usually supplied with the computer. The most common operating systems today are Microsoft® Windows® and LINUX® (for the PC), Apple® Mac® OS (for the Macintosh®) and UNIX® (for larger computers). The operating system gives the computer its 'look and feel', and generates great passion between advocates of alternative systems. See also Section B12 Systems software.

Driver

is a piece of system software supplied with a peripheral (such as a printer, a mouse, a display screen or a keyboard). It bridges the gap between the operating system and the peripheral, and converts commands from one into instructions that the other can obey. In this way, applications software such as a word processor can, for example, issue a 'print' instruction in a standard way to the operating system, without needing to know the details of the particular printer being used. The casual user may meet drivers when he or she installs or upgrades a peripheral.

Filter

including: graphics filter
is a piece of software used in conjunction with an application, which allows data stored in one format to be accessed by an application that uses another format. For example a word-processing package, such as Microsoft® Word, will provide filters for documents created in its major competitors, such as WordPerfect®. In this way, users will not be dissuaded from buying Microsoft® Word because all their previous work was created in WordPerfect®. Even between software created by the same manufacturer, a filter may be necessary, for example to import a spreadsheet into a database package. It may not always be possible to convert every feature supported by one format into another format. The user is unlikely to be aware of a filter unless he or she encounters an error message reporting the failure or absence of an appropriate one.

A **graphics filter** is a particularly common form of filter. There are many alternative formats for the storage of graphical data, not necessarily associated with any one commercial package. To be able to work with these formats, an image process-ing program (see *image compression*, page 389) must provide appropriate graphics filters to allow images to be loaded or saved.

Figure A2.1 Filters

Some filters that enable data to be imported into a word-processing program.

ORGANISING DATA

File

also known as: document
including: filename
is a collection of data items stored in the computer, and handled as a single unit. How and where the data is stored will be organised by the *operating system* (see page 9). Files are given **filenames**, so that the user can later access the correct one. Systems software also creates files in order to keep track of the operation of the computer. As the word 'file' is largely a technical one, some applications software refer to files as **documents**, even though these may be spreadsheets, databases or images as well as text-based files.

File type

including: filename extension, file associations
is the type of data that is held in a file. This might be an executable program or data structured for a particular application.

To assist the user in recognising the appropriate file, many computer systems use a short three-or four-character **filename extension** added to the name, to identify the file type. Thus, the file 'timetable.doc' is seen to be a Microsoft® Word document, 'message. txt' a text file, 'barbecue.bmp' a bitmap graphic, and so on. A short table of common extensions is given in Table A2.1; a fuller table is found in Section G3, page 456.

As well as assisting the user, **file associations** may be created, so that all files with a given extension will be linked to a specified software package. With appropriate associations set up, it is possible for the user to simply double click a filename, say 'barbecue. bmp', and this action will launch the chosen image-processing program and load the graphic file for editing or printing. In this way, the user is encouraged to focus on the data rather than on the programs that process it.

Folder

also known as: directory
including: nested folders, subfolders, subdirectories
is the name given to a collection of files, for organisational purposes. By keeping related files in the same folder, the user can select from the files he or she is working on without being distracted by files to do with other work. Folders are also known as **directories**. A well thought out directory system can make computer use easier. To this end, the user can create **nested folders** with one or more folders stored in another. For example, a folder of word-processed documents can contain **subfolders (subdirectories)** for letters, for research, for diaries and so on. See also *directories*, page 423.

THE SIZE OF THINGS

Bit (BInary digiT)

is a single digit in a binary number; it is either a 0 or a 1. It is the smallest unit of storage, since all data is stored as binary codes. Many computers are described as '16 bit' or '32 bit' and so on; this usage is explained under *word* (see page 14).

Byte

including: kilobytes, megabytes, gigabytes, terabytes
is a group of bits, typically eight, representing a single character. This is normally the smallest grouping used by computers, but see *flag* (page 193). The capacity of a computer and of its peripherals is measured in bytes – or more conveniently in multiples such as **kilobytes, megabytes, gigabytes** or **terabytes** (see Section G2 *Units*, page 453). Thus, a computer may have 512 megabytes of memory, and an 80-gigabyte hard disk.

A single byte can represent one of 256 values, either between 0 and 255 or between −128 and +127.

Table A2.1 Common filename extensions

File type	Filename extension	Comments
Document (word processor)	.doc	A word processor file will typically contain formatting and layout information, as well as the text
Text file	.txt	A text file has no formatting information, and is accessible by many applications without needing processing. It is much smaller than a word processor file
Web page	.htm or .html	A text file, but one that uses 'tags' that will enable it to be displayed properly in a web browser (see **HTML**, page 248, and **browser**, page 83
Program	.exe	A file containing a program. Double clicking on an '.exe' file will normally cause it to execute, rather than to open in an associated application
Portable document format	.pdf	A PDF file is specific to the Adobe® Acrobat® system. Although a commercial product, the Acrobat® Reader is widely and freely available, enabling documents prepared using a variety of applications to be accessed by users who may not own the original application. The software for creating '.pdf' files, is available free
Still images	.bmp, .gif, .tif, .jpg	Various still image graphics formats (see Table F3.1, page 391)
Video	.avi, .mov, .wmv	Various moving video formats (see Table F3.1, page 391)
Audio	.wav, .mp3, .aiff, .wma	Various sound formats (see Table F4.1, page 410)
Transfer format	.csv or .tsv	A text file used for transferring data between spreadsheets or databases. Use of these extensions guarantees that the file is formatted with distinct data items separated by commas (.csv, comma separated variables) or by tab characters (.tsv, tab separated variables). Empty or missing items would be recorded as successive commas or tabs
Rich Text Format	.rtf	This is a text file generated by an application such as a word processor that allows users to choose different fonts and text effects, such as italics, underlining etc. The .rtf file simply contains the text, mixed with special 'tags' similar to **HTML** (see page 248) that allow the formatting to be recreated when the file is opened in an application with an appropriate **filter** (see page 9)

Table A2.1 (*Continued*)

File type	Filename extension	Comments
Temporary	.tmp	A temporary file that may safely be deleted. Most users only see .tmp files when an application crashes or the computer fails and temporary files that would normally have been deleted when no longer required are left occupying space on the user's disk
Compressed	.zip or .hqa	A file that has been compressed to save space, and that must be decompressed before the contents can be accessed
Backup	.bak	A backup file, an exact copy of another file
Initial data	.ini	Many applications use initial data files to store data used in customising an application, so that it can open each time looking as the user last saw it
Data	.dat	A general-purpose data file
Library	.dll	A dynamic link library file (specific to Windows®). Such files contain common software routines used by several applications that extend the capability of an existing application

Word

including: word length

is a group of bits that can be addressed, transferred and manipulated as a single unit by the central processor. The size of a word, the **word length,** is determined by the width of the data pathways within the computer and is usually larger than a *byte* (see page 11) possibly consisting of 16, 24, 36 or even 64 bits. Large word sizes mean that a computer can transfer data in larger groups than a computer with a smaller word size, and this generally means faster operation.

OPERATION

Macro

including: macro recording, script, script language

is a small program to perform a repetitive task and which can be created and stored for later use by a user. It allows the user to perform a task by using the macro rather than having to enter the individual instructions. If the task is likely to be used many times it is much easier, and more user friendly, to use a macro. This requires one operation rather than the user performing the same complex set of instruction many times. Macros can also be run from on-screen buttons allowing customised applications to be constructed. See also *customise* (see page 15).

Many applications programs such as word processors now provide a macro facility. These macros can be used as if they were part of the built-in functions of the software. Macros are created by entering commands, which are recognised by the application software, to form a program. These commands may be entered by typing, recording or by using a *wizard* (see page 425). The program can then be run by selecting it from a menu or on-screen button.

Examples include routines to open a window in a database and configure it for a new record, print a page of information from a spreadsheet or sort a complex set of data.

Macro recording records the actions of the user, as the user performs the tasks, to create the program. Each significant action is analysed and converted into the equivalent commands.

Scripts are a form of macro used mainly with multimedia software. They enable the designer to specify, or program, a sequence of actions. This includes determining the order in which elements will appear, the times between elements and making choices if a user selects a specific on-screen object.

Script language is the set of commands understood by the application software. Different software usually have different script languages and the scripts cannot always be used with other products.

See also *macro instruction*, page 211.

Figure A2.2 Two examples of customising

The dialogue box on the top allows the user to select which word processor functions will be marked by special characters on the screen. That on the bottom allows the user to add or delete commands on the menus.

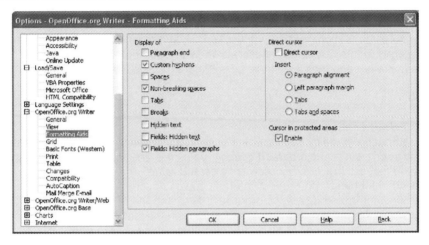

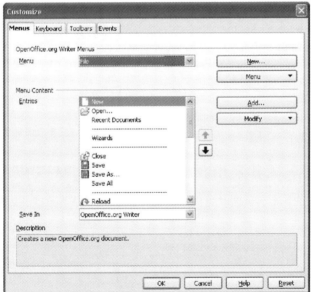

Customise

including: workspace

is to tailor an application package or even a whole computer system to the preferences of a specific user. Usually, the user can make cosmetic changes as well as operational ones. The colours and layout of the desktop might be customised, as might the sounds that the computer generates to signal (for example) an error. The sizes of text and icons may be changed, as indeed may the language in which messages are displayed. The operation of a software package may also be 'tuned' to suit the user's preferences. Short-cut keys can be defined to carry out operations that the user has frequent need for, the space left for margins may be defined or the number of decimal places used in displaying a number can be specified. The changes made to the basic operation of the package are saved when the application is closed, so that it will re-open with the same customisation as before. Sometimes, it is possible for different users to save their own customisation, known as a **workspace**, and to call up their own preferences subsequently. In this way, different users of the same computer can still benefit from an application tailored to their own needs. See Figure A2.2 on the previous page.

Default

including: default option, default value
is an assumption made by computer software in the absence of explicit instructions to the contrary. This may be a **default option** – your files are listed in alphabetical order, unless you request date or size order – or a **default value** – the computer prints one copy of a document, unless you request multiple copies. A common default option is seen in the 'Print' command in a word processor. Pressing the print button on the toolbar normally prints one copy of the entire document on the 'default printer' nominated by the user. To access another printer, to print multiple copies, or to print selected pages, requires the user to select the more complicated print dialogue box. See Figure A2.3.

Figure A2.3 Default options

Pressing the 'print' button (7th from left) on the toolbar shown at the top causes the same effect as the options shown in the full print dialogue below (one collated copy of the entire document on the Epson R1800 printer). However, in the dialogue box, none of these is assumed, and any or all of them may be changed.

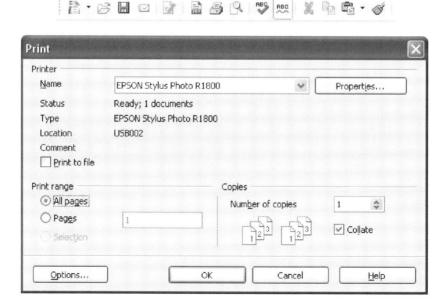

The best software is designed so that the most frequently used options are all available as defaults, so that users are not troubled by the need continually to specify such values. It is often possible for users to customise software, by selecting their own choice of defaults.

Object linking and embedding (OLE)

including: embedded object, linked object
is the insertion of data items in one format into data in another format, for example a picture in a text file. Information such as the location of the data and its format may be included as links to the data, or the data may be embedded in the file. A program using the data can load the correct program to edit that particular type of data without the user having to export the data, edit it and later import it back again (see page 19). Each item is an *object* (see page 188).

Embedded objects are inserted as part of the data and saved with it. Later changes made to the original do not appear in the copy.

Linked objects are stored separately and only loaded when they are needed; the location (usually a filename) is stored in the main data. Changes made to the linked object automatically apply to the main data.

Operational mode

including: batch processing, transaction processing, multi-access systems, time-sharing, real-time system, interactive processing, remote access, tele-processing, offline processing, online processing
is the way a computer system is used and operated. Decisions about operational modes are made during systems design. Often the *operating system* (see page 9) manages the functioning of the operational modes in use.

The terms in this section are not necessarily mutually exclusive, and more than one might be applicable to any particular computer system.

In **batch processing** all the data to be input is collected together before being processed as a single efficient operation. This method is also used when computer users submit individual *jobs* (see page 181) that are processed together as a batch.

Transaction processing deals with each set of data from a user as it is submitted. This is normally used in commercial systems where a transaction may be a booking, an order or an invoice. Each transaction is completed before the next is begun.

Multi-access systems allow several users apparently to have individual control of the computer at the same time. One method of implementing a multi-access system is by allocating a period of time to each user; this is called **time-sharing**. See also *time slice*, page 180.

A **real-time system** is one that can react fast enough to influence behaviour in the outside world; for example, this is necessary in air-traffic control systems and desirable in online reservation systems.

Interactive processing provides the user with direct, immediate responses from the system. There is often some kind of dialogue with the system. Examples include the booking of airline tickets and requesting information about a bank account through a cash-dispensing machine.

Remote access or *tele-processing* is the use of a geographically remote computer system via communications links. See also *remote job entry*, page 181.

Offline processing occurs when computer devices are not under the immediate control of the main computer, for example data entry to disk or tape storage.

Online processing allows the user to interact directly with the main computer.

Channel

including: channel number, handle, port, port number
is any physical path along which data may be transmitted between two points. The physical path may be a separate wire, a group of wires or may be shared with other channels on a single wire (see *multiplexor*, page 341).

The data a channel carries may be a radio or TV signal, communications between two computer devices (for example music systems), or between a computer and its peripherals. Although different devices work totally differently, they are simply sending or receiving data, but along different physical routes.

A *channel number* is given to each channel. A device can select the source of the data being received (or where it is sent to) simply by altering the channel number and allowing the electronics to redirect the data stream.

An example is a music system, where a generated tune could be saved to a suitable disk, or played by a variety of output devices. Each output device can be linked to a separate output channel of a *MIDI* (see page 411) that switches the output to one or more devices simply by setting and altering channel numbers.

Within a computer system channels identify which peripherals data is being sent to or received from, particularly between a central processing unit and a peripheral device or, by extension, between the user's program and a file on backing store. The channel number acts as a short cut and avoids the need to initialise the peripheral each time data is sent or received. It allows great flexibility in switching between peripherals and adding peripherals to the system.

A *handle* is similar to a channel number but used within a computer program to identify a resource. For example, a file handle will identify a file currently available for access by the program.

A *port* identifies where a channel enters or leaves a computer system. These are physical locations where peripherals or other components can be plugged in and often include an interface to convert the data into the appropriate form. For examples see *interface board*, page 335. Within the computer system each port may be given a **port number** that allows the computer to select peripherals easily.

Overtyping

also known as: overwriting
including: inserting
is to replace text on a screen with other text entered from the keyboard (or possibly read from a file) during the process of entering or editing a document. When overtyping, new characters replace those already on the screen. Contrast this with ***inserting*** text, when existing text moves to make space for the new characters.

Cut and paste

including: clipboard, notepad
is the technique of transferring a section of data (text in a word processor, or diagrams and text in a page makeup package) from one part of a document to another part of the same document, or to another document. The user first selects (highlights) the data to be moved and then 'cuts' it from the document (it is usually possible to copy it, rather than necessarily cut it out). The cursor is moved to the new position, and the data is 'pasted' in place. In most applications, the data is held in a temporary storage area called the ***clipboard*** or ***notepad***.

Data held in these storage areas will normally remain there until overwritten by new data, so allowing one exact copy of the original to be pasted in more than one place.

WYSIWYG (what you see is what you get)

(pronounced 'wizzy-wig') refers to a screen display that matches the eventual printed output in layout, highlighting and underlining, font etc. Such displays are particularly helpful in applications such as *desktop publishing* (see page 368) and *spreadsheets* (see Section F2, page 382).

Export

including: import
is to create a data file using one piece of software so that it can be read by a different piece of software. ***Import*** is the corresponding read process to accept a file produced by some other software.

Often there is a specific version of a particular package whose file and data formats are chosen by its manufacturer to be the standard version for exporting from and importing into that package. Using these formats reduces the problems of data transfer between different software applications. See also *filter*, page 9.

Control panel

is a small display/keyboard on a device that enables the user to set options. On a printer this may be used to set the print style or change the paper source.

Scrolling

including: scroll bar

is the action of 'rolling-up' a screen. As each new line appears at the bottom, the existing top line disappears off the top. Where an application occupies more than a single screen, it is usual to provide a **scroll bar** to move the displayed portion of the application up or down the screen (vertical scrolling) and sometimes left and right across the screen (horizontal scrolling), see Figure A2.4.

Figure A2.4 Horizontal scroll bar

Status bar

is a line of information displayed on the screen, usually either at the top or at the bottom, which shows some of the conditions in the task at the moment, such as the page and line number in a word-processing application.

Install

is to transfer software onto the medium from which it is to be run. Installation is normally onto a hard drive but could be onto a CD-ROM or a network.

Uninstall

also known as: deinstall

is the reverse process to *install*, see above. It may release the space from the storage medium. If there is a licence to install a limited number of copies, then deinstallation re-credits the licence manager. See *key disk*, page 169.

Deinstall is also the name of proprietary applications that carry out the action of uninstalling.

A3 COMPUTING IN EVERYDAY LIFE

Computer technology is a major part of everyday life. Many devices, such as phones, TVs, game consoles and household equipment, use a powerful computer processor. Each device is optimised for a specific purpose, but they are becoming increasingly capable of a variety of tasks given suitable input and output components. For example, you can write an email on a smartphone, but you might find it easier to prepare a complex document on a desktop computer. These devices are often connected to the internet, enabling them to be controlled in flexible and intricate ways. This complex control network is sometimes referred to as the **internet of things (IoT)**.

The speed at which computer systems carry out tasks, and their ability to access large or remote databases, are benefits of the technology, but the trail of data left when using the systems might be detrimental to a user's privacy. To get the most out of these devices and to avoid negative consequences the user needs a basic understanding of computing.

Computing in everyday life links the different elements of computer science and information technology, both of which are seen to be essential for an individual to play a full part in life. These elements include the use of computers as a tool (**information technology** or **IT**), how to develop new computer systems and understand how to get the best out of existing systems (**computer science** or **CS**) and understanding how modern technology is affecting our lives (**digital literacy** or **DL**).

Information technology provides the basic skills to operate the computer systems that are needed both at home and in the workplace. Typical applications include word processing, finance applications (including spreadsheets), communication, media production and the internet.

Computer science builds on this by developing an understanding of how and why computers operate as they do. This is useful because it enables users to understand how to get the best out of their software, how to customise it using various forms of macros and how to design new systems.

Digital literacy ensures individuals are aware of the social, ethical, moral, legal and cultural impact of technology. Without this awareness, they can be disadvantaged. It can also work to limit the negative aspects of technology through the political process.

A key component of computing is **computational thinking**. This is the cognitive skill that helps to give an individual the ability to produce his or her own solutions to real-life problems.

DIGITAL LITERACY

Digital literacy (DL)

is the understanding of how computers work and the effects of computer technology on the way people live, including the effects on society and the individual.

Having decided that using a computer to solve a problem is appropriate, a key aspect of DL is the ability to choose and use hardware, software and web-based resources while working safely, efficiently, responsibly and confidently

- to undertake a task;
- to develop ideas;
- to produce a solution to a problem.

Digital divide

is the effect of the inequalities in the availability of computing and digital literacy. The digital divide is related to the lack of opportunity for those without the ability to use modern technology or without access to an internet connection.

We are already at a stage where it is impossible to apply for many jobs without computing facilities and skills. It will soon be difficult to interact effectively without these same skills, thereby compromising effective participation in society. See also *Social aspects*, page 24.

This particularly affects the less well off, the elderly, those with mental or physical illness, the educationally disadvantaged and the learning disabled.

Aspects of everyday living

are the ways the continuing development of computing is changing the way we live. Some of these aspects are the effects of:

- communication, such as phone calls, email, texting, social media;
- access to information, such as knowledge banks and expert systems;
- access to media, such as on-demand TV, video and music streaming, media downloads;
- the digitisation of events, such as photo and video sharing;
- the digitisation of artefacts, such as the scanning of museum collections.

Some examples of the changes to the way we live are:

- being able to access to the internet while on the move;
- being able to communicate rapidly and comprehensively with friends, family, colleagues and others;

- the availability of on-demand, and on-the-move, access to media;
- the use of smartphones as scanners;
- the availability of geo-data as online maps and overlays.

Ethical aspects

are the ways the continuing development of computing is affecting the fairness with which people are treated. Some of these aspects are:

- specific groups being disadvantaged by the way computers are used;
- individuals being manipulated, personally or financially, including fraud;
- individuals being exposed to ridicule;
- the use of data in systems to monitor employees' work, for example by tracking emails.

Moral aspects

are the ways the continuing development of computing is changing the way ideas of right and wrong are dealt with. Some of these aspects are:

- the perception of victimless crime, such as *copyright* (see page 167);
- *computer misuse* (see page 159);
- respecting intellectual property;
- the use of *robotics* (see page 143) and *artificial intelligence* (see page 142) to make decisions affecting individuals.

Aspects of information access

are the ways the continuing development of computing affects access to news and the quality of the information, including:

- control of the news provided;
- how news is accessed, such as using social media;
- the rapid distribution of new information;
- the ability for anyone to comment on news and ideas;
- the validity of the information provided;
- the bias of the information provided;
- the digital culture, where the traditional arts, such as plays, films and music performances, are being made available electronically.

Legal aspects

are the ways the continuing development of computing requires new types of laws. Some of these aspects are:

- the protection of intellectual property, such as registration, *copyright* and patents (see page 167);
- the protection of personal data, such as medical records, emails and political allegiances. See also *Data Protection Act*, page 157;
- the protection of commercial data. See also *Computer Misuse Act*, page 159;
- the prevention of malicious actions, such as introducing viruses and hacking. See also *Computer Misuse Act*, page 159;
- the right to view information held by public authorities. See also *Freedom of Information Act*, page 158.

Social aspects

are the ways the continuing development of computing is changing our lives at work and at home. These aspects might be good or bad, and include:

- a *digital divide* forming between those who can access technology and those who cannot (see page 22);
- the effects on individuals and families of cyber-bullying;
- the easy availability of extreme materials, such as pornography;
- the pressure to react immediately to new situations, for example answering emails out of working hours, perhaps on holiday;
- individuals accessing information to participate more effectively in protecting their situations;
- families being able to stay in touch even when physically separated;
- crime prevention, such as using CCTV, automatic number plate recognition, face recognition and DNA identification;
- the effects of new forms of advertising;
- the changing requirements for the workforce and associated creation or loss of jobs.

Economic aspects

are the ways the continuing development of computing is changing the way we work. Some of these aspects are:

- the introduction of new technology, such as 3D printers that are revolutionising the production of small mechanical parts;
- the changes in skill levels needed within society;
- the de-skilling of some types of jobs;

- the changes in the values associated with different jobs;
- an increased value of information;
- automation in producing goods;
- the changes in the types of jobs needed;
- the opportunities to work at home because a physical presence is not required at the workplace;
- the development of international trade;
- the introduction of new marketing methods.

Political aspects

are the ways the continuing development of computing is changing the way society is run. Some of these aspects are:

- an increase in the quantity of information available;
- the availability of much more complex information;
- an ability to distribute unreliable information and smear others;
- an ability to organise political activity using social media;
- the introduction of electronic voting, which might lead to greater and more frequent involvement;
- greater involvement of the wider society, for example consultations and referenda in public policy making;
- wider access to the political process by smaller groups, such as environmental groups.

BASIC COMPUTER SCIENCE CONCEPTS

Problem solving

is a structured process that enables a task to be understood and a solution to be found that is effective, reliable and complete. This is particularly important when including a computer because the steps need to be clearly identified before they can be described and coded. The formal way to do this is defined by the *system development cycle*, page 32. For a less formal way of structuring problem solving see *computational thinking*, page 26.

Logic in computing

is making decisions by comparing the data to fixed criteria to establish if a relationship is **true** or **false**. See *logical operator*, page 106. Knowing if a relationship is true or false allows a computer program to choose between different courses of action. It also involves understanding how these logical values of true and false are combined to produce different decisions.

Computational thinking

including: algorithmic thinking, decomposition, generalisation, abstraction, evaluation
is a systematic approach to solving a problem where each stage is worked through carefully and evaluated to ensure that all possible issues are resolved. This involves using different conceptual approaches that, not used in any particular order, include:

Algorithmic thinking is identifying the logical steps (processes) needed to solve the problem, the order in which they must be carried out and the rules by which these steps are applied.

Decomposition is identifying the subtasks into which identified tasks can be split and simplified to a level where they can be implemented.

Generalisation is the ability to identify similarities and patterns in data and processes. This enables a previous solution, or part of the solution, to be applied to a new problem.

Abstraction is removing unnecessary detail from a problem so the main processes involved can be more easily identified and understood.

Evaluation is an objective review of what has been achieved to establish whether it meets the required criteria. The evaluation might also look at the wider context, the user needs and whether there are any undesirable consequences introduced into the solution.

The *system life cycle* (see page 30) describes the steps usually followed to produce a computer system.

IMPLEMENTING BASIC COMPUTER SCIENCE

Educational programming languages

including: Scratch, Kodu®, Greenfoot, Alice, RoboMind®, Flowol, Python®, Visual Basic® (VB. net), Visual Basic® for Applications (VBA)
are provided through simple *integrated development environments* (see page 40) that allow a user to enter a program, run it, observe the results and refine the code if necessary. This enables the user to solve problems within the limitations of the environment. These programs typically cannot be run outside the environment.

The output from simpler systems is in the form of a two-dimensional graphical window enabling the user to handle visual problems and develop the pedagogy of turtle graphics from earlier languages such as *Logo*, (see page 246). Users can later move to a full programming environment, such as *Eclipse*, and a powerful programming language, such as *Python*, see page 27.

Scratch is an introductory programming environment. It is based on the syntax of the *Pascal* programming language and so has some similarities to *Visual Basic®* and *pseudo-code*, see page 220. Its special feature is a 'key' system that makes programming different program structures easier.

Kodu® is an icon-based environment that provides users with the experience of programming 3D environments.

Greenfoot, *Alice* and *RoboMind*® are introductory programming environments that are based on the *Java* programming language, which has some similarities to the various C languages.

Flowol is an introductory programming environment. It allows the user to design a program as a *flowchart*, see page 220, which can then be run. The input and output is provided either by external interfaces to other equipment or by a simulation of the situation on the screen.

Python® is a popular language used in secondary schools and by some professionals. Python® combines an object-oriented approach with a simple syntax that makes use of layout and white space in structuring programs, similar to the user-friendly syntax of *Pascal*.

Visual Basic® (also known as *VB.net*) is used in secondary schools, usually to develop projects for GCSE and A-level courses. It is a free-standing language for programming systems using a *WIMP environment*, see page 420, for Windows®-based computers.

Visual Basic® *for Applications* (*VBA*) is provided with Microsoft® Office and is a version of Visual Basic®. It allows programming in the context of Microsoft® Office, and, for example, it might be used to validate data within a Word document or Excel® spreadsheet.

PIC microcontroller

including: peripheral interface controller, programmable intelligent computer
is a microprocessor designed to control a wide range of external devices, such as alarm systems, garden control systems, traffic lights and car park barriers. It is very widely used in producing commercial electronic control systems. It is optimised to control a wide range of devices efficiently and cheaply.

An engineer will construct a simple circuit board containing the PIC microcontroller, other specialised microprocessors and input/output sockets. The PIC microcontroller program is developed on a PC using simulation software, similar to Flowol, see above. The final program is downloaded to the PIC microcontroller. The circuit board is then installed into its working location to produce an embedded system.

Originally PIC microcontroller programs were stored on an *EPROM*, see page 305, and the program was transferred using a special device confusingly called an EPROM programmer. Modern PIC microcontrollers can be reprogrammed while still on their circuit board.

The acronym PIC stands for **peripheral interface controller** or **programmable intelligent computer**.

Raspberry Pi

is a small computer designed to be used as an educational tool and for the development of computer systems. All the components are mounted on a single *motherboard* (see page 334) and USB sockets are provided to connect external devices such as keyboards. The cost is kept as low as possible, for example by the use of SD memory cards for the backing store and open source software, such as the LINUX® operating system, so that it is affordable to schools and hobbyists. It is powerful enough to work with multimedia and to run office software as well as to control a wide range of external devices.

BBC micro:bit

is an educational tool for pupils' development of computer systems. It is a programmable controller (similar in function to the *PIC microcontroller*, page 27) that can be programmed to control external devices. All the components are mounted on a single 4 cm by 5 cm *motherboard* (see page 334), which also contains a variety of sensors (including push buttons, a compass and an accelerometer) and outputs (including a 25 LED array and pin connectors). Pupils use another computer or device, using a variety of programming languages, to construct the program before *compiling* it (page 177) and downloading it to the micro:bit.

A4   SYSTEMS DESIGN AND LIFE CYCLE

Related topics can be found in Section F5 User interface and documentation, Section A5 Describing systems, Section C5 Describing programs and Section C6 Testing and running programs.

There is an enormous difference between the large-scale commercial production of software and an individual writing a computer program for their own use. The problems are much larger, too large for one person to manage, and usually have to be tackled by a team. A formal approach to the task is essential, to plan and to enable members of the team to communicate both during development and afterwards. In contrast an individual writing a small program can do much of the visualisation and planning in their head.

For a purpose-built computer system, usually designed for a specific customer (for example, a large company), it is essential to establish exactly what the customer requires. The designers need to avoid the traditional complaints 'Yes – but what I really meant was ...' and 'Yes – and while you're about it, can you just ...'. The aim is to produce a reliable system that prevents errors, is produced at the right time and for the expected cost.

When designing software that will be marketed in volume, such as word processors and spreadsheets, there is commercial pressure to ensure that it is useful to as many people as possible. For example it should:

- have a range of attractive features absent from competing software;

- work within the limitations of the currently accepted level of hardware and, in particular, within the limits of any networking and communication systems;

- be able to be upgraded easily and cheaply from earlier versions (rather than users being tempted to buy a competitor's product);

- make it easy for users of competing products to use, for example by offering the ability to read (or import) files prepared in other software packages, or by designing the user interface so that it has similarities with competing products.

The development team of a computer system or software application may also have to take into account the various rules that the designers of the operating system (such as Windows®, Mac OS® or UNIX®) have defined. This ensures that the software works reliably and will work in the future when the operating system is improved or upgraded. Designers must provide a robust system that will cope with future changes in what are usually fixed values. The designer would have to take into account any financial constants referred to by a system (such as the VAT rate).

There is the need to establish precisely what the customer requires; to organise the design and coding so that teams of people can work together; to keep track of the many changes that will inevitably be necessary; to provide suitable documentation for the future maintenance of the software, and suitable documentation for the user. This can be done using a defined development procedure, so that each member of the team knows exactly what is expected, and can follow this procedure in a professional way.

This chapter defines terms and methods that are generally accepted for the development of computer systems. More detailed methodologies such as Structured Systems Analysis and Design Methodology (SSADM) and Rapid Application Design (RAD) have been developed and are used commercially to provide a reliable method of computer systems development. Other methods include Agile development and service-oriented architecture.

Typically a **feasibility study** is done before any development starts. Estimates are made of costs, effort, effectiveness, reliability and the benefits to be expected from the new or improved system. A decision is then taken whether to proceed based on the costs involved and the value of the benefits achieved. The development team then conduct an analysis of any existing system and of the requirements of the new system (**systems analysis**). The new system will be designed (**systems design**) and a **systems specification** produced of the desired system. This sets out the hardware and software requirements, data organisation, and the organisational and human implications. Only when all these stages are complete will work begin on the production of the system (**implementation of the design**). The final system will then be tested (**systems testing**) and installed (**installation**). When in use the system will probably be adapted and modified (**maintenance**) by a different team. Documentation is created at each stage.

It should be clear that designing computer systems (which may include hardware, as well as software and manual procedures) is a task that requires considerable management and discipline. The computer system may also need to meet criteria relating to the legal and contractual procedures for handling data and a long life. The development of large, complex systems (on which safety as well as profits may depend) is very similar to the design and construction of engineering projects such as bridges or buildings.

CONCEPTS

System life cycle

also known as: system cycle
including: spiral model, waterfall model
is made up of the various stages that have to be completed to create a new or modified computer system. These stages form a cycle because after a period of time the system will need modifying or replacing and the process has to be repeated.

The system may include both hardware and software or just software. To ensure that a system is developed effectively a planned approach is usually taken, which defines how the development takes place, see also *design methodology* (page 33).

The traditional understanding of the system life cycle is shown in Table A4.1. The individual stages are described later in this chapter. See pages 33–36.

Table A4.1 System life cycle

Stage	Description
Feasibility study	Of the users' requirements, including a preliminary analysis of the required system
Analysis	Of the system requirements, to provide a specification
Design	Of the new system, both the overall structure and details of the system components
Implementation (of the design)	Using the design from the previous stage, development of the software follows a similar set of stages generally known as the *software development cycle* (see page 32)
Testing	The implemented design: software, hardware and manual procedures
Installation	Of the new system in its working environment
Maintenance	Of the new system to keep it working

- Formal documentation will be produced at each stage

- Each stage may be reviewed and repeated until the result is acceptable

- See pages 33–36

In an effort to improve the speed and reliability of development the system life cycle can be viewed in different ways. Other interpretations, or models, include:

Spiral model is an abstract description of the system life cycle where there are four defined quadrants – planning, risk analysis, use of design methods, client and management evaluation. Once one stage of development has gone full circle, the next takes place, and so on until completion.

Waterfall model is an earlier abstract description of the system life cycle where each identified stage of development flows from the previous one and down to the next one. Feedback from each to the previous takes place independently of the forward flow. The process is complete when all reviews (see *project management*, page 36) are satisfied.

System development cycle

is the various stages in designing and implementing a new computer system. These stages – typically *analysis*, *design*, *implementation*, *testing* and *installation* – are part of the system life cycle performed by the main design team. Each individual stage is described separately elsewhere in this chapter.

Software development cycle

including: software life cycle
is the various stages required to produce the software component of a new computer system. The software development cycle is part of the *implementation* stage of the *system life cycle* (see page 30).

Software is often the most complicated part of a system. Hence the software development cycle is often considered separately although the stages are very similar to those of the *system development cycle* (see above). A typical software development cycle is shown in Table A4.2.

Table A4.2 Software development cycle

Stage	Description
Overall design	Identifies what is required of the software and splits it into self-contained modules
Module design	Decides how each module will perform its task
Module production	Produces a computer program for each module (coding)
Module testing	Makes sure that each module works independently
Combining the modules	Produces the new software system
Integration testing	Makes sure that the modules work together

The **software life cycle** includes the additional stages of *feasibility*, *analysis*, *installation* and *maintenance*, which may be considered separately from the rest of the system. See pages 33–36.

The relationship between the system life cycle, the software life cycle and the system development cycle can be confusing. The systems development cycle is, in fact, simply part of the system life cycle. Similarly the software development cycle is simply part of the system development cycle. The software life cycle is the same as system life cycle when the system being designed consists solely of software. Figure A4.1 shows the relationship between these various concepts.

Figure A4.1 Relationship between the three cycles

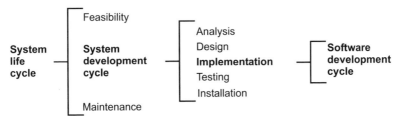

Design methodology

including: Agile development, service-oriented architecture, SSADM (Structured Systems Analysis and Design Methodology), Rapid Application Development (RAD), Jackson Structured Programming (JSP)
is a set of rules to be followed when designing a computer program or a computer system. This ensures that all the steps of the system development cycle are followed. Using the same methodologies means that different people can work together as a team. Design methodologies include:

Agile development describes the responsive development of a system made of small software modules (often web-based applications) by a group of collaborators who work concurrently and closely under a leader who ensures engineering best practice and delivery of the customer requirement.

Service-oriented architecture describes the building of software modules as reusable components (web services or business processes) that can interact with each other over internal or external networks irrespective of the programming languages or communications protocols on which they are based.

SSADM (Structured Systems Analysis and Design Methodology) is the standard method of analysis and design of large-scale software packages used within government departments in the UK and is widely used commercially. SSADM is very precise and divides the method into many small stages.

Rapid Application Development (RAD) is a design strategy that includes online development and repeated prototyping and evaluation. It is particularly suited to interactive systems.

Jackson Structured Programming (JSP) is a structured programming technique that uses diagrams as a step to developing programs. *Structured programming* (see page 45) emphasises an orderly approach to program development, breaking down large tasks into smaller subtasks. JSP is a particular form of this diagrammatic method that enables the design process to be efficiently managed.

STAGES

Feasibility study

is the preliminary investigation of a problem used to decide if a solution is possible and how it may be done. It may be carried out by the main design team or by a separate team, which will allow a suitable main design team to be chosen. It is similar to the *systems analysis* (see below) but at a much simpler level. It often:

- describes the context of the problem;
- contains an evaluation, or simple analysis, of the problem;
- identifies, and justifies, ways in which the problem may be solvable;
- involves a cost–benefit analysis to decide if a solution is affordable.

Systems analysis

is an investigation into a problem and how a new system will solve it. The analyst will usually:

- research how the previous system and other similar systems work using inter-views, observation, existing documentation, questionnaires and experience. In some cases this may be formally documented to provide a basis for the new design;
- identify the main requirements for the system: the *requirements specification*, see page 45;
- identify what is input to the system and what is output from the system;
- describe the system using *data flow diagrams* (see page 49) and a commentary;
- define the input, output and processing requirements for each process identified;
- develop a *data model* (see page 94). This may include normalised entity descriptions and *entity-relationship diagrams* (see page 51);
- identify the likely hardware and software constraints;
- specify the hardware and the software required to carry out the development.

Systems design

is the production of a detailed description showing how the new system will be constructed. One or more overall designs will be produced and then detailed designs will be produced for the preferred solution. It will usually include:

- the overall design using a system diagram and commentary describing and justify-ing the solution;
- detailed design of user interfaces, and the validation and verification of the input data;
- detailed design of reports and other outputs;
- detailed design of the storage and organisation of the data;
- detailed specifications and structure diagrams of each process. See *functional spec-ification*, page 45;
- a test plan for both the individual functions and the system as a whole. This will include the test data to be used.

Implementation (of the design)

is the process of constructing the working computer system. It will usually include:

- identifying the modules to be used and specifying them;
- identifying the main data structures within the program;
- identifying the main algorithms to be used, describing them in *pseudo-code* (page 220) or as *structure diagrams* (page 54);
- producing the program and any other elements of the system.

Systems testing

is making sure the system works as described in the specification. This is done by following the test plan:

- to test each individual system function;
- to test that each individual function works with extreme or invalid data;
- to test the whole system to ensure that the system produces the correct results for the data input.

Installation

also known as: systems implementation
including: parallel running, pilot running, direct changeover, big-bang, phased implementation
is the process of starting to use an information system in a real situation after having designed and developed it. It may enable final testing in a real situation. Different approaches are used depending on the size of the system and the properties of the data being processed.

Parallel running requires the new system to operate for a short period of time alongside the older system. The results can be compared to ensure that the new system is working correctly.

Pilot running requires the new system to operate alongside the old system but only processing part of the data. The results can be compared to check that the system works correctly but pilot running cannot test how the system will operate with the larger quantities of data of the real situation.

Direct changeover or *big-bang* requires that the new system replaces the old system without any overlap. In some cases the nature of the system prevents parallel or pilot running and a direct changeover is the only option, for example with an emergency control system.

Phased implementation involves replacing part of a system with a new system while some tasks continue to use the old system. This enables training and installation to be spread over a period of time. For example, a supermarket chain might install a new system in a few of its branches to begin with and phase the introduction into its other branches as they are refurbished. This initial phase of the implementation will inevitably involve some parallel running.

Maintenance

is ensuring the system continues to run smoothly and to meet changed requirements, for example:

- addressing problems not previously identified;
- modifying the software when circumstances change, for example the amount of data increases, the system is to be used in a new area or the data needs to be processed slightly differently (for example changes in legal requirements);
- replacing the computer hardware;
- adding new facilities to the software.

Documentation

including: technical documentation, maintenance documentation, systems documentation, program documentation
is the written information and diagrams that enable the development of the system to be planned professionally, help users use the system and enable the maintenance and development of the system. The documentation usually consists of *technical documentation*, *user documentation* and if appropriate installation instructions (see *Installation* page 35).

Technical documentation describes how the system works. It is written for the computer professional rather than the user and the reader will need to have expert knowledge. It will include both *systems documentation* and *program documentation* (see below). Some parts will be technical, for example the specifications of peripherals and their configuration. It is mainly used to develop and later adapt the system. It is sometimes known as **maintenance documentation**. See also *project documentation*, page 37.

Systems documentation describes the results of the systems analysis, what is expected of the system, the overall design decisions, the *test plan* and *test data* (see page 228) with the expected results.

Program documentation is the complete description of the software, intended for use when altering or adapting the software. It usually includes a statement of the purpose of the software, any restrictions on the use of the software, the format for input data, printed output produced, flowcharts, program listings and notes to assist in future modifications.

PROJECT MANAGEMENT

Project

is the organised production of any predefined piece of work. A project is self-contained, with a defined start and finish. The start of the project is the decision to go ahead and produce the piece of work. The completion of the project is the evaluation of the piece of work compared with the requirements. Any project will include, sometimes implicitly, analysis, design, implementation, testing and evaluation. See also the *system life cycle*, page 30.

A project can produce a physical artefact, for example a car, or a service, such as a payroll system for a business. Some activities within a project can themselves be treated as separate projects, for example a feasibility study is usually prepared as a separate project.

Stakeholders

are groups of people concerned with the success of a project. These include clients, users, team members and senior management.

Project management

is the organised production of the piece of work to the agreed goals of quality and standards, completion date, costs and product produced.

Suitable *project management software*, see page 38, may be used throughout the project to check tasks are completed by the set deadlines to ensure continued development. The documentation relating to the progress of the project is kept.

Project documentation

is a complete record of the progress of the project and includes the proposal, detailed specifications, approved updates, agendas and minutes of all review meetings, records and hand-over material relating to the testing of the product. Often a proposal is a project in its own right.

Project lifetime

is the period of time between completing the project proposal and the completion of the project. The project concludes with the client's acceptance of the product or service, after the user testing and delivery of all elements of the project.

Project proposal

is where the goals and the methods of solution (expertise, equipment and methodologies) are agreed by relevant stakeholders.

Project team leadership

is the planning, organising, leading and controlling the team as they produce elements for the project. This includes *peer review* (see page 38) of the product and each team member's contribution, communication with stakeholders and taking decisions in the light of the agreed goals.

Project review

including: peer review, external review
meetings evaluate the progress made and agree any changes experience has shown are required. They include both internal peer review within the project team and communication with stakeholders about progress at milestones of the project to log achievement, to identify problem areas and to establish appropriate response.

Peer review is a review by members of the team, who will understand the project and be able to compare what has been achieved with the expectations.

External review is a review conducted by independent consultants who can assess the project's progress with more objectivity and advise how to proceed if the requirements are not being met or costs are too high.

Project schedule

is a plan of the project giving each stage and its planned start and stop times. At each stage the activities (tasks and subtasks) will be named; the costs and the resources will be identified.

Project management software

allows the planning of complex tasks using a computer. The software allows the project to be split into activities (tasks and subtasks), each of which can be planned separately. The various parts of the project can be linked together so that the computer can construct a plan or calendar of how the project will proceed. This should ensure that later components are not waiting for earlier related components to finish.

Gantt chart

is a type of bar chart that displays the start and finish dates of the elements of a project and shows the dependencies (relationships) between elements. Gantt chart software can be used to show current schedule status using 'per cent-complete' shadings and a vertical 'TODAY' line.

Figure A4.2 An example Gantt chart

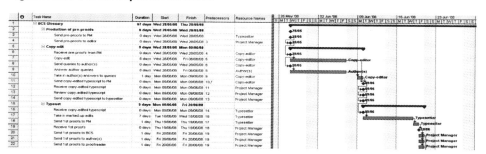

Critical Path Analysis

including: Critical Path Method (CPM), float time, dependencies
is analysing a set of project activities so that delays and conflicts are resolved to reduce the project lifetime to a minimum. One way is to use the *Critical Path Method (CPM)*.

Critical Path Method (CPM) is a mathematical algorithm for scheduling and displaying a set of project activities. The essential technique for using CPM is to construct a model of the project that includes:

- a list of all activities required to complete the project;
- the time (duration) that each activity will take to complete;
- the dependencies between the activities. Dependency may involve the materials and staff available and the completion of some activities before a new activity can start. See also *dependencies*, page 40.

Using these values, CPM calculates the earliest starting and latest finishing times for each activity. It will reveal the chain of activities whose schedule is critical to the completion of the project in that any delay to these tasks will delay the whole project's completion. This is called the **critical path**. There are also some activities with 'float time' whose scheduling is less critical. The project manager will be especially aware of the critical activities and may add suitably experienced staff to an activity after a review reveals a problem that may mean failure to achieve the goal time. See Figure A4.3, an example of Critical Path Analysis.

Figure A4.3 An example of Critical Path Analysis

Procure software

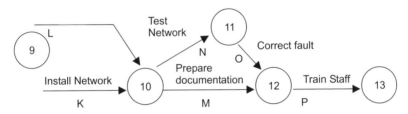

With Activity Dependency Table

	Activity	Duration Days	Preceding Activities
K	Install network	15	D, E, I, J
L	Procure software	28	A
M	Prepare documentation	15	K, L
N	Test network	10	K, L
O	Correct fault	6	N
P	Train users	10	M, O

Full Detail of Node Entry

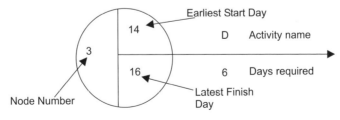

Float time is the length of time an activity can be delayed or overrun without the whole project being affected. For example, setting up a printer can be done at the same time as installing the computer but will not take as long. Float time exists because the printer could be set up at the start of the installation process or at the end. The project manager can use this to optimise the project, for example to reduce staff costs.

Dependencies are where activities can only be undertaken after another activity is completed. For example, the printer software can only be installed after the computer and printer are both set up, so dependencies exist between the software installation and both the computer and printer set up.

Integrated development environment (IDE)

also known as: integrated programming environment
is software that performs the various stages of software design and implementation in a single integrated system. It will usually include facilities for project management, design, graphical design, programming, testing and producing documentation.

An integrated programming environment enables increased automation, for example simple designs can be automatically converted into program code. It also will perform *version management* (see page 41), to ensure the correct (usually the latest tested) versions of each module are used in each version produced. See also *version*, page 44.

GENERAL

Benchmark

is a standard set of computer tasks, designed to allow measurements to be made of computer performance. These tasks can be used to compare the performance of different software or hardware. Examples of tasks are: how long it takes to copy a 1 Mb file across a network, how many pages can be printed in one minute, how long it takes to save 1000 database records to disk. Users seeking to buy software or hardware may be able to obtain some information about the performance of possible purchases.

Benchmarks may also figure in *acceptance testing* (see page 43) of a computer system, by specifying performance that must be achieved before the system is considered finished. See also *software metric*, below, for a description of the theoretical equivalent of the more practical benchmark.

Software metric

is a value that can be associated with a piece of software to describe its efficiency, performance, ease of development, and other properties. *Benchmarks* (see above) measure how software actually behaves, while software metrics attempt to describe performance from a study of the program code alone. Simple and sometimes not very helpful metrics include the number of lines of code and the space occupied in memory.

Commissioning

including: decommissioning
is putting a new system into use. The suppliers make sure the system is ready to be used and the customer accepts that it meets the specification. The customer will have checked the operation of the system and can start using it to do the job it was designed for.

Decommissioning is taking an old system out of use. This involves more than simply switching it off. Data will have to be transferred to a new system or saved in a way in which it can be accessed later. Records will need to be made of outstanding problems that still need to be dealt with and the hardware will need to be disposed of safely.

Compatibility

including: backward compatibility, downward compatibility, upward compatibility
describes how well different computer systems work together.

Backward compatible (also known as **downward compatible**) is used to describe a computer system designed to work with older systems. For example programs can load files from older versions of the program or computer hardware will run software designed for older types of computer. Backward compatibility ensures that new software can be acquired without needing to buy new hardware and that the data from the old computer system can continue to be used.

Upward compatible is used to describe a computer system designed to be extended and improved without the need to retrain staff or to alter any stored data.

Configuration management

also known as: version management
is the tracking and monitoring of changes to a system during its development and operational life. This ensures that everyone involved (both users and developers) are working with identical systems, with the same features available and consistency of performance.

Although usually applied to software systems, it can also apply to complete systems involving hardware upgrades, software revisions, telecommunications maintenance, security issues and new versions of documentation. See also *version*, page 44.

Bespoke system

is a system developed for a specific customer. It might include unusual hardware and will have to be specially programmed. This is expensive to do but may be the only solution to the customer's needs, particularly for a large organisation. It will take longer to develop and test but the customer will get an efficient system that meets the requirements. In contrast a *customised system* (see page 42) may not provide exactly the facilities wanted although it is cheaper, quicker to develop and will need less testing.

Customised system

including: customised application, turnkey system
is a system consisting of standard hardware and software that is then adapted to suit the customer's requirements. Many users do not have the skill or resources to set up a new computer system. Such users will purchase a customised system from a supplier. See also *bespoke system*, page 41.

- The supplier may simply alter the *defaults* (see page 16) and provide special templates to the customer's requirements.

- A standard application program can be further customised for the customer by constructing a special user interface, with menus, macros and buttons. This allows actions the customer will need, such as loading a specific template or producing a specific report, to be performed quickly, efficiently and with less training. See also *menu*, page 420, *macro*, page 211, and *screen button*, page 421.

- In a more complex system several commercial programs may need to be combined to produce the required system. The cost of writing standard programs such as word processors or databases is very high and it is much more cost-effective for a standard database, for example, to be purchased and a small program written to access it in the most efficient way for the user. See also *application program interface*, below.

Customised application is a customised system developed by customising a particular software application, such as a spreadsheet. Usually no special hardware is needed. This kind of system will rely on the ability to create an efficient client specific *user interface*, see page 416.

Turnkey system is a complete system, developed and tested in advance, that is quickly installed and when the user switches it on it functions without further configuration. The supplier often supplies the same system to several customers and customises the interface specifically for each customer in advance.

Application program interface (API)

is the way a supplier of a software application enables a user to integrate this application with the user's own programs and indeed with other software applications. This enables *customised systems* (see above) to be constructed easily and quickly using standard software packages. For example a program may be written to take data from a payroll program and use the facilities of a spreadsheet program to present it as charts.

The application program interface usually takes the form of standardised machine code calls to subroutines in the software application. The supplier can alter the program code of the application and adapt the application program interface to work with the new program. The users' programs will still work because the way the application program interface is accessed has not changed. See also *customise*, page 15.

Developmental testing

including: alpha testing, beta testing, acceptance testing
is the repeated testing of a system so that the results can be used for further design and development. Commercial software is developed to an incomplete state, with some questions of design, command sequences and defaults left unresolved.

Alpha testing is the issue of the software to a restricted audience of testers within the developer's own company. This version may not be completely finished and may have faults.

Beta testing is when a version is released to a number of privileged customers in exchange for their constructive comments. This is after the results of the *alpha testing* have been studied and appropriate changes made. Beta test versions are usually similar to the finally released product. They are made available to computer magazine reviewers, authors of independent 'how to' instructional manuals, and developers of associated software or hardware products, who can work over a period of time with a near-complete package, so that the final launch can be accompanied by valuable and informed publicity.

Acceptance testing is the testing carried out to prove to the customer that the system works correctly. This testing is done when system development is complete and the system is ready to be handed over to the customer. It will test all parts of the system and compare it with the requirements specified in the design. It is designed to ensure that the customer will get what they ordered. If the system fails any of the tests then the supplier is obliged to correct the faults.

Formal methods

including: formal specification
is the name given to the mathematical techniques used to attempt to prove that software works, without having to test every possible route through the programs. With large complex computer systems, it is impossible to test that the system behaves properly under every possible combination of circumstances. Therefore individual parts of the system will have a precise **formal specification** including inputs that they will recognise and outputs that they will produce, which can be linked together with mathematics.

Process

also known as: subtask
is an activity that is carried out as part of a computer system. Each process is identifiable, independent and of manageable size. The results from the process will then be passed to other processes.

Examples include inputting a set of data, printing a report, editing a record or sorting a file. An individual process may be repeated in a short period of time, for example printing a set of reports may be seen as repetition of the process of printing a single report.

Processes may reflect a user view of the system (for example when printing a report) or its internal design (for example when validating an item of data). Processes can also occur at different levels and a complex process may be split into simpler processes. The aim and quality are defined by criteria and boundaries so that these can be checked at the review stages.

Prototyping

including: prototype, storyboard
is the construction of a simple version of the program, a **prototype**, which is used as part of the design process to demonstrate how the system will work. The prototype generally consists of the working *user interface* (see page 416), but will not actually process any

data. The prototype can be reviewed by the user and changes made to the system at the design stage.

A *storyboard* is a diagram that shows the planned sequence of screen displays in a user interface. Unlike the storyboard for a film (which is linear) the storyboard may be a branching diagram showing the different paths available to the user.

Reverse engineering

is the analysis of existing software to produce an equivalent design. It is used if the original design documentation is lost to enable the maintenance of the system or the development of a replacement system. It might also be used illegally to reveal the techniques used in a competitor's product.

Shrink-wrapped software

is a computer application that is sold prepackaged for the user to install onto their own system. As the software is prepackaged it can be sold through a variety of outlets such as computer retailers or even supermarkets. Help and support is likely to be limited to the manuals (or online/on-screen documentation) provided, and possibly from a telephone support desk.

Software engineering

also known as: information systems engineering
is the science of designing and constructing new or modified computer systems, based mainly on computer software (programs). The software engineer will develop a new system following the *system development cycle* (see page 32). This will help ensure that the new system has the required characteristics of functionality: *ease of use*, *robustness*, *flexibility*, *reliability*, *portability*, and *ease of maintenance* (see page 46).

Software upgrade

including: version, migrate
is a new version of a program, or computer application, which is based on an older system but has been improved either to fix problems or to add new features. When purchased the software upgrade often just consists of the files required to convert the older version to the newer version.

Version is a reference, generally a number, which indicates how old that particular program is. The version number is important because files produced by one version are not always usable by a different version. Having a newer version of the program may cure errors that were present.

Migrate is to move from using one version of a computer application to either a new version or to an application supplied by a competitor. This process may be quite complicated as staff might need training to use the new program, and files might need to be converted so they can be used by a new program.

It is also possible to upgrade a computer system from one set of hardware to a different hardware setup. See also *portability*, page 46.

Specification

including: requirements specification, systems specification, functional specification
is a written document that precisely defines aspects of the system. Specifications may be written at different parts of the development cycle and serve different purposes. For example:

Requirements specification is that part of the system documentation that sets out the customer's requirements for the system. It is produced as part of *systems analysis* (see page 34). It may be drafted as a formal contractual agreement between the customer and the software system developers. It will describe what is expected of the system and allow the final system to be assessed, making sure it meets the customer's expectations.

Systems specification sets out the hardware and software requirements, as well as the organisational and human implications. It is produced at the end of the *design phase* (see page 34) and is used by the programmers and others to produce a system that works as intended.

Functional specification describes exactly how the system will behave, showing what happens at each stage of the system as each process is performed. It is usually part of the *systems specification* (see above).

Structured programming

including: structured planning technique, modular design, modules, top-down programming, stepwise refinement, functional decomposition, bottom-up programming, object-oriented design
is a methodical approach to the design of a program that emphasises breaking large and complex tasks into smaller subtasks. This is also referred to as **structured planning technique**.

Modular design is a method of organising a large computer program into self-contained parts, **modules**, which can be developed simultaneously by different programmers or teams of programmers. Modules have clearly defined relationships with the other parts of the system, which enables them to be independently designed, programmed and maintained. Some modules may be independently executable programs, while others may be designed to provide facilities for the suite of programs to which they belong.

Top-down programming or **stepwise refinement** is a particular type of structured programming, where the overall problem is defined in simple terms and then split into a number of smaller subtasks. Each of these subtasks is successively split and refined until they are small enough to be understood and programmed. It is an axiom of this approach that new ideas that were not in the original global design should not be added. This ensures elements are not missed.

Functional decomposition is a method similar to top-down programming where overall functions of the system are defined and then these functions are successively split down into smaller functions until they are small enough to be programmed.

Bottom-up programming involves designing a number of small modules before designing the larger structure. This is considered bad practice as it is often difficult to ensure that an efficient system is developed.

Object-oriented design involves identifying self-contained objects, which contain both program routines and the data being processed. A program is split down into very small units, called objects, which can then be used by other objects to build a more complex system. Object-orientated design requires the use of an object-oriented programming language. See also *object-oriented programming*, page 188.

System characteristics

including: ease of use, robustness, flexibility, reliability, portability, ported, (hardware) platform, ease of maintenance
are the general properties (which may be good or bad) of systems or programs that determine how successful the system may be in general use. The good properties that programmers will attempt to produce are:

Ease of use means that users will be able to operate the system or program with limited training and support.

Robustness is the ability to cope with errors and mishaps during program execution without producing wrong results or stopping. Events (such as a jammed printer) should not make the computer system fail. See also *fault tolerance* (page 118).

Flexibility is the ability to be easily reconfigured by the user or adapted for use in a different situation. This may enable a system or program to be sold more widely or to be adapted to changing circumstances.

Reliability is how well a system or program operates without failing due to design faults.

Portability is the ability to be used on different computer hardware. Many large commercial systems remain in use for much longer than the original hardware and will be adapted or ported to new types of computer hardware, thus saving the expense of rewriting the system. Most software packages will only work on particular combinations of hardware and operating system, which are sometimes referred to as **(hardware) platforms**.

Ease of maintenance allows modifications that have to be made during the life of a system to be carried out easily and cheaply. *Program maintenance* (see page 196) is a major expense in the use of a computer system. *Structured programming* (see page 45) enables software to be designed in a way that enables ease of maintenance.

Undocumented feature

is a facility included as part of a computer system that is not described in the official specification or documentation. The feature may not be fully tested or may be provided to help engineers diagnose faults. The user cannot rely on the feature since it may be altered or removed at a later date.

Visual programming tools

allow the developer to design and prototype applications rapidly with less traditional coding. System elements such as the input and output user interfaces are presented and manipulated graphically; the controls such as event buttons are linked to coding subroutines. Microsoft®'s Visual Studio® is a good example of such a software tool.

A5 DESCRIBING SYSTEMS

This section is concerned with the written comments and graphical illustrations that form the description of a system. The symbols and layout conventions referred to are those given in British Standards BS 4058:1987, BS 7738:1994 and in ISO 19501:2005. Related topics can be found in Section F5 User interface and documentation, Section A4 Systems design and life cycle, Section C1 Programming concepts, Section C5 Describing programs and Section C6 Testing and running programs.

Software systems will require some modification during their lifetime. If this is to be done satisfactorily, it is vital that good, complete and understandable documentation is available. Requests to modify software may arise for a number of reasons, which could include changes in company procedures, requests for improvements, errors in the software that were not found at the testing stage and changes in government regulations (for example, new taxation law). The resources required at the maintenance stage of the **systems life cycle**, which is covered in Section A4 Systems design and life cycle, frequently equal and indeed sometimes exceed the initial resources required to deliver the software in the first instance.

The original teams that did the analysis and design, and the implementation, of the software may not be available to carry out the maintenance stage. This makes it all the more important that good, up-to-date documentation is available throughout the life of the software.

A standard form of documentation may be followed, which may be specified by the company involved. There are a number of recognised system development methodologies, for example **SSADM (Structured Systems Analysis and Design Methodology)**. These specify, at various levels of detail, what documentation should be produced and in what form. Software tools also exist, such as **CASE (computer-aided software engineering)** tools, which can help to produce consistent documentation of changes. Additionally, visual programming tools and IDEs are available for developing systems online.

Documentation produced at the design and analysis stage will include the **requirements specification**, which is sometimes 'signed off' as a formal agreement between the customer and the software group. As the design develops, a range of diagrams will be produced; these can include:

- diagrams showing the relationships between the data in the data model (**entity-relationship** or **entity-relation diagrams**);

- diagrams showing the relationships between the data and the processes or programs that manipulate and transform the data (**data flow diagrams** or **system diagrams**);

- interface designs;

- **UML (Unified Modelling Language)** combines all these techniques in a consistent structure in an object-oriented manner.

The design task will be tackled in a hierarchical way, gradually breaking it down into smaller parts (subtasks). Often diagrams use different shapes to indicate the use of a particular device or medium, in the same kind of way that icons are often used in a graphical user interface. Further design of the data model into **third normal form** may be needed.

As the programs are designed and developed there will be other documentation for the programs. These have particular forms and are covered in Section C5 Describing programs. Alternative techniques such as object-oriented or event-driven programming are covered in Section C1 Programming concepts.

Block diagram

is a diagram made up of boxes labelled to represent different hardware or software components and lines showing their interconnections. See Figure A5.1.

Figure A5.1 An example of a block diagram (courtesy Acorn Computers)

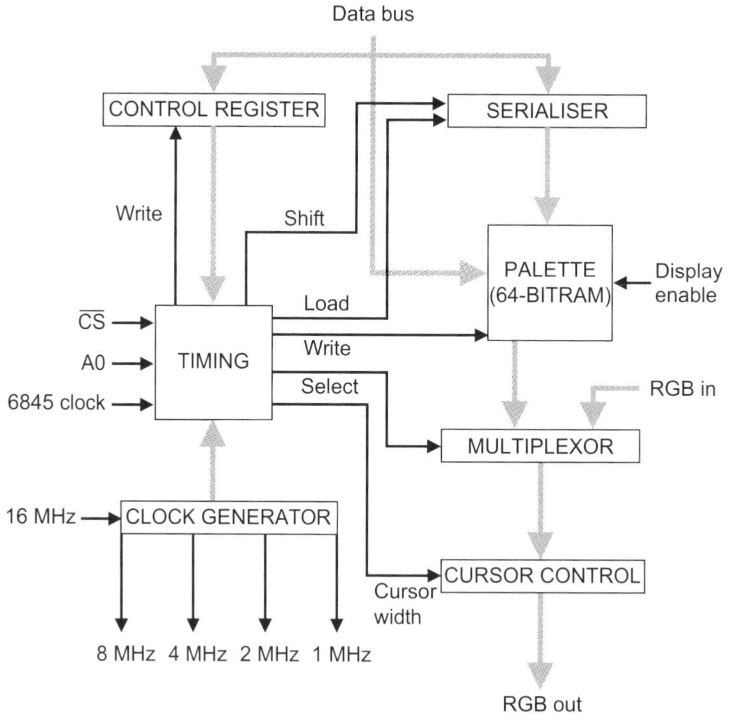

Information flow diagram

is used to show how information moves between the various parts of a business organisation. It demonstrates what happens at an organisational level and includes the boundaries with external entities. See Figure A5.2, information flow diagram symbols, and Figure A5.3, an example of an information flow diagram. These are often used by business analysts, and are equivalent to level 0 *data flow diagrams* (see below).

Data flow diagram

shows how data moves through a system. It demonstrates what happens at the overall system level. It identifies where the data comes from in the wider organisation, the processes it passes through and where the data goes to in the wider organisation. It is an essential part of *SSADM* (see page 33).

It is developed from the *information flow diagram* (see above) and shares its context. The level 0 data flow diagram identifies how the data needs to be processed in the overall computer system. Each arrow on the information flow diagram can be thought of as a process in the data flow diagram.

Figure A5.2 Information flow diagram symbols

Figure A5.3 An example of an information flow diagram
This describes the information flow in a simplified online ordering system. The internal functions are Orders, Payments and Warehouse. The external organisations are the Customers, Bank and Suppliers.

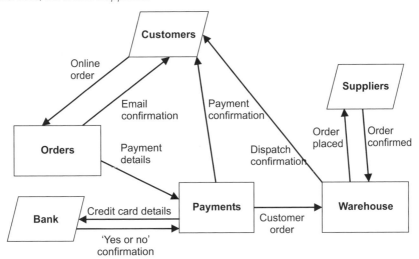

Lower level data flow diagrams show increasing complexity in the processes and deliver detail in the context of the relevant stages of development.

Data flow diagrams are used in *systems analysis* (see page 34) to show what happens to the data throughout the whole organisation, in both computerised and manual systems. Such a diagram is not usually linear and does not try to place the processes into any order. This is done with a system diagram in the design stage. More detail of each process can be shown by a level 2 data flow diagram.

Figure A5.4 shows a widely used set of symbols used for data flow diagrams and Figure A5.5 shows a level 1 data flow diagram for a traditional payroll system. Compare this with Figure A5.8 on page 53, which is the system diagram for the same scenario.

Figure A5.4 Data flow symbols

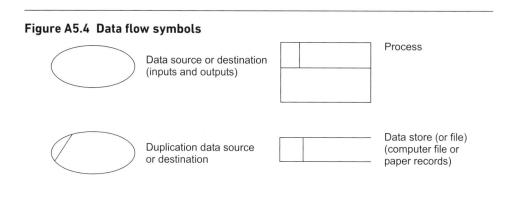

Figure A5.5 Level 1 Data flow diagram of the payroll process

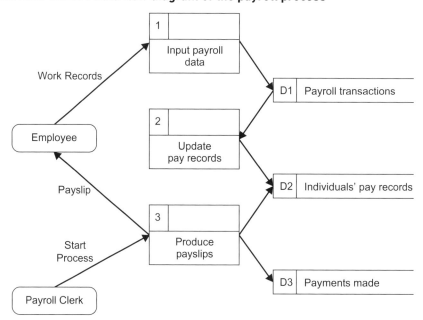

Entity-relationship diagram

including: entity relationship
is a diagram used to show how the entities in a data model are related to each other. It is a conceptual representation of the data. For example, how the different layers of data in a database are related and how access to one layer of data will automatically achieve access to related data items and related layers.

It demonstrates what happens at the data structure level. An **entity relationship** is a formal statement of the way in which one data item is related to another, or of the way in which a class of data items is related to items in another class. See also *data model* (see page 94).

Figure A5.6 illustrates two different classes of entity relationships, many-to-many and one-to-many.

System flowchart

also known as: system diagram
is a diagram used to describe a complete data-processing system. It demonstrates what happens at an individual process level. The flow of data through the operations

---

Figure A5.6 Entity-relationship diagram used in designing a database

In the top diagram, two entities, aircraft and route, are identified. Attributes are not shown, but they might include the plane number, its type, passenger capacity, and so on, for the aircraft, and the starting point and destination for the route. There is a relationship between these entities: an aircraft can be used on many routes, and a route can be travelled by many aircraft. Such many-to-many relationships are not easy to implement in a database, so the designer breaks this relationship and invents a new entity called trip, *which represents one specific journey over that route by one specific aircraft. One aircraft now makes many trips, but each trip is made by only one aircraft. Similarly, one route has many trips over it, but each trip is over just one route. Two such one-to-many relationships are more efficient to implement than one many-to-many relationship.*

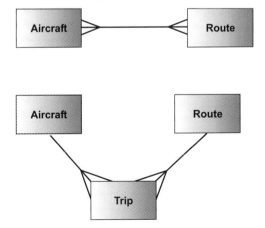

is diagrammatically described, down to the level of the individual programs needed to achieve the system requirements. Symbols of flow are used (either an arrowed line showing the sequence of operations or an arrowed split line showing communication of data). The details of programs are not included, since these are covered in the *program documentation* (see page 36). See Figure A5.7, system flowchart symbols.

The flowchart in Figure A5.8 describes the part of a payroll process where the wages information for each employee is processed. The transactions are validated, sorted and then used to update the wages master file.

The descriptions (printer, disk etc.) may be altered, according to the particular medium being used. Alternatively, the descriptions may be omitted completely, if a less specific flowchart is required.

Figure A5.7 System flowchart symbols

Input/Output symbols		Used for any input or output of data however achieved.
Interaction input symbol	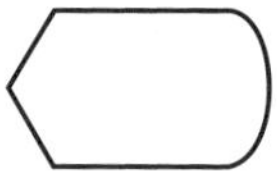	Used to indicate data input by keyboard or other operator-controlled input system such as a bar-code reader. It may also be used for online interrogation.
Document output symbols	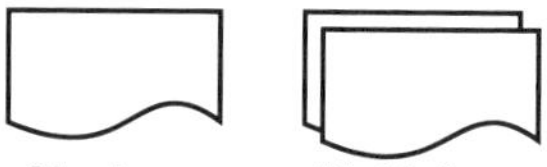 Single document Multiple documents	Used to indicate that data is to be printed.
Process symbol	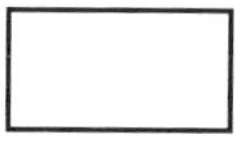	Used for the processing of data, for example by a computer program.
File symbols	 Online data	Used for data held on any online file, whatever the purpose.
	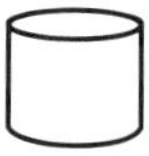 (Magnetic) disk file	Used whenever the data is held on a disk.
	 (Magnetic) tape file	Used whenever the data is held on a tape.

Figure A5.8 An example of system flowchart using alternative symbols

This flowchart uses alternative British Standard symbols to show a typical payroll process. The annotation on the right of the flowcharts has been used to describe the function of the symbols. A similar annotation method can be used to provide an explanatory commentary on the algorithm or process represented by the flowchart diagram. The document symbols can also be used for the input of data to a system by means of documents (e.g. written orders).

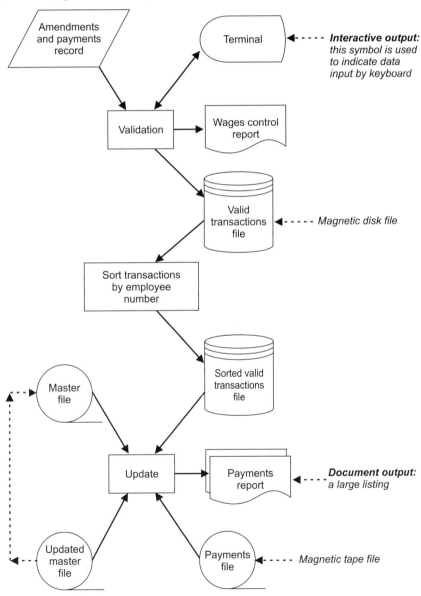

Structure diagram

is a means of representing the design of a program or system.

The structure diagram, Figure A5.9, shows another way of representing the payroll process shown in Figure A5.8. It is based on the *Jackson Structured Programming (JSP)* method (see page 33). The hierarchical structure diagram is displayed in a top-down, left-to-right manner. At each successive level (labelled 1, 2, 3, ...) the tasks are described in greater detail. The lower boxes expand the description of the task defined in the box in the level above to which they are connected. This process of expansion is continued to varying depths in different parts of the diagram until it is judged that sufficient detail is given.

Figure A5.9 A structure diagram for the payroll process

The numbers are used to identify the boxes uniquely. The actual numbers are not significant although they can be used to indicate levels. In this case the first digit indicates the level, for example 3.59 would indicate a box at level 3.
Note: In UML *(see page 56) structure diagrams are different.*

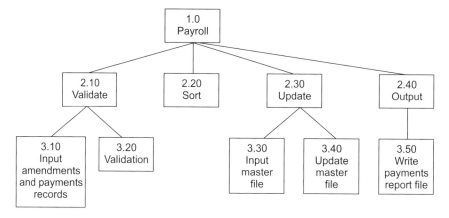

At greater levels of detail it can be helpful to draw the expanded version of a section in the structure diagram, in this case the validation section, as a separate diagram, Figure A5.10.

In this example horizontal and vertical connecting lines are used. It is of no importance which type of connecting line is drawn although it is normal to be consistent.

Flowchart

including: flow line
is a graphical representation of the operations involved in a process or system. *Flowchart symbols* (Figure A5.11) are used to represent particular operations or data, and **flow lines**, which connect the flowchart symbols, indicate the sequence of operations or the flow of data. Flow lines may use arrows to indicate sequence, or a top-down, left-right convention may apply if there are no arrows.

Different shapes indicate the various kinds of activity described by the diagram. Sometimes highly formalised shapes are used, each having a specific meaning; in other

Figure A5.10 Expansion of process 3.20 in Figure C5.9

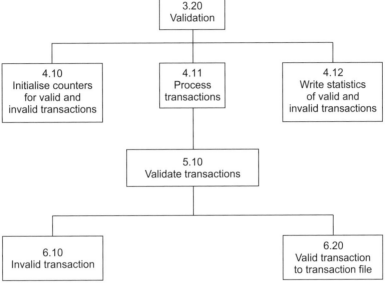

Figure A5.11 Flowchart symbols

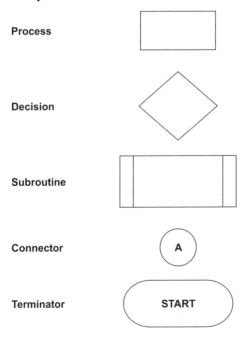

situations very simple boxes with words are used. Provided the meaning is clear, either method is an equally acceptable way of representing a process or system. Examples of how these symbols might be used are given in Figure A5.12.

Unified Modelling Language (UML)

including: use case diagram, sequence diagram, activity diagram, class diagram, statechart diagram (also known as state diagram)
is a notation of symbols and diagrams to communicate object-oriented analysis and design. It also documents the construction of a software system, including the business model, where the dynamic behaviour is represented.

Figure A5.12 An example of a flowchart
This flowchart shows the order of the processes when making an online purchase in a typical online ordering system.

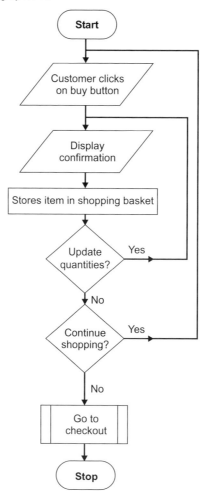

In the UML notation, structure diagrams emphasise what things must be inside the system being modelled and document the architecture of the software system. These include diagrams of:

- classes and their attributes;
- components and their associations;
- deployment on to hardware;
- objects;
- packages or their logical groupings.

Each concept in the system is described as a class.

The notes on UML follow the industry-accepted standard ISO 19501: 2005.

Use case diagram shows the functionality of the system from the users' perspective and is essentially non-technical. The system boundary is represented by a rectangle surrounding the use cases (ellipses) and the users or actors (stick figures, although they can also represent non-human hardware or another system). See Figure A5.13.

Sequence diagram shows the interaction between objects and messages over time. Time being the vertical axis and objects (or classes) depicted left to right horizontally. The named message is shown between objects. See Figure A5.14.

Activity diagram shows a variation of the *statechart diagram* (see page 58) where events are replaced by internal flows. An action state is represented by a box with rounded ends; a diamond represents a decision with its exclusive outcomes. Joins and forks are shown as bars. 'Swim lanes' separate different actions. See Figure A5.15.

Figure A5.13 An example use case diagram

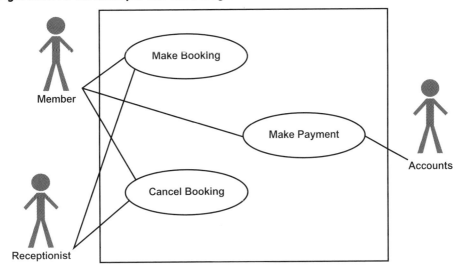

Figure A5.14 An example sequence diagram

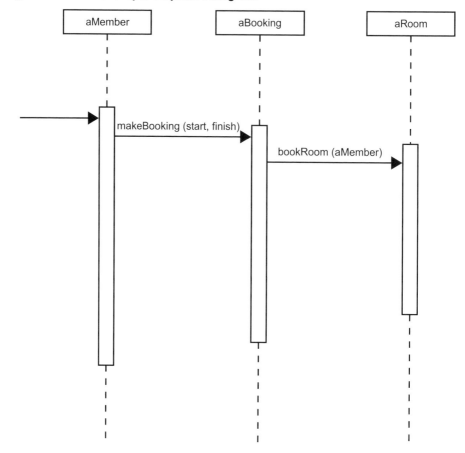

Class diagram shows a *class* (see page 189) represented by a rectangle labelled by its name, attributes and operations. Classes may be associated similar to *entity relationships* (see page 51). See Figure A5.16.

Statechart diagram (also known as **state diagram**) shows the various permitted states that an object may be in (an object is an instance of a class). States are represented by a rectangle with rounded corners and labelled with a unique name. Transitions from state to state are represented by arrows labelled with the trigger condition (the event name) and any changing attributes. See Figure A5.17.

Figure A5.15 An example activity diagram

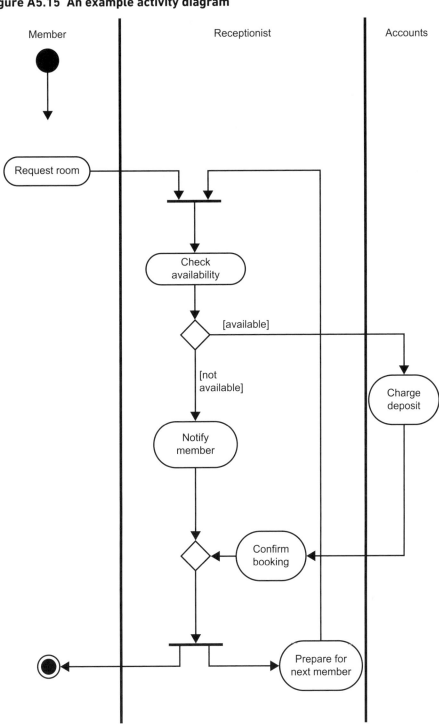

Figure A5.16 An example class diagram

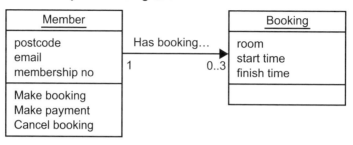

Figure A5.17 An example statechart diagram

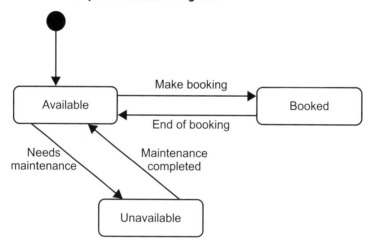

PART B: CONCEPTS

This section contains terms that might be met by any computer user working with applications in any of the areas covered. The chapters in Part B are concerned with general issues involved with well-defined areas of computer use. Some contain terms that might have been placed in other parts but they were kept with other related terms for completeness; this is particularly true of the chapters covering the internet and computer security because they have become more prominent aspects of computer use. Some terms have references to terms in other parts that will provide readers with pointers to other associated terms and concepts.

B1   PERSONAL USE OF THE INTERNET

This section is concerned with terms you are likely to meet when using the internet. Other related terms can be found in Section B2 The internet.

With the rapid spread in the availability of the internet, almost everybody can now have personal access to the services it provides. This has occurred as demand made it profitable for telecommunications companies to find solutions. The solutions include using domestic telephone lines and fibre optic cables to carry fast internet communications, the cheapness of wireless networking (Wi-Fi) and the ability of mobile phone signals to carry fast internet communications at an affordable cost. In remote areas, Government subsidies have been used to provide an almost universal infrastructure.

This widespread access to the internet has transformed our lives, perhaps as much as the invention of the telephone or the motor car did. We have quick and effective access to a wide range of information, from train times and hotel vacancies, to do-it-yourself help videos and general knowledge. We have fast communication to help us run our jobs, our lives and manage our leisure.

These changes have also has been driven by the increasing power of mobile devices, such as mobile phones and tablets, which not only act as phones and internet terminals but can communicate with other nearby IT equipment. These mobile phones are called smartphones. They usually contain a sound recorder, camera, video camera and location finder. The increased functionality of smartphones has led to uses such as route navigation and video conferencing. New applications (apps) for smartphones and mobile devices are emerging all the time, such as for health monitoring, central heating control, security systems control and cashless payments.

The connection of everyday devices to the internet (known as the **internet of things – IoT**) is enabling individuals to control their own environment in a very powerful way.

As well as giving people many new opportunities, the ease of internet access and the wide range of internet use gives us several challenges in managing the threats it brings to our personal security, such as privacy violation, financial fraud, child exploitation and other criminal activities.

Some uses of the internet can potentially become addictive, such as social networking, entertainment and gaming, especially when it is practised in excess and to the exclusion of other means of social interaction. This addictiveness can lead to problems in both adults and children who cannot live without the internet. Legal systems are slowly developing that protect users of the internet, but until they are mature and adopted worldwide, users need to understand the dangers and know how to protect themselves.

The difficulty of protecting children is an area of internet use of major concern. Children, even very young ones, use smartphones to keep in touch with their friends and family. They might not realise that every comment they make, or picture they post, might be seen by people they do not know – this might be by accident, such as a message sent to the wrong person or to a group of contacts. Once published, messages might be exploited by a bully or by a contact who takes offence and circulates them for revenge. The complexities of social networking systems might even hide vulnerabilities that allow private messages to be seen by others unauthorised to do so.

These and other issues might mean that children are befriended by unprincipled adults who use the youngsters' naivety and trust to obtain exploitative images or even to meet them. The internet makes it relatively easy for the people the children are communicating with to hide their true identity and feelings. It has also proved easy for people and organisations with extreme political views to promote them to children who do not have the breadth of experience to assess them properly.

Adults can also become involved with immoral individuals. Embarrassing images can be distributed widely. Like children, grown-ups might be harassed or bullied by unwanted emails or social media postings, which might originated from anywhere in the world.

The rapid development of social networking has provided a platform for individuals to become involved in wider debates. Some individuals, who might not be used to the conventions and legal boundaries of these debates, stray into unethical behaviour of abuse or misrepresentation of their opponents. However, laws are slowly evolving and wrong-doers can be prosecuted for abuse or libel.

One area that gets a lot of attention is copyright (more properly known as intellectual property rights or IPR). This is because much of our entertainment, which might be text, music or video (generally known as media), has been produced at considerable expense and our society considers that the creators, such as authors, musicians and artists, should be paid appropriately. However, much of the information available publicly on the internet is free, but actually paid for as a form of advertising, by philanthropic individuals or by political pressure groups. This has led to a culture where it is thought to be acceptable to obtain media content free.

There is also the concept of the 'dark web', which consists of elements of the normal internet that are either invisible or unintelligible to the normal user. This includes websites that do not have normal addresses and messages that are relayed around the world to make them difficult to trace or which are encrypted so they cannot be understood. These techniques have produced a conflict between the need to send information securely, such as to prevent fraud, and the need for security agencies to read messages to prevent and investigate crime and terrorism. Governments and big business need to ensure that their secrets are not read by other governments or commercial opponents, while still being able to identify criminal activities and plots.

The need for security software is often overlooked, even on the relatively secure smartphone. This is to prevent criminals fraudulently obtaining money or obtaining personal information leading to identity theft. This is more fully covered in Section B11 Computer security, abuse and related law.

GENERAL

Netiquette

also known as: net etiquette
including: friends
is a set of informal rules indicating how users of the internet are expected to behave. For example, it is considered inappropriate and impolite to compose emails and forum postings all in capital letters – this is interpreted to be the equivalent of SHOUTING.

Like any other human communication, if users are not careful how they express themselves they might be misunderstood or cause unintended offence. Keeping to the common conventions of an etiquette helps prevent this.

'Friends' are contacts added to a social media website – they enable a user to restrict comments and information to a selected group of people.

Online abuse

including: cyber bullying, cyber stalking, flaming, troll
is the use of the internet or mobile technologies to bully, hurt or embarrass the victim. The effect is similar to physical abuse except that the bully can be more difficult to identify and harder to avoid given how closely we link our lives to our online presence. Online abuse can take a number of forms:

Cyber bullying is sending the victim abusive messages, critical messages and embarrassing pictures.

Cyber stalking is a campaign of online harassment or cyber bullying that might take place over a substantial period of time. It can involve tracking online someone's daily life and movements without ever making contact.

Flaming is an abusive or aggressive reply to an individual's views expressed in social media, particularly on bulletin boards and discussion forums. It attempts to discredit a view by discrediting the individual.

Troll is an individual who viciously abuses victims, individuals or organisations. The troll uses social media while keeping their identity hidden and is often a complete stranger.

Internet identity

is the name by which an internet user is known when contributing to an online environment. It might be made up or be similar to the users' real name. It provides some degree of anonymity and might be easier to use online than the user's full name. Users are often required to add numbers if their name is duplicated to make sure it is unique. They can use the same online identity on a range of websites and discussion forums.

Internet presence

is whether an individual is active on the internet and by which forms of communication they can be contacted. Some social media websites might flag contacts as being online and available at that time. Other users might have a less visible presence on the internet, but still read information posted on social media websites and forums, without contributing. See also *lurk*, below.

ONLINE CONTENT

Illegal content

is information found on the internet that is illegal to upload, download or access. This might be because it is protected by *copyright*, see page 167, it is illegal pornography, or it is material unsuitable for children.

Forum

also known as: discussion forum, bulletin board
including: newsgroup, posting, frequently asked question (FAQ), lurk, moderated newsgroup, thread
is a message storage area that is dedicated to a particular special-interest subject. Users post messages to the forum where they are stored and made available to other users of the forum. An interested user can read these messages and perhaps contribute. Forums are sometimes known as discussion forums. They enable contact and debate between people who do not necessarily know each other but have a common interest. Forums were originally known as bulletin boards because short messages could be quickly posted and made available when internet technology was limited.

Newsgroups are similar to forums, but they have a distinct structure arising from their origins as an email-based system. In particular, a posting can be automatically emailed to members of a newsgroup.

The nature of forums has allowed a specialised vocabulary to develop, including:

Posting is both the act of sending a message to a newsgroup and the message itself.

Frequently asked question (**FAQ**) is often presented within a list of other FAQs with their answers that have been posted on a newsgroup. The purpose is to save time by avoiding the questioner having to send a popular question and wait for replies. The term now has a much wider use in all areas of society.

Lurk is to read messages in a forum or newsgroup, but never to post any.

Moderated newsgroup has a person checking all messages before they are made available. This prevents the misuse of the newsgroup by irrelevant, obscene or insulting messages being posted.

Thread is an initial posting and all associated comments linked to it. A contribution might be linked to an existing thread or start a new one.

Cookie

is small file that is placed on a user's computing device by a website that the user has visited. On a subsequent visit to the same website, the cookie is detected so the website knows that the user has visited it before and does not request again any personal information that the user has previously entered. The owner of the website can build up a picture of what the user sees on repeated visits.

Under EU legislation, websites must give users the right to block cookies. Many users routinely do so because of suspicions they have about what information is being gathered about them.

Cloud storage

is storing information on other computers that can be accessed using the internet. For example, this allows digital music to be accessible to the user's computer, phone or any other device with internet connectivity.

- Advantages of cloud storage are that it is very easy to use and that small amounts of storage are freely available, with more space being available by paying a subscription. The cloud provider will often also ensure the data is *backed up*, see page 115.

- Disadvantages of cloud storage are that is more vulnerable to data theft and information loss, for example data might be deleted if the company providing it thinks you have broken their rules or if it goes out of business.

The term cloud is used because the actual location of the data is unknown. See also *cloud computing*, page 88.

File sharing

is accessing data files stored on another computer. This can be organised by a central website, such as YouTube®, a *peer-to-peer network*, see page 133, or between linked computers in the home, such as accessing a music library from a smartphone.

The most common files that people want to share contain photographs, digital music and video, although much digital media is protected by copyright and so should not be shared. Many users use websites such as YouTube® to share files legally with a wider audience.

Other websites might use peer-to-peer *file sharing software*, see page 89, often to distribute illegal music and video content.

Instant messaging

including: chat, chat room
is a development of *email* (see *electronic mail*, page 86) that allows real-time exchange of messages. Both users wishing to communicate must be connected to the internet at the same time, and software that allows messaging normally allows users to nominate a group of preferred correspondents who will be notified automatically when they log on the internet.

The principle can be extended to allow discussion between several users, when it is generally known as **chat**. Different topics might be under discussion in separate **chat rooms**, and users might join or leave these at will. Chat programs usually offer a small window in which all contributions to the typed conversation are displayed – the window is small so that a user can view and discuss other programs running on the computer at the same time.

Social networking

including: Facebook®, Linkedin®, YouTube®, Picasa®, Flickr®, Second Life®
is the use of social media websites, which allow users to create 'profiles' of themselves with pictures, biographies and comments. These include **Facebook**®, which first appeared around 2006, and its professional equivalent, **Linkedin**®. Users can link to other profiles on the website, creating a network of *friends*, see page 65. Typically, friends will be automatically alerted whenever a profile changes.

Initially an electronic form of 'vanity publishing' and self-promotion, social networking has developed as a means of publicising important issues and campaigning.

The internet allows users to upload short video clips to social media websites, such as **YouTube**®, where they can be accessed by anyone. Similarly, users can 'share' photographs on social media websites such as **Picasa**® and **Flickr**®.

Perhaps the most developed of these websites are those that allow the creation of 'virtual communities', such as **Second Life**®, which can be regulated and developed by the users, and even require a separate virtual currency.

Tweet

is a message sent across the internet using the Twitter website. Twitter provides a form of *social networking* where messages are very short (140 characters maximum) allowing for rapid communication to take place.

GATHERING INFORMATION ONLINE

Grooming

is befriending an individual for the purpose of eventually exploiting the relationship. For example, paedophiles might befriend a young person in the hope that they can develop a sexual relationship. Children, young people and vulnerable adults can be targeted using the internet because the groomer can pretend to be someone else, even using a false picture.

Identity theft

is the use of personal data by a fraudster to impersonate another individual. If the fraudster has enough personal information they can act as if they were that person, using their good reputation and creating a situation where the victim gets the blame for the illegal actions. The data needed for identity theft is often obtained by *hacking*, see page 159.

Malware

including: spyware, key logger
is the general name for malicious software, which includes viruses, worms and Trojan horses. Malware is often inadvertently downloaded. For a fuller description of threats, see *online security*, below. Two common forms of malware are:

Spyware seeks to record secretly the user's actions on the computer – actions that may include typing passwords or other personal details over what the user believes to be a secure connection.

Key logger records all typing, and later sends this secretly across the internet. As a defence, many secure websites require users to select letters or numbers from an image on the screen as part of any authentication process.

Phishing

is the practice of persuading individuals to disclose private information, such as bank account details or passwords, by sending an email pretending to be from an official body and requesting 'reconfirmation' of data that the organisation should already have. Often, the credibility of the email is enhanced by directing the recipient to a website that appears to be the official website of the organisation, see also *pharming*, below.

Early 'phishing trips' were not very sophisticated and aroused suspicion by their immature language and poor spelling; the fraudsters have become more sophisticated now. It is worth reminding anyone who uses a computer that no reputable organisation will ever request secure data through email or over the telephone.

Pharming

is the use of fake websites, made to look like the legitimate websites, used by fraudsters to collect users' personal and financial information. The fraudsters often use a very similar website address to the legitimate website, so users might find the fraudulent website using a search engine or an email might be sent with a link to fraudulent website. See also *phishing*, above.

ONLINE SECURITY

Online security

is protecting the computer from threats on the internet. This might be technical protection or ways of using the computer to minimise risk. Data stored on or accessed by a computer linked to the internet can be threatened by:

- *hacking*, see page 159;
- *phishing*, see above;
- *malware*, such as *spyware* (see above), *viruses* and *worms* (see page 166) and *Trojan horses* (see page 167).

Protection of data from threats is enhanced by ensuring:

- an up-to-date *firewall* is installed, see page 160;
- up-to-date *antivirus software* is installed, see page 166 – this is often integrated with the firewall;
- an *internet filter* is used, see below;
- *parental control software* is used, see below;
- *security updates* are installed, see page 71;
- *encryption* is used where necessary, see page 163;
- simple rules, such as not opening unknown emails, are followed;
- an *acceptable use policy* is followed in the workplace, see below.

Acceptable use policy (AUP)

is a set of rules provided by an organisation to its employers to ensure that they do not undertake activities that are not in the best interest of the organisation. The organisation makes clear to users the standards expected and can discipline them if they do not maintain the standards. This reduces the possibility of users acting illegally or not in the company's best interest. It provides procedures for users to follow that help an organisation:

- keep its data confidential;
- reduce the vulnerability of the system to hacking;
- ensure electronic communications are conducted ethically;
- ensure it users do not indulge in time-wasting activities;
- ensure its users do not indulge in criminal or unethical activities, which might affect the organisation's reputation.

Internet filter

also known as: web filter
including: parental control software
is a program that checks each internet request made for inappropriate information. This might be done using a variety of methods, including by blocking known inappropriate websites or by checking the text for known inappropriate words. Internet filters are used by organisations (as company policy), internet service providers providing public access and as part of parental control software.

Parental control software can be installed by parents on their children's computers to block access to inappropriate web material or limit the times when their children can have internet access. Parental control software is password protected so only parents, as authorised users, can set control parameters or override its use.

Security updates

are modifications to programs running on a computer (usually the operating system, browser and security software). The updates correct security vulnerabilities that might be exploited to gain unauthorised access to data, for example, by a hacker. Despite thorough testing, computer systems often contain program flaws that allow a hacker to gain control of the computer. When these flaws are found the manufacturer releases a security update containing new code that prevents access. Security updates are often downloaded automatically from the internet. See also *updates*, page 232.

Junk mail

including: spam, spam filter
in the context of computers, is unwanted emails, usually attempting to sell something, but also possibly spreading *viruses* and other *malware* (see page 69). Online junk mail is often called **spam**. It is sometimes applied to automated messages sent using other online systems. The enormous amount of online junk mail circulating is largely due to the ability to send thousands of copies of an email for the same effort as sending one, combined with a lucrative market in lists of email addresses obtained from newsgroups and websites.

It is the online equivalent of the paper junk mail delivered to homes but, as well as being cheaper to send than paper, online junk mail is much more profitable. From the thousands of emails sent out, only one or two people need to respond for the sender to benefit. Unsolicited emailing is now illegal in several countries.

A **spam filter** will attempt to detect spam before it is delivered, and either delete it or ask the user to confirm that it is unwanted. Some filters simply work by recognising keywords in the message or its subject. Others attempt to 'learn' what is spam by getting the user to identify initially unwanted messages for long enough for the filter program to be able to recognise them. Powerful commercial filters might use other approaches, such as creating addresses (honey pots) with the only purpose of being a target for spam; there is no legitimate reason to send emails to these addresses, so any message received is sure to be spam. A further approach – recognising that most spam is automatically transmitted – is to reply on behalf of the recipient and ask the sender to verify that they are a genuine correspondent by typing in a word displayed as an image on the screen: an automated program will necessarily fail this test.

Private browsing

also known as: privacy mode, incognito
is a feature of most web browsers that, when turned on, stops the browser permanently storing information about the websites visited, such as the *browsing history* and *cookies*, see page 67.

Private browsing also prevents the saving of passwords and prevents search engine results being affected by the previous search history. It cannot prevent some tracking of browser activity by remote websites that record the IP address of the browsing computer.

B2 THE INTERNET

This section is concerned with terms likely to be met when using the internet. Many internet terms are concerned with the transmission of data between computers within networks. Some of these terms and other related terms can be found in Section B7 Networking, Section E6 Communications components or Section E7 Communications technology.

The internet – also known as 'the Net' – began in the 1960s as a US military initiative to create secure and robust communications in times of conflict. The important concept was of a network of computers, each communicating with several other computers in the network, but not with all of them. A data transmission from one computer to another thus generally travelled by stages, handed on from one computer to another. What created the required robustness was that if any link in the chain was destroyed by enemy action, there would be other paths, through other computers, to the same destination. To facilitate this, and to create the desired security, transmissions would be broken down into small 'packets', each including the 'address' of the destination computer. These portions of the transmission would travel separately, possibly by different routes, and the complete transmission would be reassembled only at its destination. Thus, if the enemy managed to eavesdrop or intercept a transmission, they would be unlikely to capture all of it.

The internet grew as more and more computers were linked to it. Universities in particular saw the internet as an increasingly important way for researchers to communicate. This underlined another design strength of the internet: if, say, a university already maintained its own internal network linking all its staff and students, it was only necessary to link one of these computers to the internet and at once all the existing computers could access every computer anywhere on the internet – the first links being through the university's own network, and the later ones through the global communications.

To ensure that this all worked, it was necessary to define strict protocols – rules – that specified the exact format of an internet transmission, how data items were to be divided into packets and recombined, and what an internet 'address' was. This was done successfully very early in the development of the internet, through the **Transmission Control Protocol (TCP)** and **Internet Protocol (IP)**: sets of rules that have remained essentially unchanged as the internet has grown. The success of this approach is shown in the way that the internet connects computers of different makes, using different operating systems and running different software – but all adhering to these protocols.

This physical structure of the internet – its hardware – was matched by the development of software to make use of the potential. One significant step was the creation of the **World Wide Web**. This used a standard way of referring to data anywhere on the internet – its **Uniform Resource Identifier Locator (URL)** – to create documents. These documents, usually in the form of **web pages**, arranged as **websites**, are assembled from text and graphics that can easily be on different computers. The web also used the idea of the **hyperlink**, something that had already been introduced in educational software: certain parts of a web page would be 'active' so that selecting them with a pointer, such as a mouse or screen tap, would load a new document. This is now so familiar that it is hard to recollect what a revolutionary idea it was.

The internet is also used for sending files of data, usually containing audio, video, text or graphics. The basic protocol here is the **File Transfer Protocol (FTP)** that allows a user to connect to a computer elsewhere on the internet and to request the transfer of a file. As multimedia files are large, the power of the internet has been harnessed in an innovative way, through **file sharing** – rather than by downloading all of a possibly massive file from one source, a request is sent to all computers known to hold copies of that file, and the transfer is made in separate packets from several of these.

Another application of the internet is **electronic mail,** now more commonly known as **email**. This allows messages to be sent from one internet user to another. It took longer in this case for a universally recognised system of **email addresses** to emerge, but the eventual spread of the form john@bcs.org.uk reintroduced the almost defunct bookkeeping symbol @ into everyday life.

The development and rapid growth of the internet has not been without its problems. In part, these problems occur because the internet is simply a transmission network without 'intelligence' of its own, and hence it has no security or monitoring features. The ease of sending emails created **spam** – electronic junk mail. The growth of commercial applications required users to send personal details such as bank account details across the internet, and the existing protocols were found not to be secure enough against fraud. The relatively unregulated nature of this worldwide communications tool encouraged the growth of near-illegal websites – offering pornography or pirated software, for example.

ACCESSING THE INTERNET

Internet

also known as: the Net, information super highway
is a worldwide communications system linking computers in geographically separate locations through the use of a variety of telecommunications links including local area networks, telephone lines, satellites and wireless. It enables fast communication between computers (or devices such as mobile phones or tablets), and the transfer of data between these. Messages and data are passed from the source computer, through other computers, until the destination computer is reached.

Any computer can be linked to any other computer attached to the internet, communicating through intermediate computer systems. This is achieved by having common technical standards, a common identification system for computers and a common reference system for data files. See also *protocol*, page 348.

The internet can be used to provide a reliable communications network for any application that links computers over a short or longer distance. Examples of applications include:

- The *World Wide Web*, see page 79, allowing information to be made widely available;
- *Distributed information systems*, see page 77, allowing direct access for customers to input data and obtain results;
- The *internet of things* (*IoT*), see page 74, where everyday items have embedded processors enabling them to be controlled and monitored over the internet;
- *Cloud computing*, see page 88, allowing information to be stored by a computer services company and processed remotely;
- *VoIP*, see page 90, allowing telephone calls to be made using the internet, rather than older technologies;
- *Social networking*, see page 68, allowing individuals to communicate with others in an online group sharing personal and social information, pictures and video.

Internet of things (IoT)

is a use of the internet where many everyday devices are connected to the internet allowing remote monitoring and control. Each device has an embedded computer processor that can communicate with the internet (*internet enabled*). This means individuals can monitor and, if required, control their environment in a very flexible and sophisticated way. Examples include:

- smart watches that monitor your health;
- CCTV to protect your property from thieves;
- fridges that monitor their contents;
- kettles that can be switched on remotely;
- central heating systems that can be monitored and controlled remotely.

Cyberspace

is an extravagant name for the complete set of facilities and resources that can be accessed using the internet. It can be thought of as an imaginary or virtual world, made up of all the sites and all the files available. This virtual world can be explored electronically in the same way as we might explore a real area of the world by moving around and looking for interesting things. The term does not have any precise meaning outside politics and journalism.

Internet service provider (ISP)

is an organisation that has direct links to the internet and accepts transmissions from users over *dial-up* or *broadband* connections (see page 75), and passes these on to the internet. Most individual users of the internet access it through any one of a number of commercial internet service providers.

Dial-up connection

is one made using a *modem* (see page 340) connected to an ordinary telephone line. The connection sends the data using the voice frequencies of the telephone system. In consequence, the speed available is limited and dial-up connections are rarely used except in remote areas. See also *broadband*, below.

Broadband

including: asymmetric DSL (ADSL), symmetric DSL (SDSL)
is the generic name given to internet connections using a technology capable of high communication speeds. This might be achieved by fibre-optic technologies or transport management techniques such as those deployed in **digital subscriber lines (DSL)**. DSL uses the physical connections of the telephone system, but transmits data in a way that does not interfere with the voice frequencies. The data can be transmitted very much faster than over a dial-up connection. See also *mobile broadband*, below.

Asymmetric DSL (ADSL) offers a very high data transmission speed from the internet to the user, but a relatively slow speed in the opposite direction. This asymmetry is quite acceptable to most individual users, who download far more data than they transmit.

Symmetric DSL (SDSL) offers high speeds in both directions, and is less common.

Mobile computing

is the concept that describes the ability of users to access computer facilities while on the move, including the internet. At its simplest this might be using a portable computer, but access to the internet is considered an essential. The more powerful mobile phones (*smartphones*, see page 290) are linked to the internet (either through Wi-Fi or the mobile phone network) enabling them to provide users with the ability to work while moving (in a car, train or even walking). These smartphones are convenient to use because they can access the internet to provide personal services, such as directions to a favourite restaurant or the time of the next train. See also *mobile broadband*, below.

Mobile broadband

including: 3G, 4G, WiMAX, LTE, tethering, hotspot
is the delivery of an internet service using mobile phone technology. The mobile phone operator provides a data service as part of their wireless phone service, either to a traditional computer or a specially enabled mobile phone. Most mobile phones can access the internet using mobile broadband. To provide mobile broadband to a computer a special adaptor (sometimes called a *dongle*, page 168) is used to connect to the mobile phone operator's communications network allowing the user to access the internet. There are several ways of providing mobile broadband including:

3G, which are mobile phone signal transmission standards in widespread use. The '3G' identifies it as the third generation of these standards.

4G, which are also mobile phone signal transmission standards and which are more powerful and expensive than *3G*.

WiMAX and *LTE* are two of the alternative standards for *4G* phone networks.

Tethering, which uses a short range wireless connection such as *Bluetooth*, see page 140, to allow mobile computers to connect to a nearby mobile phone and so to the internet using the standard *3G* or *4G* connection.

Hotspots, which are public access points to allow mobile computers to connect to the internet using the standard *Wi-Fi* (see page 140) wireless system.

Internet café

also known as: cyber café
is a place where customers can make use of computers for a small fee. An internet café provides a number of computers and facilities for accessing the internet, and might be true enough to its name to serve refreshments as well. Such cafés have spread around the world and provide a convenient means for travellers to keep in touch through email while away from home, without the need to carry a computer with them.

Client-side processing

including: server-side processing
is when data is processed by the user's computer. When a user is carrying out a series of transactions over the internet, data transmission (the slowest part of the process) can be enhanced if as much processing as possible can be done on the user's computer – on the **client side**. For example, when making a travel booking, simple programming contained in the downloaded page can check that the user has filled in all the required data, that any dates selected are sensible (e.g. they have not already passed) and that the format of items such as email addresses is correct. In this way, the request for a booking will not need to be returned from the server for correction.

Server-side processing is when the processing is done by the internet server. In the example above, some processing, such as actually making the booking, can only be by the server. For example, is impossible for the user's computer to know if seats are still available on a selected date. See also *server*, page 134.

Point of presence (PoP)

is an access point to an internet service provider's network. This is usually the telephone exchange where the transmitted data leaves the public telephone network and enters the internet service provider's own network. See also *ISP*, page 74.

Internet protocol (IP)

including: HyperText Transfer Protocol (HTTP)
is a standard set of rules used to ensure the proper transfer of information between computers on the internet. Internet protocols define how data is to be structured, and what control signals are to be used.

Some protocols primarily deal with how particular types of data are structured, such as *File Transfer Protocol (FTP)*, see page 89 and *HyperText Transfer Protocol (HTTP)*, see below. Other protocols are essentially technical, governing how the individual data elements are communicated over the internet.

HyperText Transfer Protocol (HTTP) is a protocol that defines the process of identifying, requesting and transferring multimedia web pages over the internet. These web pages are usually constructed using *HTML* (see page 248). A secure variant, HTTPS, also exists.

Distributed information system

including: distributed information system design, scaling, replication, failure tolerance, concurrency
is an information system that involves distributed access, distributed storage or distributed processing. It can be accessed from multiple locations across a wide area. In practice this usually means using the internet as the communications system enabling many users to access or retrieve data using a specialised website, while the data might be stored and processed at several dispersed locations. This is subtly different from *distributed processing*, see page 136, where the processing is shared across multiple sites to provide robustness and failure tolerance.

Distributed information systems, where there is distributed input and output, allow clients to directly input data to the system, and view the results, almost eliminating the need for specialised data input teams and customer service departments. This approach provides additional challenges to the developers. For example, the numbers of clients accessing the system at any one time can vary enormously and the system might also have to cope with many new clients joining it.

For a distributed information system to meet these challenges, the designers have to take into account the following specific characteristics, as well as the *system characteristics*, page 46, which are common to all computer systems;

- **scaling**, is expanding the system to allow a much larger number of clients to access the system effectively;
- **replication**, is the provision of facilities, including storing copies of the data, at different locations to prevent data loss and improve performance because the processing can be performed at several locations.
- **failure tolerance**, is ensuring that the system will continue to provide a service if some elements fail;
- **concurrency**, is the ability to perform several tasks at the same time. For a distributed system where the processing is at different locations, it has to ensure *data consistency*, see page 157;
- *security*, is ensuring customer data and organisation data are kept secure and *hacking* is prevented, see page 159;
- *migration*, is the need for the system to adapt efficiently to new hardware, see also page 44;
- *access*, is the need for users to have efficient access using the internet;

- *performance*, is the need for the system to respond to users requests in a reasonable time;

- *location*, is where the storage and processing occurs in different countries, to ensure performance and legal compliance.

Distributed information system design is planning a computer system that is accessed using the internet and might incorporate distributed storage and processing. This is different from the conventional *system design*, because it has to incorporate the unique characteristics required by a distributed system.

ORGANISING THE INTERNET

Uniform Resource Locator (URL)

also known as: Uniform Resource Indicator (URI)
is the recognised method for referring to resources on the internet. Each resource, which is usually a file, has a reference that, in full, is similar to:

http://www.bcs.org.uk/index.htm

In order, the components of the URL are: the protocol for accessing the resource (http://), the server on which the resource is stored (www), the *domain name* (bcs.org.uk), see below, and the filename with any extension required (index.htm).

Even though most internet resources are accessed by clicking on *hyperlinks* (see page 82), and it is rarely necessary to type a URL in full, most *browsers* (see page 83) have defaults for portions of the URL. If the protocol is omitted, http:// is assumed, because this is the commonest protocol. If the filename is omitted, index.htm is normally assumed. Even where the filename is given, htm (or the equivalent html) will be assumed if no extension is present.

Domain name

including: domain name servers, top-level domain, subdomain, redirection, IP address, static IP address, dynamic IP address
is the name for the apparent location, or site, of a resource on the internet. Each location has a unique domain name. Domain names are allocated and registered by international organisations contracted to do this. Once registered, domain names are stored in a number of large, publicly accessible databases known as **domain name servers**.

The structure of a domain name such as bcs.org.uk can give clues to the type of organisation holding the data. The **top-level domain** (uk) is often geographic (see Section G4, page 460). Any **subdomains** (there is usually at least one) such as org will identify the type of organisation: in the UK, you will find **co** (a commercial business), **ac** (part of an academic community), **org** (a semi-public organisation), **sch** (a school) and **gov** (government agency).

Most individual users with *websites* (see page 80) use space on the servers of their *ISP* (see page 74); the domain name of this will naturally reflect the ISP and not the individual. It is possible to make use of **redirection** services, which allow a user to register a domain name of their choice, but to have any requests for web pages diverted to the true location of the site. A similar facility allows personalised *email addresses* (see page 87).

Domain names are human-friendly, and thus memorable; however, separate from these 'logical' addresses, each computer linked to the internet has a physical address, a number called its **IP address**. The IP address (Internet Protocol address) uniquely identifies the physical computer linked to the internet. The domain name server converts the domain name into its corresponding IP address, which is of the form 158.152.1.58. Some computers are potentially connected to the internet at all times – these always have the same IP address, a so-called **static IP address**. Others, which access the internet through an ISP (see page 74), are assigned a **dynamic IP address** when logging in, one of the range allocated to that ISP; this address might be different on subsequent log-ins.

ITU (International Telecommunications Union)

also known as: CCITT (Comité Consultatif International Téléphonique et Télégraphique)
including: Internet Society, Internet Architecture Board (IAB)
is the international organisation that coordinates worldwide telecommunications. It is part of the United Nations. Originally it was based in France and known as the *CCITT*, an acronym by which it is still widely known. It seeks to obtain agreement on the setting of and adherence to international standards for data telecommunications.

Various other organisations work with the ITU:

The **Internet Society** is an organisation representing the major internet network owners.

The **Internet Architecture Board (IAB)** is a committee of the Internet Society and considers the use of appropriate internet standards and protocols.

W3C (World Wide Web Consortium)

is the international body responsible for defining the standards of the World Wide Web – in particular the development of the 'languages' used for designing web pages, such as *HTML* (see page 248). Their work has not always been strictly adhered to, largely because designers of *browsers* (see page 83) are eager to implement new and up-to-date features and often do so without waiting for international agreement. As a result, there still remain frustrating differences in the way web pages are displayed in different browsers.

THE WORLD WIDE WEB

World Wide Web (WWW)

also known as: the web
including: surfing
is the name given to the collection of information available to computers connected to the internet, and which is therefore available for anyone to access. The information is made up of *web pages* structured into *websites* (see page 80). Websites are

often interactive, allowing users to supply information to the server or to customise the web pages they are viewing – a concept originally described as *Web 2.0*, see below.

The process of searching **the web** for information and following links to other information is known as **surfing**, after an earlier use of the word to describe a television viewer switching rapidly between channels to find something worth watching.

Web page

is a 'document' accessed in a *browser* (see page 83). It will generally contain text and graphics and might well also contain audio or video. Aside from the text, these elements are not stored in the web page itself, but are loaded into the page by the user's browser from the location specified by a *URL* (see page 78) contained in the page. For large files, such as video or audio material, *streaming* (see page 392) might be used.

Most web pages are written in *HyperText Mark-up Language (HTML)*, see page 248.

Website

including: home page
is a collection of *web pages* (see above) at the same domain, often with a common theme and usually maintained by a single individual or organisation. The user moves between pages by clicking on *hyperlinks* (see page 82); this causes a new page to be loaded, or parts of the existing page to be refreshed with new information (see Figure B2.1).

Home page is a webpage that usually describes the website and provides hyperlinks to other pages. The home page usually loads by default when the website is first accessed. Generally, a user accessing a website for the first time will be aware of the existence of the site, but will have no information about the individual pages it contains.

Web 2.0

was the concept used by internet-based systems to enable individuals to work more effectively with others. It is now an accepted part of the internet. It enables users to contribute to the content instead of only being a consumer. Technologies currently being used include the ability for the user to customise the view of a website, websites adapting automatically to the needs of the user and specialist servers to share information. These technologies enable the identification and storage of user behaviour by web providers, enabling targeting of information to identified users (*pushing information*, see page 86) and enabling users to find information more effectively (*pulling information*, see page 86). Examples include the use of a *wiki*, see page 85, to create the data dictionary and a *blog* (see page 85) to provide integrated development records for a software project. This is an extension of the original *World Wide Web*, see page 79.

Figure B2.1 Anatomy of a website

Picture 1 shows the home page of a village website; although it is not apparent, this page is laid out in three independent frames. In picture 2, this is demonstrated when the user clicks on a link in the left index frame, which loads new content into the main frame on the right, without altering the heading or the index. When the user clicks on one of the tabs in the heading (picture 3), both the main content and the index change. The site also makes use of a rollover image (picture 4): when the mouse hovers over the picture of the village sign, it shows the other side. To make it easier to print the content without the heading or index, one link opens a new window with just the content (picture 5). And finally (picture 6), the 'contact us' link takes the user to a completely new site that provides a form for the user to complete with their comments.

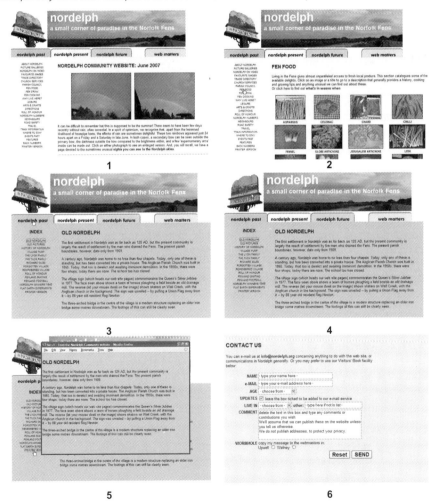

Semantic web

is the linking of data using its meaning to form a web of data. The relationships between data are based on meanings that enable automated systems to produce sensible real-world conclusions. In the context of the internet (World Wide Web) this means each web object (such as a webpage) has *metadata* (see page 97) describing its meaning, enabling it to be linked automatically, for example by a search engine. Few websites are effectively implemented as a semantic web. See also *semantic net*, page 145.

Webmaster

is the person responsible for maintaining the contents of a website. It is normally possible to email the webmaster directly with contributions, comments, complaints or criticisms of a website.

Webcam

is a video camera, usually physically small and of low resolution, that is connected to the internet and might be accessed remotely through a browser; it might also provide audio. Webcams can be used to increase the immediacy or interest of a web page. For example, allowing viewers to see live, moving images from a tourist resort, examine skiing conditions on the top of a mountain or watch rare birds on their nests. They may also be used to add a visual component to a spoken conversation over the internet (see also *VoIP*, page 90).

Hyperlink

is an area of a web page, usually a section of text or an image, that contains a link to another location on the web – often another page in the same website, but possibly a location on the current page or even another site entirely. When the user's mouse hovers over the hyperlink, the shape of the cursor changes, generally to a 'hand' symbol (see Figure B2.2), to indicate that clicking here will cause the page to change.

Figure B2.2 Hyperlink
These words on a web page are all hyperlinks; when the mouse is moved over one, the designer has arranged for the link to be underlined and the cursor changes to the hand shape. Clicking at this point will load the linked page.

ROLL OF HONOUR
NORDELPH NUMBERS
NEIGHBOURS
ROAD SAFETY
TRAVEL

ROLL OF HONOUR
NORDELPH NUMBERS
NEIGHBOURS
ROAD SAFETY
TRAVEL

Browser

also known as: web browser, internet browser
including: Edge, Internet Explorer®, Firefox®, Google Chrome®, Safari®, Opera®, bookmark,
favourite
is the application running on a user's computer that allows a user to interact with the
internet. It is responsible for requesting the text and graphics of web pages from servers
on the internet and for assembling them for display. The browser also runs programs
embedded in the web pages and allows data to be returned to a website's server. Most
functions that involve the internet are now managed using web pages processed in the
user's browser. Although all browsers attempt the same task – displaying a web page
as the designer intended – there are many differences between them, some trivial and
some significant. Not all browsers implement the full set of features defined by the
World Wide Web Consortium, see page 79.

At the time of writing, the commonest browsers are Microsoft®'s **Edge** and **Internet
Explorer**®, Mozilla® **Firefox**®, Apple® **Safari**®, Google **Chrome**® and **Opera**®.

Bookmark or **favourite** is the page address (the *URL*, see page 78) of a website the user
intends to visit often. Most browsers allow the user to save these addresses, referring to them as bookmarks or favourites. These websites can then be accessed by
selecting from the list of bookmarks, rather than typing in the full URL.

Search engine

including: crawler, robot, bot
is an application accessed over the internet that maintains indexes of web pages. Users
wanting information on a particular topic will access the search engine over the internet
and submit a topic or list of topics. The search engine will compare this list with the
pages in its index and generate a page of *hyperlinks* (see page 82) that the user can click
to go to the most relevant pages. See Figure B2.3.

As most search engines index many millions of pages, there is great importance for
commercial websites in being among the first few hyperlinks reported. In creating
these reports, search engines attempt to rank pages in terms of usefulness, by noting
how often the words searched for appear on the pages, or how often other pages link
to that page.

Crawlers or **robots** ('**bots**') search the web continually, looking for new pages and
recording information they find there. This enables search engines to compile their
indexes automatically, although websites can also be submitted for consideration.

Cache

is a store of recently accessed web pages and the images they contain, kept by a
browser. Because transmitting more information than is strictly necessary over the
internet is inefficient, if a user revisits a page that is already stored in the cache, it can
be reloaded from the local copy, without needing access to the internet. Further, as
commercial websites frequently repeat the same information (such as a company logo)
on different pages, it is not necessary to download all this data again.

Figure B2.3 Search engine
The first five (of about 142,000) references to the BCS Glossary found using the Google search engine.

This process is not without its pitfalls. The user may be accessing a web page regularly to see if there is anything new. If the page is reloaded from a cache, it will of course appear identical to the last visit. Browsers allow the cached files to be deleted periodically, or for the user to force a page to reload over the internet even when it is already in the cache.

Web pages are also cached by (for example) internet service providers or search engines – in fact by any organisation that wishes to save bandwidth by minimising data transmission.

Portal

is a website designed to be one that a user will want to visit first whenever accessing the web. There are obvious commercial advantages for the portal in attracting as many users as possible because the owners can sell advertising on the site. To be useful to the individual, the portal site must offer services that the user needs regularly, such as search facilities, news updates and so on.

In many cases, a portal site allows the user to create their own customised page, made up of links to information that the user chooses. For example, the latest news headlines might be displayed: these will be loaded from a news site, but will appear on the portal.

Syndication

including: Really Simple Syndication (RSS), aggregator
is a method of feeding the contents of one website to another; for example, a *portal* (see page 84) might include a feed of the latest headlines from a news site, or a weather report from a meteorological site. Syndication software can be used for any item that might change – not only 'news', but also changes to a website you are interested in, the addition of new material to a *blog* (see below), revisions to a document held on the internet and so on.

Really Simple Syndication (RSS) is a common format for syndication.

Aggregators are programs that check for RSS information. Once information about a syndicated item is in RSS format, an aggregator can check the RSS feed for changes and respond accordingly.

Wiki

is an online information management system designed for the collaborative development of a body of knowledge, usually textual. A *wiki* starts as an empty shell into which authorised users can add information and hyperlinks to other entries. Initially there is no particular structure, relying on the information provided and the hyperlinking to develop it. This enables it to be quickly developed as users add their own knowledge. An example is a manual for an application, where the developers can add and edit descriptions of features as they are developed and solutions for faults are found.

If the *wiki* allows wide editorial access then the information might be unreliable.

Blog

including: blogger, vlog, vlogger
is an online diary where entries are made and presented in chronological order. Blogs are designed for sharing information, ideas and trivia over an extended period. A host website provides a software platform onto which a **blogger**, a person who writes blogs, can add diary entries. It also enables them to be read, and sometimes commented on, by other users. The entries can include text, video, images and hypertext links to other resources.

Vlog is a blog that is produced as a video.

Vlogger is an individual who produces a vlog. The vlogger will talk to the camera to convey ideas, rather than present them primarily as text.

Web application server

including: SharePoint®, web widget
is a specific form of database software that manages the content of complex web pages. Each element on the web page, often taking the form of a panel (sometimes known as a *web widget*, see page 86) within the web page, is managed by the web application server. The element can be altered by the server to reflect the context or previous inputs. This enables each user to have a personalised customised view.

SharePoint® is a common web application server produced by Microsoft®.

Web widget is a small application that can be embedded into a web page usually providing specific additional functionality such as a clock or a weather report. See also *widget*, page 420.

Push information

including: notification
is to send (push) information, usually by an internet server, to a user whether the user wants it or not. This can be used by developers to ensure software is kept up to date and by advertisers to ensure users read their adverts. Usually the client is running an application that is able to receive and act on the information pushed to it. Some applications allow preferences to be set to determine the type and frequency of push notifications.

Notification is the system provided by the many operating systems to allow information to be pushed to a tablet or smartphone.

Pull information

is to request information from an internet server in order to receive it.

Electronic mail

also known as: email
including: email client, webmail, web-managed email system, mailbox, bounce, receipt, carbon copy, blind copy, simple mail transfer protocol (SMTP), Post Office protocol 3 (POP3), internet message access protocol (IMAP), multi-purpose internet mail extensions (MIME)
is a system for sending messages from user to user through the internet. These messages are the equivalent of traditional letters or memos; there is no provision for two-way conversation (but see also *instant messaging*, page 67). Messages are delivered automatically and usually very quickly to anywhere in the world where the internet can be accessed.

Most email systems provide both a *web-managed email system* and an *email client* to manage their emails. Each user is assigned a unique *email address*, see page 87, to which mail can be sent, and which is protected by a password.

Many organisations have internal email systems running on their own private networks, which can provide additional confidentiality. Email is relatively inexpensive, and the senders and recipients do not have to be using their computers at the same time, so it is a popular way to communicate around the world.

Webmail or *web-managed* email system is an email system managed by a website, where the emails remain on the server. The user logs on to view and compose emails through a webpage. This can be useful, for example, when travelling and accessing the internet through a public computer or *internet café*, see page 76.

Email client is software installed on the user's computer to manage emails. The software downloads and stores the emails locally, communicating with the email server regularly to check for new messages and to send composed emails.

Mailbox is the term used to describe the location of the storage of emails, each email address being linked to storage located on an email server. A correctly addressed email can normally be delivered to the recipient's mailbox at any time, regardless of whether the recipient is connected to the internet at that time.

Bounce is when the recipient's mailbox cannot be located and a message to that effect will be returned to the sender. It will occur if an email is sent to a non-existent email address or if the inbox of the email recipient is full.

Carbon copy (cc:) is an identical copy of the email sent to a different user or users, usually for information.

Blind carbon copy (bcc:) is an identical copy of the email sent to a different user or users, but where the existence the recipients is hidden and their email addresses remain confidential.

Simple mail transfer protocol (SMTP) is an internet protocol used in the transfer of emails between computer systems. The user's incoming mail is stored on the service provider's computer. SMTP does not automatically download the email as soon as the user connects to the server, but requires a specific request to do so. See also POP3, next.

Post Office protocol 3 (POP3) defines the transfer of email between computer systems. It provides more facilities than *simple mail transfer protocol*, above. The emails are usually downloaded in one operation for the email client to process.

Internet message access protocol (IMAP) is an internet protocol used in the transfer of emails between computer systems. It allows considerable flexibility and is used with both web-managed systems and email clients. It allows for the synchronisation of things like folders and message status between the email client and server enabling the system to be used with multiple clients.

Multi-purpose internet mail extensions (MIME) is a very common protocol used to specify the structure of an email including *attachments*, see below. On receipt, some attachments (such as image files) might be displayed within the message, while others might need to be detached, saved and opened separately. Transmission of the email will use one of the transmission protocols above.

Email address

including: address book
is the way of giving the destination of an email message. It generally takes a form such as **john@bcs.org.uk**, and has a similar structure to a *domain name* (see page 78). As with domain names, it is possible to redirect emails, so that users can have a personally relevant address, while using facilities on (for example) their ISP's servers.

Address book is a list of frequently used email addresses maintained by the email system. A user can refer to intended recipients by a name of their choice and it is unnecessary to type the email address in full.

Attachment

is a file sent with an email. While email messages are generally simply text messages, it is possible to attach a file to a message as a convenient way of transmitting data without using a more complex method such as *FTP* (see page 89). To do this, it is necessary that sender and recipient computers share the same protocol for file transmission via email. The commonest such protocol is ***multi-purpose internet mail extensions (MIME)***, see page 87.

Postmaster

is the person responsible for maintaining an email system in any organisation large enough to use several email addresses. The postmaster allocates addresses, accepts messages concerned with the running of the system, and deals with messages that have arrived at the correct domain name, but are not addressed to a proper address – that is, the part of the address **after** the @ sign is correct, but there is no recipient corresponding to the part of the address **before** the sign.

List server

is an automated email distribution system. The list server can receive requests from people to join (or leave) the mailing list; these requests are processed automatically. A user on a mailing list can send an email to the list server, which will copy it to all users currently on the mailing list. This is a useful way of distributing information to a group of users who have a common interest.

OTHER INTERNET APPLICATIONS

Cloud computing

is using the internet to provide services that would normally be provided by a *local area network* (*LAN*, see page 129). These services include data storage, email, virtualised software, backup, specialised printing and remotely hosted applications. They are usually provided by large computer systems companies who use *server farms* (see page 128) to host the services for many users. It can also be focused more easily on the needs of individual users enabling the provider to adapt quickly to changes in user requirements. The services can be used from any suitable computer which has an internet connection, allowing users to be much more flexible in how they work.

The physical location of the software used and the data stored may not be known and it is not necessary to store any data locally. For example, a user located in the UK might have their data stored in Australia, emails in America and blogs in Argentina. It also allows users to collaborate effectively from anywhere in the world using a wide range of IT devices from large computers to mobile phones. Remotely hosted applications allow the software and associated database to be located by the supplier at a convenient location. The software is operated and data updated from any suitable computer across the internet. This enables the provider to give a secure and reliable system because the supplier only has one software system to maintain and differences in hardware are no longer a potential source of error. It is a form of *distributed networking*, see page 131.

App

is a computer program run on a smartphone or hand-held computer. App is an abbreviation of *application* (see page 6) used in the context of mobile computing. Apps are usually relatively small programs that perform a single function. They are easily purchased on the internet and downloaded by casual users. Many are provided free as a form of marketing. An example app is one that might allow you to book at a local restaurant and then provide directions to it using the built-in GPS facility of the smartphone.

File transfer

including: file transfer protocol (FTP), anonymous FTP
is the movement of files across the internet. Users can access a *server* (see page 134) holding the required file and request that it be downloaded to them; alternatively, a user can send a file to a server that will accept uploads – it is in this way that most personal web pages are delivered to the web server where they are stored.

File Transfer Protocol (FTP) is the commonest protocol for such transfers. It is used so often that 'FTP' has become a verb: 'It took only a few minutes to FTP the files'; 'I FTP'd it up to the website.'

When a user downloads files through FTP, they are given greater access to the file server than (for example) to a web server. They can usually see a listing of all the files and folders, and might be able to navigate through the directory structure. For this reason, passwords and usernames are frequently required, and verifying these is an added task for the server.

Anonymous FTP (Anonymous File Transfer Protocol) is a convenient way of offering public downloads without the need for password checks; sites that offer such downloads will always accept 'anonymous' as both username and password.

Peer-to-peer file sharing

also known as: P2P
including: supernode, BitTorrent
is the use of the individual computers that make up a network to share large files between those computers. Each computer in a peer-to-peer file sharing network sends data it has received on to other computers when requested. This allows peer-to-peer file sharing to work effectively by allowing data that has already been downloaded to a computer to be sent to any other computers requiring this data. This means that data can be obtained from several sources reducing the load on the network connection (usually the internet) to the original source. This is often configured automatically without the user really being aware of it happening. Provision is also made to resume an interrupted download automatically.

Peer-to-peer file sharing is a solution to one of the problems created by the asymmetric nature of *broadband* (see page 75). Although ADSL connections can download very quickly, they upload comparatively slowly. It is easy to forget that every download from the internet begins life as an upload to the internet, and that as a result the overall speed of data transmission is limited by the upload speed. This is not a problem when accessing a large website where the server has a fast connection to the internet, but can be when many individuals want to download the same files.

Peer-to-peer file sharing uses the power of the internet in an innovative way. It is not always easy to separate the technology from the service that coordinates the file sharing. Early services such as Napster and Kazaa maintained a directory of small individual users who had copies of the files; when a new user wanted to download one of these, it would be requested in smaller blocks from several other users and assembled from these blocks on arrival. As this is essentially the way all internet communication works, the system only required the maintenance of a directory in order to work smoothly.

Supernode is any computer in a peer-to-peer file sharing network that sends data it has received on to other computers.

BitTorrent is a file sharing protocol used by many peer-to-peer file sharing services. It efficiently breaks down large files for sharing over the internet. Some peer-to-peer file services can allow individuals to share files illegally such as music or video (see also *copyright*, page 167). However, the technology is also used legally for distributing TV programmes over the internet and by games companies to update computer games automatically and securely.

VoIP (Voice over Internet Protocol)

including: Skype®
is a method of using the internet to make 'ordinary' voice telephone calls. Digitised speech is just data and can be sent over the internet as with any other data.

With appropriate software a user can talk with any other user connected to the internet for free. As a chargeable service, commercial VoIP providers make it possible to call ordinary telephone numbers – VoIP is used to take the call to a place from which a short local call over ordinary telephone lines completes the call. Further, users can be allocated a 'telephone number' that allows them to be called on their computer from an ordinary telephone.

Skype® is a popular VoIP service allowing free calls, for individuals, between computers, with the option of chargeable calls to telephones. Skype® also provides video calls and *video-conferencing*, see below.

Podcast

is a digital recording of a radio broadcast or similar programme made available for downloading over the internet to a personal audio player. The name derives from Apple®'s portable audio player, the iPod®, although the facility is not limited to this make of player.

Video-conferencing

is the use of the internet to conduct business meetings between several people who are geographically separated. It is usual to see the other participants on a screen.

Teleworking

is the use of information technology to allow people to work in their own homes, while still being in easy contact with the office. As well as the use of *email* (see page 86), it is usual for the teleworker to be able to access their company's central computer. This can be done either directly via a *virtual private network* (see page 133) or via an *intranet* (see page 137) using a secure connection.

Ecommerce

is the use of the internet for ordinary commercial tasks such as retail sales and publishing. This reduces the need to exchange physical contracts in face-to-face meetings or by post. The advantages include the ability to:

- reach worldwide markets at a fraction of the normal advertising costs;
- eliminate the need for an expensive range of shops;
- provide the service 24 hours a day;
- test the range of customers' needs without extensive market research;
- shorten the time from ordering to despatching goods;
- shorten the time between launching products and advertising and launcing update.

In the case of 'soft' goods (such as text, graphical images, computer software or electronic games) the delivery can itself be made using the internet.

Bitcoin

is a currency unit used for online transactions. Each bitcoin is based on a data string constructed to prevent copying. It uses a system of distributed databases that anonymously record every transaction. The bitcoin owner uses his private key to encrypt the data string. The system can verify ownership using the individual's public key. Hence bitcoins are difficult to trace and users remain generally anonymous. See also *public key cryptography*, page 164.

Dark web

also known as: deep web
are computers connected to the internet that are not easily accessed and not included in the results of search engines. They are often accessed using software that provides the user with anonymity, such as *Tor*, see page 92.

The dark web can be used both for good and bad purposes. Communication using the dark web is often used for illegal or extreme activity, such as for selling illegal goods or communicating illicit materials. However, there might be other cases where it allows data to be protected from industrial or other espionage.

Tor

is software that encrypts internet traffic and routes it in a complex way so the user can remain anonymous. Websites that require Tor to access them are commonly known as the *dark web*, see page 91.

INTERNET PROBLEMS

Scams

There are many attempts at fraud and mischief circulating on the internet. One long-standing version identifies the sender of an email as a crooked politician who has access to large sums of money, which he or she will share with the recipient, in exchange for their bank details. Many people learn – to their surprise – that they have won a prize in a lottery that they cannot recall participating in: the proceeds will be transferred to their bank as soon as they submit their details.

A common scam at one time was to send an email (with a request that, in the public interest, it be circulated as widely as possible) describing some *malware* (see page 69) that might have infected the recipient's computer. In following the instructions to locate this, the user invariably found it because it was usually a part of the operating system. They might then foolishly follow the final instruction to delete it.

Denial of service (DoS)

including: distributed DoS (DDoS)
is the inability of a *web server* (see page 135) to service clients' requests for web pages. Most often this occurs when a web server receives so many near-simultaneous requests for pages that it cannot service them all, and frequently refuses to function at all. This might happen if a well-publicised and popular website creates a lot of interest; this happened, for example, when the UK Census data for 1901 was first made freely available on a website. However, it is more likely to be the result of a malicious attack from *hackers* (see page 159) deliberately seeking to damage a website.

Distributed DoS (DDoS) attack is conducted by spreading a *virus*, see page 166, which causes all infected computers to access a particular website without knowledge of the users, with the intention of causing the website to be made inaccessible.

B3 DATA HANDLING AND INFORMATION RETRIEVAL

Although a computer can store enormous amounts of data, this data is useless without appropriate links between individual data items. Imagine, for example, what a (printed) telephone directory would be like if it was simply two separate listings of telephone subscribers and their numbers, without the connection that is made by the printed layout between a particular subscriber and their telephone number. The data is also useless if it cannot be easily retrieved when required – imagine the telephone directory in random rather than in alphabetic order.

The same applies to computerised collections of data. These are generally referred to as **databases** and can vary between such things as a simple name-and-address listing and a massive collection of structured data that provides information for a large business. It is easy to be deceived when one is experimenting with techniques for accessing databases. If a demonstration database is constructed with tens (rather than millions) of entries, many of the techniques can seem unnecessarily long-winded. If you were certain that your data would never extend to more than 100 entries, it would be sensible to store it in a simple table. When it grew, despite your plans, to millions of entries no table would be capable of holding it, and your program would need to use sophisticated methods of data management.

Large databases usually have many potential users. Allowing simultaneous use of the same data files may lead to operating system problems – the solution to these problems is usually embedded in a complex piece of software, known as the **database management system (DBMS)**.

The concepts used in designing and setting up a large database are complex and require specialist developers. Simple user interfaces are often provided to help the inexperienced to access the data. Some applications running on the internet offer 'web style' interfaces and have enhanced security systems. Also many applications access data without need of any direct human interaction. For example, in the retail sector an online order may launch purchase, stock movement and invoicing systems.

Database

is a (large) collection of data items and links between them, structured in a way that allows it to be accessed by a number of different application programs. The term is also used loosely to describe any collection of data.

Data model

including: entity, attribute, relation(ship)
is usually a diagram of a database. Designers of a large database will normally construct a diagram of the planned database. This will show the things represented in the database (the entities) and the information held about them (the attributes). The relationships between entities are also shown, and from this model the most efficient arrangement of the data will be worked out. See also *entity-relationship diagram*, page 51 and Example B3.2.

Entity identifies a group collection of information, which describes the subject of that entity. That subject may be a physical object such as a person or a stock item, or an abstract object such as a medical record. Each individual set of data described by the entity is referred to as an *instance of the entity* and is often physically stored as a single record within the database system.

Attributes describe each individual data item within the entity. So for an entity called 'Person' the attributes could be information such as Name, Address and Date of Birth. The actual data stored within an *instance of the entity* ('John Smith', '1 High Street', '10/08/2008') are often physically stored as *fields* within the database system.

Relationship describes a link between two entities. So if 'Person' and 'Address' are understood as separate entities then a relation 'lives at' can be defined, which, for a particular *instance of the entity*, means 'this Person lives at this Address'. Where data items are related to each other they are usually linked together by pointers stored in the database. See *key*, page 261.

Database management system (DBMS)

is software that can find data in a database, add new data and change existing data. The database management system works automatically without users knowing how. It deals with finding the requested data, updates the data and performs other tasks, including maintaining indexes.

The DBMS may provide its own simple user interface or may just communicate with other programs that request and use the data available to the database. Large computer systems will have programs written for particular tasks. These programs use the DBMS to handle the complexities of managing the database because it is easier than directly accessing the data files.

Communication between these programs and a DBMS usually uses commands in a special programming language, a *data manipulation language*, the most common of which is *Structured Query Language (SQL)*, see page 105.

Information retrieval

also known as: data retrieval
is extracting useful information from large amounts of stored data, such as a database. This usually involves specifying some form of *query* (see page 105) and also stating display and sorting instructions. This enables large amounts of data to be searched and the results to be output efficiently.

Figure B3.1 How a database management system works

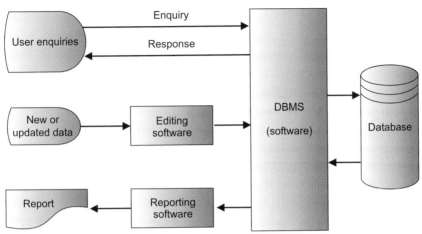

Data dictionary

also known as: data directory
is a file containing descriptions of, and other information about, the structure of the
data held in a database. The data dictionary is not usually accessible to users. It is a tool
for the managers of the database, for example when they need to alter the way data
is stored. Typically it contains such items as field name, data type, field size, format,
default value, entity, whether a primary key.

Distributed database

is one where several computers on a network each hold part of the data and cooper-
ate in making it available to the user. If the particular data required is not available at a
particular computer it will communicate with the others in the network to obtain it. Often
each computer will keep a separate copy of frequently used data. Special methods are
needed to ensure that the latest data is used.

Flat file

is a database held as a table and stored in a single file. The data will be structured
with a row for each *record* (see page 260) and a column for each *field* (see page 261).
This allows only very simple structuring of the data, which can only be considered as a
two-dimensional table (hence 'flat'). See Figure B3.2.

Hierarchical database

is a database where the data is held in a *tree* structure (see page 257). Users can think
of each data item as existing on one of a number of levels. There are links to related data
items at the higher level and sometimes at a lower level. The data items at a lower level
hold more detail about the item that they are linked to above. See Figure B3.3.

Figure B3.2 A flat file or two-dimensional table

A two-dimensional table consisting of names and addresses

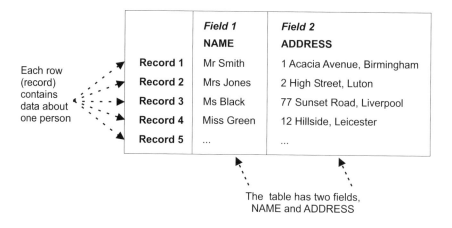

The table has two fields, NAME and ADDRESS

Figure B3.3 Hierarchical database

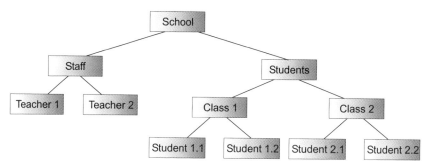

Object-oriented database

is a type of database system normally making use of *relational database* structures, and applying the concepts of *object orientation* (see page 188). The most common type is the object-relational database, in which the rows of a relational database *table* represent objects and the definition of the table itself represents a *class*.

New *table* types can be created from existing tables, by *inheritance* (see page 189). That is a new table can be created from an existing one by adding and/or removing *attributes* (see page 94). An advanced technical feature is the association of *methods* with data items (tables or attributes) that can be used to perform processing specifically related to those items.

Object-oriented databases have the advantages that they can be used to represent object-oriented systems more directly and can deliver more efficient and faster data storage and retrieval.

Relational database

including: table, view
is a complex database structure designed to hold a variety of different data. Where data items are related to each other they are linked together internally by pointers. See *pointer*, page 277.

Relational databases are especially powerful, because the method of storing data in tables makes no assumptions about how the applications programs will access the data, and hence does not restrict the *queries* (see page 105) in any way.

Table is the name for each group of similar data with rows for each instance of the *entity* and columns for each *attribute* (see page 94).

View is how a particular type of user sees the data. The (relational) *database management system* (see page 94) provides tools for linking tables together and selecting items from within tables. In this way, each user can be given a different view of the data. An example of a view may be a table set up for a particular type of user, such as a medical receptionist, who may work with a view containing only data relevant to their job (name, address, appointment) and denied access to views containing sensitive medical information.

Schema

including: subschema, data description language (DDL), metadata
is the precise description of the data items to be stored, and the relationships between them, in a database system.

Managing the large amounts of data of different types stored in a modern database requires that descriptions of the data items are held, as well as the data items themselves. The description, the schema, will be written in a *data description language*. The *database management system* (see page 94) may reformat the data before presenting it to the user, and will make use of individual subschemas that describe the data a particular user can access (see *view*, above).

Subschema consists of the data items and their relationships as seen by a particular type of user. This allows the same set of data to be used in different ways and access restricted to the particular attributes appropriate to that class of user.

Data description language is a way of describing the physical characteristics of data within a database. Many systems now use *XML* (see page 248) as the data description language, allowing portable and flexible system design.

Metadata describes the characteristics of data stored in a system: that is 'data about data'. It allows *identifiers* to be attached to key data to enable it to be structured, retrieved and used. In some cases this will be information such as *data types*. A *data description language* is often used to produce the metadata. See Figure B3.4 – a screen that allows the user to choose the identifiers or items of metadata that are displayed by default on a digital image.

Figure B3.4 Sample metadata listing for a digital camera image

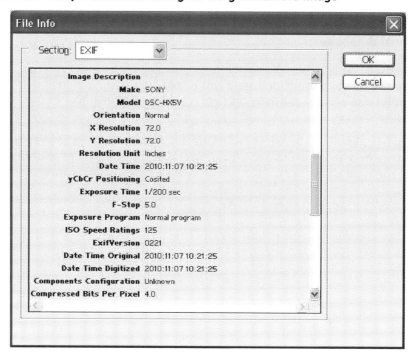

Typically metadata contains such identifiers as title, creator or rights holder, source and language, subject and intended audience, description, publisher, type and format or standard, date created, date modified. The example of the metadata attached to a digital photograph (Figure B3.4) shows that date and time taken can be useful in correctly ordering images of a particular event.

Normal form

including: first normal form (1NF), second normal form (2NF), third normal form (3NF)
is a way of structuring the data in a *relational database* (see page 97) according to formal rules, in order to avoid problems of efficiency and security in accessing and maintaining the data.

The *schema* (see page 97) is progressively refined with logical processes. If the schema for a database is in third normal form then errors and inconsistencies will be reduced. See Example B3.1.

In **first normal form (1NF)** data, all *attributes* (see page 94) are indivisible and *entities* (see page 94) do not have repeating groups.

Example B3.1 An example of organising data in normal form

The source data is given below. This is an example of data in un-normalised form:

Student name	House	Course
Smith	Yale	French, Mr Green, Room LA1 Computing, Mrs Brown, Room CP3 Maths, Mrs Brown, Room CP3
Aziz	Cornell	Geography, Mr Violet, Room HU2 Chemistry, Miss Grey, Room SC5 Maths, Mrs Brown, Room CP3
Jones	Yale	Computing, Miss Grey, Room SC5 Chemistry, Miss Grey, Room SC5
Smith	Cornell	Chemistry, Miss Grey, Room SC5

This data is **not** in first normal form because

- There is no sensible unique KEY
- Each student can take several courses (a repeated group)

Stage 1 - first normal form – no repeating groups

This table satisfies First Normal Form:

Stud_ID	Student name	House	Course_ID	Subject	Teacher	Room
485	Smith	Yale	1023	French	Mr Green	LA1
485	Smith	Yale	1156	Computing	Mrs Brown	CP3
485	Smith	Yale	7865	Maths	Mrs Brown	CP3
907	Aziz	Cornell	2367	Geography	Mr Violet	HU2
907	Aziz	Cornell	3112	Chemistry	Miss Grey	SC5
907	Aziz	Cornell	7865	Maths	Mrs Brown	CP3
322	Jones	Yale	1157	Computing	Miss Grey	SC5
322	Jones	Yale	3112	Chemistry	Miss Grey	SC5
678	Smith	Cornell	3112	Chemistry	Miss Grey	SC5

For the KEY to be unique we have a compound key: **Stud_ID+Course_ID**

This data is **not** in second normal form because

- Student name and House are independent of Course_ID
- Similarly, Subject, Teacher and Room are independent of Stud_ID

Note: Bold attributes indicate a key and * indicates a foreign key

Stage 2 - second normal form – non-key attributes are fully dependent on the key

The data is split into three tables to satisfy second normal form:

Stud_ID	Student name	House
485	Smith	Yale
907	Aziz	Cornell
322	Jones	Yale
678	Smith	Cornell

Course_ID	Subject	Teacher	Room
1023	French	Mr Green	LA1
1156	Computing	Mrs Brown	CP3
2367	Geography	Mr Violet	HU2
3112	Chemistry	Miss Grey	SC5
7865	Maths	Mrs Brown	CP3
1157	Computing	Miss Grey	SC5

Stud_ID	Course_ID
485	1023
485	1156
485	7865
907	2367
907	3112
907	7865
322	1157
322	3112
678	3112

There are 3 keys:

Stud_ID, Course_ID and a compound key: **Stud_ID+Course_ID**

This data is **not** in third normal form because

- Teacher and Room are dependent (each teacher always teaches in the same room)

Stage 3 - third normal form – non-key attributes are independent of each other

The Course table is split into two tables to satisfy third normal form:

Stud_ID	Course_ID
485	1023
485	1156
485	7865
907	2367
907	3112
907	7865
322	1157
322	3112
678	3112

Stud_ID	Student name	House
485	Smith	Yale
907	Aziz	Cornell
322	Jones	Yale
678	Smith	Cornell

Course_ID	Subject	Teacher_ID*
1023	French	T001
1156	Computing	T002
2367	Geography	T003
3112	Chemistry	T006
7865	Maths	T002
1157	Computing	T006

Teacher_ID	Teacher	Room
T001	Mr Green	LA1
T002	Mrs Brown	CP3
T003	Mr Violet	HU2
T006	Miss Grey	SC5

Example B3.2 An example of data modelling

This example has been illustrated by inspection of the data, *data analysis*.

If data anomalies do not appear in the example data then this solution may not be correct. For example occasionally teachers may teach in different rooms, invalidating the model.

An alternative approach is *data modelling*, see page 94.

Data modelling – an alternative approach

Data modelling uses the attributes identified and attempts to use contextual information to organise them. So the data in un-normalised form becomes:

Students_Course (Name, House, Subject, <u>Teacher, Room, Teacher, Room, Teacher, Room</u>)

Note: Bold attributes indicate a key, * indicates a foreign key and <u>underline</u> indicates a repeated group.

Stage 1

Inspection identifies that the attribute *House* depends on the *Student* the data is about.

Also, inspection identifies that *Teacher* and *Room* depend on the *Subject* studied.

An initial model could be:

Student (**Stud_ID**, Name, House, Course_ID*, Course_ID*, Course_ID*)
Course (**Course_ID**, Subject, Teacher, Room)

Stage 2

This, however, has a repeated group and we introduce an extra table 'Course Taken':
Student (**Stud_ID**, Name, House)
Course_Taken (**Stud_ID***, **Course_ID***)
Course (**Course_ID**, Subject, Teacher, Room)

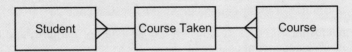

Stage 3

Inspection identifies that we may need more flexibility for the rooms allocated and a decision can be taken whether to move 'room' into the Course_Taken entity or perhaps give it an entity of its own.

These decisions are balanced against the need for efficiency in the system, but the ultimate data model could be:

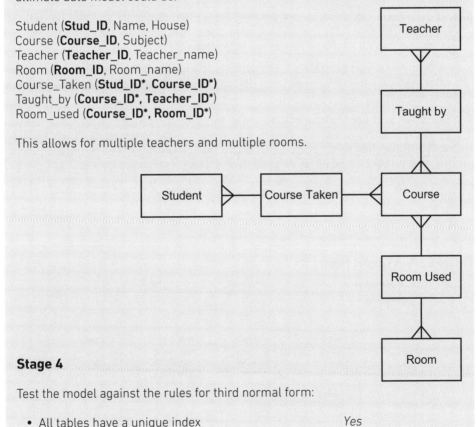

Student (**Stud_ID**, Name, House)
Course (**Course_ID**, Subject)
Teacher (**Teacher_ID**, Teacher_name)
Room (**Room_ID**, Room_name)
Course_Taken (**Stud_ID***, **Course_ID***)
Taught_by (**Course_ID***, **Teacher_ID***)
Room_used (**Course_ID***, **Room_ID***)

This allows for multiple teachers and multiple rooms.

Stage 4

Test the model against the rules for third normal form:

- All tables have a unique index   *Yes*
- No repeated attributes   *Yes*

- Non-key attributes are fully dependent on the key   *Yes*
                                       (no compound keys in main entities)

- Non-key attributes are independent of each other   *Yes – by inspection*

In **second normal form (2NF)** data, *relations* (see page 94) are in first normal form and non-key attributes are fully dependent on the *key* (see page 261).

In **third normal form (3NF)** data, relations are in second normal form and all non-key attributes are independent of each other.

Report

including: report definition, report layout, report format, display order, sort list, presentation order
is the presentation of selected data from a database. A report is usually printed in the form of a table. Reports may be defined in advance so that the user does not have to set up the report definition each time it is needed.

Report definitions require a query, a report layout and a display order to be defined. Normally the user will set a *query* (see page 105) so that the database will be searched, finding each record that satisfies the query.

Report layout or **report format** specifies which parts of the data are to be output and in what position. Often this is a list of *fields* (see page 261) to be printed as the columns of the report.

Display order, sort list or **presentation order** specifies the order in which records will be output. This is generally done by specifying the fields whose data will be used to determine the order of display. One specified field determines the main order in the display. Other fields may be used to affect the order when the records have the same value for the first field. In Figure B3.5, 'Surname' is used to determine the main order and the other fields are used when the first fields are identical.

Figure B3.5 A typical report

Title: **Mathematicians**

Query: Surname = "Sm"

Surname	Forename	Nationality	Birthdate	Birthplace
Smale	Stephen	USA	15/07/1930	Flint, MI
Smeal	Glenny	Australian	13/02/1890	Australia
Smimov	Vladimir	Russian	10/06/1887	St. Petersburg
Smith	Henry	Irish	02/11/1826	Dublin
Smith	Karen	USA	09/05/1965	Red Bank, NJ
Smithies	Frank	British	01/03/1912	Edinburgh
Smoluchowski	Marian	Polish	28/05/1872	Vienna

8 results out of 2118   Page 1/1

Query language

including: Structured Query Language (SQL), Query By Example (QBE), Data Manipulation Language (DML), report generator
is a way of accessing, and usually manipulating, the data in a database. Large *database management systems* (see page 94) must allow the user – who may not be a skilled programmer – to ask for information to be extracted: for example, 'How many invoices more than three months old are recorded in the database that have not yet been paid?' Query languages are simplified programming languages, restricted to accessing the database, although many have additional functions to add, edit and delete data items.

A few keywords are used to link the names of fields in the database, and to specify values for comparison:

```
SELECT invoices

WHERE date-sent < 16-04-2010 AND total-owing > 0
```

See also *query*, below, and *logical operator*, page 106.

Structured Query Language (SQL) is now the standard query language. The example above is in SQL. In addition to its use by programmers it can also be generated automatically by the query facilities in a database system and the SQL code is passed for implementation to the DBMS.

Query By Example (QBE) is a simple query language where the user fills in their request on a form to match the results wanted. It is simple to use but can only be used to retrieve data from a database.

Data Manipulation Language (DML) is a form of high-level language, usually part of a *database management system* (see page 94) that is designed to allow the user to retrieve (query), store (insert) and change (update) data in a *database* (see page 93). *Structured Query Language (SQL)*, see above, is an example of a data manipulation language.

Report generator is software that allows a business user, who is not necessarily a skilled computer programmer, to specify a printed report that draws on values from a database, or the results of calculations performed by the computer.

Query

including: interrogating, selecting, searching
is a question used to retrieve selected information from a database. The query is structured so that the answer is either true or false for each record in the database. To answer a query the computer must check each *record* (see page 260) of the data to see if the answer is true. The result of the query is a list of all the data that satisfies the query, and is produced as a report. Querying a database is also referred to as ***interrogating*** the database, ***selecting*** data or ***searching*** for data. See also *search*, page 280.

An example of a general request might be:

"Which pupils in Year 11 take French?"

This query is made precise by using words from the *query language* (see page 105) to link the names of the fields, 'year' and 'subject', in the database.

```
SELECT pupil WHERE year = 11 AND subject = "French"
```

Data filter

selects the set of records to be displayed. A data filter is often used in an interactive system to implement a query. Setting a filter, which is easily done but temporary, will involve entering a query. See also *query*, page 105.

Logical operator

including: logical data, true, false, truth value, AND, OR, NOT, logical value
combines **logical data**, which uses only the two values **true** or **false**. Two of these **truth values** are combined to give another **truth value**. Logical operators include **AND, OR, NOT**.

In addition to performing calculations computers take decisions on the results. The computer only has two choices, to act or not to act. Whether the computer acts or not will depend on the **logical value** of a data item. If it is TRUE the computer acts, if it is FALSE no action is taken. In reality many of these simple decisions are combined to produce complex decision-making abilities. This whole area is known as *Boolean algebra*, see page 356.

```
IF "webbed feet" AND "white feathers" THEN show picture ELSE next
item
```

This is usually done when constructing a condition to be tested such as an *if statement* or a *query*. An example may make this clearer:
TRUE and **FALSE** are the only two data values allowed in logical operations. They can be combined to determine how the computer takes a decision.

Logical value or **truth value** is the value of a logical data item. It can only be TRUE or FALSE.

AND is used when the result needs to be TRUE only when both data items are TRUE.

OR is used when the result needs to be TRUE when either data item (or both) is TRUE.

NOT is used when the result needs to be the opposite value of the data item, so NOT TRUE becomes FALSE and NOT FALSE becomes TRUE.

Data warehouse

including: data mining
refers to large amounts of data that are stored together, usually in a single location, for further processing.

Much of the data collected by large businesses with many sites is used immediately for a specific purpose and is stored where it is collected and used. This data, particularly when analysed with other data, can provide useful information for future planning. The data warehouse is where these large quantities of data are collected together from a variety of locations for efficient analysis and also provides a form of archive of the data. Since the data is only being used for further analysis it does not have to be complete or up to date.

Data mining is the analysis of a large amount of data in a data warehouse to provide new information. For example, by using loyalty cards, which connect purchases to a particular customer, supermarkets can gather information about the buying habits of individual customers. Combining all the information about customers helps them to establish long-term trends. *Pattern recognition*, see page 143, allows the recognition of correlations such as that between disposable nappies and cans of beer, from which it can be deduced that when families have young children more is spent on drinking in the home. When a customer's purchasing pattern changes to include disposable nappies the supermarket may have the opportunity to promote sales of beer to the customer.

B4 COMMERCIAL DATA PROCESSING (DP)

Other concepts related to the design and implementation of systems to carry out commercial data processing are found in several later sections, especially Section B2 The internet, Section A4 Systems design and life cycle, Section A5 Describing systems and Section D3 Managing data files.

Data processing covers those particular computing applications and activities concerned with business and commerce. Examples include:

- interfaces with retail customers and stock management;
- financial transactions and maintenance of customer bank accounts;
- the provision of booking and ticketing for travel and the leisure industry.

The public service and government sectors have become much more automated and have harnessed the internet for remote access to their services. Examples include:

- information services from local councils about planning applications and amenities;
- dealing with tax and licensing authorities directly;
- General Practitioner services allowing hospital appointments to be booked when the patient is seen.

In many business applications, quite simple tasks are carried out but repeated for a very large number of individual transactions. For example, working out one person's pay is not difficult but it has to be done for all employees, each week or month. Typical of such application areas are accounting, payroll, record keeping, route planning and stock control.

Data processing in an organisation has to provide a cost-effective and efficient service with minimum errors. The main elements in data processing involve automated data collection, prevention of errors, security of data and procedures to collect, process and use large amounts of information. The terms discussed in this section reflect this focus. The DP activity is changing to reflect the nature of **cloud computing**.

For particular applications (for example payroll or accounting), there are often standard packages. Although all users will need to use a particular type of package to do the same job, they may require a specific version because they have different hardware or operating systems or because they need to use the package in association with another application area. Data processing software can use complex interfaces to access applications on the web.

Authentication

is checking the identity of the user of a transaction handling system. There are various methods that check the applicant against known features (the 'profile') of the user and any failure results in the applicant being blocked from access to the system. See also *user identification*, page 162.

Authorisation

is checking that a user is permitted to carry out the requested transaction before any further action is taken. It may involve checking the user's *access rights* (see page 163) or referring the transaction to another user simply to check and allow the transaction. See also *verification*, page 110.

Data preparation

is the input of large quantities of data into a computer system for further processing. Input may be automatic, for example by scanning optical mark forms, or manual, when the data is typed and verified ready for processing.

Validation

including: range check, presence check, length check, type check, format check, lookup check, file lookup check, integrity check
is the automatic checking of data entered into a computer system.

Validation involves using the properties of the data to identify any inputs that are obviously wrong. Validation only proves that the data entered is a reasonable value for the computer to accept. It cannot prove that the data entered is the actual value the user intended. However, it does allow the computer to filter out obvious mistakes. The data is not processed until the validation succeeds.

The checking is done by software that can either be part of the input system or a separate program that checks the data at the following stage. For examples see the descriptions of individual validation checks below. As the data passes through the system it will also be verified; see *verification*, page 110.

Validation checks may include:

Range checks to reject any data items outside an expected range. For example an employee's age that was less than 16, or over 75.

Presence checks to reject a group of data where required fields have been left blank. For example, information about a customer would be of little use without including an identifier such as the customer's name.

Length checks to ensure that the data entered is of a reasonable length. For example it might require that a name is between 3 and 15 characters long.

Type checks to ensure a data item is of a particular data type. For example a number of items in stock will be entered as an integer (whole number).

Format checks to ensure a data item matches a previously determined pattern and that particular characters have particular values such as being letters or digits. An example is whether the data is valid as a UK postcode.

Lookup checks to ensure that the data matches one of a limited number of valid entries. For example subjects studied in a school should be selected from a list of Mathematics, English etc. A **file lookup check** is used to compare the data against a larger list of items that are held in a data file. For example the product code of an item in a supermarket will be looked up in the stock file to confirm such an item exists.

Integrity checks to confirm the value of a piece of data by comparing it with other data. For example an individual's date of birth can be compared with their current age, if known.

Check digits added to data items, which allow the items to be *verified* (see below), may also validate the data implicitly.

Verification

including: double entry verification, screen verification, check digit, batch total, control total, hash total, parity check, checksum, cyclic redundancy check (CRC)
is the use of checks to make sure data is consistent and has not been corrupted. Verification confirms the integrity of data as it is copied between different parts of a computer system. Copying should not change the data. Differences detected would mean an error in the transfer.

Verification can take place both when data is entered at the human–machine interface and when it is copied between other components within a computerised system (including from remote sensors or other computers). The data will also have been validated on input; see *validation*, page 109.

The verification checks at the human–machine interface may include:

Double entry verification to ensure data typed into a computer system is entered accurately. The data is entered twice, by different operators, and compared by the system. Any differences can be identified and manually corrected.

Screen verification to ensure data being entered into a computer system is accurate. After being entered the data is displayed on the screen, the user reads it and confirms if it is correct.

Check digits are extra digits added as part of a numeric data item (like a bar code or a stock number). They are worked out from the other digits in a way that can be repeated, enabling the data to be checked at a later stage by working out the check digit again and comparing the results.

Batch totals are the total value of one or more fields in a batch of data. They are calculated in advance (manually) and then compared with the total as calculated by the computer.

Control totals are batch totals that have a meaningful value, for example the total value of a batch of orders or simply a count of the number of transactions.

Hash totals are batch totals that have no other meaning, for example the total formed by adding all the dates of the orders or the total of all the numeric fields for a particular record.

The verification checks within the hardware of the system are of particular importance when sending data between computers. These verification checks may include:

Parity checks to ensure that a single byte or word of data has been transferred within the system correctly. A bit in each byte or word is reserved to be the parity bit. This parity bit is set to 1 or to 0 depending on the data. If the data is corrupted then the parity check is likely to fail.

Checksums to ensure that a block of data has been transferred within the system correctly. Extra words of data are added to a block that are worked out from the value of the data in the block. At later stages the checksum is worked out again, and compared with the original, to ensure the data has not been corrupted at some stage in the system. This check is more complex than the *parity check* (see above) but is more suited to verifying quantities of data larger than single bytes or words.

Cyclic redundancy checks (CRC) are a particular type of *checksum* (see above). They are commonly used to verify blocks of data stored on disks or transmitted across networks.

Transaction

is the data and processes needed to update a computer system to reflect a single change in the information held. A single change in the information can involve several changes, or additions, to the data physically stored in the computer system. There may be other changes such as to indexes used by the computer system. A transaction usually refers to a single piece of financial data or changes to a single *entity* (see page 94) in a database system. When transactions are made *authorisation* (see page 109) is needed.

Audit trail

including: journal file
is an automatic record made (in a *journal file*) of any transactions carried out by a computer system, such as updates to files. This may be required:

- for legal reasons (so that the auditors can confirm the accuracy of the company accounts);
- for security reasons (so that data maliciously or accidentally deleted can be recovered);
- or simply to monitor the performance of the system.

Archive

is the storage of information for long periods of time. The data is likely to be compressed to take less space and stored on a cheaper storage medium such as optical disks (see *optical disk storage*, page 299), freeing space on the main computer system. It can be accessed if needed, but is not so easily available as the original information. There are legal requirements on most businesses to keep data for several years and so old data will be archived. See also *archive file*, page 275.

Data capture

is the collection of data for entering into a computer. This may be done automatically, as in the scanning of bar codes in a shop, or manually, as in typing in a gas meter reading. See also *data capture*, page 118 in Section B5 Control and monitoring.

Article number

including: International Standard Book Number (ISBN), Universal Product Code (UPC), European Article Number (EAN)
is the number given to a particular product to identify it (e.g. the **International Standard Book Number (ISBN)** found on a book). This is often printed together with its *bar code* representation (see below), so that it can be read both by people and automatically by a *bar code reader* (see page 296) or some other *point-of-sale terminal device* (see page 136). The numbers are usually structured, and there are international agreements on how the numbers should be constructed for various types of goods. Two common forms of numbering systems are the **Universal Product Code (UPC)** and the **European Article Number (EAN)**.

Bar code

including: QR codes, quick response codes, tags
is a pattern of parallel lines of different thickness used to represent a code number, which can then be read automatically. It is a very cost-effective way of inputting data into a computer. For example, the article number printed on the back cover of this book is given with its bar code version above it.

It is often used by shops to identify a product at the *point-of-sale terminal* (see page 136) so that its price can be found automatically from a computer. This is an alternative to a manual system where prices are marked on goods and the prices are entered through a keypad. See also *article number* (see above).

Various two-dimensional bar codes are widespread; some are proprietary such as **QR (quick response) codes** and **tags**. These codes can represent a much larger quantity of data than a one-dimensional bar code. They include a textual message that could be for example a website address. See Figure B4.1. They were originally developed for stock control purposes by a car manufacturer.

Radio frequency identification device (RFID)

uses a small tag that can respond to a sensor operating at a short distance. A radio message is sent to the RFID tag. It is received, modified by the silicon chip in the tag, returned and deciphered by the sensor. Examples include reading season tickets on toll roads and tracking items of stock in a supermarket.

Optical mark recognition (OMR)

is machine recognition of data recorded as simple marks on a document. The special forms (or cards) are printed to match a template in the computer. The hardware detects marks made in the predetermined positions and software interprets this as data.

Figure B4.1 An example of a QR code and a Microsoft® tag

 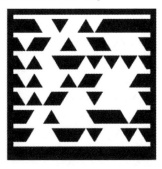

The marks may be printed or put on the form by hand, for example with a pencil. The OMR software only detects marks, not characters such as letters or numbers. It is very reliable and suited to small quantities of multiple-choice data. The numbers recorded on some lottery entry forms are an example.

Timing information

including: clock mark, clock track
is required because mechanical devices cannot operate with the precision needed by computers. An example is the **clock marks** making up the **clock track**, which synchronise the reading of the items on a mark sense document.

Figure B4.2 Clock track on a machine-readable document

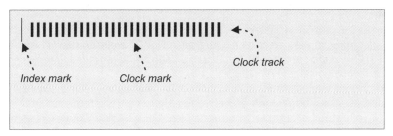

Magnetic Ink Character Recognition (MICR)

is machine recognition of stylised characters printed in magnetic ink. It is very reliable, so it is suitable for purposes needing accuracy such as banking. The commonest application is the data printed on a bank cheque: the cheque number, the branch number and the account number. These characters are both machine and human readable. It is unlikely to be used for newly designed systems because it is expensive and bar codes provide a more efficient alternative.

Optical Character Recognition (OCR)

including: editable text
is machine recognition of printed characters: for example the machine-readable section of a passport or the reading of typed postcodes when mail is automatically sorted.

Editable text results from using optical character recognition software, which can convert a page of text from a scanned image into a text data file. This text file can then be edited using a word processor. The software is not foolproof but it does include error messages to highlight characters that were not recognised. For most people, scanning an existing document and editing errors is much quicker than retyping the text. *Handwriting recognition software*, see page 294, can also produce editable text data files.

Document reader

also known as: document scanner
including: document imaging
is a *scanner* (see page 296) used in business to input documents quickly and accurately into a computer system. It usually incorporates a sheet feeder to enable many pages of a document to be input automatically. The document can then be processed in a number of ways, for example:

- using *optical character recognition* to identify typed data, see above;

- using *optical mark recognition* to identify data on handwritten forms, see page 112;

- using **document imaging**, which stores a complete image of the page for future reference, including details such as signatures. See also *archive*, page 111.

Epayment

including: electronic money, electronic fund transfer (EFT), electronic fund transfer at point of sale (EFTPOS), debit card, credit card, cash dispenser, automatic teller machine (ATM), contactless technology, home banking
is the use of computer systems to pay or receive money, replacing physical forms of money such as coins, banknotes and cheques. Epayment systems really only provide an alternative method of transferring money from one bank account to another, which is otherwise expensive. Epayment systems usually involve *authentication* (see page 109) of the user of the account and *authorisation* (see page 109) of the transaction requested.

The most common systems are:

Electronic money is the use of a device such as a *smart card* (see page 295) or contactless radio frequency identification tag (RFID, see page 112) to replace coins and banknotes. The card has credit transferred electronically to its chip or its associated account. Money can then be transferred from the card to a shopkeeper's point-of-sale terminal by a special card reader when an item is paid for. A transport system can use a similar system when a passenger enters a vehicle or a station.

Electronic funds transfer (EFT) is the use of computer networks to transfer money between bank accounts. This is done between banks, as an alternative to sending a cheque or a bankers' draft, including international transfers. Most companies now pay their employees by electronic transfer of funds into their personal bank accounts.

Electronic funds transfer at point of sale (EFTPOS) is used in retail stores as an alternative to payment with coins and banknotes, usually using a *credit card* or *debit card*, see below.

Debit cards authorise the shop's bank to transfer money from the purchaser's account directly to the shop's account. Credit and debit cards allow a person to buy goods (or services) without having to handle cash.

Credit cards authorise the credit card company to charge the value to the purchaser's credit card account and credit the value to the shop's (or service provider's) bank account. Every month the credit card company will send a statement to the purchaser requiring payment for items bought using the credit card.

Cash dispenser or **automatic teller machine (ATM)** is a machine that automatically issues banknotes to customers when authorised by a credit card or debit card (and authenticated by a *PIN*, see page 162). The user's bank or credit card account is updated with the value of the transaction.

Contactless technology allows a credit card, debit card or radio frequency identification tag to be used quickly by passing it close to a contactless reader. As there is no authentication this method is only used for low value sales.

Home banking allows account holders to carry out transfers from their account to other bank accounts by accessing it online or by telephone. They can also access an up-to-date statement and carry out other bank transactions.

Turnaround document

is printed by a computer and then used to record additional data to be input into a computer later. Examples include repeat prescriptions from GP surgeries and pupil details on forms from schools. This has several advantages:

- The data identifies the information accurately (it came from the computer system).
- The printed data only needs altering if wrong.
- Errors, for example due to poor handwriting, are reduced.
- The additional data may be simple enough to read automatically, for example using mark sense reading.

Backup

including: full backup, differential backup, incremental backup
is making copies of data or programs in case the originals are corrupted or lost. If the system fails it can be rebuilt with accurate data. Backups should be made regularly and provision made for any changes made after the last backup. These backups may be:

- a **full backup**, which copies all files to provide a complete snapshot of the data at a particular point in time;

- a **differential backup**, which copies only data files that have changed since the previous full backup;

- an **incremental backup**, which copies only those data files that have changed since the last backup, which could be a full backup or a previous incremental backup;

- a *journal file* (see page 275), which provides a record of transactions since the previous backup;

- files using the *grandfather-father-son* (see page 276) method;

- or even (as a last resort) stored on paper.

A backup of the total software of the system will be stored separately from the computer as a safeguard against physical dangers such as fire or hardware failure. However, a backup of an individual file may simply be an additional copy stored on the computer system, for example a previous version of a word processor file. See also *restore* (see below).

Restore

is to replace corrupt or lost data using copies from a *backup* system (see page 115). This generally involves copying the last full backup back onto the system, followed by the differential backup or any incremental backups. To return the system to the state when it failed usually involves restoring the latest *journal file* (see page 275) or any *transaction files* (see page 275).

B5 CONTROL AND MONITORING

Other terms related to the use of computers in control processes and devices will be found in Section C1 Programming concepts and Section E7 Communications technology.

The use of computers to make machines do what we want them to – called **control** – grew out of the extensive use of mechanical devices and electromagnetic switches (relays). In telephone exchanges, traffic lights and lifts control used to be achieved by the use of mechanically operated switching systems. Other methods were designed to control the operation of machines, made up of devices that reacted to conditions in the environment such as temperature, pressure, speed, position. Large manufacturing plants were built controlled by these methods.

The development of microprocessors and microcomputers made it possible to improve the reliability of existing systems and to make them more flexible. In a modern airliner the computer system is capable of controlling take-off and landing as well as automatically maintaining course, speed and altitude. The computers used in cars take over part of the control of the car engine from the driver. The operation of washing machines and video equipment is frequently managed by microprocessors. Control systems can also be used to improve efficiency (for example saving energy) or to be environmentally friendly (for example reducing pollution).

Control may be exercised remotely, in which case control signals are sent from the controller to the device. These signals may be transmitted in any of the ways that are used to pass data, for example through wires, or as radio or infrared signals.

Control systems may be either passive or reactive. In a **passive system** the controlled device, once it has been set going, will perform a predetermined set of activities regardless of the circumstances. A **reactive system** will vary its behaviour in response to feedback from different situations. By using programmable chips, connected to suitable sensors, systems respond to the information provided by these sensors. Combining control and observation, through the use of sensors, has made it possible to extend the scope of automatic **process control**, for example in the manufacture and packaging of chemical products. **Fault tolerant** systems are able to continue operation in the event of the failure of some of their components although the quality of the output may be degraded. This is in addition to the system characteristics of robustness and reliability.

Virtual reality systems give the user the illusion that they are transported into an environment created by the computer. Computer-controlled graphics are used to generate scenes of various levels of realism that the user can interact with and control.

CONTROL

Automation

is the use of machines or systems to perform tasks as an alternative to using people.

Actuator

is any device that can be operated by signals from a computer or control system causing physical movement, for example, devices for opening windows in a computer-controlled ventilation system.

Servo mechanism

also known as: servo
is a mechanical mechanism for remote control of machines. A simple form is the motor that operates the control surface of a radio-controlled model aircraft, where the person flying the model plays an active part continuously adjusting the position of the control levers. Servos can be controlled electronically through computer circuits that may incorporate feedback to achieve automatic control; in these situations human partici-pation may be very limited.

Data capture

including: sampling, data logging
is the *sampling* (collection at specified intervals) of output from external sensors (see also *polling*, page 334). This data may be used to control a process. *Data logging* is the capture and storage of data for later use; thus data captured in a control process may be logged for later analysis of the process.

Fault tolerance

is the ability of a system to recognise and to cope with unusual events. Examples include a traffic light system where failure to display instructions to the pedestrian by one of the two displays will not stop the use of the crossing system. Alternatively in a packet switching network system if a package is lost it will be resent.

Feedback

including: closed loop, open loop
is the use of data from sensors as input to the controlling program. In this way the result of previous actions becomes input that contributes to selecting the next action. If the response to the feedback is automatic (there is no human operator involvement), the process is called *closed loop*; if an operator is involved or feedback is not used, it is called *open loop*. In most situations where feedback is used to control position, for example stacking boxes on shelves, the correct position is achieved by an iterative process, in which a move is followed by a position check, each move bringing it closer to the required position, until the correct position is reached.

Fly by wire

is a method of controlling an aeroplane in flight. The flaps, rudder and other control surfaces of the aeroplane are operated by motors. These motors are controlled by (electrical) signals that are created as a result of actions by the pilot. This kind of flight control system involves the use of computers to analyse the pilot's intentions and thus work out the right amount of movement of the control surfaces; the computers can override the pilot in situations that would endanger the aeroplane.

Numeric control

also known as: computer numeric control (CNC)
generally refers to the automatic control of machines such as lathes and milling machines. Some numerically controlled machines simply obey a preset program of instructions, while more advanced machines can react to *feedback* (see page 118) from *sensors* (see below).

Paper tape

including: paper tape punch, paper tape reader
is sometimes still used as the means of program and data input to machine tools. A pattern of holes punched in the tape is used to represent the data. In order to prepare the tape a **paper tape punch** is attached to the computer on which the program and data are prepared while a **paper tape reader** is used as an input device to the machine tool.

Process control

including: integrated manufacturing
is the automatic monitoring and control of an industrial activity by a computer that is programmed to respond to the *feedback* (see page 118) signals from *sensors* (see below). The operation controlled may be as small as a single machine packing boxes or as extensive as the control of an automated bakery, where the mixing, cooking and packaging are controlled within a single **integrated manufacturing** process.

Robot

including: robot arm
is a computer-controlled mechanical device that is sufficiently flexible to be able to do a variety of tasks. Robots are frequently used to do jobs where consistent performance is required (such as paint spraying motor cars) or where there is some danger to humans performing the task (such as the handling of toxic materials). A **robot arm** is a relatively simple fixed robot capable of picking things up, positioning them etc.

Sensor

including: analogue sensor, digital sensor, passive device, active device
is a *transducer* (see page 344) that responds to some physical property such as pressure, rate of flow, humidity, the proximity of ferrous metal. The electrical output from the

sensor may be either analogue, an **analogue sensor**, or digital, a **digital sensor**. Some sensors, called **passive devices**, require no external electrical source. Those that require an external voltage are called **active devices**.

Stepper motor

also known as: stepping motor
is an electric motor that moves in small rotational steps. Suitably controlled and geared, a stepper motor can provide very small discrete movements, for example the movement of the paper rollers and the print head in a printer. The control circuits may involve the use of *feedback* (see page 118).

Telemetry

is the use of communications (usually radio) to monitor sensors to achieve control of machines and instruments at a distance. For example, the control of satellites and space probes, or the monitoring and control of the performance of Formula 1 racing cars, where the technicians can monitor the engine control system on the car from the pits while the race is in progress.

VIRTUAL REALITY

Virtual reality

including: immersive virtual reality, non-immersive virtual reality
is a computer-generated environment that provides the user with the illusion of being present in that situation. Virtual reality is produced by providing feedback to our various senses: vision, hearing, movement and sometimes smell. As the user moves or acts, the image seen will change along with appropriate sound and movement. It usually requires high-powered computers.

Immersive virtual reality systems provide feedback to as many senses as possible by using specialised equipment. They attempt to provide the user with a very realistic situation and are used for training in critical and stressful situations. Examples include the training of aircraft crew (a cockpit simulator using a cabin mounted on hydraulic jacks to provide movement) and training maintenance engineers to work in nuclear reactors (using specialised peripherals such as *data gloves*, see page 121, and *headsets*, see page 121).

Non-immersive virtual reality systems use limited feedback to provide the user with the perception of a particular situation without attempting to convince the user that it is real. This can be done relatively cheaply using common equipment. The environ-ment is displayed on a standard monitor using 3D graphics and can be controlled using a simple pointer device such as a special scalpel that a sculptor may use to carve a sculpture. Other examples include vehicle driver training and the ergonomic evaluation of a shop layout.

Data glove

is an input device worn on the hand by a user of a virtual reality system. Typically, it enables the position of the fingers and the orientation of the hand to be sensed by the system. In most systems, when the user 'touches' a simulated object, there is no physical sensation returned to the hand. Greater realism is possible in systems that do provide this kind of feedback. See also *haptic feedback*, below.

Haptic feedback

provides the user with a sense of feel and touch. When the user touches a virtual object the input device stops moving freely and provides resistance to the user. An example is the sculptor who uses a special scalpel that moves freely until it starts cutting the virtual object.

Headset

is an input and output device worn on the head by a user of a virtual reality system. It gives the wearer the impression of being within the computer-generated scene, with sound provided through headphones and vision through small video screens in goggles worn over the eyes. The headset senses changes of position of the head and inputs this to the computer so that the simulation can be changed appropriately. Since the user is isolated from external sounds and vision there is a very strong sense of being within the simulated environment.

Virtual reality cave

is a small room where the walls consist of back-projected displays, giving the user a more immersive experience without the need for a headset. For example, a driving simulator may consist of a car body at the centre of a virtual reality cave.

B6   MODELLING AND SIMULATION

Imagine having to consider designing and building a new bypass to divert traffic round a town. Before starting on such a venture it would be wise to check on the cost and compare this with the advantages to be gained. Although it is quite possible to produce accurate costings, it is harder to work out how wide the bypass should be (for example should it be dual or single carriageway?) or what route it should take to reduce the traffic flow through the town. By the time the road is built the money will have been spent and the bypass might not be effective. When data on current traffic flow has been collected and likely future traffic requirements have been assessed a model of the alternative new routes can be produced.

Modelling is the production of a mathematical description (the **model**) of a problem. After the modelling has been completed, the computer simulation of the problem allows solutions to be found.

Weather forecasters also use computer **simulation**. Data is gathered from many sources at different times and from this the computer predicts what weather we are likely to expect. From experience we know that weather forecasting accuracy can vary from being very good in the short term to being dramatically wrong in the long term. Economic forecasting is performed in a similar way, but often lacks the accuracy of even a weather forecast.

In any field, predictions can only be as good as the model used to produce them. All computer simulations are approximations of the real world and while some are very close approximations, others rely on assumptions that are only valid for some of the time (for example when calculating the risks on various financial investments). Similarly, many of the arguments over climate science and the extent of global warming are concerned with the assumptions used in the simulations that predict how severe the effects will be. Difficulties also arise when the process underlying the simulation is non-linear or chaotic. For such processes (for example long-term weather conditions) very small changes to starting conditions can lead to widely different outcomes. Some systems are adaptive (for example the movement of a flock of birds) rather than just complicated and current modelling methods include using social phenomena such as crowd behaviour.

Computer simulations are also used in training. A flight simulator is used to prepare pilots to cope with anything from standard flying and landing to dealing with emergencies without putting anyone's life at risk. A flight simulator can range from a simple screen display to a full-size mock-up of the flight deck with motion effects.

Computer simulation can be used to demonstrate a process that would normally be impossible to demonstrate because it would be too dangerous, too expensive, would take too long or occur too quickly. In a simulation dealing with a nuclear power station, alterations can be made that would not be allowed during a visit to such a station. Similarly, in the field of genetics, alterations can be simulated on a reasonable timescale rather than waiting months. In business some managers plan logistic operations (such as the layout of warehouses) by simulating using different business models to run a variety of future scenarios thus allowing more efficient approaches to be identified.

In silicon chip design, a simulation is used to show how the circuitry will behave. The design is adjusted until the required response is achieved. This saves the expense and time of producing, testing and having to change a series of prototypes. In these circumstances **emulation** software is used to check computer behaviour for various programs before the new chip becomes available.

Forecasting

is the use of simulations to predict future events, such as forecasting the weather. To be of any value the results of the simulation must be reasonably accurate. The programs must be thoroughly tested by comparing predictions with actual events. If the programs are shown to be accurate they can then be used regularly to aid planning. See Example B6.1.

Example B6.1 Forecasting using a computer system

In this example, we will look at how we can forecast the costs of using a mobile phone:

- The cost of a *single phone call* can be worked out by an application (a computer program) that asks for the length of the call, where it is to be sent to, the tariff and so on. This will provide an **exact answer** and the computer is simply being used as a **calculator**.

- The expected cost of the *calls for the next month* can be worked out by an application that asks for information about how many calls are expected to be made, how long they usually are, where they will be sent to, the tariff and so on. This information is not exact, so the computer will forecast an answer that is not exact but as accurate as possible given the information supplied. The computer is using a **simulation**.

- If we *don't have an application* to work out the expected cost we can design a model, perhaps as a spreadsheet, to simulate the likely cost of each call. This is called **modelling**. We can use this model to perform the simulation as if we already had a suitable simulation application.

Simulation

also known as: computer simulation
is the use of a computer program to predict the likely behaviour of a real-life system. A mathematical *model* (see below) of the system is constructed and tested. The model is usually incorporated into a program that can be used to investigate other situations.

A simple simulation can be built using a spreadsheet. A more typical simulation might produce a graphical display reacting to real-time inputs. Some complex simulations might require specialised simulation software.

Simulation software uses the model that has been developed to show the effect of different conditions on the outcome of a process. To be of any use the model used must be thoroughly tested. It is now possible to get simulation software that contains a model with tested components. It is not necessary to start from scratch each time.

Computer games might attempt to be simulations of real-life situations. These games include models of how the situation works. For example a flying game will include a model of gravity and air resistance and the accuracy of this model will affect the realism of the game.

Model

is a sequence of ideas that attempts to represent a process. At some stage these ideas may be expressed mathematically, for example as a set (or collection) of equations perhaps in a spreadsheet. The accuracy of this model is limited by the knowledge of the process being modelled, the time available to produce the model, the availability of input data and how quickly results are required.

Modelling

also known as: computer modelling
is the construction of a sequence of ideas (see *model*, above) by a mathematical analysis of the required situation. The model is refined by testing predictions with data from various known conditions.

For the example of road planning (see introduction, page 122), the model produced is a description of the rate of traffic flow at all points of interest on the town bypass. This mathematical model is then implemented as a computer model. The computer can quickly carry out the necessary calculations (many of which are repeated but are quite simple) and show the results using tables of numbers, diagrams and animations. The data in the computer simulation of the bypass can then be altered and the results reviewed; for example by increasing the expected amount of traffic on the bypass we can determine whether this causes any problems at road junctions. The bypass could then be built, with the likelihood that it will be worthwhile, or it could be abandoned as being not useful enough, having only spent the relatively small cost of the modelling. See Example B6.2.

Example B6.2 Modelling techniques

The following modelling techniques are illustrated using the example of *forecasting the cost of phone calls for next month*:

- *Formulas*, for example to work out the average length of the phone calls;
- *Decisions*, for example to use different formulas if the calls are local or international;
- *Iteration*, for example, to forecast the phone calls tomorrow and use this predicted information to work out the next day's calls;
- *Monte Carlo method*, for example, to use chance to forecast the length of each call, see below.

Emulation

is a very precise form of *simulation* (see page 124) that should mimic exactly the behaviour of the circumstances that it is simulating. See *emulator*, below.

Emulation might be used with printers to enable them to behave like a different printer. They might then be used with a wide variety of computer software.

Emulator

is a program that allows a computer to behave as if it were a different type of computer. An emulator enables:

- software to be developed that will run on computers not yet built;
- software to be used on a type of computer other than the type it was designed for;
- software to be tested when it would otherwise use expensive resources;
- a computer to be used as a peripheral, appearing to the host computer to have the characteristics expected. This enables microcomputers to act as terminals to larger computer systems.

An emulator is often much slower than the host computer because of the extra processing involved.

Monte Carlo method

A whimsical name that comes from the use of chance, usually random numbers rather than roulette wheels, in simulation. In exploring the performance of a complex system (which might be chemical, physical, biological, socioeconomic etc.) the overall behaviour of the system might be too complicated to specify confidently in mathematical terms. If the many small decisions in the system can be easily specified, then the behaviour of the system **can** be simulated, using random numbers to model a large number of small decisions.

For example, migration of people between towns in the UK might be too complicated to specify mathematically, but information is available on how many people move from London to other major cities each year. The overall behaviour of the population can be explored by selecting one resident of London, and generating a random number to see if that individual will stay or move, and if so, to where. In this way predictions about future population trends will be possible, even if the mathematics is not fully understood, see *random number generation*, below.

Random number generation

including: pseudo-random number generator
Many *simulations* (see page 124) on a computer need to make use of random numbers, in a similar way to 'tossing a coin' in order to make a decision. Most programming languages include a random number function that gives the user a suitable number, as if it had been chosen at random – numbers between 1 and 6, for example, to simulate the throw of dice in a game. Because computer programs cannot be truly random, a **pseudo-random number generator** is used, which gives numbers with the appearance of being random. This sequence of numbers can be repeated for testing and debugging purposes. See *Monte Carlo method*, page 125.

B7 NETWORKING

Other terms and concepts related to networks and communications are to be found in Section B2 The internet, Section E6 Communications components and Section E7 Communications technology.

Connecting pieces of communications and information equipment together in a network is not a new concept. The early telegraph systems, especially in the USA where the distances are so great, provided the stimulus for telegram services and the later development of telex communications, in which text information could be sent between any telex machines on the worldwide telex network using telephone lines. Passing messages internationally has been possible ever since the development of international cable links, which began in the 19th century. For over 70 years the world's newspapers depended upon organisations that gathered news around the world and delivered it to their client newspapers through the telex network. These services are still provided by some of the same organisations but in addition there are now email and other services linking computers around the world.

In a computer network a number of computers are connected together in order to exchange information. For example, an organisation having offices spread over a wide geographical area might install a network to enable employees to examine information held on computers in other offices many miles away.

The connections between computers may be wires, fibre optic cables, microwave links, communication via satellite or any combination of these. The interconnected collection of computers form the network. The computers may be large powerful machines, small personal computers or terminals. They may all be capable of running on their own but will have the added advantage of being able to communicate with each other.

In a traditional network, users must explicitly log on (that is, identify themselves to the network) and explicitly move information around on the network by issuing the appropriate instructions. A **distributed system** is normally thought of as a network in which the existence of the other machines is not obvious to the user. Programs and data held on other machines can be used as though they were held locally on the user's computer.

A distinction is usually made between networks of computers that are all situated relatively close to each other – for example in the same building or in a cluster of buildings – known as a **local area network** (a **LAN**) and those in which the computers are geographically remote, known as a **wide area network** (a **WAN**).

A network offers the possibility of sharing information and work between the different resources available. For example, if one computer has a heavy load of processing, some of the work can be moved to another machine on the network. A network makes all the resources of the network (programs, data and equipment, such as printers and disk drives) available to the whole network without regard to the physical location of either the resource or the user. Reliability is another advantage of networking. The effect of hardware failures can be reduced by switching work from a failed device to one that is still functioning. This can be particularly valuable in systems such as banking where it is important that the system can continue operating even if there are some hardware failures.

Networks of small computers can be a cheaper way of providing computer power than a single large machine. If a network of small machines has access to outside facilities, whose use may need to be purchased, such as large specialist databases, the potential of the network is greatly enhanced. Linking a network to other networks, which are themselves linked to yet further networks, makes it theoretically possible to have the whole of world knowledge available to any computer on such a network.

The **internet** now provides this kind of linking of networks. It works because there are thousands of networks each connected to other networks in such a way that it is possible for messages (data) to be sent from a computer on one of the networks to any computer on any other network, provided that both networks have access to the internet.

Network

is a linked set of computer systems, which may be capable of sharing computer power and resources such as printers, file storage and databases. Sometimes the term network is used to mean the arrangement of links between the equipment that form the network. See *network topology*, page 129.

Distributed networking

including data centre, server farm
is the sharing of resources by the (network) operating system across several computer systems. The user will not need to manage these processes. A distributed network will be based around a number of *servers*, see page 134. These servers are physically located either at a range of locations or together in a *data centre*. Client computers will use which-ever server is appropriate without the user being aware of it. In addition the various sets of data stored in the network will appear as a single set accessed by various techniques such as *tags* and *indexes*. The term distributed networking is sometimes used to describe *distributed processing*, see page 136. See also *cloud computing*, page 88.

Data centre is a central computer centre used primarily to house the large databases used by major organisations. A data centre enables efficient maintenance of the system as well as providing security, including facilities for *backup*, see page 115, and protection against power failure.

Server farm is a form of *data centre*, see above, that consists of a large number of individual linked *file servers*, see page 134. This can be cheaper and more flexible than using a small number of large computers, particularly if the data centre is performing a large number of small tasks. The flexibility of this organisation allows businesses to buy capacity independently.

Local area network (LAN)

is a network in which the computer systems are all situated relatively close to each other, for example in the same building or cluster of buildings, such as a school. Since the distances involved are small, direct physical connection is possible. The network connections are normally wire cables, wireless links or fibre optic cable. A local area network usually serves a single organisation. See also *Ethernet*, page 138, and *Network components*, page 139.

Wide area network (WAN)

is a network in which the computers are geographically remote. Wide area networks make use of a range of connection methods typically using public telephone links, undersea cables and communication satellites. Often a wide area network links the local area networks in a geographically spread organisation.

Metropolitan area network (MAN)

is a network covering a highly populated area. The network serves the inhabitants of a built-up area (often a town or city), rather than an individual organisation, using fibre optic cable and wireless to provide a powerful service. The close proximity of users makes it cost-effective.

Network topology

including: bus network, ring network, loop network, star network, central node, hub, nexus, backbone
is the theoretical arrangement of components of a network. The actual arrangement will almost certainly be determined by the buildings or other locations for the parts of the network. The network descriptions indicate how the devices on the network, the computers, printers, servers etc., are connected to each other. Since networks normally communicate serially, the actual connections will be capable of *serial data transmission* (see page 346).

Figure B7.1 A bus network with spurs
Each device is connected to the network bus cable by a spur.

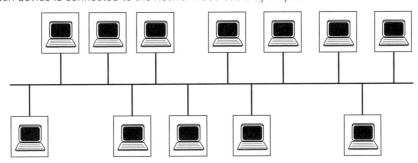

A *bus network* has each of the devices connected directly to a main communications line, called a bus, along which signals are sent. The bus will frequently be a twin cable of some kind, for example coaxial cable. See Figures B7.1 and B7.2.

Figure B7.2 A bus network

Each device has the network cable going into its network interface and out to the network interface of the next device.

A *ring network* (sometimes called a *loop network*) has each of the devices on the network connected to a ring (or loop) communications line around which signals are sent. The devices may be connected to the ring by spurs, as in Figure B7.3, or the connections may pass through the *network interface* (see *interface*, page 335, and *interface card*, page 335) in each device, as in Figure B7.4; in this case, provision has to be made for the system to continue to work if one of the devices is switched off or fails to function properly.

Figure B7.3 A ring network with spurs

Each device is connected to the network bus cable by a spur.

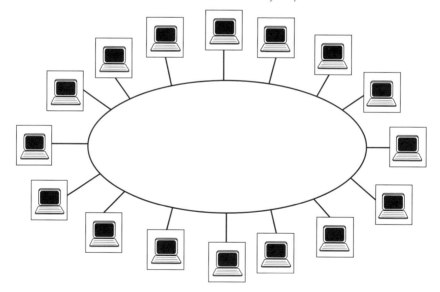

Figure B7.4 A ring network

Each device has the network cable going into its network interface and out to the network interface of the next device.

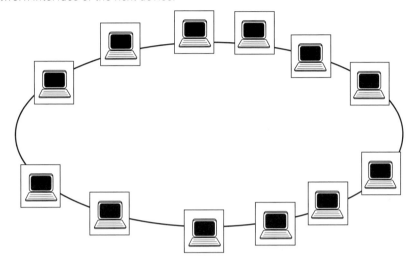

A **star network** has all the network devices connected to one central computer, which is often used as the *file server* (see page 134). The **central node** of the network, sometimes called the **hub** or **nexus**, is a computer that has separate connections to each computer or terminal. See Figure B7.5.

A **backbone** is a high-speed communication link used to provide the main links between the smaller subnetworks in large network. The connections are fibre optic cable. See Figure B7.6.

Cluster

including: cluster controller
is a group of computers in the same physical area, possibly on a network. A cluster sharing resources will usually be less formally organised than most networks. A **cluster controller** is the computer acting as controller for the cluster. See also *network controller*, page 136.

Token ring network

including: token
is a *ring network* (see page 130) in which information is sent around the ring as variable-sized packets of data. In addition to the data, a packet will contain the address of the sender and the destination address. A **token**, which is a signal that passes round the network, can be thought of as a carrier for the packet. For a packet to travel round the ring it has to be attached to a token. This is a method of avoiding data packets colliding on the ring and creating unreadable signals. In principle, the packet travels round the ring attached to the token until it is taken off at the destination address or it returns

Figure B7.5 A star network

Each device is connected directly to the central computer at the hub of the network.

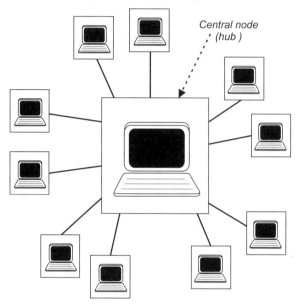

Figure B7.6 A backbone with three subnetworks

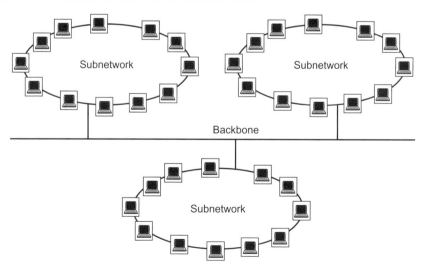

unread to the sender, where it is taken off as unread. The token then becomes free and continues round the ring ready to have another package attached to it by one of the network devices. The token continually circulates around the ring picking up, carrying and dropping packets off at their destinations.

The network topology for token ring networks is shown in Figure B7.4.

Virtual network

including: virtual private network, virtual private networking (VPN), remote desktop protocol (RDP)
is a network where a specified group of computers can communicate with each other. Several virtual networks could share the same physical connections, without a user realising any of the other virtual networks exist. Similarly a virtual network could exist across several local area networks, or even across the internet, but other users could not get access to it. Virtual networks can also be used to make a local area network structure more efficient, see *virtual local area network (VLAN)*, page 140.

A virtual network is usually managed by using the specific individual network addresses of each workstation. The security software that manages the virtual network ensures that communication is only permitted with other stations on the same virtual network. However, this technique may not be secure enough on large networks such as the internet where other techniques are used such as *virtual private networking (VPN)*, see below, or authentication tokens, see *personal identification device (PID)*, page 162.

Virtual private network is a virtual network used to protect the information being shared. Thus a business with geographically distant offices can use a virtual private network to provide a company *intranet* (see page 137) or to communicate with its own computers. Other users of the host network (which may be the internet) cannot access, or even know of, computers using the virtual private network. One technique used to implement a virtual private network is *virtual private networking* (VPN), see below.

Virtual private networking (VPN) is one way of implementing a *virtual private network*, see above, by ensuring two-way secure communications between the stations. The virtual private networking system allows a client station to communicate using the internet, with the server, to verify the authenticity of the remote computer. The data is *encrypted* (see page 163) during transmission over the internet.

Remote desktop protocol (RDP) is a secure method for one computer to control a different computer. Both computers need to be linked to the same network. The desktop of the computer being controlled is displayed on the remote computer that can then control the computer as if the user was actually working at it. This technique is usually used by engineers to diagnose and fix problems remotely.

Peer-to-peer network

is a simple network that provides shared resources, such as printers and storage, but may offer little else in the way of additional facilities, such as file security. The name comes from the fact that all the computers on these networks have equal status and can send data to and from each other. For example one station may send data to another station, which can then print it out, acting as a printer server. Similarly, one station can send data to another for storage on that station's disk drive. See also *server*, below, and *terminal*, page 136.

Client–server network

is a network organised around one or more *servers* (see below). The server maintains a database of authorised users, passwords and access rights. Usually, but not always, a server also acts as a *file server* (see below) but its prime function is to provide the security for the network. See also *terminal*, page 136.

Network relationship

including: peer-to-peer relationship, client–server relationship
describes the way two computer systems work together when attached to the same network. Most networks operate with a mixture of network relationships depending on the functions being performed. The relationships can be either peer-to-peer or client–server:

Peer-to-peer relationship is a method of network organisation in which *network stations* (or *clients*, see *terminal*, page 136) can share resources on other network stations, so one station can use a printer on another station or save data on another station's local storage. There is no concept of the resource being owned by one station and then being given to other stations. This is simple but has the disadvantage that the data is not centrally organised or controlled, leading to duplication and errors.

Client–server relationship is a method of network organisation in which *network stations* (or *clients*, see *terminal*, page 136) make use of resources available at one or more *servers* (see below). The resource can be hardware (such as a printer), data such as a database, or a software application. Many network organisations can operate with a client–server relationship. For example this kind of organisation is seen in a *star network* (see page 131), in which one computer has the role of managing a particular resource for the network. One advantage of a client–server relationship is that the server does the required processing, only the results being sent to the client thus reducing network traffic. Another advantage is that the resource is in one place and there are no problems caused by its physical distribution.

Server

including: file server, printer server, CD-ROM server, database server, internet server, web server, application server, terminal services server, mail server
is a computer on a *network* (see page 128) that provides a resource that can be used by any authorised *client station* (see *terminal*, page 136). There are a number of types of server:

A **file server** provides central disk storage for any users of the network. The file server software identifies each user's files separately so that other users cannot use them. Users can access their own files from any client station on the network or, given suitable *access rights* (see page 163), can access other users' data.

A *printer server* allows the client stations to use a printer controlled by it, and usually provides the facilities of a *printer spooler* (see page 179).

A *CD-ROM server* allows all the client stations to obtain data from a CD-ROM currently being used by the CD-ROM server computer. Often a CD-ROM server will have access to many CD-ROM and DVD disks, from a collection of several CD and DVD drives, a CD jukebox, or disk images stored on the CD-ROM server.

A *database server* manages a large database. Client stations can access data in the database and, if authorised, can maintain the database. The server usually carries out the database processing, with the query being sent by a client station to the server and the results assembled by the server and returned to the client station. This form of *client–server relationship* (see page 134) can ensure the consistency of the database, even in the simpler environment of a *peer-to-peer network* (see page 133).

An *internet server* manages access to the internet for all the users of the network. However, it is often called a *proxy server* (see page 160) since it usually combines the additional security features of a proxy server.

A *web server* provides internet pages for other computers through the internet. It often provides a cache of web pages, which are pages stored when first accessed so they can be supplied later without the delay of accessing the internet.

An *application server* stores application software (such as a word processor program). Each time a user wants to use the software it is temporarily copied from the server, making it easy to update the software centrally and to monitor its usage.

A *terminal services server* is a powerful server that both stores and runs the application software over the network for client stations. The software is not copied to the client station. See also *thin client*, under *virtualisation*, below.

A *mail server* manages the electronic mail for the network. It provides the users with email addresses, stores incoming emails until collected by users, and sends outgoing emails to their destinations.

Any expensive resource can be made available to a large number of users by a server. A specialised example is a weather station server obtaining and distributing current local instrument readings or satellite weather data.

Virtualisation

including: thin client
is the use of servers to run applications for desktop client computers. The application is stored on the server and accessed by the client computer. The processing may be carried out either by the server or sections of the application can be transferred to the client computers for local processing, if they are powerful enough. This technique allows for the centralisation of *maintenance*, see page 36, *updates*, see page 232, (with cost savings) and the use of cheaper client computers with less power.

Thin clients are client computers that rely on a server to do the processing required. They have just enough computer power to process the input, the display and communicate with the network. The thin client may not store any data and it cannot function without the network link to the server. This means they are very cheap and easily replaced if faulty but they do require a powerful server. See *client–server relationship* (page 134).

Terminal

also known as: network terminal
including: network station, station, client stations, point-of-sale (POS) terminal
is a computer or computer-controlled device that provides a user with access to a network. A network may have a variety of different kinds of equipment connected to it. For example, a supermarket network will probably have standard computers for its offices as well as the point-of-sale terminals (the checkouts) all connected on the same network. This may be linked to a wider network for the whole supermarket chain.

Network stations are any desktop computer terminals on the network that are available for use by users of the network. They are sometimes simply called **stations** or on a *client–server network* (see page 134) they are called **client stations**.

Point-of-sale (POS) terminals are the specialised terminals used at supermarket check-outs. A point-of-sale terminal will have a variety of functions, which may include *electronic funds transfer* (see page 115), as well as *bar code scanning* (see page 296) combined with getting the prices from a database on the network to produce the customer's bill.

Distributed processing

is the sharing of processing tasks between physically separated processors on a network. For example a complex set of calculations that require considerable computer power are processed by sending individual calculations to different computers over the network (which may include the internet) for processing, coordinated by a master computer. See also *distributed database*, page 95, and *distributed network*, page 128.

Network controller

including: controller
is a computer dedicated to organising a computer network. It handles the communications between users and the shared resources, such as disks and printers. Some network arrangements (topologies), such as a *star network* (see page 131), where the central computer is the network controller, can only operate with a controller; other arrangements may not use one. See also *server*, page 134.

Controller is sometimes used to mean a network controller, but normally means a computer used in control applications to monitor *sensors*, page 119, and control *actuators*, page 118.

Network operating system

including: Novell NetWare
is the software needed to enable a computer to communicate with other computers (stations) using a network. All computers on a network must have compatible network operating system software to be able to communicate through the network. Different software is required for any servers. In particular, a file server needs additional software to enable it to provide secure data storage for users. Most modern operating systems, such as Windows® (working with Windows® Server® software on

fileservers), MacOS X® and UNIX®, now include the network operating system facilities. Specialist network operating systems such as **Novell NetWare** can provide more sophisticated facilities or link client computers with differing operating systems.

Host computer

is a computer used to control a multi-user, multi-access or distributed computer system. In particular the term is applied to computers that provide access to the internet. A host computer manages the communications and storage needs of its users, who may be subscribers to an *internet service provider* (see page 74).

Network accounting software

provides statistics about the use of a network by its users. This may be about the use made of terminals on a multi-user computer system or about the use of facilities on a *peer-to-peer network* (see page 133). The information can be used to charge users for their use of resources or to monitor improper use of the network.

The information recorded can include such things as the connection time and the processor time used, a list of times and dates when the computer has been used on a multi-user system, disk storage space used, printer use, and email use on a peer-to-peer network.

The accounting software can present the overall activity on the network in a variety of ways (tables, graphs or a log) and thus assist the network manager to optimise the system and, possibly, devise charging structures.

Value Added Network Service (VANS)

is a wide area network with additional facilities such as a centrally provided database or information system for which users pay charges, which are usually based on their use of the facilities.

Workstation

is either a *station* on a network (see *terminal*, page 136), or a location where a computer, with its associated equipment, is used, such as a designer's work area; this kind of workstation may or may not be on a network.

Intranet

is a communication system, solely within a particular company or organisation. It provides services similar to those offered by the internet. For security it is usually only available to users physically connected to the company's network or possibly accessed using a *virtual private network*, see page 133. Intranets are increasingly used to provide access to collaborative working tools such as customer relations management and project management. Unsecured access is not permitted across the internet.

Extranet

is a communication system for a particular company or organisation, which can be accessed from the internet. It provides similar services to those offered by the wider internet. It is an extension of an *intranet*, see page 137, but which can be accessed from the internet with a lower level of security than an intranet. Often only a simple user ID and password are required. For example an extranet may be used to provide a service to customers who can be provided with a user ID and password to see trade prices. A physical or VPN connection is not required.

TCP/IP (Transmission Control Protocol/Internet Protocol)

is the most common general-purpose standard *protocol*, see page 348, that allows any networked computers (including those on the internet) to communicate with each other whatever their equipment.

TCP/IP specifies how individual signals are sent over the network and provides the transport and routing for the data. Originally TCP/IP was designed for the internet but has proved very flexible and is used by the majority of networking systems, reducing the need for special gateways to convert the signals into different protocols and allowing easy connection to the internet. This protocol is unusual in that it splits the data into small *packets*, see page 347, which may be sent, or *routed*, using different physical network links. See also the *OSI networking model*, page 348.

Ethernet

is the most common general-purpose *local area network* (see page 132). It provides the physical connection between the computers (see also the *OSI networking model*, page 348). Different types of computers can use the same Ethernet network at the same time. Network interfaces are available from many manufacturers. Ethernet uses wire connections, wireless links or fibre optic cable. The software that makes up the *network operating system* (see page 136) is usually incorporated in most PC operating systems but may be bought separately. Ethernet networks are frequently used in offices and schools. The transmission rate for wired systems is usually 100 Mbps although faster systems are available with speeds of 1 Gbps or 10 Gbps. Wireless systems are considerably slower.

Ethernet networks consist of groups of computers usually linked to *switches*, see also page 139, in a *star network configuration* (see page 131). These switches are then linked together to form the local area network. See also Figure B7.7 for an example of a modern network.

The local area networks can be linked to telecommunications systems using *gateways* (see page 140). The internet is the ultimate example of a *wide area network*, see page 129, formed in this way.

Figure B7.7 An example of a modern computer network

The location of each component is flexible. Switches are usually located in cabinets in different buildings with links between them. It is possible to add switches at a later date, in a new room or office. The only limitations with an Ethernet system are that the links must not form a 'circle' and the maximum distance for a single cable link is 100 m. Longer links use fibre-optic cables.

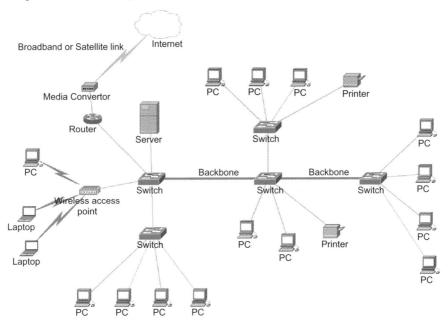

Networking components

including: Ethernet hub, switched hub, router, repeater, wireless access point, media converter, Bluetooth, gateway, bridge
are used to construct Ethernet networks from different types of networking components including:

Ethernet hubs allow any two computers connected to the hub, or though other hubs, to send data to each other. A simple hub can only deal with one link at a time and can be slow if many computers are using the same hub.

Switched hubs act as hubs but have extra circuitry, 'switching circuitry', which allows them to deal with many connections simultaneously. They are much more efficient than simple hubs.

Routers are sophisticated switched hubs. They hold information about the addresses of computers attached to the network and can forward data efficiently to the correct location via an appropriate route. They are generally used as *gateways* (see page 140) where a local area network is connected to a larger network such as the internet.

Repeaters are used to link two cable segments. Because of the loss of signal strength in network cables, a repeater amplifies the signals it receives before passing them on.

Wireless access points are hubs on the local area network that allow wireless connection. Any computer with a wireless network interface, which is within range, can communicate with the local area network by radio to the wireless access point.

Media converters change the physical signals where different types of network link meet, for example between fibre optic cable and twisted pair cable.

Bluetooth is a short range wireless communication standard. It allows Bluetooth-equipped devices to communicate with other Bluetooth devices in a *peer-to-peer relationship*, see page 134. If one of the devices is a computer then it can act as a gateway onto a network. An example is a mobile phone with a separate earpiece linked using Bluetooth wireless communication.

Gateway is a computer system that links two dissimilar computer networks. Gateways usually provide a single point of entry to a secure computer network. The gateway converts data passing through it into the appropriate form for the second network. The gateway can monitor usage and also limit access between the networks to authorised users. In a network that uses the Internet Protocol (IP) a *firewall* (see page 160) provides most of the functions of a gateway.

Bridge is a device that links two local area networks. It may also convert the data into the appropriate form for the other system. It is simply a link, and there is no concept of it providing an entrance to a computer network.

Wi-Fi

including: wireless mesh
also known as: wireless Ethernet
is a way of connecting computers to a network by wireless. Each computer has a Wi-Fi wireless interface that connects to a *wireless access point* (see above) attached to the network. It is the most successful of several competing technologies, which include **wireless mesh**. The name Wi-Fi is simply a marketing tool to imply a relationship to Hi-Fi (high fidelity) music.

Routing

is the management of the route for data being sent over a network. This involves identifying the destination and deciding on the best route across the network via the intermediate computers or specialist routers. Different parts of the data (see *packets*, page 347) travel using different routes depending on the availability of the various routes. If links become unavailable, available or busy, routes may be changed dynamically while the packet is in transit. In a local area network routing usually uses the *internet protocol (IP)*, see page 76. See also *signal routing*, page 346.

Virtual local area network (VLAN)

is part of a local area network that appears as a separate network and is separated from the rest by the use of sophisticated *switches*, see page 139. This allows a local area network to be split into several virtual networks that work independently. A network split onto VLANs is much more efficient as it reduces the conflicts between the network traffic. The special switches act as *gateways* (see above) between the VLANs. See also *virtual network*, page 133.

B8 ARTIFICIAL OR MACHINE INTELLIGENCE

Artificial or machine intelligence (AI) is the study and modelling of the relationships between all aspects of intelligence. We have common sense notions of (human or animal) 'intelligence' or 'creativity'. In describing the behaviour of machines we tend to use these terms for activities that would require intelligence or creativity when performed by people.

Reasons for developing AI include:

- making machines more capable;
- understanding human behaviour (cognitive science) better;
- understanding intelligence in all its forms.

Current applications of AI include:

- knowledge-based or expert systems;
- image processing;
- vision;
- natural language processing including voice recognition;
- machine learning;
- project planning and optimisation.

These applications use many techniques for representing problems and searching for their solutions. Such techniques include: neural networks, genetic algorithms and genetic programming, semantic nets, fuzzy logic and rule-based systems.

Many techniques originally developed by AI researchers have been adapted for use in other areas such as the inspection of items on a production line using pattern recognition.

The study of AI is almost as old as computing itself, dating back to the 1950s and Alan Turing. He gave a great deal of thought to AI and thinking machines. He posed the famous Turing Test, a test to see if computers could convincingly mimic human-like behaviour. Neural networks also date from about this time.

Early successes in AI include programs to play draughts and chess. In games such as these it is easy to see that an exhaustive search might well provide good answers, but such a search seems doomed to fail because of the sheer number of possibilities. Such seemingly intractable problems are within the capabilities of even the most modest machines of today because of the increase in speed and memory capacity together with the development of new search techniques that learnt how to use these increases.

One of the most important insights originating from AI is that tasks that seem complex may be easier for a machine while a trivial task may prove very difficult for a machine. For example flying an aircraft may be easier for a machine than picking up an egg without breaking it.

There are two main types of strategy employed when trying to automate human tasks. These are the 'knowledge poor' and the 'knowledge rich' strategies. For example, a neural network solves a problem by searching for a set of parameters that fit, much as one might try to find a straight line through a set of data points. The fitting uses no knowledge of what the data represents. This is known as a 'knowledge poor' strategy.

Expert systems, on the other hand, often need very specific rules that encapsulate lots of knowledge about the problem. They are said to be 'knowledge rich'.

Artificial intelligence (AI)

also known as: machine intelligence
is the study of relationships between all aspects of intelligence of all forms and modelling them by computer systems. Many of its applications involve systems capable of learning, adaptation or error correction. These include:

- knowledge-based or expert systems;
- image processing;
- vision;
- natural language processing;
- machine learning.

Cognitive science

is concerned with human thinking processes and covers a wide range of subjects. The goal of cognitive science is the understanding of the nature of the human mind.

Some of these subjects, such as *artificial intelligence* (see above) and *human–computer interaction* (see page 416), are directly concerned with computers. Others are concerned with how people function: for example cognitive psychology including mental processes and memory; language processing and vision; learning, perception and attention; and social interaction. Some cognitive scientists find it helpful to describe how humans function in terms of a computer model of information processing.

Neural network

also known as: neural net
is a simple model of a primitive brain used as an alternative to traditional programming. The network is a collection of nodes linked to each other by one- or two-way connections. Some nodes are also connected to the external world providing the input

or output for the network. Each connection has a 'weight' and, in simple networks, each node calculates the weighted sum of all of its inputs and gives an output. Even simple networks have proved to be computationally very powerful.

Neural networks are 'knowledge poor' (the representation of the problem does not seem to be related to the problem itself). The power of neural networks is contained in the *algorithms* (see page 191) that find the weights from examples. The hope is that we could give a neural network data relating to a problem such as examples of cancer cases, from which the network may predict its occurrence in other populations.

Neural networks are particularly applicable where conventional algorithms are difficult to write. Different applications include language processing, *pattern recognition* (see below), finance and control.

Pattern recognition

is the process of identifying objects in a digitised picture, or in some cases digitised sounds, through analysis of the digital representation of the objects and comparison with stored knowledge about similar objects.

Some pattern recognition systems are based on 'knowledge rich' *algorithms* (see page 191) that 'know' lots about the potential scene. The 'knowledge rich' systems might, for example, measure the distance between the eyes as a distinguishing feature.

Other systems rely only on having many examples and expect the computer to learn to recognise (say) faces by comparison.

This area has been extended to include the process of *data mining* (see page 107) for information, finding patterns that are not clear from the way that the data has been structured. One controversial use of pattern recognition is the analysis of sales data by supermarkets to find patterns in our buying habits.

Cybernetics

including: robotics
is the study of computer control of processes, for example an industrial process or a robot. **Robotics** is the study and design of robots. See also Section B5, and *robot*, page 119. Other definitions of cybernetics have been proposed but the essential issues are the use of information processing to organise and control systems of communicating individuals. The applications of cybernetics extend from engineering and robotics to the management of companies.

Expert system

also known as: (intelligent) knowledge-based system (IKBS), (KBS)
including: knowledge base, rule base, heuristics, knowledge engineer, inference engine, shell
is an application of artificial intelligence to a particular area of activity where traditional human expert knowledge and experience are made available through a computer package.

Expert systems are very 'knowledge rich', that is, the subject is often represented as 'facts and rules' in the expert system and the resulting representation is close to the language of the subject itself. Such systems are 'expert' in their fields. Important examples of expert systems include: Prospector, which is credited with having found valuable mineral deposits where geologists had not expected any; MYCIN, a system that was 'expert' in the identification of bacterial diseases.

Experience of expert systems suggests that a good design strategy is the separation of the subject knowledge from the rules of logic (or inference) that are to be used. Thus an inference engine and a knowledge base are essential components of an expert system. To be useful any such program will also need an interface to the user, allowing interactions such as inputting queries and obtaining results. A strategy for self-improvement or a learning component, as well as a means of explaining or justifying an answer are also essential for the success of the system.

Once a knowledge base has been constructed, an expert system is ready to be interrogated or consulted. The system requests the user to provide information and then uses (searches) the knowledge base to find appropriate advice for the user. From time to time the knowledge base is updated when new information becomes available on the results of its use.

Knowledge base is that part of an expert system that holds knowledge about the application area (or domain), such as drug side effects. Often much of the knowledge is held as **IF...THEN...** type rules and this knowledge is called a *rule base*. For example:

> **IF** a patient has high blood pressure AND is anaemic **THEN** avoid the use of a certain kind of drug.

Heuristics are rules that are not derived purely from logic but are derived from the experience (of a person). These are also known as 'rules of thumb'. Many of the rules in an expert system are of this type.

Knowledge engineers are the people who collect the information for the knowledge base. This information is acquired from a variety of sources in a variety of ways; one of the most important is eliciting information through talking to experts. The knowledge obtained is then formulated as a set of rules and facts.

Inference engine is a piece of software in an expert system that interrogates the knowledge base and as a result draws inferences or conclusions.

Shell is a piece of software that is an 'empty' expert system without the knowledge base for any particular application. The user enters the appropriate rules and facts. Expert systems have a clearly identifiable internal structure, which is illustrated in Figure B8.1.

Turing test

is a test to discover whether a machine's response is distinguishable from a human response. Turing believed that machines could be so intelligent as to be able to produce

Figure B8.1 An expert system structure

The user communicates with the system through the user interface, which passes requests for advice to the inference engine. The inference engine processes the request, obtaining information – rules and facts – from the knowledge base as required and finally returns the answer to the user interface, and hence to the user.

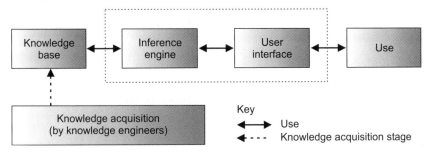

answers to questions that were indistinguishable from answers produced by a human. In 1950 he devised what has come to be called the 'Turing test'. For this test a human and a machine are able to produce output in response to a 'player'. The player knows the others as X and Y but does not know which is the computer. By addressing questions to either X or Y the player has to discover which is the human.

Turing believed that by the year 2000 the chances of the player's success would be less than 30 per cent. Unfortunately, despite great advances in both hardware and software by 2000, computers were still not able to pass this imitation test.

Genetic algorithm

is a search algorithm that uses a mechanism similar to evolution to improve a set of solutions to a problem. Such an algorithm starts with a set of possible solutions and combines them using analogues of mutation and breeding (among others) to produce a new set of solutions that are on average better than their predecessors. By repeating this process one can expect the population to improve until it contains 'good' solutions to the problem.

Genetic programming

is the use of *genetic algorithms* (see above) to optimise computer programs. In fact the idea has been used recursively so that better programs are developed using genetic programming. Compare this with robots making better robots.

Semantic net

including: arc
is a net whose nodes are concepts that are linked to each other. A semantic net is used to represent a body of knowledge. Its nodes are ideas linked by **arcs**, lines that are labelled with the relationship between the nodes. For example, we could draw the structure of the *Glossary* and add any other knowledge as needed. See also *semantic web*, page 82.

Fuzzy logic

is a means of working with uncertain knowledge. Whereas in classical logic we treat statements as being either true or false, in fuzzy logic we give each of these possibilities a certainty factor between zero and one.

Fuzzy logic is used in searching for text in a document or index: if the given text is imprecise fuzzy logic allows the software to find the 'match' that has the greatest degree of truth and is close.

B9   COMPUTER PERSONNEL

The are two main classes of people who use computers. People who make use of software to perform an aspect of their job are known as 'users'. These 'users' would make use of hardware and software without making major changes from the original configuration in order to perform their tasks.

For people who are employed for their IT/computing skills and are recognised as 'experts' then the term 'practitioner' is used. Practitioners come from a wide range of expertise and respond to users' requirements. They help specify systems; design, test and build systems; develop and enhance existing systems; implement and manage systems; and liaise with and train the users.

In simplistic terms a person performing an administrative role would generally be classed as a 'user' in their use of IT, whereas an IT technician would be classed as an IT practitioner. Most of the discussion in this section concerns the roles of the IT/computer practitioner. Practitioners will normally need a qualification or training in their field of expertise in order to practise their skills and it is useful to have an understanding of the disciplines that exist:

- **Computer science** involves a number of disciplines: designing and developing computer software, devising new ways to use computers, developing effective ways to solve computer problems, planning and managing organisational technological infrastructure.

- **Computer engineering** is the development of systems that involve software, hardware and communications.

- **Information technology** focuses on computing infrastructure and needs of individual users; tends to involve a study of systems (perhaps just software systems, but perhaps also systems in support of learning, of information dissemination etc.).

- **Information systems** is computing in an organisational context, typically for use in businesses.

- **Software engineering** deals with large-scale software systems; employs certain ideas from the world of engineering in building reliable software systems.

Further areas of research and work include **bioinformatics, computational science, computer science and mathematics, gaming and animation, health informatics programs**. For more details see Section F6 Specialised computer applications.

In many organisations, both the number and the range of tasks that computers are required to perform are still on the increase. This expansion of use has to be managed in a controlled and professional manner. Many computer-related job descriptions and responsibilities have changed, and many users' jobs have also been affected.

IT practitioners have job tasks identified by the SFIAplus (Skills Framework for the Information Age) descriptions maintained by BCS, see www.bcs.org. Desirable personal qualities to work successfully in these roles are:

- good communication skills and ability to work as part of a team;
- ability to enquire independently, reflect, conclude and document;
- technical and problem-solving competences, including creativity;
- understanding of the standards required and ability to work to 'good practice';
- willingness to carry out continual professional development.

The professional skills described by the SFIAplus fall roughly into six categories that encompass the 86 skills:

- **Strategy and architecture** – covers skills such as consultancy, security and information management.
- **Business changes** – covers skills such as project management and business modelling.
- **Solution development and implementation** – covers skills such as systems integration, testing and network design.
- **Service management** – covers skills such as network support, IT management and system software.
- **Procurement and management support** – covers skills such as asset management, quality assurance, education and training delivery.
- **Client interface** – covers skills such as marketing and selling.

Each skill has a level number depending on the experience and training gained by the individual. A task such as **Corporate Governance of IT** will have a level associated with it, in this case level 6. The level descriptors are:

1. Follow
2. Assist
3. Apply
4. Enable
5. Ensure/advise
6. Initiate/influence
7. Set strategy/inspire

It is thus much clearer to define roles within the computer industry using the SFIAplus framework.

IT practitioner

responds to users' requirements. They help specify systems; design, test and build systems; develop and enhance existing systems; implement and manage systems; and liaise with and train the users. Practitioners come from a wide range of expertise.

IT user

including: IT end-user
is a generic term for an individual or organisation who uses IT (often desktop applications) on a regular basis in their work activity. An **IT end-user** is anyone who uses an IT product. This could include withdrawing money from an *ATM* (see page 115) or using a mobile phone.

Outsourcing

is the purchase of services from outside contractors rather than employing staff to do the tasks. See page 5.

Systems development personnel

including: developer, programmer, systems programmer, applications programmer, information systems engineer, systems engineer, coder, systems analyst, business analyst, risk manager, systems designer, software engineer, website developer, quality controller

- A **developer**, or **programmer**, is the person responsible for writing and testing computer programs. Those involved in the writing of operating systems, general utilities (such as printer drivers) and specialist tools (such as a graphical user interface) are usually called **systems programmers**. Those writing programs for specific needs or user applications, such as database management systems, are known as **applications programmers**. Those programmers working on the design and testing of computer systems, hardware as well as software, are often called **information systems engineers**, or **systems engineers**, while those who are mostly involved in translating statements into machine-readable form are called **coders**.

- A **systems analyst** is the person responsible for the analysis of a system in discussion with the user to assess the need for any changes or upgrades to existing processes. A **business analyst** may be called to review business processes and the associated information. A **risk manager** may be called to identify processes carrying a high premium on their performance. Where change is decided upon, the **systems designer** will be responsible for building on the analyst's report to create the system and will normally work up to the point where programmers can sensibly take over. The designer will employ 'standard methodologies' to produce design for processes and data structure. (See Section A4 Systems design and life cycle.)

- A **software engineer** normally works as part of a team on a large installation, and will have skills in a specialist area. However, they may be expected to undertake any of the roles from systems analysis, through design, implementation (or service delivery), testing and project management. They may be responsible for the design or enhancement of integrated computer systems including networks and telecommunications. They are also often employed in designing and implementing the software in *embedded systems* (see page 4).

Website developers design and develop websites and web pages. This involves not only designing the appearance and content, but also designing the function to strict performance criteria. For example, the customer accessing a sales site should be able to explore information about products and place orders with ease, confident that credit card or bank account details are, and remain, secure. A team designing websites will include people with artistic skills as well as systems designers with technical skills and experience. The *webmaster* (see page 82) of an organisation will be responsible for maintaining and updating the corporate website.

Quality controllers are involved in the development of procedures that ensure products or services are designed and produced using business and engineering disciplines to meet customer requirements.

Information management personnel

including: data-processing manager, information manager, database administrator (DBA), database manager, information officer, decision support specialist, data entry staff, data controller, security administrator

A *data-processing manager* is the person responsible for the overall running of a data-processing department.

An *information manager* is the person who manages the interface between the computer system and the organisation's user community.

A *database administrator (DBA)*, also known as *database manager*, or *information officer*, is the person in an organisation responsible for the structure and control of the information in the organisation's databases. See also *database management system*, page 94.

A *decision support specialist* is responsible for organising database interrogation procedures to allow business managers to access management information in appropriate formats.

Data entry staff are those responsible for organising and entering data into the computer system. Data entry is increasingly undertaken as part of other jobs, such as administration, or by automated methods.

A *data controller* (previously designated a Data Protection Officer) is the named person in an organisation who is responsible for seeing that the organisation's registration is adhered to under the *UK Data Protection Act (1998)* (see page 157). Any public organisation must allow access to information under the *Freedom of Information Act (2000)* (see page 158).

A *security administrator* is the person in an organisation who is responsible for monitoring the information system infrastructure:

- to ensure that it complies with the established security policy;
- to ensure that the procedures are by controlled by audit;
- to respond to unauthorised activity.

User support personnel

including: technical support staff, asset or configuration manager, software support staff, help desk, hot line, training
are those involved in the day-to-day running of an organisation's computing installation, who respond to queries from computer users.

Technical support staff (also called **asset managers** or **configuration managers**) are computer specialists who are concerned with the integrity and functionality of the computer system. They may be hardware-oriented and responsible for matching the requirement to the capabilities of the system in a cost-effective manner. They may need to log activities and resources, plan 'change over' procedures and prepare for 'disaster recovery'.

Software support staff are often employed by software houses or specialist vendors in order to respond to questions relating to the use of particular pieces of software. Support staff are often referred to as a **help desk** and may be contacted quickly using the telephone **hot line** to give advice on problem solving. They may 'talk through' a solution using a particular piece of software. These staff may also be responsible for **training**.

Systems support personnel

including: network manager, computer operator, computer service engineer, computer engineer, maintenance engineer, service engineer
are those who deliver, operate and monitor the computer systems in an organisation. These include:

Network manager is the person with overall responsibility for the smooth running of a network. This will generally include communications (software, hardware and telecommunications), access (user identifications and passwords) and shared resources such as common data storage. One of the network manager's responsibilities will be the disaster recovery procedures of the network.

Computer operator is the person responsible for the operation and monitoring of larger computer systems including backup and archiving. Where appropriate, they respond to requests, which may be from the operating system or from remote users in a networked or time-sharing system.

Computer service engineer is the person responsible for the maintenance of the hardware, and is often employed by a specialist servicing company under contract. They are also known as **computer engineers**, **maintenance engineers**, or **service engineers**.

B10 PROFESSIONALISM AND ETHICS

Society expects reliable and effective products and services. Employers need to feel confident that there are codes of professionalism, conduct and ethics that their staff adhere to. In this section we describe the professionalism and ethics of people working in the IT and computing industry. This is often achieved by membership of the appropriate professional body.

BCS, The Chartered Institute for IT, is one of the professional bodies that supports the IT and computing industry. It was formed in 1957 and now has around 70,000 members. It supports its members, but also promotes the industry in the UK and abroad. Government and national bodies come to BCS for advice and guidance on matters related to computing and IT. Its mission statement is to make IT good for society. Other professional bodies are, in the UK, **The Institution of Engineering and Technology** (**IET**), and in USA, **The Institute of Electrical and Electronics Engineers Computer Society** (**IEEE CS**) and **The Association of Computing Machinery** (**ACM**).

To achieve membership of these professional bodies, IT and computing practitioners need to demonstrate their skill, knowledge and experience. They can also attain chartered status through the **Engineering Council**. A chartered professional is someone who has achieved a recognised standard showing that they have the necessary experience and qualifications as well as having demonstrated professionalism. They are bound by a code of conduct and a code of practice, which means they can be struck off (recognition withdrawn) for inappropriate behaviour.

Professional bodies can also define standards used in the industry.

Professionalism

describes the standards of behaviour of people working in the IT and computing industry. Nearly every business uses IT systems in order to operate. All of these IT systems need to be maintained and adjusted on a regular basis. This involves a standard of competence, reliability and independence. IT professionals who do this need to be trusted in a number of ways:

- They need to be technically capable of carrying out these tasks and doing so to the specified quality;
- They need to ensure that this is done in a manner that minimises disruption to the operation of the business;

- They need to be trustworthy because they might have access to sensitive data and information, for example personal information about staff, which needs to be kept safe, secure and not divulged. See also *Data Protection Act*, page 157.

Ethics

are the principles of a group of people. They reflect the agreed moral values of the group. Members of BCS agree the principles to be expected of an IT professional and these are incorporated in the *BCS Code of Conduct*, see below.

Code of conduct

is a set of rules that govern the personal conduct of individual members of the group. They are also required to notify the society of any significant violation by another member. Any breach of the Code will be brought to the attention of the society and is considered under disciplinary procedures.

The *BCS Code of Conduct* for IT professionals specifies the professional standards required by BCS as a condition of membership. It applies to members of all grades, including students and affiliates. It defines four obligations:

- Public interest
- Professional competence and integrity
- Duty to relevant authority
- Duty to the profession

Code of good practice

is a set of rules that describe standards of practice relating to the many IT demands found in today's workplaces. The *BCS Code of Good Practice* can be adapted for the particular needs of individual organisations. It is more specific than their Code of Conduct (see above). It is intended to help members personally by providing a framework of guidance into which their particular needs can be fitted. The code covers the following areas:

- Common practices
- Maintaining your technical competence
- Adhering to regulations
- Acting professionally as a specialist
- Using appropriate methods and tools
- Managing your workload efficiently
- Participating maturely
- Respecting the interests of your customers
- Promoting good practices within your organisation
- Representing the profession to the public

IT Technician

also known as: ITTech
IT technicians register with The IET and work in a range of jobs that involve the support or facilitation of others to use IT equipment and applications. They are required to use IT knowledge and understanding when applying technical and practical skills and contribute to the design, development, testing, commissioning, installation, operation, migration or maintenance of IT products, processes, systems or services.

Incorporated Engineer

also known as: IEng
is a qualified engineer who is registered with the Engineering Council as having the scientific and technical knowledge to satisfy its professional requirements. This is not as high a professional qualification as Chartered Engineer.

Chartered IT Professional

also known as: CITP
is an IT professional who is qualified and registered with BCS, The Chartered Institute for IT, as having the technical knowledge and skills along with practical experience to satisfy its professional requirements. They usually specialise in managing large, complex IT systems.

Chartered Engineer

also known as: CEng
is an engineer who is qualified and registered with the Engineering Council as having the scientific and technical knowledge and practical experience to satisfy its professional requirements. Engineers qualify in various areas such as Electrical Engineering, Mechanical Engineering, Civil Engineering or Information Systems. The latter usually specialise in managing large, complex IT systems.

B11 COMPUTER SECURITY, ABUSE AND RELATED LAW

This section includes terms from legal aspects of computing and terms relating to the security and control of data in computer systems.

Modern society is very dependent on computer systems and the data they contain. This dependence provides opportunities for antisocial behaviour ranging from the annoying to the criminal. This section considers security measures and legislation that attempt to deal with computer abuse.

Computer abuse describes a wide range of behaviour, such as:

- unfair use of personal data, for example cross-referencing that reveals new, unrelated and perhaps embarrassing information;
- electronic vandalism where software or data is deliberately damaged, or where the operation of the computer system is affected;
- creation of virus software that cause random damage to software or data;
- theft of valuable information.

These problems are dealt with through the deterrent effect of legal punishment under the Data Protection and Computer Misuse Acts and through using a variety of security measures to make abuse difficult.

The **Data Protection Act** protects individuals from unreasonable use of their stored personal data. This data may be very embarrassing or perhaps be used for blackmail – even if the individual has done nothing illegal. Computer data is potentially more dangerous than paper documents because:

- data can be retrieved electronically from a computer anywhere in the world;
- it can be searched very quickly to find patterns that are not obvious but which could be personally damaging or embarrassing;
- data from a range of computers can be combined, so apparently unrelated data can produce damaging information.

The **Computer Misuse Act** defines electronic vandalism, unauthorised access to computer systems and theft of information. It makes these activities criminal. There are penalties for individuals who attempt to interfere with another person's use of computers, such as:

- hackers who try to beat security measures as a 'game';
- vandals who damage the software or data of a computer;
- virus writers whose viruses can cause damage at random;
- thieves who break into computer systems to gain access to valuable information.

Security measures that can be taken may use either physical or software methods. **Physical** methods include:

- providing workstations with locks or keycards to prevent unauthorised use;
- locking offices containing workstations;
- positioning screens so that visitors are not able to see their contents.

Security measures using **software** include:

- using screen savers to hide the contents of the screen if the user leaves the work-station;
- using passwords to ensure users are authorised;
- ensuring passwords are changed frequently;
- limiting the range of tasks that can be carried out at a particular workstation;
- setting access rights so that only some users can carry out some operations;
- having barriers (such as firewalls) to restrict access to a computer system by external users.

In addition to Data Protection and Computer Misuse legislation, and the **Freedom of Information Act**, there are also copyright laws that enable software producers to protect their investment in software development. These laws provide the means to penalise people who copy or use software without permission.

Computer systems in manufacturing, real-time processes and safety-critical applications need to meet particular design standards and their implementation may have to conform to quality assurance standards. Product Liability and Consumer Protection legislation, particularly in the USA, imposes severe penalties on the producers of poor quality computer products.

DATA SECURITY

Data protection

including: data consistency, inconsistent data, data integrity, data privacy, data security is ensuring that data is correct and is kept confidential and safe. These concepts apply to all data, not just personal data. Data about individual people is particularly sensitive and is legally required to be managed under the terms of the *Data Protection Act* (see page 157).

Data can be corrupted, taken or lost in many different and unexpected ways, both by accident and design. It is essential that these are prevented (as far as possible) and that the data can be recovered if required. Failing to protect data can be disruptive and often very expensive.

Data protection involves the following issues:

Data consistency is the relationship between the input data, the processed data and the output data, as well as other related data items. If the system is working properly the data will be correct at each stage (allowing for the processing done) and is said to be consistent.

Inconsistent data is found either when the result of a process is wrong or if two pieces of related data have the wrong relationship. For example if a person's recorded age is not the same as their age when calculated using their date of birth, this would be inconsistent. This inconsistency could be caused by the age or the date of birth being input wrongly, an error in the calculation program or a variety of technical faults.

Data integrity describes the correctness of data both during and after processing. Data may be changed by the processing, but will still have integrity. Safeguards are needed to make sure that the data has integrity by detecting any accidental or malicious change to the data. See also *corruption*, page 281.

Data privacy is the requirement that data is only to be accessed by, or disclosed to, authorised persons. The *Data Protection Act* (see below) provides legal protection for individuals' data. Data privacy requires systems managers to build safeguards into their systems (both physical arrangements and software checks) to reduce the risk of unauthorised access.

Data security involves the use of various methods to make sure that data is correct, is kept confidential and safe (providing data protection). Data security includes ensuring the integrity and the privacy of data, as well as preventing the loss or destruction of the data. An important part of data security is planning to ensure reliable backing up of the data and testing that it can be restored effectively. See also *backup*, page 115.

Data Protection Act (1998)

including: data controller, Information Commissioner, data subject, sensitive personal data, data protection principles
is the UK Act of Parliament that sets out requirements for the control of stored data about living individuals, both on computer systems and in other forms (such as paper). The Act covers many aspects of data privacy (see *data protection*, page 156). The Act also defines **data controllers**, the individuals who are responsible for the uses made of the computerised data.

Data controllers are required to notify the **Information Commissioner**, providing details about the data they hold for the data protection register. This register enables any individual to find out if personal data relating to them is likely to be held and they have the right to ask for a copy of the data from the data controller. If the data is incorrect, the individual (as the **data subject**) is entitled to ask the data controller to have the data corrected.

The Act provides special protection for **sensitive personal data** such as an individual's race, politics, religion, trade union membership, health, criminal record and sexual orientation. The few exemptions under the Act mainly relate to data held for certain limited purposes by government agencies, the police, the courts and the security services. There are also some exemptions for data intended for use by journalists or broadcasters.

The 1998 Act defines eight *data protection principles*, which are given here in a simplified form:

1. Data should be fairly and lawfully processed (for example there should be no deception in the collection of the information and the subject should be told how the data will be used).
2. Data should be only used or disclosed for the specified notified purposes.
3. Data should be adequate, relevant and not excessive.
4. Data should be accurate and kept up to date.
5. Data should not be kept any longer than necessary.
6. Access must be provided for individuals to check and correct their data, with a right of explanation when a computer takes automated decisions based on the data.
7. Security measures should prevent unauthorised access to, or alteration of, the data.
8. Data should not be transferred outside the European Union except to countries with adequate data protection legislation.

The Act only applies to data about living individuals, known as 'personal data'. The 1998 Act replaces a 1984 Act with new legislation to comply with European Union requirements. There are many changes to the 1984 Act, which was extended to cover non-computer data such as paper records.

Freedom of Information Act (2000)

is the UK Act of Parliament that allows the public a right to information held by public authorities. Scotland has its own Act (2002). Public authorities include central and local government, the health service, schools, colleges and universities, the police and other bodies.

The authority is bound to deal with all requests for information made by individuals and must respond within 20 working days giving reasons if they withhold information. They may refer to the *Data Protection Act* (see page 157) or other statute in their decision, refuse to disclose information that might be harmful to the wider public interest (there are 23 exemptions) and make small charges. If responding to the request will cost them a significant amount of money the authority can refuse.

An individual can appeal to the *Information Commissioner* (see page 157).

Computer abuse

has no legal definition but it is generally taken to be the wrongful use of computer systems and software for improper, antisocial or illegal purposes. Examples of computer abuse are the spreading of *viruses* (see page 166), data terrorism (actions against computer systems and data), computer-based fraud and computer pornography. Almost all examples of computer abuse involve breaches of laws such as the *Data Protection Act* (see page 157) and the *Computer Misuse Act* (see below).

Computer Misuse Act (1990)

including: computer misuse
is the UK Act of Parliament aimed specifically at *hackers* (see below). It defines **computer misuse** as the unauthorised use of computer systems and relates both to hardware (for example using a computer without permission) and software (for example accessing parts of a computer system without authorisation). The Act created new offences relating to unauthorised computer access and the unauthorised access to, the modification of, or the deletion of data.

Hacking

including: hacker
is attempting (with or without success) to gain unauthorised access to a computer system. This may be the unauthorised use of a computer or simply unauthorised access to particular programs or data stored on a computer (see *access rights*, page 163). A **hacker** is someone experienced in attempting to gain unauthorised access into computer systems.

Hacking often involves an unplanned approach to the attack on the computer system and the use of unusual and complicated techniques to solve problems as they arise. The term 'hacking' is also used to describe this approach when applied to the design and use of a computer system. The resulting software is prone to errors and difficult to fix and maintain.

Digital signature

also known as: electronic signature
is part of a message that is specially encrypted and is used to indicate that the sender of the message is who they claim to be. If the recipient of the message can correctly decipher the digital signature then forged data is unlikely to have been substituted. The digital signature confirms the identity of the sender; it does not encrypt the information. The message (including the electronic signature) will usually be encrypted again so the content is hidden as well. See also *digital certificate*, below, and *public key cryptography*, page 164.

Digital certificate

including: certification authority, trusted service provider, trusted third party, certificate
is an encrypted message provided by a certification authority that confirms that the individual is who they claim to be in an online communication. It includes a *digital signature* (see above), which can be confirmed by sending a secure message to the certification authority.

The **certification authority,** also known as a **trusted service provider** or a **trusted third party**, is a business that provides online certification facilities. These organisations are trusted to check the identity of the online users and provide them with encrypted messages (the certificates) that can be confirmed by checking the **certificate** with the certification authority.

Key escrow

is a method of storing *cryptographic keys* (see page 164) to electronic communications so they are accessible to authorised agencies (usually governments). The keys to electronic communications are stored by an independent company, which will release them to appropriate government agencies in certain circumstances. This is primarily to allow the police access to criminal communications.

Secure Socket Layer (SSL)

including: Secure Electronic Transaction (SET)
is a *protocol* (see page 348) that enables an encrypted link to be created between two computers using the internet. It protects electronic communications from interception and allows a computer to identify the server it is communicating with. It is the standard security protocol used to provide security for commercial transactions (such as buying goods) taking place over the internet.

Secure Electronic Transaction (SET) is a more sophisticated protocol developed by some major international banks. It is not as widely used as the Secure Socket Layer protocol.

Firewall

including: personal firewall
is a computer application used in a network to prevent external users gaining unauthorised access to a computer system. A firewall may be software running in the main computer or a separate computer physically located between the system and the external access (see Figure B11.1). It limits the data and instructions that can be received from or sent to external users. For example, the firewall could block certain types of data, only allow access from specific computers or require additional user identification. It is usually used with a *proxy server*, see below. The firewall may restrict authorised users' external access to a small part of the system and may allow limited public access, for example to a web server. The firewall can prevent a user (including users with limited authorisation) accessing data or executing any programs in the rest of the system.

A **personal firewall** provides the same protection for a personal computer where a single user may be linked to the internet, a potentially hostile network.

Proxy server

is a computer application that accesses data on a different computer system or network. It controls the access of authorised users to data and allows the operation of the system to be isolated from control by external users. Proxy servers are often also *internet servers* (see page 135).

This application receives requests from users, verifies them, accesses the required data and communicates the requested information back to the users. External users cannot run

Figure B11.1 Firewalls and proxy servers

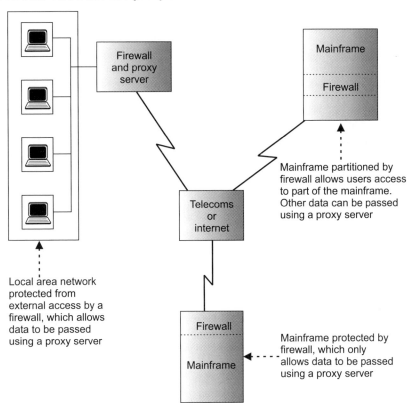

programs on the protected system but rely on the proxy server to access data for them. Instructions to the protected system itself are limited to specific types of requests, the effects of which can be controlled. Proxy servers can provide data for both external and internal users. External users cannot access the main system directly while the internal users can be provided with controlled access to external systems, such as the internet.

Intrusion detection system (IDS)

monitors the operation of the network and the data transmitted to detect and warn when illegal access is attempted. The system may be server based, detecting attacks on the operation of the file server, or may be network based, watching the pattern of traffic across the network.

Logging in

also known as: log in, logging on, log on
is the procedure needed for a user to gain access to a computer system. It might provide access to a computer network, a multi-access computer system, a specially set-up

stand-alone workstation or just a specific application program. Logging in is a part of the security procedures to prevent unauthorised access.

Logging out

also known as: log out, logging off, log off
is the correct procedure to be followed when ending a session on a computer system. It cancels the authority to use the system obtained from the *logging in* procedure (see page 161). Logging out is a part of the security of the system preventing the workstation or applications program being used until an authorised user logs in again. A user may be logged out automatically if the session has not been active for a predetermined time or the network connection is lost.

User identification (user ID)

also known as: username
including: password, personal identification device (PID), keycard, swipe card, personal identification number (PIN)
is a unique name or code used to identify a user to a computer system when gaining access (known as *logging in*, see page 161). The *network manager* (see page 151) or systems management software allocates user IDs to new users.

Checks must be made to verify that the person logging on is the correct 'owner' of the user ID. Methods of establishing and checking include passwords, personal identification devices and personal identification numbers.

Passwords are words or codes that should only be known to the user. A password is linked to a specific user ID. Although a user ID may be generally known to others, access can only be gained with the correct combination of user ID and password.

Personal identification device (PID) is a computer readable object (such as a *magnetic stripe card*, see page 295) carrying data that identifies the owner and acts as an electronic key. This information can be read by a computer and used as a user ID. Unauthorised use is made difficult because a user must physically have the personal identification device. Additional protection can be provided by the use of a *personal identification number* (see below). **Keycard**, or **swipe card**, are other names for a personal identification device in the form of a plastic card. See also *smart card*, page 295.

Personal identification number (PIN) is a number used as a password, particularly with bank cards and credit cards. For example a bank card is the personal identification device, which provides the user ID, and is used with a personal identification number to obtain cash from an *automatic teller machine*, page 115.

Biometric

is a unique physical characteristic of an individual that can be checked automatically by a computer. The individual's biometric is measured by a special scanner and used with the *user ID* (see above) in a similar way to a password. Finding physical characteristics that can not be copied has been difficult but viable systems include fingerprints, iris scans and retina scans (the pattern of veins at the back of the eye). Face recognition and voiceprints have so far proved to be unreliable for use as biometrics.

Access rights

also known as: network privileges, privileges
including: ownership, password protection
control the extent to which a particular user can use or edit a program or data file. Each user is assigned access rights that determine whether the user:

- can access the file;
- can copy, change or delete the data or file;
- can read but not edit the data;
- has no access at all.

Computer support staff may have more comprehensive rights than most users, including the right to alter other users' access rights. Access rights can also restrict the use of a file to a particular workstation or a particular user.

With the simpler operating systems used on stand-alone computers, the actual user may not be identified. The access rights can easily be changed but do provide a way of preventing some mistakes (for example deleting important files).

The more complex network operating systems provide a way of identifying individuals (for example by a user ID and password). The extent to which each individual user can access the resources is determined by the access rights (or privileges) set by the network manager. The user may have **ownership** of some files and can then set the access rights to restrict who else can use the files.

Some files have additional access restrictions provided by **password protection**. When a user attempts to gain access to one of these files an additional *password* (see page 162) will be requested before access is allowed. This provides extra security since knowing a user's system password is not enough to gain access to the data. The password is often used as part of the *encryption key* (see page 164) to encrypt the data, making the data meaningless even if unauthorised access to the system is achieved.

Authorisation code

is a type of password needed to install or run a piece of software. By providing software that is protected in this way the supplier can ensure that the software is used only by authorised users who have been provided with the authorisation code. In some cases the user's identity is hidden in the code allowing illegal copies of the software to be traced. This method usually involves some form of encryption.

Encryption

including: scrambled data, decryption, encryption key, decryption key, enciphering, coding, encoding, deciphering, decoding
makes data in a computer system unintelligible. The encrypted data appears to be meaningless and is sometimes described as **scrambled data**. Encryption provides security for the data (by preventing it being understood), both when stored electronically

and when transmitted between computer systems. **Decryption** is converting the unreadable data back into an understandable form.

An **encryption key** is a word or code selected by the user to govern the encryption process. A **decryption key** is needed before the data can be understood.

In many systems both encryption and decryption keys are the same and therefore all users must have a copy of the key. If the number of users is small and the concern is for the security of stored data, a single encryption key is usually sufficient. If transmission, rather than storage, requires extra protection then different encryption and decryption keys may be used. See *public key cryptography*, below, and *data encryption standard*, below.

The terms **encryption, enciphering, coding** and **encoding** are often used loosely with the same meaning, as are **decryption, deciphering** and **decoding**.

Data Encryption Standard (DES)

including: Advanced Encryption Standard (AES)
is a standard method of encrypting data, developed by the US Government. The method specifies how a *key* (see *encryption*, page 163) is used to encode the message in a standard way. It was believed that the method was complex enough for the encrypted data not to be decrypted without knowledge of the key, even though the method was known. This meant that the method could be published allowing computer manufacturers to develop software and hardware to encrypt and decrypt the data. Since it is a standard method, the Data Encryption Standard allows encrypted data to be sent between any computers whose manufacturers have implemented it.

The **Advanced Encryption Standard (AES)** algorithm is newer and much more complex. It may eventually replace the Data Encryption Standard.

Public key cryptography

including: public key, private key, one-way functions, trapdoor functions, RSA algorithm
is a very secure encryption method where different keys are used to encrypt and decrypt the data. The key has two parts, a **public key** and a **private key**, which form a matched pair. The *public key* and *private key* are linked and data encrypted with one key needs to be decrypted with the other key. To send data the sender uses the known *public key* to encrypt the data. It can only be decrypted using the *private key*, which only the receiver has.

However, it would be easy to replace a message with a forgery (since the *public key* is well known). To prevent this a *digital signature* (see page 159) is used. This often uses public key cryptography in reverse: the sender uses a *private key* to encrypt the data that can only be decrypted using the known *public key*, showing the sender must have used the *private key* and so is genuine. To enable large numbers of users to use these digital signatures they are often managed using *digital certificates*, see page 159.

The principles behind public key cryptography involve complex mathematical functions. Some mathematical operations are easy to do, but in practice impossible to undo. As a simple example, it is easy to multiply together 11 and 13 to get 143, but it takes an amount of trial and error to work back from 143 to the (only) factors 11 and 13. If the numbers involved had hundreds or thousands of digits, rather than just two, the amount of trial and error involved would mean that even a fast computer might be unable to find the factors in an acceptably short time. Such operations – easy to do, and impossible to undo in a realistic time – are known as **one-way functions**. If the operation is one like the multiplication above, where some secret knowledge (like the numbers 11 and 13) provides a short cut, they are known as **trapdoor functions**. These can be used as the basis for a simple but secure coding system, as shown in Figure B11.2. The best known such function was developed by the mathematicians Rivest, Shamir and Adleman, and is, unsurprisingly, called the **RSA algorithm**.

Figure B11.2 How a public key cryptosystem works

	A public directory is published – for everyone in the code system, it tells the whole world what key is used to send messages to that person. This is a (big) number that can be used to encode messages. The decoding part is secret: only one person knows it.
	I want to send a message to you. I write my message out, substituting A = 01, B = 02, etc. and get a (long) number that represents my message.
	Now I look up your key in the public directory and use it to turn my message into another long number – this is done in a way that no one except you can decode – even I can't, unless I look back at my original message.
	You can receive my message and, using your very secret decoding method, turn it back into the original message.
	How do you know that the message was really from me? Anyone could lookup your key in the public directory and send a misleading message that claimed to be from me. I can prove it was from me, like this:
	With my message, I include my name and address, but before I code this, I use my own secret decoding key to turn the name and address part into a scrambled version.
	Now I code the whole message – the message itself and the previously scrambled name and address.
	You receive this two-part message and use your secret decoder to extract the plain message and the scrambled name and address. You read the message and need to check that it is from me.
	You take the scrambled part, look me up in the directory and see what my public coding key is. Using this will unscramble the name and address, and you are confident that it was from me, because I am the only person in the world who knows what my secret key is.

VIRUSES AND MALICIOUS CODE

Virus

including: payload, infection, parasitic virus, macro virus, email virus, worm
is a program designed to copy itself between and within computers, to make a computer system unreliable. The virus includes instructions to do the copying automatically, via a disk or network. The virus may also include instructions to damage data (in the memory or on a disk) or affect the computer's operation, such as displaying silly messages or filling up the computer's memory. These effects are often referred to as the virus's **payload**. They are often activated when some predetermined conditions occur (such as a particular date). Most viruses are specific to a particular operating system.

Infection occurs when a virus has copied itself onto a computer system, usually to its hard disk. Because of the potential damage a virus can cause, it has to be removed, see *antivirus software*, below.

There is an increasing use of viruses with a malicious purpose. Viruses often exploit weaknesses in the security of either the operating system or the applications software.

Viruses include:

Parasitic viruses that hide themselves by attachment to a file that already exists until a specific event causes the virus to take action.

Macro viruses that attach themselves to the data files associated with the more complicated application programs that allow users to add *macro programs* (see page 211) to their documents.

Email viruses that are attached to an email and usually propagate themselves by sending emails automatically to contacts in the user's own address book.

Worms that are programs that spread themselves via network connections to other systems. Unlike a traditional virus, a worm does not require a host program or data file, but is a stand-alone executable program that exploits the facilities of the host computer to propagate.

Antivirus software

also known as: vaccine utility
including: antivirus monitor, virus checking, disinfection, quarantine, computer hygiene
is used to detect and remove *viruses*, see above.

Antivirus monitors are programs loaded permanently in memory continually monitoring the system for the tell-tale patterns indicating the presence of any of the thousands of viruses that have been identified. If any change is detected, the file is prevented from being run and a warning message is given. New data read into the computer is also screened for viruses and appropriate action taken.

Virus checking scans the files on a computer system to detect viruses.

Disinfection is the removal of viruses that have been detected.

Quarantine is the isolation of a file suspected of containing a virus. The file can then be investigated and the operation of the virus can be analysed.

Computer hygiene is the term used to describe the prevention and cure of problems caused by viruses.

Trojan horse

also known as: Trojan
including: logic bomb, backdoor Trojan, trapdoor Trojan
is a program that performs a normal process in the computer while also performing another, possibly harmful, process at the same time. Just as parasitic viruses attach themselves to other files, Trojan programs are often hidden in other valid programs. Trojans have been used by hackers (see *hacking*, page 159) to copy data from secure files or to record information about security measures. Types of Trojan programs include:

Logic bombs are small programs included within a larger system and designed to acti-
vate when a particular set of circumstances occur. For example a programmer may include a logic bomb in the system he or she is developing to cause damage if his or her name is deleted from the company payroll. They are used for revenge attacks and for blackmail.

Backdoor Trojans, also known as *trapdoor Trojans*, are programs normally left by a hacker that permit access to a computer system without the use of valid authentication codes or passwords. They enable the hacker to avoid the computer's normal security systems. See also *trapdoor functions*, page 165.

COPYRIGHT

Software copyright

including: software licence, licence agreement, end-user licence agreement (EULA), single-
user licence, multi-user licence, site licence, public domain software, freeware, shareware,
concurrent user licence
is the legal protection that authors and publishers have regarding the use of their software. It is not always realised that computer software is covered by similar copyright laws to those that apply to books and other publications. The Copyright, Designs and Patents Act (1988) protects 'intellectual property' and establishes the rights of the author.

When software is purchased there will be a *software licence* (also known as the licence *agreement* or *end-user licence agreement, EULA*) that sets conditions for the use of the software. These conditions vary considerably between products. Any use of the software not allowed by its licence is illegal. In practice, this means that copying software bought by someone else is likely to be an offence. Special licences are needed for some cases, for example multiple use on a network.

Various types of licence are used and the specific terms of each licence must be adhered to. Examples of the types of licence include:

Single-user licence where the software can be used on only one computer. This is the usual type of licence.

Multi-user licence where an organisation may install the software on an agreed number of computers. A reduced fee is paid for each computer.

Site licence where any number of computers may use the software at a single location. One payment is made to allow the multiple installation. These are not common outside the UK educational sector.

Public domain software has a licence waiving all rights and allowing free use of the software. This is a US legal concept that rarely applies in the UK. See *freeware*, below.

Freeware has a licence allowing free use (and usually distribution) of the software. The licence usually does not allow alteration or sale. The author usually provides little, if any, help and support. In the UK freeware is often called *public domain software*, above.

Shareware has a licence allowing free use (and usually distribution) of the software for a trial period. If the user wishes to continue using the software a fee must be paid, usually in return for improved versions, manuals and support.

Concurrent user licence agreements allow the user to operate the software on an agreed number of computers. The actual computers to be used do not need to be specified providing the total number in use at any one time does not exceed the number of licences.

Piracy

also known as: software piracy
including: protected software, unprotected software, copy protection, dongle, installation disk, key disk
is the illegal copying of software whether for personal use or resale. Software publishers lose considerable potential income due to illegal copying of their products and take a variety of measures to prevent it.

Protected software is supplied in a form designed to be difficult to copy. It may have copy protection or use a *key disk* (see page 169).

Unprotected software has no special precautions against copying and relies on the legal authority of the *software licence* (see page 167).

Copy protection uses some physical changes to the data on the disk to prevent copies of the disk being made.

Dongle is a piece of hardware used to reduce the possibility of software piracy. It usually plugs into a standard interface on a computer. Without the correct dongle the protected software will not run.

Installation disks contain the software in encrypted form. The software is copied onto the computer's hard disk before it can be used. The installation program may only allow the software to be installed a limited number of times. It may also make further copying difficult by embedding the owner's name or computer serial number within the installation disks.

Key disk is a floppy disk or CD-ROM disk used to install software that contains credits that are reduced by one on each installation. It may also be a disk that is required every time a program is run to ensure it can only be used by one computer at a time. See also *software copyright*, page 167.

B12 SYSTEMS SOFTWARE

Other related material can be found in Section A4 Systems design and life cycle, Section A5 Describing systems and Section C7 Programming languages.

A computer system requires a layer of software that enables users to operate it without having to know about the underlying processes that are going on all the time inside. This includes the **operating system** and other forms of **systems software**.

A computer needs separate instructions for even the most elementary tasks. Computer users are interested in solving their problems without having to program every detail into their computer. The systems software is provided by the manufacturer and enables a user to give a few simple instructions that the systems software translates into the millions of minor operations needed for the computer to function in an easy-to-use way.

Every computer is provided with an operating system that controls the vital parts of the computer's operation – using the keyboard, screen display, loading and saving files and printing are some examples.

Additional programs (such as disk formatters and device drivers to control peripherals) are provided, which are useful in the operation of the computer. They do not enable the user to get answers to problems (**application programs** do that) but they do make using the computer easier, by allowing resources to be organised and controlled better. They improve efficiency by making the computer easier to use.

Systems software can be classified in a variety of ways depending on whether it:

- is necessary to run the computer (**operating system software**);
- provides other useful functions for operating the computer (**utility programs**);
- provides for frequently required tasks (**library programs**);
- enables software to be produced and maintained (**compilers** and **assemblers**).

Software that is essential to the running of a computer is usually sold with the computer. Other systems software may be purchased separately to enable the computer to be used for particular types of task.

In brief, systems software is the collection of programs available for the total control of the running of a computer system.

CONCEPTS

Systems program

is one of the programs that control the operation of a computer system, enabling the computer system to be developed and to be more efficient. Examples of systems programs are compilers, performance monitoring programs, defragmentation programs, network software and print spoolers. Many systems programs are part of the *operating system* (see page 172).

Systems programs can be contrasted with *applications programs* (see page 6), which perform some end-user tasks. These tasks, such as producing a letter, are not part of the actual operation of the computer. See also *utility program*, page 172.

Boot

also known as: bootstrap
including: booting up, booting, boot file, bootscript, reboot
is the process of starting up the computer by loading a short sequence of machine-code instructions, which in turn load and initialise an operating system ready for use. These instructions are normally held in read-only memory and activated when the machine is switched on. This process is sometimes referred to as **booting up** or **booting**. See also *BIOS*, below.

A **boot file**, sometimes called a **boot script**, is used to control the start-up of the computer by placing the required commands in it. This file will be executed automatically by the computer after it has booted the *operating system* (see page 172).

To **reboot** the computer is to restart the system. This might be after the system has *hung*, see page 234. The system might also need to be rebooted to complete the installation of some hardware and software. The computer will start up as if it had just been switched on, so data that had not been saved by the user, or saved automatically, will be lost. See also *recovery*, page 235.

BIOS (basic input output system)

is a machine-code program that handles the low-level *input* and *output* operations such as those relating to the keyboard and screen of the system. It provides an interface between the hardware and the operating system. Suppliers usually provide the BIOS with the hardware in the form of *firmware*. It is usually considered to form the lowest layer of the operating system.

In order to make it possible for a range of different operating systems to be installed without the supplier having to modify the operating system for different hardware platforms, the BIOS has to comply with one of a range of agreed common standards (as does operating system software).

The BIOS in most systems can be updated. This allows a newer version of the BIOS to be loaded.

Some changes in hardware configuration can be coped with manually by altering the settings of the BIOS, for example CPU speed.

Operating system

including: disk operating system (DOS), Android, Windows®, MS-DOS®, UNIX®, LINUX®, Mac OS-X
is a program or suite of programs that controls the entire operation of a computer. It is normally provided through the supplier and manages the internal functions of the computer, such as memory management, multi-users, handling what has been typed in, displaying data on the screen and loading from and saving to backing store.

Most modern operating systems include some *utility programs* (see below) that make the operation of the computer easier, such as a program to change the resolution of the display screen. At a technical level the operating system handles the basic and central functions such as *input* and *output* operations (see *BIOS*, page 171), *interrupts* (see page 331) and *multi-tasking* (see page 180).

Most operating systems today also include a *Graphical User Interface (GUI)* (see page 417). Some systems use a *command line interface* (see page 417) or a *menu selection interface* (see page 417) such as found on mobile phones.

Windows ® is a widely used system from Microsoft® that combines the operating system and a graphical user interface. Users do not need to be aware of what operating system commands are used because the Windows® interface offers most of the required system operations. There have been many versions of Windows®.

UNIX ® is an operating system originally written for larger machines. Versions are now available for a variety of machines ranging from mainframes to personal computers. It was designed to improve software portability. It is easily customised for the specific requirements of each multi-user or networked system. Currently there are versions with a graphical user interface but the underlying system is unchanged.

LINUX ® is an operating system based on UNIX®, and including almost all of its features. It can be downloaded from the internet free of charge, although commercially supported versions also exist.

OS-X ® is the operating system and associated graphical user interface used in Apple® Mac® personal computers. It is also the basis for iOS, which is used by various Apple® portable computers, such as the iPad®. Like many modern operating systems, the technology has been based on UNIX®.

Android is an operating system based on UNIX®. It is designed for use with portable devices, such as smartphones and tablet computers. It is designed as an *open system*, see page 348, which allows different suppliers to use and customise it at limited expense. This leads to many variations of the software.

Utility program

is a program that performs some specific task in the operation of the computer. It is a type of *systems program*, see page 171, because it makes the operation of a computer easier, rather than doing a productive task.

Some utility programs are supplied as part of the operating system, but others can be bought from other software suppliers. Utility programs might be used to back up files, test memory, analyse disk space, manage power usage, compress data and schedule tasks.

Network utilities are used to measure network performance, identify the location of network problems, configure settings and identify data flow around the system. See also *operating system*, page 172, and *backup*, see page 115.

Software library

also known as: library, program library
is a collection of software held on backing store that is always available to the user. It will include complete software packages, package modules that will only be required occasionally, and machine-code routines for loading into user programs. Software libraries might be built up by a user or they might be provided as part of the system, particularly where the computer architecture or operating system are non-standard and commercial software cannot be used.

Configuration file

including: registry
holds the shared information that defines the set up of the computer. The operating system of a computer can be configured in a variety of ways that will be automatically saved so that on subsequent booting, the system will look the same. A configuration, for example the location of program files and libraries, will be stored in configuration files or a configuration database.

The **registry** is the configuration database in the Windows® operating system. The registry is stored in main memory, but a copy on disk is always kept updated to allow the computer to start up quickly and reliably. The configuration is loaded as part of the *boot process*, see page 171.

Login script

is a file of commands that will be executed automatically by the computer when a new user has logged on to the system. This allows instructions to be executed when the computer starts up to ensure a certain configuration, even if the stored configuration is corrupted. This is particularly useful in a network environment because the login script can be easily changed globally, perhaps for new network settings, rather than change each computer's configuration.

Plug-in software

also known as: add-on software
is a (generally small) optional program that, when installed, extends the facilities of an existing software package. For example, a photo-editing package might have a range of plug-ins to provide special effects such as an 'old picture' or an internet browser might need a plug-in to display certain types of document.

Disk Operating System (DOS)

is the part of the operating system that handles the storage of data on disk drives and other forms of backing store. Historically the disk operating system was the most complex part of the complete operating system and the efficiency of the computer depended on the efficiency of its disk operating system. Also the design of the disk operating system might have to be different for different backing store hardware. As a consequence, many older operating systems were referred to as 'the DOS' or had 'DOS' in their titles, such as MS-DOS®. In fact these operating systems provided the full range of operating system facilities.

The design of an operating system is modular, allowing new types of backing store to be added and other new hardware to be accommodated by supplying a new program module. This allows other manufacturers to supply the latest hardware without also having to supply a new operating system, just a module that has to be installed onto the computer. As hardware has become more standardised, many more modules have been provided as part of the core operating system. The *network operating system* (see page 136) is another module that provides similar facilities for use with local area networks.

Firmware

Including: flashing
is a program stored in *non-volatile memory*, see page 300. This means it is available immediately and does not need to be loaded from backing store. The reliability of the system is ensured because it is also difficult to corrupt the program.

Firmware is usually used for the *BIOS*, see page 171, so a computer can start up quickly. It is also used for the operating system and other key software on mobile devices such as mobile phones.

Flashing is the updating of the non-volatile memory holding the BIOS or operating system. Special software is used to access the memory (in older systems by applying a higher than usual voltage) to change the program code stored. Flashing has to be done carefully because it is easy to destroy the non-volatile memory chip.

DEVELOPMENT

Library routine

is program code that users can incorporate into their own programs to carry out common tasks such as file operations. Programming environments such as *Java* provide large pre-prepared libraries to carry out standard operations such as drawing shapes on the display or interpreting the input received.

Example B12.1 shows how library routines are used in the C programming language.

Example B12.1 The use of library routines in the C programming language

```
#include <graphics.h>              This defines commands in the graph-
                                   ics library which can then be used
int main()
{
   int gd = DETECT, gm;            The programmer can now use instruc-
                                   tions such as initgraph and circle
                                   to draw on the screen
   int x = 320, y = 240, radius;

   initgraph(&gd, &gm, "C:\\TC\\BGI");

   for ( radius = 25; radius <= 125 ; radius = radius + 20)
      circle(x, y, radius);

   getch();
   closegraph();
   return 0;}
```

Translator

is a computer program used to convert a program from one language to another (for example from a low-level language to machine code). This is a general name for the three types of translation programs, *assemblers* (see below), *compilers* (see page 176) and *interpreters* (see page 177). See also Section C7 Programming languages.

Assembler

also known as: assembler program
including: macro assembler, cross-assembler
is a program that translates (assembles) a program written in assembly language into the machine code of the *processor*, see page 324. Assemblers are usually used to produce system programs where general purpose programming languages are unable to work effectively with specific hardware requirements or where extreme efficiency (usually in execution speed) is required (such as in a computer game). See also *assembly language*, page 243.

In essence, each assembly language instruction is changed into one machine-code instruction but there are further refinements to make programming easier such as *macro instructions* (see page 211).

The assembler program is often provided as part of the systems software, since the assembly process automates the task of producing machine-code software required to operate the computer.

A *macro assembler* is a more complex type of assembler that offers the facility of expanding *macro instructions* (see page 211).

A *cross-assembler* is an assembler that runs on one type of computer, but produces machine code for another. It enables software developers to produce programs for computers that are still being designed or to convert software between different types of computer.

Compiler

including: source program, source code, source language, object program, object code, dynamic compiler, virtual machine, cross-compiler
is software that translates a program or module, written in a high-level language, into one written in a low-level language such as the computer's machine code. Generally each high-level language instruction generates several low-level language instructions. The computer produces an independent program that can be run without reference to the original program, although a *run-time system*, see page 232, might be needed.

Source program, also known as **source code**, is the original program, written by the programmer, in a high-level language. It is written using a *text editor* (see page 367) or a more specialised program-editing environment (see *integrated development environment*, page 40). A source program cannot be run directly because the instructions are in a language designed for humans to read rather than the binary codes understandable by the computer.

Source language is the computer programming language in which the source program is written.

Object program, also known as **object code**, is the resulting derived program that can be run on a computer system.

The resulting object program might be machine code that can be executed immediately by the computer, or *intermediate code* (see page 243) that can be translated by a small *interpreter* program (page 177). An example is a program written in Java, a high-level language, which is then compiled. This compiled program is distributed and can be used on any computer for which Java virtual machine software has been written and which has been installed on the specific computer.

The source code is kept in case any changes have to be made, when the modified source program would be recompiled. It is not generally possible to modify the object code, which is why the object code rather than the source code is distributed.

The intermediate code translator may be a **compiler**, an **interpreter** or a **dynamic compiler**.

Dynamic compiler is a translator in which the generation of the machine code is delayed until run time. This allows for optimisation of the machine code depending on the data being processed, which cannot be known before run time. Statements in the source code that are not encountered during execution are not translated (similar to the action of an interpreter), but those that are translated are stored for use later in the run. Dynamic compilation is used by the Java Virtual Machine.

Virtual machine is a layer of software that allows one computer to simulate another. The computer simulated does not have to exist as hardware but might be a theoretical concept for which we can design software. The same virtual machine implemented on many hardware platforms improves the portability of software. An example is the Java Virtual Machine. See *intermediate code*, page 243. A virtual machine is also known as an *emulator*, see page 125.

Cross-compiler is a compiler that runs on one computer platform, but produces code for another platform. It enables software developers to produce programs for computers that are still being designed or to convert software between different types of computer. For example, mobile phone software can be developed using a larger computer.

Compilation

including: lexical analysis, syntax analysis, code generation
is the translation used by a compiler that produces an equivalent program in a low-level language. Compilation involves analysing the language structure of the source program, determining if it is valid, and producing suitable machine code. Compilation involves a number of steps:

Lexical analysis is the stage in the compilation of a program that puts each statement into the form best suited to the syntax analyser. The standard components of each statement, such as PRINT, IF etc., are replaced by their tokens (a unique fixed length code) and programmer-defined names are entered into a *symbol table* (see page 178). The lexical analyser also removes unnecessary characters such as spaces.

Syntax analysis is the stage in the compilation where language statements are checked against the rules of the language, errors being reported if a statement is not valid.

Code generation produces a machine-code program that is equivalent to the source program.

See also Section C6 Testing and running programs.

Interpreter

is software that executes programs not in the machine code of the computer. It reads a statement and immediately performs the required action. This means that a sequence of instructions can be performed without the complexity of producing and then executing a compiled version of the program. However, it is slightly less efficient than a compiled program. For example, when an interpreted program contains a loop, the speed of execution will be reduced because the analysis of each statement has to be repeated for each time round the loop. See also Section C7 Programming languages.

The program to be interpreted is usually in a high-level language. The interpreter is also used to execute programs, macros or script languages (see *macro*, page 14), testing programs in a test environment or programs compiled to an intermediate code. The intermediate code is distributed across the internet for users to download. (See *intermediate code*, page 243.)

Command line interpreter

including: batch file, command file
is the portion of the operating system that analyses a system command typed by the user and performs the appropriate actions. Earlier operating systems worked by asking the user for commands to be typed in, as a line of text after a *prompt* (see page 424), analysing the commands and taking appropriate action. Modern operating systems provide a *graphical user interface* (see page 417), which is often easier to use, but usually the command line interpreter is still available.

Some graphical user interfaces simply convert information from the mouse into an equivalent system command that is processed by the command line interpreter. Commands might be:

- read from a text file (called a **batch file** or **command file**);
- provided remotely from a peripheral or another computer through an interface;
- provided from within a program.

These commands are all automatically processed by the command line interpreter.

Disassembler

is a program that translates from machine code back to an assembly language. They are generally used to decipher existing machine code by generating equivalent symbolic codes. This is useful for programmers maintaining and modifying machine-code programs.

Loader

including: linking loader, linking, linker, link editor
is a program that copies an *object program* (see page 176) held on backing store into main store ready for execution.

Linking is providing the actual machine code locations of the routines that are provided already compiled in a *library* (see page 173). This also involves completing address links to and from the program.

A **linking loader** performs the linking at the same time as the program is loaded at run time, that is when the program is used to perform its task.

A **linker**, or **link editor**, performs the *linking* when the program is compiled. It is a software tool that allows already compiled object code files or modules to be combined with the compiled program and then converted directly into an executable file.

Symbol table

also known as: name table
is the table relating programmer-defined names to machine addresses. It is created and maintained by a *compiler* (see page 176) or *assembler* (see page 175). It might also hold information about properties of data, such as *data types* (see page 263).

When translating a program the compiler or assembler works through the program for the first time (the first pass) replacing some parts with tokens and building the symbol table that contains the actual address in memory of each variable, label or subroutine. The program is then processed a second time (the second pass) when each identifier can be replaced with its actual address in memory.

Parsing

is the breaking down of high-level programming language statements into their component parts during the translation process, for example identifying reserved words and variables.

OPERATIONS

Spooling

including: printer spooler, print job, print queue
is the temporary storage of input or output data, as a means of compensating for the different operating speeds of the systems. It is most commonly used with printers, storing printouts until the printer is ready and queuing output from different systems to a single printer by means of a *printer spooler* (see below).

Printer spooler (or **print spooler**) is an operating system program that stores data ready to be printed. When the data to be printed has been received from a program and is complete, the printer spooler can send this data to the printer. Several programs or workstations can send data at the same time for printing, because the data is stored in data files by the printer spooler and sent to the printer when appropriate. If a printer spooler is used, programs do not have to wait while printing is being done (printers work more slowly than computers do). This is particularly important with personal computers and interactive computing because users do not want to waste time waiting for data to be printed out. See also *printer server*, page 135.

Print job is one set of data to be printed. It is usually a single document (which could be many pages) but could be a batch of similar documents of other data such as an image.

Print queue is a list of work waiting to be printed by a printer spooler. Normally it is a list of the files holding data ready for printing. Each file will hold the data from a particular *print job*, which will be sent to the printer by the printer spooler when the printer is free.

Multiprogramming

including: time slice
is a method of benefiting from the speed of a central processor compared with slower peripheral devices, allowing two or more programs to be processed apparently simultaneously but actually in bursts, controlled by an operating system. For example, while one program is waiting for an input or output operation to be performed or is using a

peripheral, another might have access to the central processor. To control this process, priorities might be assigned to jobs.

A **time slice** is the predetermined maximum length of time for the bursts during which each program is allowed to run in a multiprogramming system.

Executive program

also known as: monitor program, supervisor program
is a control program that schedules the use of the hardware required by the programs being run in a multi-task or multiprogramming situation.

Multi-tasking

including: single-tasking
is a method of organising computer use that allows several different tasks or applications to be available at the same time. The users of a *multi-access system* (see page 17) will be working on different tasks apparently at the same time, although only one program is actually being executed at any one time. Similarly, modern personal computer operating systems allow users to have several tasks apparently running at the same time, with the user switching freely between applications or tasks.

Single-tasking operating systems allow only one program to be in use at any time. Single tasking is used by some operating systems that do do not support *multi-tasking*, such as some control systems.

Thread

including: multi-threading, concurrent thread, single thread
is the processing performed on a single set of data in the system.

Multi-threading is the use of a single copy of a program to process several sets of data that are at different stages of processing. This is most useful in a multi-tasking situation where tasks might need to be launched at any time. Only one copy of the program needs to be loaded, which saves memory. The program design ensures that the data for each thread is kept separate and that the appropriate program instructions act on the thread that is being executed.

Concurrent threads are two or more threads being executed at the same time using *multi-tasking* (see above).

A **single thread** is one set of processing. This might be the traditional simple program (which is not designed to multi-thread) or one thread out of several being processed in a more complex system.

Processing mode

is the way in which the processing tasks carried out by a computer system are organised to make the most of the potential of the system. Sometimes the choice of mode is given to the user. For example, the user might have a choice between *single-tasking* or *multi-tasking* (see page 180) when running a program, or a choice between *foreground* or *background processing* (see below).

Different processing modes can also be selected by the central processor for different types of tasks. For example, some types of instruction might only be available to the operating system, reducing the possibility of a user program affecting the rest of the computer's operation.

Job

including: job control language (JCL), job queue
is a data-processing term for a package of work regarded by the computer as a single unit. Typically, a data-processing department will run programs on behalf of its clients. These programs might be small (a single report) or large (a complete payroll). Once started, each program will proceed automatically to completion and, from the data-processing department's point of view, each is a single task or job to be run.

- The **job control language (JCL)** is a specialised language used to control the execution of a job in a computer. It enables the operators to specify the requirements of a job (such as which printer to use) when the job is executed. The programmer does not need to deal with these decisions when writing programs. A *job control language* also enables a series of small jobs to be linked together and executed in one larger and more efficient operation.

- A **job queue** is the list of jobs waiting until the computer system is ready to execute them in a *multiprogramming system*, see page 179, or a *batch processing system*, see page 17. This will normally be in the order they are submitted although in some systems priority levels can be assigned to jobs to ensure some are executed earlier than other less urgent jobs.

Remote job entry (RJE)

is the use of a remote terminal to initiate a *job* (see above) on a computer within the network to which the terminal is attached. One example is the use of a terminal in a supermarket to transmit the record of the day's transactions to the central computer for the chain and initiate the appropriate funds transfer and ordering routines. Another very simple example is a request for a bank statement from a customer using a cash machine.

Foreground/background processing

including: foreground job, background job
is a method of organising a computer system so that certain important tasks are able to claim the sole use of the computer when required, while other less-pressing tasks utilise the remaining time.

- The **foreground job** is the task that a computer will give priority to and process if possible.

The **background job** is the task that a computer will process if higher priority tasks cannot continue. This is usually because they are waiting to receive data, for example from an input or storage device, or send data, for example to an output or storage device. Typical background jobs used in modern personal computers include antivirus scans and downloads from the internet.

For example, a user can continue typing at a word-processing program (the foreground job) while the computer sends data to a printer (the background job) using processing time that is idle while waiting for user input.

The same concept applies to a *multiprogramming system* (see page 179), where the foreground job will have priority, but if the processor is idle (for example, waiting for disk access) then a background job will use that time.

Segmentation

including: segment, interleaving
is splitting a large program into a number of smaller programs or **segments**. Each segment is a complete program that is executed separately. The function of the large program is achieved by running segments consecutively.

Segmentation allows a large program to be executed on a computer with insufficient memory to store the whole program.

Interleaving is when segments of several programs are run as required allowing several programs to be run at the same time (although no two segments can use the processor at exactly the same time). Interleaving allows several large programs to be run concurrently, in parts, to make optimum use of resources. These techniques are not widely used now due to the relatively large memory of modern computers. Similar techniques are *overlays* (see page 197) and *paging* (see page 328).

Scheduling

including: round-robin
is the method by which central processor time is allotted in a multi-access system. The scheduling algorithm might be as simple as the **round-robin** or as complex as a scheme of priorities distinguishing between users and between tasks.

Round-robin is a simple scheduling algorithm which deals with each user equally in turn.

Free space

including: garbage collection, memory leak, fragmentation, defragmentation, defrag
refers to areas of the computer's storage, either *main memory* (see page 299) or *backing store* (see page 299) that are not currently being used to store data. Programs can use some of this free space to store new data. These areas can then be released later as free space for the same program or other programs to store other data. Poorly written programs do not release the space when they no longer need the data, leading to inefficient use of computer memory. This is resolved by *garbage collection*, see page 183.

As programs claim free space in different size blocks and then release that space, the available memory could become fragmented. Subsequent claims on the free space might require more memory than is available in any one block. This makes the data processing slower, resulting in poor computer performance. A similar problem arises with backing store if files are stored with several parts of the files in different locations. Both these issues are resolved by *defragmentation*, see below.

Garbage collection is the identification of data in the main memory of the computer that is no longer used by a program. This data is marked as free space and a *defragmentation* routine collects these fragments of memory together so they can be reused. Library routines are available to do this but they have to be correctly implemented by the programmer to be effective. *Multi-tasking operating systems*, see page 180, might also use garbage collection techniques as programs are loaded and deleted when finished with.

Memory leak occurs when a program fails to release unused memory correctly. After a period of time the computer will slow down as programs have trouble finding free space until eventually there is no free memory available and the computer will *crash*, see page 234.

Fragmentation occurs where data (either in memory or within a file) is split and stored in different parts of the store (usually either main memory or a disk drive). The access speed of the memory and hence the performance of the system will be reduced. This is particularly significant for backing store when the backing store is almost full or with slower backing store devices, such as magnetic disk drives.

Defragmentation, or **defrag**, is the reorganisation of memory or backing store to improve efficiency. This involves collecting together the separated data stored in different locations of the memory. If the data is stored in the same part of the memory then access to the data will be quicker. Also if the free space is collected into larger groupings then future fragmentation is reduced. *Utility programs*, see page 172, are available to *defragment* backing store. When dealing with defragmentation of disks then the usual grouping of data is the *block*, see page 302, in which case a *disk map*, see page 306, is often used to graphically display where data is stored on a disk.

PART C: PROGRAMMING

This part is concerned with terms relating to writing computer programs. These are frequently considered to be associated with computer science, as opposed to the terms in Parts A and B, which are concerned with the needs of computer system users, and Part E, which provides some technical information that might be helpful to both computer users and to students following courses requiring some knowledge of computer systems and peripherals. Part F is concerned with the way software is used.

The range of terms covered in Parts C and D and the depth of treatment of individual terms has been influenced by knowledge of the difficulties encountered by students who are studying courses that involve computer science, whatever the title of the course.

C1   PROGRAMMING CONCEPTS

The terms defined in this section cover a variety of techniques and concepts used to communicate ideas and algorithms. These terms are used both to communicate ideas before a program is written and to describe the program design so that other programmers can maintain the program at a later date. Related terms can be found in Section A4 Systems design and life cycle (system characteristics), Section C2 Programming (flow of execution), Section C3 Programming (subprograms), Section C4 Program syntax, Section C5 Describing programs and Section C6 Testing and running programs.

The construction of any effective computer program is time-consuming and complex, requiring the application of a wide range of techniques, skills and processes. The programmer has to work at a very detailed level to make the computer do what is wanted, so that the resulting program works reliably and at a reasonable speed.

The actual computer program run on the computer has to be in the machine code used by the computer. There are ways of speeding up and simplifying the production of this program, such as using object-oriented programming styles, higher-level computer languages, program generators and specialised computer languages designed to produce particular types of programs, for example database managers. Many of the principles used by these various methods involve the same standard techniques that are used in traditional programming and much of the technical language used is of value to anybody involved in developing computer software.

Regardless of the method used to develop computer software, the designer has to balance the properties of cost, speed, ease of use and reliability of the final product. A slow program can be used with a larger computer, but at a greater cost in computer time. Similarly a complicated program will be more expensive to test. However, if software is well designed, using a professional approach, then more efficient software can be developed at lower cost.

A computer programmer has to be prepared to choose between alternative programming strategies in order to get a usable program. The obvious method of solving a problem may be inefficient, as the user will not be prepared to wait while the computer carries out some apparently simple task. To avoid this, the programmer may use a variety of strategies (expressed as algorithms), some of which may be complex, but without which it may not be possible to produce a usable program. One skill a programmer must have is the ability to understand and adapt a wide range of existing algorithms to new situations.

The user will expect a program to work reliably and produce no errors. The programmer may use standard algorithms developed and tested by other people as one way of reducing possible errors in a program. The program must be able to deal with any mistakes the user makes without introducing any errors, for example in the input data.

OBJECT-ORIENTED TECHNIQUES

Object-oriented programming (OOP)

uses the concept of self-contained objects, which contain both program routines and the data being processed. An object-oriented program is designed as a collection of objects which interact by sending messages to each other. Object classes may be used in other programs.

Object-oriented programs are more reliable because the objects are self-contained, simple and so easier to program. The same types of object may be able to be used in different contexts within a program and there is no hierarchical structure as in traditional top-down design.

Object

including: encapsulation
is a group of data and associated program routines used within an object-oriented programming system. An object is designed to be self-contained and contains both the program routines (called *methods*, see below) that affect the object and the data that is being processed.

Each object may contain several program routines (called *methods*, see below) that act differently on the data (called *properties*, see page 189). When an object-oriented program is run it may contain several objects of the same class containing different data. Since the program routines are linked to the data and copied with it there is no possibility of a routine accessing the wrong data. It is also possible for the object to be defined differently in different situations. See *overloading*, page 189, *polymorphism*, page 189, and *inheritance*, page 189.

Encapsulation is where the technical details of methods or properties are hidden within the object and data can only be changed by using the appropriate methods, which will have been thoroughly tested. Ideally all the methods and properties in an object will be encapsulated.

Method

also known as: member procedure, member function
including: constructor, destructor
is a program routine contained within an *object* (see above) designed to perform a particular task on the data within the object. For example, an object working out the total of a set of numbers would have a method to add a data item to the object, a method to return the results of the calculation or even a method to print the results directly to the installed printer. There are some methods that should always be provided when programming an object.

These include:

Constructor a method that correctly initialises and sets up a new class of the object when it is created based on the object *class* (see below).

Destructor a method that deletes the object, if necessary saving any data, warning other objects and freeing the computer's memory.

Property

also known as: data member
is data within an *object* (see page 188). For example the properties of an object display-ing some text on the screen will include the text to be displayed and may have additional properties that control how the text is displayed, such as its colour and font size. Another example would be an object which has a method to work out the total of a set of numbers, which would have a property storing the values of the numeric data.

Class

also known as: object class
including: instance of the class, class library
defines the methods and properties for a group of similar objects. It is a template speci-fying program routines used for the methods and the data types of the properties.

Individual objects can be defined based on the object class but with specific properties. Each specific object is known as an **instance of the class**. The methods in the object class will be thoroughly tested and a programmer can rely on this for the individual objects created, reducing programming errors and programming time. See also *inheritance*, below.

The **class library** is the set of class definitions, which are built up over time and may be reused.

Inheritance

including: derived class
is the means by which the properties and methods from a *class* (see above) are copied to another class so that only the differences have to be reprogrammed.

A **derived class** is a class resulting from the inheritance process.

Overloading

including: polymorphism
is when a method is defined more than once in a class for use in different situations. The different situations involve different types, or quantities, of data being input into the *object* (see page 188) and the types of parameters supplied determine which method is used.

Polymorphism is a specialised form of overloading which allows us to create very general object structures, which can be used with a wide range of data types.

189

TRADITIONAL PROGRAMMING TECHNIQUES

Address

including: memory location, absolute address, base address, offset, relative address
Each piece of data or program instruction is stored separately in the computer's memory and it is located by its address. The address is the number for the position of a word of storage in the main memory. This number is used by a program as the identification of a particular **memory location**, which may contain a data item or the next instruction, when a machine-code program is branching.

If the address is the real address used by the internal electronics of the computer, it is known as the **absolute address**. Many machine-code programs and operating systems use a method of addressing that allows a program to have its own (imaginary) addresses and convert these to the real addresses as the program is executed. The real addresses are worked out from a starting address number, called the **base address**, by adding another number, called the **offset** or **relative address**, to it.

One use of relative addressing is storing arrays. The location of any particular element of the array can be calculated from the element number and the base address of the (array) variable.

Array (machine-code programming)

The use of arrays is a fundamental technique in machine-code and low-level programming, since they make it possible to handle large amounts of related data efficiently. Each element in an array will be held sequentially in memory and an *index register* (see page 327) or *relative addressing* (see above) can be used to access each element in turn. Since the array is stored as a single block of computer memory the programmer has a variety of methods that can be used to manipulate the data easily, for example copying the entire block as one operation. See also *array*, page 258.

Algebraic notation

including: infix notation, prefix notation, postfix notation, reverse Polish notation
is the way mathematical and logical processes are described when writing a computer program. Infix, prefix and postfix notations are different ways of writing the algebraic (and logical) expressions used by a program.

Mathematicians normally use **infix notation** (where the operators are placed between the operands, such as A+B). **Prefix notation** places the operator first (such as +AB), while **postfix notation** places the operator last (such as AB+). See Table C1.1.

Prefix and postfix notations are easier for a computer to execute. Modern computers are sufficiently powerful that most users do not need to use either prefix or postfix notation.

Reverse Polish notation is a form of postfix notation where brackets are not permitted (and not needed). No rules about precedence are needed for different operations, which are carried out in the order met in the expression.

Table C1.1 Examples of different algebraic notations

What has to be worked out:	Work out the perimeter of a rectangle, which is twice (**L**ength plus **B**readth)
*The formula in **infix** notation:*	2*(**L+B**)
*The formula in **prefix** notation:*	*2+**LB**
*The formula in **postfix** notation:* (*also called **reverse Polish** notation*)	2**LB**+*

Reverse Polish notation has the advantage that any algebraic expression can be processed strictly from left to right. It is widely used by compilers, which convert the infix notation that a programmer has used into Reverse Polish notation. This Reverse Polish notation is then easily converted into a machine-code program. It was derived from work by the Polish mathematician Jan Lukasiewicz.

Program algorithm

is a sequence of steps designed to perform a particular task. An algorithm may be constructed to describe the operation of a complete system or to describe a particular part of it. Standard algorithms have been developed to do specific common tasks, such as a particular method of sorting a set of data. Many have been published and are available for general use.

Algorithms include precise details about the operations to be performed and in what order. An *algorithm* is a sequence of instructions including information such as when sections are repeated or choices made.

Algorithms can be written in any suitable form, such as a programming language, *pseudo-code* (see page 220) or as diagrams. Often they are written in pseudo-code, which is easily communicated and easily translated into any suitable programming language, see Figure C1.1.

Code

including: program code
refers to the actual set of instructions that form a program. This is either the source text of a program, which is later compiled, or the actual instruction codes of a machine-code program.

The term *program* (see page 212) is often applied to a complete software system (including items such as spellchecker dictionaries) but *program code* applies specifically to the instructions that make up a particular part of the overall system. See also *relocatable code*, page 198, and *absolute code*, page 198.

Figure C1.1 An example of an algorithm in pseudo-code

Algorithms become complicated when covering all possibilities.

```
To count the number of words in a line of text:
begin count words                                   for a space at the start
    set words = 1
    set character = space
    while not end of line
    begin
      make previous character = character    for unnecessary spaces
        get next character from line
        if character = space
           and previous character not space  two spaces together
        then add 1 to words
    end
    if character = space then subtract 1
        from words                                  space at end of line
end count words
```

Assignment

is an instruction that gives (assigns) a value, which could be the result of a calculation, to a specified variable. The value is placed in the memory location corresponding to the given variable. See Figure C1.2.

Figure C1.2 An example of an assignment statement

Working out an area:

```
area:=height*width;
```

calculates 'height' *times* 'width' *and assigns the result to the variable* 'area'

Event

is an external change that is notified to the program by the operating system. This may be a key being pressed or a mouse button being clicked.

The term event has a specific connotation related to multi-tasking operating systems used by personal computers. Events are occurrences that may apply to any of the programs running and are put into context by the operating system communicating with the programs. Events should not be confused with normal input, which is directed to a particular program nor with *interrupts* (see page 331), which are usually dealt with by the operating system. One effect of an interrupt may, however, be to generate an event.

Events are an important element in the design of multi-tasking programs where the operating system handles the input (e.g. from the keyboard) and output (e.g. to the screen). When a new input is received, a message is sent to the program informing it of the event and allowing it to take appropriate action.

Flag

including: set, unset, status word, status byte
is an indicator that has two states, often called **set** or **unset**. It enables the program to record whether a particular event has occurred, for example whether (or not) a list of numbers has been sorted, whether an interrupt has been sensed (or not sensed).

In a high-level language a variable may be used as a flag. If a *Boolean* or *logical data type* (see *data type*, page 263) is used, the two states, true and false, are equivalent to the flag states set and unset. To begin with the flag may be unset (false) and when a particular case is detected it is set (true); when the action has been completed it is unset again (back to false).

Only one bit is needed to store a flag, so a machine code programmer may use the bits in a single *word* to store several flags, which can be easily manipulated in machine code using a mask (see *mask*, page 194, and *masking*, page 333). Most central processors have a **status word** or **status byte**, which is the group of flags used in the control of the arithmetic/logic unit. When individual bits are used as flags, the two states are referred to as 0 or 1.

Carry flag

including: overflow flag
is a flag within the *status word* (see *flag*, above) of the central processor that is set to 1 (or true) when a carry condition occurs, otherwise it is set to 0 (or false). This may be tested by the programmer if some special action may be appropriate, such as producing an error at that point.

Similarly the **overflow flag** is set to 1 (or true) when overflow occurs during an arithmetic operation, because the result of a calculation is too big for the computer to store.

Heuristic program

is one that attempts to improve its own performance as a result of learning from previous actions within the program. See also *heuristics*, page 144.

Initialise

including: initial value
is to set counters or variables to zero, or some other starting value, usually at the beginning of a program or subprogram. These values are known as **initial values**. A common programming error is to fail to initialise a variable. In this case the program may execute correctly but could produce wrong results.

Default option

is the action to be taken automatically by the computer if no specific instruction is given. For example, in some versions of BASIC arrays do not need to be declared, in which case they are given bounds 1 to 10. This is the default option. See also *default*, page 16.

Look-up table

is a table used to convert one set of values to another set.

The table normally has two columns. The first column holds a list of data items and the second column holds a list of related values. For example, the first column might hold product codes and the second column their prices.

Another example is a tax table (for VAT). Each product has a tax code, which is looked up in a look-up table to find the tax rate to be used. Look-up tables are particularly useful for non-linear values and tax rates are often non-linear.

A further example is a SINE table. Values of the mathematical sine function are calculated for a range of values and stored in the memory. Each time a sine is required it is found in the look-up table rather than being worked out again. This speeds up the program because calculating sines is very slow.

Logical operation

including: AND, OR, XOR, NOT operations, mask, shift
is the use of logic (see *logical operator*, page 106) within a program. Logical operations are frequently used to determine the future progress of a program within selection statements, such as IF statements, REPEAT and WHILE loops.

Logical operations include **AND**, **OR**, **XOR** and **NOT**, which, when used with Boolean values, produce the results described in *logic gates* (see page 359). For example when using a simple database of information about birds, a search might be written:

```
IF 'webbed feet' AND 'white feathers' THEN show picture ELSE next
item
```

Both the expressions 'webbed feet' and 'white feathers' can be either true or false; what happens next depends on the truth value derived from 'ANDing' them.

Logical operations can also be performed on *bytes* or *words* (see page 14) when a group of *bits* (see page 11) is processed together. Logical operations simply compare each bit and the result is assigned to the equivalent bit of the result. An example of their use is the manipulation of a *status word* (see *flag*, page 193) by the operating system.

These operations can be performed using a **mask**, which is a user-defined binary pattern, to select which bits are to be changed while the other bits remain unchanged. See Figure C1.3. See also *masking*, page 333.

The bits in a byte, word or register can also be shifted. A **shift** moves the whole bit pattern one or more places to the left or right. Bits that move out are lost and empty spaces are filled with a '0'. See also *shift*, page 331.

Figure C1.3 Logical operation on a bit pattern

The byte holds colour information:

> The intensity of red is held in the colour byte below in the third and fourth bits from the right:
>
> 0 0 0 1 **1 0** 1 1   *The bold digits **1 0** are the red intensity.*
>
> 0 0 0 0 **1 1** 0 0   *A **mask** to select the bits we require.*
>
> **0 0 0 0** 1 **0 0 0**   *The result of an **AND** operation on the mask and the colour byte: unwanted bits are set to 0.*
>
> 0 0 0 0 0 0 **1 0**   *The result of a **right shift** of two places.*
>
> equals 2 (denary)   *The intensity of the colour red is 2.*

Machine-code instruction

including: operation code field, address field, operand field, operand
is a binary code that can be directly executed by the computer. Each type of computer has a set of binary codes that are recognised by its processor as instructions, see *instruction set*, page 325.

Each type of processor has a different instruction set. These are the only instructions that can be used to control the computer. Other instructions (such as those written in BASIC or Pascal) must be converted into appropriate machine-code instructions before they can be executed by the computer.

Each instruction is a binary pattern that can be decoded by the control unit. It consists of several fields, including the *operation code field* and usually an *address field* (see *single-address instruction*, below).

The **operation code field** is the part of the binary code for the instruction to be carried out (for example 'add' or 'jump').

An **address field** gives the *address* (see page 190) where the data to be used in the operation can be found. It is sometimes called the **operand field**, or simply the **operand**. See also *address calculation*, page 327.

Single-address instruction

also known as: one-address instruction
including: multiple-address instruction, two-address instruction
is the most common format of a *machine-code instruction* (see above). It consists of two fields, the operation code field and the address field.

A **multiple-address instruction** has more than two fields. There is always an operation code field and at least two address fields (giving several pieces of data that can be used by a single operation). In particular a **two-address instruction** has three fields, the operation code field and exactly two address fields.

Other designs of processor may have different structures. For example, stack-based processors do not need address fields at all, just the operation code. Another example is microprocessors, which often use several bytes of storage, instead of one word, for each machine-code instruction. These are loaded separately but then treated as a single-address instruction.

For general-purpose computers, single-address instructions are more economical than other formats.

Mnemonic

including: symbolic addressing
is a code for an operation that is easily remembered. The meaning of the instruction is normally abbreviated into a related alphabetic code.

Mnemonics are particularly used in *assembly languages* (see page 243) where each binary *operation code* (see *machine code*, page 243) is replaced with a mnemonic, for example ADC could represent the binary instruction for ADD WITH CARRY. Mnemonics rather than binary numbers make writing programs faster and make errors easier to find. Assemblers are used to convert the instruction mnemonics into the binary machine-code instructions (see *assembler*, page 175).

The use of mnemonics or words to specify the address of a store location is called **symbolic addressing**. This is used in assembly language programming where the address of a store location is specified by means of an *identifier* (see page 217), normally in the form of a word or mnemonic, rather than the numeric value of the memory address. See also *symbol table*, page 178.

Program maintenance

including: corrective maintenance, adaptive maintenance, perfective maintenance
is the modification of a software application or system after its implementation has been completed. This may be needed to correct errors found in the system, that is, **corrective maintenance**. Maintenance may be necessary to adapt the system to changes within the organisation using it, to external changes such as new legislation or to allow the system to operate with new hardware, that is, **adaptive maintenance**. Additionally, it may be advantageous to make changes that will enhance the performance of the system, that is, **perfective maintenance**.

Maintenance cannot normally be carried out by the user and specialist staff are employed, often the team that designed and wrote the original system.

Maintenance is much easier if the program is well designed, well structured and well documented (see *structured programming*, page 45). *Ease of maintenance* (see page 46) is a desirable characteristic of a computer system.

Overlay

including: overlays
is the process by which only parts (the **overlays**) of a large program are brought from backing store for processing, as needed. Only those overlays currently requiring processing are held in main store. The major part of the program (which also manages the overlays) is always held in the main store.

The use of overlays is a technique that enables programmers to reduce the amount of memory needed by a program. Similar techniques are *segmentation* (see page 182) and *paging* (see page 328); the latter is used by operating systems to make efficient use of available memory.

Pretty printer

including: printf, PRINT USING, format
is a subroutine that displays a line of text (on the screen or on paper) in a neat way. This may mean splitting the line between words, justifying it and displaying numeric variables to a defined number of decimal places.

Many operating systems provide pretty printers as machine-code subroutines for use by programmers and some programming languages have predefined functions or procedures (such as the function **printf** in C and **PRINT USING** in some versions of BASIC). See Figure C1.4.

Figure C1.4 Examples of display and print format statements

Using the **writeln**, **PRINT USING** and **printf** functions

If the variables a, b and c have the following values:

$$a: = 3.14159 \; b: = 1.5 \; c: = 1.5$$

In *Pascal:*

```
writeln('Answers', a:4:2,b:4:2,c:4:2);
```

will display: Answers 3.14 1.50 1.50

In *BASIC:*

```
PRINT USING "Answers #.## #.## #.00",a,b,c
```

will display: Answers 3.14 1.5 1.50

In *C:*

```
printf("Answers %0.2f %0.2f %0.2f",a,b,c)
```

will display: Answers 3.14 1.50 1.50

(Continued)

The examples display variables:

a rounded to two decimal places as 3.14

b has the trailing 0 discarded by the PRINT USING statement, a facility not available as standard in the equivalent C and Pascal statements

c padded to two decimal places as 1.50

A pattern, known as a **format**, is used to determine features such as total width and the number of decimal places (Table C1.2).

Table C1.2 Examples of formatting numeric and date data

#.##	Numbers will be displayed rounded to two decimal places	2.52
#.00	Numbers will be displayed to two decimal places, with trailing zeros if needed	2.50
00000	Numbers will be displayed as a five-digit integer, with leading zeros if needed	00123
#.##e+00	Numbers will be displayed to three significant figures using scientific format	2.56e + 02
(£#,##0)	Numbers will be displayed as a currency, with brackets for negatives	(£3,250)
dd/mm/yy	Date in European form, with obliques	31/12/12
mm.dd.yy	Date in American form	12.31.12
Mmmm d, yyyy	Date in American form, with month in words	December 31,2012

The formats used vary between software; these are from a typical spreadsheet.

Relocation

including: relocatable code, absolute code, position independent code
is the moving of a program from one area of memory to another by the operating system. This allows the operating system to make best use of memory, for example during compilation. Code that can be moved in this way is known as **relocatable code**, whereas **absolute code** must reside in a particular area of memory.

When a program is relocated, any memory addresses must be suitably altered, in particular any addresses in *jump instructions* (see page 204). This means that programs may need to be written in a special way to be relocatable. See also *relative address*, in *address*, page 190.

Ideally, when relocating a program it should not be altered, which will take time. It is possible, using special techniques, to write a program that will operate correctly wherever it is loaded into memory. Such a program has **position independent code**.

Packing

is the compression of data in order to make the best use of storage space. If a computer has a large word length, much space can be wasted when occupied by small pieces of data. For example, a character may only need 6 bits to store it, so a computer with a word length of 24 bits could pack four such characters into one word of storage that would otherwise only store one character. Packing is sometimes done automatically by the operating system.

Self-documented program

is where the program code describes the operations being carried out. This can be done by the use of comments, statements with meaningful variable names, formatting and clearly visible structures.

These features are in addition to the normal program documentation but are valuable because they help to avoid mistakes being made when a programmer modifies the program. Modifications should always be based on the full program design documentation, otherwise the other effects of introducing changes cannot be predicted.

The use of a *fourth-generation language*, page 238, helps this process, because these languages describe the underlying design of a system rather than the detail of its implementation. They rely on powerful compilers to convert the design into an executable system.

Terminator

also known as: rogue terminator, data terminator
including: rogue value
is a specified value, not normally expected in the data, that is used to mark the end of a list of data items. The program can process the data in order until it reaches the terminator. The number of data items can vary and the number of data items does not have to be known in advance.

The term **rogue value** often implies a numeric value (see *numeric data type*, page 270). It may also describe a special value, at some point in the data, used to indicate a particular situation, for example a deleted record.

Common values used as rogue terminators are 0, −1 and 9999. If the data is being entered from a keyboard then simply pressing the enter key can be the terminator (a blank input). When data is stored as a data file a special terminator, called the *end of file marker* (see page 261), is used to show where the data finishes.

C2 PROGRAMMING (FLOW OF EXECUTION)

Concepts and terms to do with programs in general are in Section C1 Programming concepts. Other related terms can be found in Section C3 Programming (subprograms), Section C4 Program syntax and Section C5 Describing programs.

Computers derive much of their power from their ability to repeat groups of instructions within a computer program and to choose which instructions to execute. The effect is that the programmer can control the flow (or order) of execution depending on the data being processed.

The instructions that enable a programmer to do this are known as control structures. When using a high-level language, specific instructions are provided for control structures. However, when using assembly languages the control structures have to be constructed from combinations of simpler instructions and, in particular, jump instructions.

Control structure

is the general term for the different ways in which a group of instructions can be executed. Control structures allow the group of instructions to be repeated a variable or fixed number of times, or to be selectively executed depending on the data currently being processed.

The main control structures provide for sequencing, selecting and iterating as the program executes. There are *loops* and *conditional* statements, provided by programming language statements such as **for** loop, **repeat ... until** loop, **while** loop, **if ... then** and **case** statements (see page 204).

Loop

including: nested loop, iteration
is a group of instructions that is repeatedly executed. For example, to produce payslips for several workers, the instructions for one payslip are repeated many times with different data.

The instructions may be repeated a fixed number of times (as in a *for loop*, see page 201) or a variable number of times, with the instructions being repeated until some specified condition is satisfied (as in a *while ... do* or *repeat ... until loop*, see page 202).

A **nested loop** is a loop contained within another loop. The inside loop will be executed a number of times for each single execution of the outer loop.

Iteration is the process of repeating a sequence of steps. Iteration will involve a loop that is repeated (iterated) until the required answer is achieved. The first time the instructions in the loop are executed is the first iteration.

Count-controlled loop

including: for loop, do loop
is a type of loop (see page 200) that is executed a fixed number of times. This may be a constant (if the number of repetitions is known when the program is written) or may depend on the data being processed (but the number of repetitions is still fixed at the start of the loop).

With a high-level language this is often called a **for loop** (*for ... next loop*) or **do loop**; the names are derived from the program statements used to implement it. Traditionally the variables 'i', 'j' and 'k' are used as the control variables that record the number of repetitions executed. See Figure C2.1.

Figure C2.1 Examples of count-controlled loops

In *Pascal*:	`for i: = 1 to 10 do`	**i** *is a variable that holds the number of the current repetition*
	`begin`	
	`...`	
	`end;`	
In *BASIC*:	`FOR i = 1 TO 10`	
	`...`	*... indicates an instruction (or several instructions)*
	`NEXT i`	
In *C*:	`for (i = 1; i <= 10; i++)`	
	`{`	
	`...`	
	`}`	

Infinite loop

including: breaking, escaping
An infinite loop is a *loop* (see page 200) from which there is no exit and the instructions in the loop will continue to be repeated for ever. This may sometimes be useful, for example in a program controlling a set of traffic lights that continuously repeats the same instructions.

In most cases an infinite loop prevents any other use of the computer. Interrupting an infinite loop may mean having to switch the computer off to reset it, but in a multi-user computer system the operator should be able to terminate the program without affecting other users. This is called **breaking** out of the program or **escaping** from the program. Control will return to the operating system and the user can issue further commands.

An infinite loop that cannot be interrupted results in a *hung computer* (see page 234).

Condition-controlled loop

including: repeat ... until loop, while loop
is a type of *loop* (see page 200) that is executed continuously and only finishes when particular conditions are met. This enables loops to be written where the number of repetitions is unknown. The advantages of this approach include:

- the amount of data being processed need not be known in advance;

- mathematical algorithms can continue until an answer is found;

- more than one exit condition can be used, for example the loop could continue until the result is obtained or an error is found.

Figure C2.2 Examples of condition-controlled loops

*In **Pascal**: a **Repeat loop***

```
i:=1;
repeat
    ...
    i:=i+1;
until (i=10) or (flag=true);
```

*a **While loop***

```
i:=1;
while (i<10) and (flag=false) do
begin
    ...
    i:=i+1;
end;
```

*In **BASIC**:* i=1

```
REPEAT
    ...
    i=i+1;
UNTIL i = 10 OR flag=TRUE
```

i=1

```
WHILE i<10 AND flag=FALSE
    ...
    i=i+1;
ENDWHILE
```

*In **C**:* i=1;

```
do
{
    ...
    i++;
}   while (i<10 && flag==0)
```

i=1;

```
while (i<10 && flag==0)
{
    ...
    i++;
}
```

Two forms of condition-controlled loops are usually provided by high-level languages. These are often called **repeat ... until loops** and **while loops**: names derived from the program statements used to implement them.

Both *repeat ... until loops* and *while loops* act in a similar way. The *repeat ... until loop* tests for its exit after executing the instructions; *while loops* test for exiting before any instructions are executed, thus allowing for situations where no action needs to be taken. See Figure C2.2.

If statement

including: else
is the name for a statement allowing selection within a program. A group of statements may be executed or ignored, depending on the data being processed at the time. The name is derived from the program statement used to implement this control structure. See Figure C2.3.

Figure C2.3 Examples of selection statements

if... then ... else statement

In **Pascal**:
```
if k=1 then    k is a variable that holds the data on which the current
                      selection depends

begin

   ...

end

else

begin

   ...

end;
```

In **BASIC**:
```
IF k=1 THEN

   ...                      ... indicates an instruction (or several instructions)

ELSE

   ...

END IF
```

In **C**:
```
if (k==1)

{...}

else

{...}
```

It is possible for the program to choose between two alternative groups of statements by using an additional keyword **else**.

Jump

also known as: branch
including: conditional, unconditional
allows the order of execution of the statements in a computer program to be changed. Normally instructions are executed in the sequence they are stored but this can be changed by a jump instruction, which enables a program to choose which instruction to execute next.

Machine-code program instructions are stored consecutively in memory and the control unit works through them sequentially using the *program counter* (see page 326). A jump alters the program counter and thus changes the next instruction to be executed.

Jumps are not normally used with high-level programming languages because they make the program harder to write without causing *logical errors* (see page 230). However, compilers change instructions such as *for, while* ... , and *repeat ... until* loops into suitable combinations of jump instructions.

A jump may be either **conditional** or **unconditional**. An unconditional jump is always executed. A conditional jump is only executed if required by the result of a test, for example 'is a certain variable zero?' or 'has the loop been executed ten times?'.

Case statement

is a statement allowing multiple selection within a program. One of several groups of statements may be executed depending on the data being processed at the time. The other groups of statements are not executed. This enables complex selections to be programmed easily and more reliably than using combinations of *if statements* (see page 203). The name is derived from the program statement used to implement this control structure. See Figure C2.4.

Figure C2.4 Examples of multiple selection

In *Pascal*:

```
case k of
      1:... ;
      4:... ;
      9:... ;
    otherwise end;
```

k *is a variable that holds the data on which the current selection depends*

In *BASIC*:

determine

```
CASE k OF
WHEN 1:...

WHEN 4:...

WHEN 9:...

OTHERWISE ...

ENDCASE
```

labels such as 1: *and* 4: *are matched against the control variable data to*

which group of instructions is executed

In *C*:

```
switch (k)
{
case 1:

    ...

   break;
case 4:

    ...

   break;
case 9:

    ...

   break;
default:

    ...

}
```

... indicates an instruction (or several instructions)

205

C3 PROGRAMMING (SUBPROGRAMS)

Concepts and terms to do with programs in general are in Section C1 Programming concepts. Other related terms can be found in Section C2 Programming (flow of execution), Section C4 Program syntax, Section C5 Describing programs and Section C6 Testing and running programs.

One of the most powerful techniques available to a programmer is the use of subprograms. **Subprograms** enable a program to be split into a number of smaller and more manageable sections. They can be called in any order, any number of times, so the use of subprograms is very flexible.

The design technique of splitting a program into subprograms, each designed and programmed separately, has certain advantages:

- Each subprogram is more easily understood, so reducing errors.

- Each subprogram may be small enough to be assigned to one programmer, rather than a programming team.

- The subprograms can be tested separately and more thoroughly than a single large program.

- The subprogram can (and should) be written so that it cannot cause errors in other parts of the system.

Another benefit of subprograms is to avoid having to write the same routines many times. The same piece of program code can be used by different parts of the program, which means it only has to be written and tested once. Routines that perform general tasks, such as controlling the screen display, can be reused in different programs thus saving programming time, testing effort and expense.

When using high-level languages, subprograms are usually implemented by defining **functions** and **procedures**. In machine-code or assembly language programming, subprograms are often called **subroutines**.

The supplier of the operating system will provide subroutines that allow access to the basic operation of the computer – such as displaying a character on the screen or reading data from a file. Operating systems often provide more sophisticated facilities, such as complex screen drawing routines, loading and saving complete files to backing store and spooling printout. These are all accessed as machine-code subroutines, which enables them to be shared between programs. They are effectively a library of subroutines always available to the user through the operating system.

206

Subprograms generally require data. With functions and procedures, the data is normally passed using **parameters**. Ideally these parameters and any other variables will be **local** to the subprogram, so that the operation of the subprogram cannot affect variables in any other part of the program. If the results from a subprogram are required by the program, then the variables will be passed **by reference**. It is possible for a subprogram to act on **global variables** but this is generally an unwise process, since it could produce adverse effects in other parts of a large program.

Function

is similar to a *procedure* (see below) but returns a single value. The name of the function is usually used as a variable having that value. Every time the name is used in the program, the function will be executed and the result will appear like any other variable.

Procedure

is a *subprogram* (see page 208) that is generally written using a precise formal definition. The procedure is defined and given an identifier (or name). This identifier can be used subsequently just like any other program instruction.

A procedure receives data from the program, manipulates it in some way and makes the results available to the program.

Such procedures are usually associated with high-level languages, although sophisticated assembly languages also allow procedure definitions.

Standard function

is a function provided by a compiler or an interpreter that is so common that it is worth providing as part of the language. For example, almost all languages provide standard functions to work out mathematical results such as *log*, *sine* and *square root*.

Figure C3.1 An example of a function

*In **Pascal**:*

*The function **square** is defined like this:*

```
function square (number:integer):integer;
begin
        square:=number*number;         number is the parameter
end;
```

then it could be used as follows:

```
answer:=square (5);
or  if square(x)=25 then...
```

Routine

is a part of a program to do a specific task. It may simply be a section of the main program or might be formalised as a procedure, function or subroutine.

Machine-code subroutine

is a subprogram stored in machine code. It may be called from another machine-code program, from an assembly-language program or from a high-level language program. The operating system often provides machine-code subroutines for common tasks, such as screen updating and printing, which can be called from any user program in any language.

Usually, when a subroutine is called, the current machine status is stored on the system *stack* (see page 260) and when the subroutine is finished, the previous machine status is restored and the computer can continue running the program from where it left off.

When writing a machine-code subroutine, the programmer is directly manipulating the memory and there is no concept of local variables. If appropriate, the programmer could reserve a section of memory for use by the subroutine.

Common machine-code subroutines are often stored as a *subroutine library* (see below). These machine-code subroutines are often designed as *modules* (see page 45) and are frequently described as machine-code modules.

Subprogram

including: subroutine, call, return, exit, subroutine library, closed subroutine, open subroutine
is a set of program instructions performing a specific task, but which is not a complete program. It must be incorporated into a program in order to be used. Different types of subprogram are known as *procedure*, *function*, *routine* (see above) or *machine-code subroutine* (see above).

The terms **subroutine** and *subprogram* are generally interchangeable, but sometimes each of these terms could mean something more precise, such as implying a machine-code routine.

A program that uses a subprogram must have an instruction to transfer control to the subprogram. This instruction is known as a **call** to a subprogram. When a subroutine, procedure or function is called the computer will start executing it.

When the subprogram has completed its task it must transfer control back to the calling program, which can only continue from its calling position. This is generally done by a **return** (or **exit**) statement in the subprogram. A subprogram may have more than one return instruction.

Commonly used subprograms are stored in a **subroutine library**. This contains a number of prewritten and pretested subprograms, available to a programmer, which perform common tasks such as display a window, sort a set of numbers or save a file.

Subprograms can be used as either *open* or *closed* subroutines depending on which is more efficient.

In a **closed subroutine**, separate calls to the subroutine use the same piece of program code. A closed subroutine should make the program shorter, although the program could be slower because of the extra instructions required to call the subprogram and return from it.

In an **open subroutine**, the instructions become part of the main program. The skeleton code of the subroutine is modified by the parameters passed to it and the resulting code is copied into the program where required. In some situations open subroutines may have advantages, for example avoiding the extra time taken to call closed subprograms.

Recursive subprogram

including: stopping condition
is one that includes, among the statements making up the subprogram, a call to the same subprogram. The subprogram will continue calling itself recursively, so it must have a means of finishing and continuing the calling program. This is done by a **stopping condition**, which causes the subprogram to exit rather than call itself again.

Some mathematical techniques involve repeating a process an indefinite number of times using the results of the previous calculations (see *iteration*, page 201). One method of managing this is the use of recursion where the same subprogram is called repeatedly (with the revised data). When the result is found, the automatic way in which the computer handles the return from the subprogram ensures that execution will continue from the calling point. See Figure C3.2.

Figure C3.2 Examples of a recursive subprogram

The factorial of N is calculated as:

$$1 \times 2 \times 3 \times 4 \times \ldots N$$

(up to the number N).

So *factorial*(5) is $5 \times 4 \times 3 \times 2 \times 1$

which is also $5 \times factorial(4)$

and *factorial*(4) is $4 \times factorial(3)$ and so on.

*In **pseudo-code**, the function **factorial** can be defined:*

```
function factorial (N)

    if N<=1 then factorial:=1; return    we stop and go back when we get
                                          to 1

    factorial:=N*factorial (N-1)          recursive call

    return                                return to previous call of function
```

Parameter

including: parameter passing, formal parameter, actual parameter, argument, by value, by reference
is information about a data item being supplied to a function or procedure when it is called.

With a high-level language the parameters are generally enclosed in brackets after the procedure or function name. The data can be a constant or the contents of a variable. See Figure C3.3.

Figure C3.3 Examples of parameters

*In **Pascal**:*

when the function **length(side)** is called,

the **parameter** is the variable **side**

when the function **length('Fred')** is called,

the **parameter** has the value **'Fred'**

when the function **SIN(60)** is called,

the **parameter** has the value **60**

When a function or procedure is defined, a formal parameter, which is a *local variable* (see page 214), is declared and this can be used in the program code for the function or procedure.

When the function or procedure is used, the calling program must pass parameters to it (***parameter passing***). The ***formal parameter*** links the data in the calling program (which will change) to its use in the function or procedure. The data item supplied, known as an ***actual parameter*** or ***argument***, is passed to the local variable. See Figure C3.4.

Actual parameters can be passed to functions and procedures either ***by value*** or ***by reference***. If a data item is passed by value, a (local) copy of the data is used, which is discarded when the subprogram exits. If the data is passed by reference, the location (in memory) of the data is used. This means that any changes are retained after the procedure or function has been completed. Effectively, a single variable has two identifiers, with the subprogram using a pseudonym for the data item involved.

Re-entrant program

is one where the same physical copy of the program code can be used by several different tasks. The program must be written so that data about different tasks does not get mixed up. This is particularly important with systems software, where the computer can be executing the subroutine and an interrupt transfers control to a different program, which may then use the same subroutine. If this subroutine is not re-entrant then data may be corrupted and errors may occur.

Figure C3.4 Examples of parameter passing to a function

The value of fred *after execution of the function will be different depending on whether the* parameter fred *is passed* by value *or* by reference. *The variable* fred *will still be 2 if passed* by value, *but it will be 3 if passed* by reference.

Function definition:

```
function increment(number:integer):integer;
```
                                    local variable is number

```
begin
```
```
number:=number+1;
```
                                    adds 1 to number

```
increment:=number;
```
                                    function returns the value assigned to increment

```
end;
```

Main program:

```
begin
```
```
fred:=2;
```
                                    variable **fred** *starts at 2*

```
bill:=increment(fred);
```
                                    fred *is the* **parameter**; *its* **argument** *is 2*

```
write(bill);
```
                                    variable **bill** *is now 3*

```
end;
```

One example is an interrupt handling routine, which may still be handling one type of interrupt when a different type of interrupt is received.

Another example is the use of a high-level language interpreter on a time-shared system, where a single copy of the interpreter is used by the different users with different data depending on whose time slot is currently being executed. See also *multithreading*, page 180.

Macro instruction

also known as: macro
is a sequence of instructions, usually in a low-level language, defined as a single object. When a macro is encountered the complete sequence of instructions is substituted into the program at that point. The program may then include the same sequence of instructions several times.

A commonly used routine can be defined as a macro instruction and given an identifier. Then the user can simply *call* (see page 208) the macro instruction, using the identifier, to save time and reduce errors. This is different from a *subroutine* (see page 208), where the program jumps to the code to be used, and returns to the same place in the program.

C4 PROGRAM SYNTAX

This section considers the various elements that make up a computer program rather than how they are used. Related material can be found in Section C1 Programming concepts, Section C2 Programming (flow of execution), Section C3 Programming (subprograms) and Section C7 Programming languages.

A computer program, which must be written in a very precise way, is written in a programming language. Programming languages have a vocabulary of only a limited number of words with precise rules describing how they may be combined.

Unless a program is written in machine code (which is very rare) it needs to be translated into some form of machine code before it can be executed. A program can be **assembled**, **interpreted** or **compiled**, which are all forms of **translation**.

Program

including: program suite
is a complete set of program statements that can be executed by the computer to perform some task. The program statements may be written in assembly language or in a high-level language. In order to be executed, the program will need to be translated by a translator program into machine code.

If a program is not complete, it will not work successfully. A correctly written program can be thought of as a specification of the algorithm that the design process has produced. Large software systems are normally ***program suites*** of several programs to do all the tasks required.

Syntax

is the precise way program statements must be written to be understood by the computer. It is the set of rules for combining the elements of a programming language (such as characters and reserved words) into forms that the compiler, interpreter or assembler can understand. The set of rules does not define meaning, nor the use of the final construction, but it does allow programmers to know if a statement they are making is a correctly structured statement.

Semantics

is the meaning of the individual elements that make up a computer language statement, such as the words, symbols and punctuation. The overall meaning of any statement, which is made by combining these individual elements, is uniquely determined by the semantics of the programming language.

Program statement

is any one of the instructions within a program. Program statement is usually taken to mean a statement in a source language instruction, which is human-readable, rather than a binary code instruction. When a program statement is translated it often generates several machine-code instructions.

Block

including: block structured language
is a group of program statements that are treated as a single unit. Special *reserved words* (see page 213) or symbols are used to show which statements form a block. Blocks enable complex programs to be constructed from simple elements without any confusion about how statements will be executed. See Figure C4.1.

Figure C4.1 Examples of block structure

```
In Pascal: begin

                   ...              ... indicates the statements that form the block

           end;
In C:      {

               ...

           }
```

Programming languages that encourage the use of blocks are called *block structured languages*.

Declaration

is a statement in a program that gives the translator information it needs. It is not an operation carried out as the program is executed but is needed for the correct translation of the program. For example, in Pascal the declaration:

```
var area: integer
```

informs the translator that whenever the program uses the variable 'area' it must be treated as an integer (a whole number) rather than as a real number, a string or other data type. Declarations provide information about such things as array sizes, variable types, constants, functions, procedures, library routines and memory allocations. See also *directive*, page 218, and Figure D1.4, page 259.

Label

is an identifier (normally a name) that identifies a particular statement in a program. Labels are normally only needed to indicate the destination of a *jump* (see page 204), which is the next instruction to be used after the jump instruction.

Variable

including: global variable, local variable, strongly typed languages, dynamic variables, static variables
is the identifier (or name) associated with a particular memory location used to store data. By using a name the programmer can store, retrieve and manipulate data without knowing what the data will be.

Global variables can be used anywhere in the program but **local variables** are defined only for use in one part of the program (normally a function or procedure). They come into existence when that part of the program is entered and the data they contain is lost when execution of that part of the program is completed. Using local variables reduces the unplanned effects of a variable being used in another part of the program and accidentally being changed. In a large system, global variables should only be used for data that needs to be shared between sections and should be clearly documented at the design stage.

The data that is identified by a variable can be a number (such as integer or real), a character, a string, a date, a set, a file, an array, a sound sample or any other kind of data. This is called the *variable type* or *data type* (see page 263). In a high-level language, the type may need to be declared when the variable is first used, so that adequate storage space is provided. In a machine-code program, the programmer has to manage the different types of data although they still need to be identified and defined in the design process.

The special features of the data types provided in many high-level languages enable a programmer to write better programs (see *system characteristics*, page 46).

These features include:

Strongly typed languages, which validate (see *validation*, page 109) the data and prevent the wrong kind of data being assigned to a variable.

Dynamic variables, which store the data in the most efficient way, often by using a pointer to locate the data, which is held in a different location. The programmer has limited control over how or where the data is stored.

Static variables are stored in a known format in a known location allowing the programmer to use unorthodox methods to manipulate the data. Static variables can also be used to preserve local data between the calls to a subprogram.

Scope

is the range of statements for which a *variable* (see above) is valid. This will normally be the subprogram in which it is declared and any other subprograms embedded within that subprogram. A variable cannot be used outside its scope as it appears not to exist.

This concept enables the same identifier to be used in different parts of the program for different purposes without conflict. This concept defines which variable will apply

in any given situation during compilation. In a large software project several programmers may be employed but this characteristic of variables means they will not have to
coordinate their use of identifiers.

Dummy variable

is a variable (or identifier) that appears within a program but which is not actually used.
This may be because the syntax of the programming language requires a variable but
the data contained is not needed.

One use of a dummy variable is illustrated in Figure C4.2. An assignment statement
is used to produce an outcome that is desirable and a dummy variable has to be present
to accept the (unwanted) result of the assignment.

Figure C4.2 An example of the use of a dummy variable

In line 120, the statement GET *provides the code of the key being pressed and this is
stored in the variable* dum. *This value is not needed and is ignored.*

```
110    PRINT "Press any key to continue"

120    dum = GET

130    CLS
```

The identifiers used in the definition of a *procedure* or a *function* (see page 207) have
sometimes been called dummy variables because they will be replaced by other identifiers when the program is executed. Better descriptions for these would be *parameters*
(see page 210) or *local variables* (see page 214).

Operator

*including: binary operator, unary operator, arithmetic operator, string operator, relational
operators, Boolean operator, truth value, logical operators*
is a symbol used to indicate that a particular operation is to be performed and gives a
shorthand method of indicating in a computer program how data is to be manipulated.
An obvious example is the '+' sign to mean 'add', but most programming languages now
provide a wide variety of operators for different contexts. See Figure C4.3.

Figure C4.3 An example of '+' operator

Two different uses of the '+' operator

> 5 **+** 7 *means* 12

> > *in the context of the addition of numbers.*

But 'Fred' **+** 'Smith' *means* 'FredSmith'

> > *in the context of the concatenation of strings.*

The important distinction between an operator and a program instruction is that an operator manipulates one or more pieces of data. Most operators are **binary operators**, which combine two pieces of data, although **unary operators**, which act on a single piece of data, are commonly used. See Figure C4.4.

Figure C4.4 Examples of unary and binary operators

In **Pascal**:

unary operators:	**not** end_of_file
	- 5
binary operators:	result **and** end_of_file
	length **+** width
Operators are in **bold**.	

Arithmetic operators manipulate numbers by carrying out normal arithmetic tasks such as addition or subtraction.

String operators combine or manipulate strings by performing such tasks as concatenation (joining strings) or replication (copying part or all of a string).

Relational operators compare data and produce an answer of true or false (see *truth value*, page 106). This answer can control the flow of a program using **IF**, **WHILE** or **REPEAT UNTIL** statements. Examples of relational operators include equals '=' and less than '<'. See Figure C4.5.

Figure C4.5 Examples of relational operators in pseudo-code

In these examples, the operators = and > are shown:

Are two numbers equal?	
maybe	if age = 18 then ...
Is a string alphabetically after another string?	repeat ...
maybe	until word > 'FRED'

Boolean operators combine *truth values* (see page 106), using operators such as *or*, *and*, *not* to produce another **truth value**, which can only be *TRUE* or *FALSE*. This result can control the flow of a program using **IF**, **WHILE** or **REPEAT UNTIL** statements. In other contexts Boolean operators may be known as **logical operators**. See *logical operation*, page 194, and *data type*, page 263.

Identifier

is a name or label chosen by the programmer to represent an object within a program. The object could be a variable, a function, a procedure, a data type or any other element defined within a program. It is wise to make identifiers as meaningful as possible by using longer, more descriptive words (such as 'sales' rather than 'S'). See also *variable*, page 214.

Constant

is a data item with a fixed value. In a high-level language it is assigned to a variable that cannot be changed when the program is executed. For example, if the following declaration is used:

```
const pi = 3.14159265;
```

then the programmer can use the variable name **pi**, which will make writing the program easier. Similarly the declaration:

```
const tax_rate = 20.0;
```

allows the programmer to use the variable name **tax_rate**, the value of which is also easy to change at a later date if circumstances change. However, the program would need recompiling. Only one *declaration* (see page 213) would need altering and not the many occurrences throughout the program.

Machine-code programs also use constants in the form either of a directive assigning a value to a particular mnemonic, or of a data item stored when the program is assembled, which makes it part of the program rather than its data.

It is generally more efficient to use constants because the data is inserted directly into the program code, rather than variables, which the computer will have to retrieve from memory every time they are required.

Reserved word

also known as: keyword
is any word in the vocabulary of a programming language that can only have the meaning that is defined in the language.

For example, many programming languages have an instruction **for**, which is a reserved word and a variable or other identifier cannot be named **for**.

Directive

is a statement in a program that influences the translation process. Examples include: controlling the use of memory; production of a program dump; producing debugging information; or the use of declarations. While a declaration provides information for the program, a directive affects the environment of the translation process. See also *declaration*, page 213.

C5 DESCRIBING PROGRAMS

This section is concerned with the written comments and graphical illustrations accom-
panying a program. The symbols and layout conventions referred to are those given in
British Standards BS 4058:1987 and BS 7738:1994. Related topics can be found in Section
F5 User interface and documentation, Section A4 Systems design and life cycle, Section A5
Describing systems and Section C6 Testing and running programs.

Program documentation is the documentation that is produced for those stages of
the **software life cycle** that are concerned with module development and integration.
Program documentation is particularly important at the maintenance stage of the
system life cycle.

Software will need to be modified during its lifetime and the original programming
team is unlikely to be fully available to assist with modifications, hence the team
making the modifications will need to rely heavily on the original program and system
documentation.

Each module will need to be documented individually at various levels of detail, depending upon its size and complexity. Some of this will be within the programs, using
comment facilities to describe, for example, the data used and the processes carried
out. This notion of a **self-documenting program** is an important element in program
documentation. As well as the use of comment facilities, there are other functions,
which can improve the readability of code; these include the use of indentation (for
example, for the body of a loop) and the choice of meaningful names for identifiers.

The history of a module is important: for example, who wrote it, where and when it
was written, when it was modified and by whom, details of modifications made, testing
history including some test data and the results obtained. As with other information
about a module, some of this can be included in the module listing as comments. This is
often included at the start of the listing where a standard format to the header defines
the information expected.

Diagrams, such as a set of **program flowcharts** or **JSP (Jackson Structured
Programming)** structure diagrams, help to show the flow of a module. They can be
particularly valuable for showing how modules are integrated into subsystems and then
into the completed fully integrated software as it is to be delivered.

Another tool that is also helpful at the module design stage is **pseudo-code**, which is a
formalised English-like way of describing the steps involved in a program routine.

Listing

also known as: program listing
is the printed sequence of program statements. This may also include lists of the data required for the program. See also *statement*, page 213.

Program flowchart diagram

also known as: program flowchart
including: flow line
is a graphical representation of the operations involved in a computer program. Symbols are used to represent particular operations and **flow lines** indicate the sequence of operations. Arrows on flow lines may be omitted if the flow is from top to bottom or from left to right.

A program flowchart forms part of the permanent record of a finished program; it is needed for maintenance purposes. Examples of program flowcharts are given in Figure C5.8, Figure C5.9, and Figure C5.11.

ECMA (European Computer Manufacturers Association) symbols

are standard symbols used in system and program flowcharts. Examples of the use of some ECMA symbols in *system flowcharts* are shown in Figure A5.7 and Figure A5.8. Their use in *program flowcharts* is shown in Figure C5.8 and Figure C5.9. In addition there are British Standards for flowcharts.

Pseudo-code

is a method of describing a program or system design. It uses control structures and keywords similar to those found in programming languages, but without the strict rules of programming languages. It may be presented in a form that looks like a combination of English and a programming language. (See the example of *pseudo-code*, Figure C5.10.)

Decision table

is a table that specifies the actions to be taken when certain conditions arise.

The example, in Figure C5.1, illustrates possible decisions in the problem of how to go to work. Y and N indicate the values of the condition (Yes and No). X indicates that the action is possible. Blank entries indicate that the action is not possible or that no action decision is needed. For example, column four indicates that on a weekday, after 8.00 a.m. (which is also after 7.00 a.m.) the decision has to be to go by bus without having breakfast.

Program flowchart symbol

is a formalised symbol used in a program flowchart diagram. Different shapes indicate the various kinds of activity described by the flowchart. Sometimes highly formalised shapes are used, each having a specific meaning; in other situations very simple boxes with words are used. Provided the meaning is clear, either method is an equally acceptable way of representing a process or system.

Figure C5.1 A decision table

Condition	Value of condition			
Action	Value of action			
Weekday	N	Y	Y	Y
Before 7.00 a.m.		Y	N	N
After 7.00 a.m.		N	Y	Y
After 8.00 a.m.		N	N	Y
Breakfast		X	X	
Walk		X		
Go by bus			X	X

Examples of program flowcharts showing how these symbols might be used are given on pages 224–226. In Figure C5.11 rectangles are used for all processes while more formal shapes are used in Figure C5.8 and Figure C5.9.

Connector symbol

also known as: continuation symbol
is used to indicate that the flowchart is continued elsewhere at an identically labelled connector point. To simplify layouts, connector symbols may be used to replace lengthy flow lines, or to indicate that the flowchart continues on another page.

Figure C5.2 Connector or continuation symbol

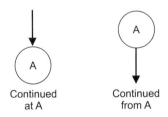

Continued   Continued
at A   from A

Input/output symbol

also known as: input symbol, output symbol
is the program flowchart symbol used for any input or output operation. The description in the box may include the device or medium for the process.

Figure C5.3 Input/output symbol

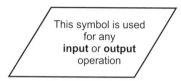

Decision symbol

also known as: decision box
is the flowchart symbol used to indicate points in a program where decisions are made. There are a number of different ways of representing decisions diagrammatically. One set uses the diamond shape in a variety of ways. A decision box may have more than two exits. Four forms are shown in Figure C5.4.

Figure C5.4 Alternative forms of decision box

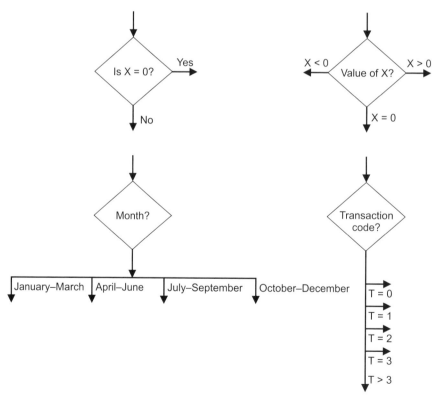

Process symbol

also known as: operation box, process box, operation symbol
is a box used as a flowchart symbol for any operation or sequence of instructions that does not involve a decision. The box can be any suitable size. See Figure C5.5.

Figure C5.5 Process symbol or box

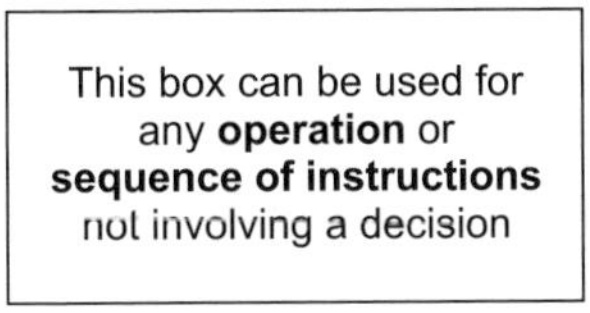

This box can be used for
any **operation** or
sequence of instructions
not involving a decision

Start/stop symbol

also known as: start/stop box
is the flowchart symbol used for both starting and stopping points in a flowchart. A flowchart will have only one start point but there may be more than one stop in a flowchart.

Figure C5.6 Start/stop symbol or box

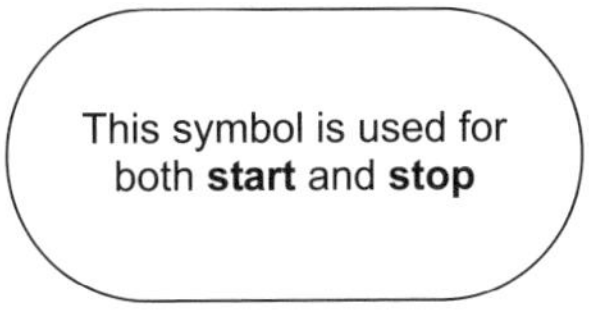

This symbol is used for
both **start** and **stop**

Subroutine symbol

is used to indicate a subroutine call

Figure C5.7 Subroutine symbol or box

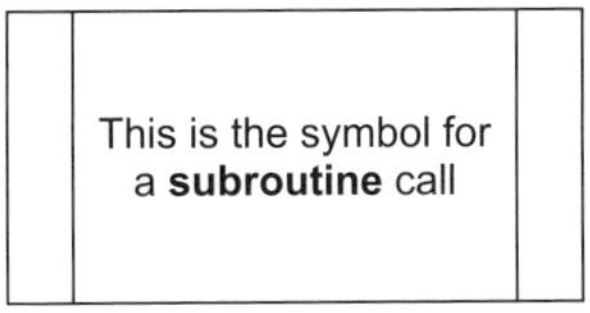

This is the symbol for
a **subroutine** call

An example of a program module

This program module reads a series of records from a transaction file and uses the valid transactions to update a master file. Details of invalid transactions are output on a

223

line printer, together with a summary of the numbers of valid and invalid transactions processed. Figure C5.8, Figure C5.9 and Figure C5.11 give flowcharts for this module.

Figure C5.10 shows the module expressed in pseudo-code. In this method of presenting the program module, an English-like approach is combined with the use of a structured layout, which is closely akin to some computer languages.

Figure C5.8 An example of program module flowchart (in traditional form)

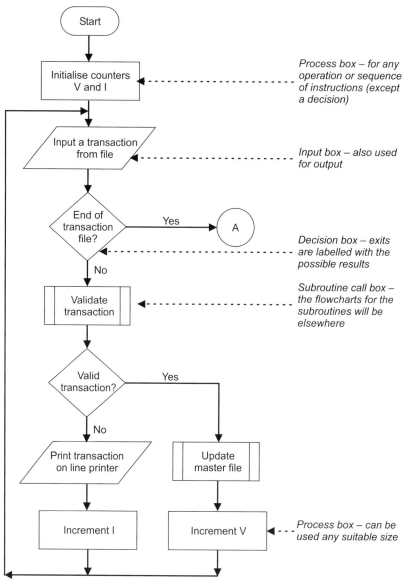

Figure C5.9 An example of program module flowchart (continuation)

Arrows on flow lines may be omitted, as they have been here, if the flow is from top to bottom (or left to right).

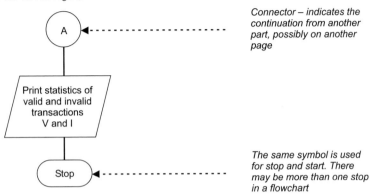

A
Connector – indicates the continuation from another part, possibly on another page
Print statistics of valid and invalid transactions V and I
Stop
The same symbol is used for stop and start. There may be more than one stop in a flowchart

Figure C5.10 Program module in pseudo-code

```
BEGIN
Initialise counters V, I
WHILE more transactions
   BEGIN
   Input transaction
   Validate transaction
   IF valid transaction
         THEN BEGIN
              Update master file
              Increment V
              END
         ELSE BEGIN
              Print transactions
              Increment I
              END
   END
END WHILE
Print statistics of valid and invalid transactions
END
```

Figure C5.11 An example of program module flowchart (using very simple boxes)

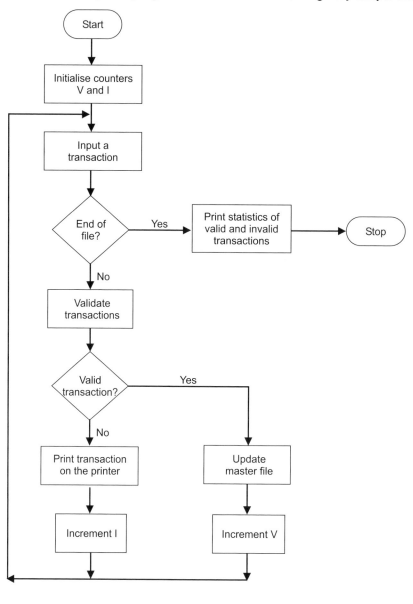

C6 TESTING AND RUNNING PROGRAMS

Other related material can be found in Section A4 Systems design and life cycle, Section C1 Programming concepts, Section C2 Programming (flow of execution), Section C3 Programming (subprograms), Section C4 Program syntax, Section C7 Programming languages and Section B12 Systems software.

Computer systems need to be reliable. Depending upon the task they are designed to do, different levels of reliability are appropriate. Software on these systems ranges from that used for office activities, such as word processors and spreadsheets, through software used in financial institutions, all the way to safety-critical software such as that used for controlling aircraft in flight.

The way software is developed and tested ultimately affects its reliability. A long process of development and testing is undertaken to ensure that it works well for the customer.

The complete software development cycle is described in Section C1 Programming concepts. This section describes the methods and tools used to produce software.

Software systems are normally designed as small interacting modules, possibly by different teams of people. These modules can be independently **coded**, **compiled** and **tested**. Errors found during the testing are investigated and corrections made to the module (**debugging**). This cycle is then repeated until the criteria are satisfied that specify the level of performance to be achieved. The modules are then combined one at a time (**integration**), tested at each integration stage (*integration testing*) and debugged. Once all the modules are successfully combined, the whole system should be tested (**system testing**) and the remaining known errors corrected.

The testing process for each phase is carried out using a **test plan**, designed to test the widest possible range of situations. However, software can be highly complex. This means that, in most cases, without infinite time and resources it is impossible to test every logical path through a program. As a result, test cases must be carefully designed to execute the areas of software, or trigger conditions within the software, that are most likely to provoke errors. There are various techniques that are used to improve the effectiveness of testing, some of which are supported by software tools. All these techniques can be classified as either **black box** or **white box**.

Testing should not be delayed until an executable program is completed. Before the software is coded, requirements, specifications and design documents can all be inspected to eliminate errors early on in the software development life cycle. An inspection is most likely to be performed by a team consisting of designers, developers and clients. Guided by a checklist, the team will review the documentation and look for errors. Code can also be inspected, or may be subjected to a manual **walkthrough**, to determine if there are any errors.

The later an **error** is detected in a piece of software the more costly that error is to fix. It is therefore good practice to aim to catch errors as early as possible in the software development life cycle or, better still, to prevent errors being made in the first place. Unfortunately, even after testing has been completed and software is released, errors may remain and will need to be corrected. Some errors may not be detected until the software has been in operation for a period of time. Some time after the initial software release a new version or **patch** may be issued, which fixes many of the known errors. However, software that has been adequately specified, well designed and thoroughly tested will have a minimum number of errors remaining.

Execution

also known as: program execution
is the operation of a computer program. Unless the program is being interpreted (see *interpreter*, page 177), it must be in machine code. If the machine code is produced by compiling a high-level language program, it is the *object program* (see page 176) that is executed. If the machine code is produced from an assembly language program it is the assembled program (see *assembler*, page 175) that is executed.

Testing

including: test plan, test data, test case, black box, white box, inspection, walkthrough
is the process of detecting errors in a piece of software. It can be carried out at all stages of the *software development life cycle* (see page 32). For each stage a ***test plan*** will exist. The plan will describe each item that needs to be tested. It will provide instructions or operations to be carried out and ***test data***, which are the inputs to be used. It will also provide the expected outcomes. Each set of test data and its expected outcome forms a ***test case***.

Unfortunately there is an infinite number of test values that can be applied to a piece of software. However, various techniques can be applied that aid the selection of test cases, which will force out the largest number of errors. These can be split into black box and white box techniques.

Black box techniques see the software as a 'black box' with inputs and outputs, but no understanding of what is happening within the black box. When testing, suitable inputs are selected based upon the interfaces of the system or module.

White box techniques analyse the structure and logic of the program. This is then used both to help monitor the depth of testing and to guide selection of appropriate data that will cause areas of code to be run that have not yet been executed.

Test cases are usually applied to code that is executed. However, errors can also be found by examining the code manually, such as using inspections and walkthroughs.

Inspection is a technique where a small team will read through the code during a group meeting, analysing it with a checklist. The checklist documents common problems, which the team will be explicitly looking for during the inspection.

Walkthrough is a similar technique. In this case the team will manually execute the code using inputs from defined test cases. This is a formalised team version of a *dry run* (see below).

Debugging

including: diagnostic aid, debugging tool, diagnostic program, debugger, cross-referencer, trace, variable check, step mode, single stepping, post-mortem routine
is the detection, location and correction of faults (or bugs) causing errors in a program. The errors are detected by observing *error messages* (see page 230) or by finding unexpected results in the test output. The location of the faults may be obvious (identified by the error message) or may require extensive investigation. Tools are available to help in this process, particularly with assembly language programs, where comprehensive error reporting may not exist. These **diagnostic aids** and **debugging tools** include:

Diagnostic programs attempt to detect and locate faults in another program or a system by supervising its operation and providing additional information about possible errors.

Debuggers are programs that provide a range of facilities enabling the programmer to investigate the conditions when errors occur.

Cross-referencers are programs that identify where variables are used in a program. This allows errors such as unplanned use of duplicate names to be identified.

Traces are printouts that show the statement tables executed as the program is being run and may include the values of variables. The program flow can be compared with the trace to identify where an error has occurred.

Variable checks list the contents of variables at specific points in the program. This allows their contents to be compared with the expected values, perhaps from a *dry run* (see below). *Breakpoints* (see page 232) provide a way of stopping the program to look at the contents of variables.

Step mode (or **single stepping**) is the execution of a program one statement at a time under user control. It allows the user to observe the effects of each statement after it has been executed.

Post-mortem routines display or print the values of variables at the point when a program failed. In some systems it is a list that indicates where the program failure occurred and gives the latest values of registers, stacks and other variables. See *register*, page 326, and *stack*, page 260.

Dry run

including: trace table
is working through a section of a program manually. This is useful for locating errors, particularly run-time errors. A dry run can be performed on a section of an assembler

program or on a high-level language program. A dry run is usually carried out on parts of a program rather than on a whole program.

Working from the listing of a section of a program, a **trace table** is constructed with a column to identify the instruction executed and columns for the contents of each variable. The programmer follows the instructions from the listing, adding a new line to the trace table each time an instruction is executed. The new line of the trace table should indicate the instruction, either by its machine address or by its line number, and show any changes to the variables. See Figure C6.1.

Error

including: bug, error message, listing file, execution error, run-time error, compilation error, linking error, syntax error, statement syntax error, program syntax error, structure error, logical error

is a fault or mistake in a program or information system causing it to produce wrong results or not to work. A **bug** is a fault in a program that causes errors. Most computers attempt to indicate the likely source of an error by producing **error messages**. Usually these messages are produced either on the user's screen, if the error is attributed to the user, or on the operator's console for more serious errors.

When a program is being developed, many simple errors will be detected during the compilation process. A **listing file** can be generated during compilation; this will contain the source program with error messages and other diagnostic information.
The many types of error can be classified as follows:

Execution errors or **run-time errors** are errors detected during program execution. These errors, such as overflow and division by zero, can occur if a mistake is made in the processing algorithm or as a result of external effects not catered for by the program, such as lack of memory or unusual data.

Compilation errors are errors detected during compilation and are usually *syntax errors* (see below).

Linking errors occur when a compiled program is linked to library routines. For example, if a particular subroutine is not present in the library or the number of parameters provided is wrong.

Syntax errors occur either when program statements cannot be understood because they do not follow the rules laid down by the programming language, **statement syntax errors**, or when program structures are incorrectly formed, **program syntax errors** or **structure errors**. Examples of statement syntax errors include wrong punctuation and misspelling of reserved words and variables. Examples of program syntax errors include control structures incorrectly nested or incorrectly terminated.

Logical errors are mistakes in the design of a program, such as the use of an inappropriate mathematical formula or control structure, recognised by incorrect results or unexpected displays. It is unlikely to generate an error message because the error is in the program design.

Figure C6.1 Examples of trace tables

*Example of a **trace table** for a very simple program in an assembler language:*

Current address	Instruction	Accumulator	&98FF	&9800	&9801	Display
&8001	INP &98FF		5			
&8002	INP &9800		5	15		
&8003	LND &9800	15	5	15		
&8004	. . .					

*Example of a **trace table** for a very simple program in a high-level language:*

Program statement	H	W	A	Output	Comment
1: Input H	5				Get height
2: Input W	5	15			Get width
3: A = H * W	5	15	75		Calculate area
4: Print A	5	15	75	75	Print area
5: GoTo 2					Go back for new pair of values This is an error, this line should be GoTo 1
2: Input W	5	20	75		Get width – we haven't updated the height
3: A = H * W	5	20	100		Calculate area

*An alternative **trace table** for the simple program in a high-level language
(showing the position after statement 4 of the program):*

*Many programs simply use a box for each variable, making changes to the
boxes as instructed by the program but without constructing a formal trace table:*

Statement	H	W	A	Output
1 2 3 4	5	15	75	75

Run

including: run-time

is putting a program or information system into action so that it can perform the data processing it was designed to do.

Run-time is the time during which a program or information system is in operation. Often data has to be provided during run-time and some effects, such as *run-time errors* (see page 230), can only be detected when the system is operating.

Breakpoint

is a position within the program where the program is halted as an aid to debugging. While the program is halted, the programmer can investigate the values of variables, memory locations and registers. This provides additional information to help locate errors, particularly run-time errors.

This facility is often used with assembly language programs and may be incorporated into the operating system or provided by a *debugger* (see page 229). The machine code addresses of breakpoints can be set, the progress of the program can be monitored and the program will halt when the instruction at a breakpoint address is reached. A debugger allows the contents of computer memory to be displayed. It may be possible to resume execution after stopping the program at a breakpoint.

A programmer may insert breakpoints in a program as part of a testing strategy. These will be deleted when the tests are successful.

Dump

including: screen dump, memory dump, core dump

is to copy the contents of a file, or the contents of part of immediate-access store, to backing store or to an output device. The output is known as the dump, and may be used to test the integrity of a data file or to assist in program error detection. A dump may also be made as part of a backup process. There are various types of dump including:

Screen dump is a representation of the screen stored as a data file or produced as a printout. A screen dump is an easy way of printing data collected together on the screen and produces a copy of the current screen display.

Memory dump is the output of an area of memory to a file or the screen, usually showing the information in binary or hexadecimal numbers.

Core dump is a memory dump of part of the main memory of the computer. It usually occurs when a program is abnormally terminated by an internal error.

Patch

including: service pack, update

is a small fragment of code, provided by a software supplier, to enable a user to modify or correct their copy of software without requiring a complete replacement. A **service pack** is a collection of programs and data files that correct problems in released software. It is installed to overwrite parts of the originally released software. An **update** is a minor release of software that incorporates corrections, but does not usually include any significant new features. It is common for manufacturers to publish these updates on their website, enabling users of the software to download them. See also *software upgrade* (page 44).

Run-time system

is the complete set of software, including any *library programs* or *library routines* (see page 174), that must be present in a computer before a particular program can be executed.

Process state

including: ready, running, blocked, suspended, stopped, completed, deadlock, deadly embrace
is the status of a program submitted to a computer system for *running* (see *run*, page 231). The concept is particularly useful with *multiprogramming systems* (see page 179) where several programs may be being processed at the same time. This includes multi-user computer systems, which will be operating using some form of multiprogramming.

Programs submitted to a computer, either for batch or interactive processing, are added to a job queue and are then in one of a number of process states. See Figure C6.2.

Figure C6.2 Program process states

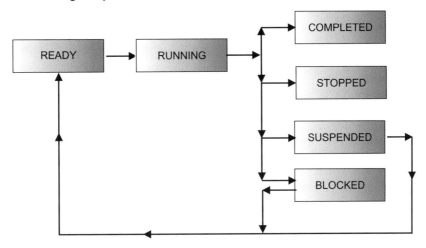

Ready: a program waiting to continue execution by the central processor. Several programs may be ready at any one time, waiting for execution.

Running: a program being executed by the central processor. A central processor can only execute one program at a time, so only one program will be running (except in a computer with several processors). Execution may be interrupted, in which case the program will be either suspended or blocked.

Blocked: a program waiting for a peripheral. The peripheral may be in use by another program or already committed to a task for this program. When the peripheral becomes available, the status returns to ready, allowing the central processor to continue executing the program when it can.

Suspended: the operating system decides that a program has to be interrupted, perhaps because it is taking up too much time. The program status will be returned to ready to await a further time allocation.

Stopped: a program has been aborted (see *abort*, page 234).

Completed: a program has run to a proper conclusion. It will then be deleted from the job queue.

Deadlock or ***deadly embrace***: a condition in which no processing takes place at all and the system appears to be *hung* (see below). This could be the result of a number of situations, for example process A is blocked, waiting for process B to complete, which it cannot do until process C is complete, which it cannot do until process A is complete … . The chain could, of course, be even longer.

Down time

is the time when a computer system is not available (down) to the user. This may be because the computer is being maintained, it has broken down, there is a failure in the operating system or there is a communications failure.

Abort

is stopping the execution of a program or system before it has reached its normal conclusion. The run may be aborted by the program itself, the operating system or an operator.

A program may be aborted if an error is detected or if the operator requests it. An error such as a missing file will cause a program to be aborted. If the program appears to be working incorrectly, the operator may request that it is aborted. Sometimes the operating system may not be able to abort a run; in this case the computer will not respond and will have to be reset. See also *hung*, below.

Crash

also known as: bomb
including: system crash, hung
is the term used to describe the situation when a computer system unexpectedly stops working correctly. This could be caused by a hardware failure, an error causing the program to *abort* (see above) or an error causing the computer to be hung.

A ***system crash*** is a major failure of a computer leaving it inoperable and all users unable to continue.

A ***hung*** computer does not produce any output, and appears to have ceased to operate. This is often caused by an *infinite loop* (see page 201). The operator will then attempt *recovery* (see page 235) but if that is not possible, the computer will need to be *reset* (see page 235).

If a crash occurs, it is possible that any recent unsaved alterations to work or data will be lost.

Recovery

including: warm start, cold start, reset
is the process of returning the system to normal operation after an error. The procedures may differ, depending on the type of program in use and the type of error (whether due to hardware, software or data). Recovery will include identifying any data that has been corrupted and deciding on the restart process.

Warm start: execution is continued from the point at which the error occurred, using data that may already have been processed and stored in memory. Because the computer's memory is not initialised, there is a risk that corrupted data may cause further errors. A warm start enables a fast recovery of the system, if it is possible.

Cold start: the system is started again from the beginning. See also *reboot*, page 171. The computer's memory is initialised and the system should now work as expected. This can be a slow recovery, since the system may have to repeat processing already performed. See also *crash*, page 234.

Reset: the system is returned to its initial state, as if it had just been switched on or started. This is often used after a program has caused a computer to crash or behave erratically, when the computer may continue to work, but corruption of the contents of critical areas of memory may lead to erratic behaviour and loss of data.

Immediate mode

is the use of a command or program language statement outside the program that has been running. The instruction is executed and any results are produced before the user can enter the next instruction. Usually, immediate mode is only available with *Interpreter*, see page 177.

C7 PROGRAMMING LANGUAGES

Other related material can be found in Section A4 Systems design and life cycle and Section B12 Systems software.

Programming languages are the means of generating the software that makes the computer work. A computer operates by executing a **program**, that is, following a sequence of instructions. This is held in memory as electronic patterns, known as **machine code**. The programmer starts with a design of what the program or algorithm is intended to do, then writes it in a programming language. The written program is known as the **source code** and is translated into **object code** (or machine code).

Programming languages are not the same as human languages – most obviously because (at present) they are only written and never spoken. But the term 'language' is a very appropriate one. Languages have a **grammar** (or **syntax**), which states the rules of the language. This makes it possible to recognise 'wrong', ungrammatical uses of language, to avoid spending time and effort trying to understand something that has no meaning. The syntax of a language is not simply a collection of 'correct' uses – it is a set of rules that allow programmers to combine elements of the language into a statement and know it is acceptable to the computer. Statements in languages also have meanings (or **semantics**). One important difference between human and computer languages is that computer languages are never ambiguous – a statement always has just one meaning (even if it isn't the meaning that the programmer intended).

Historically, the first languages were developed to simplify the process of programming the electronic patterns instead of entering them as 1s and 0s – binary digits, or bits. If the pattern 101010 was the code for ADD, it was easier to allow the programmer to write 'ADD' and let the computer substitute the appropriate code. These languages are known as **assembly languages** because they 'assemble' instructions that could be coded directly as bits. The instructions are translated into machine code by **assembler** programs. Assembly languages are very close to the actual machine code of a computer. A different assembly language is needed for each type of computer. Because of this close link, such languages are known as **machine-oriented** or **low-level languages**.

As programming became more sophisticated, languages were designed to allow programmers to write instructions that are closer to the way they think about the problem. If a running total is located in 1101101 it is easier to give this location a name, e.g. TOT, and let the computer substitute the location. The programmer can work more efficiently and has less to remember so mistakes are less likely. A translation program will turn, for example, a mathematical calculation expressed in mathematical symbols, into the (often quite lengthy) sequence of machine-code instructions to perform that calculation. This also allows the programmer to use a single language for different computers, provided that the language is translated by a translation program appropriate for the computer in use. Such languages are at a different level from the details of how the machine works, and they express programming steps in a way more suited to the problem than the computer. These languages are known as **problem-oriented languages** or **high-level languages**, an example being Visual Basic®.

With a completely developed program, the translation process is only performed once so it need not be very fast, provided that the machine code that is produced is efficient. There are several ways of organising the translation. Some translators take in a written program and produce working machine code; others translate into assembly language, and use an existing assembler for the last stage of translation. Yet another way is to produce **intermediate code**, which is easier to translate than the original program during execution. Java is of this type.

Translation programs that produce another program at a lower level (machine-code, assembly language, intermediate code) are called **compilers**. After compilation, programs can be executed again and again without needing the original translation program any more.

Some programs are translated while they are being executed, a process known as **interpreting**. This allows the programmer to make changes easily without long delays waiting for compilation. A disadvantage is that all of the translation program, known as an **interpreter**, needs to be present when the program is executed, so even a quite small program will need a lot of memory when it is running.

Interpreters normally translate and execute programs line-by-line, converting each program statement into a sequence of machine code instructions and executing these instructions without retaining the translated version. In a program with a loop, this means that the same statement will be translated each time it is encountered. For this and similar reasons, interpreted programs are usually slower in execution than compiled ones. Nevertheless, both the disadvantages, space and time, may be outweighed by ease of use.

Interpreters begin execution of a program immediately and they can work on an unfinished program, hence they are commonly used interactively, where it is important to see the results as soon as possible. Compilers are best used for software that will be used many times without change – such as systems software and applications packages.

Over a period of time a number of programming techniques have developed and programming languages have been written with characteristics that support the various programming styles. However, machine code is **imperative**: that is, it specifies the operations, the order in which they must be carried out and the memory locations to be used. All other language types such as **declarative**, **functional** and **logical** languages have to be translated (compiled or interpreted) into an imperative form for execution. Programming techniques such as **structured**, **procedural** or **object-oriented** programming are designed to enable effective programs to be developed and maintained, particularly when several people are involved in the design.

New languages are designed when existing ones no longer provide adequate facilities – specialist graphics and statistics languages have emerged, for instance. At present, their translators are often written in a particular high-level language called C (or its successors C++ and C#), which has its own features to allow the easy design of such systems software. Specialised tools are available to simplify the process further.

Computer users are becoming increasingly aware of **mark-up languages**. These are not programming languages in the normal sense, but rather a way of defining the structure and format of a document – for example a web page.

Comparative information about some significant early programming languages that are no longer used for program design appears in Table C7.1 (see page 239) and about programming languages used today for program development are given in Table C7.2 (see page 241).

LEVELS OF LANGUAGE

High-level language

including: problem-oriented language, third-generation language (3GL), fourth-generation language (4GL), application generation language
is designed to help a programmer express a computer program in a way that reflects the problem that is being solved, rather than the details of how the computer will produce the solution. These languages are often described as ***problem-oriented languages***. The programmer will certainly be allowed to use long descriptive names for the variables, and to structure the program into subroutines or functions to help keep the logic of the solution clearly visible. Certain mathematical notation will be permitted, allowing calculations to be specified in the same way as in written mathematics. When the language is translated, the *compiler* (see page 176) or *interpreter* (see page 177) will take care of the details of the many machine-code instructions necessary to cause the computer to execute the program. Compare this with the definition of *low-level language*, page 243.

Languages that were developed at the time of *third-generation computers* (see page 288) are known as ***third-generation languages (3GL)***, and many are still in current use.

Fourth-generation language (4GL) is used to describe languages aiming at end-users rather than specialist computer practitioners. A characteristic of these languages was the recognition that computing power was becoming more freely and more cheaply available, and that popular software reduced the time taken to develop users' programs. 4GLs are also known as ***application generation languages***.

Some comparative information about some significant high-level languages appears in Table C7.1 (see page 239) and Table C7.2 (see page 241).

Table C7.1 Early programming languages

Language	Date	Derivation of name	Translation	Characteristics	Notes
Ada	1975–83	after Countess Lovelace	compiled	imperative	mainly used for large military systems, sponsored by US Dept of Defense
ALGOL	1958–68	*ALGO*rithmic *L*anguage	compiled	imperative	originally for (paper) description of algorithms - an influential language with several distinct versions (Algol-60, Algol-68)
ALGOL 68	1968	*ALGO*rithmic *L*anguage	compiled	imperative	developed from Algol with more structure
APL	1957–68	*A P*rogramming *L*anguage	interpreted	functional	easier to write than to read; it uses symbols not always found on regular keyboards - requires large memory. Operates on vectors
COBOL	1959–60	*CO*mmon *B*usiness *O*riented *L*anguage	compiled	imperative	easier to read than to write; large memory requirements, hence a mainframe language; highly structured data suited to business use
FORTH	late 1960s	pun on 'Fourth'	mixed	unique, functional	very different from other languages: used in control and graphics applications
Pascal	1968–71	after Blaise Pascal	compiled	imperative	mainstream general-purpose structured language of the 1970s and 1980s
PL/1	1963–64	*P*rogramming *L*anguage *1*	compiled	imperative	union of COBOL and FORTRAN, introduced new simple concepts but never gained popularity
POP-2	late 1960s	author: Dr R. J. Popplestone	interpreted	functional	artificial intelligence uses

(Continued)

239

Table C7.1 (Continued)

Language	Date	Derivation of name	Translation	Characteristics	Notes
RPG	1964	Report *Program* *Generator*	compiled	imperative	almost an applications package for business reports
Simula	1965	from *simulation*	compiled	object-oriented	Simulation. First object-oriented language
SNOBOL	1962–68	StriNg Oriented SymBOlic Language	compiled	functional	string manipulation language

Generally no longer used for program development although some are still in use.
The **date** is that of initial development; most languages have been continuously improved since invention.
Translation indicates the most usual method, not necessarily the only one.
Characteristics indicates:

- whether the language is used by giving instructions on how to solve the problem (an algorithm, or conventional program) – '**imperative**';
- whether it is based on functions or procedures applied to sets of data '**functional**';
- or whether its basic structure is that of an **object-oriented** programming language.

Table C7.2 Programming languages

Language	Date	Derivation of name	Translation	Characteristics	Notes
Ada 95	1995				superseded Ada, see Table C7.1, page 239
BASIC	1964	Beginners All-purpose Symbolic/nstruction Code	interpreted	imperative	easy to learn and (in modernised versions) the world's most frequently encountered programming language, especially in schools
C	1972	see notes	compiled	imperative	systems programming language, derived from 'B', which derived in turn from BCPL, which derived from CPL
C++	1979-83	C plus a bit more	compiled	object-oriented	object-oriented features added to C
C#	2001		compiled	object-oriented	client-server distributed applications – pronounced C sharp
Delphi	1995		compiled	object-oriented	Object Pascal extension to Pascal by Borland
FORTRAN	1954-57	FORmula TRANslation	compiled	imperative	mainstream scientific programming language; language still reflects punched-card input – too early to be a structured programming language
FORTRAN 2003					there have been different generations
Java	1991-95	Its 'exotic, exciting, adrenaline-pumping connotations' linked to Java coffee beans	compiled to intermediate code then compiled dynamically	object-oriented	platform-independent related to C++ for the internet use of applets, and bytecode for distributed applications across the internet
Lisp	1959	List Processing	interpreted	functional	artificial intelligence uses – an influential language, in that many other languages have been derived from it

(Continued)

Table C7.2 *(Continued)*

Language	Date	Derivation of name	Translation	Characteristics	Notes
Logo	1966–68	Greek for 'thought'	interpreted	procedural, list processing	based on list-processing features, but noted for its 'turtle graphics' subset; popular in education as it is considered to teach thinking as well as programming
Prolog	1972	*PROgramming in LOGic*	interpreted	declarative	artificial intelligence uses – a very different language
Smalltalk	1972–80	to emphasis nature of language interface	interpreted	object-oriented	forerunner of most graphics interfaces
Visual Basic®	early 1990s	*GUI-based extension of BASIC*	interpreted or compiled	imperative	provides quick and easy means of creating interface applications for Microsoft® Windows®
VBA		Visual Basic® for Applications	interpreted	imperative	later development of Visual Basic®
Perl	1987	Originally Pearl	interpreted	object-oriented procedural	general purpose, used for text processing, web development, GUI development
JavaScript	1995		interpreted	object-oriented procedural	scripting language, superset of ECMAScript standard
Python	1994		interpreted	object-oriented procedural	

Typically used today for program development.
The **date** is that of initial development; most languages have been continuously improved since invention.
Translation indicates the most usual method, not necessarily the only one.
Characteristics indicates:

- whether the language is used by giving instructions on how to solve the problem (an algorithm, or conventional program) - **'imperative'**;
- whether it is based on functions or procedures applied to sets of data - **'functional'**;
- or whether its basic structure is that of an **object-oriented** programming language.

Intermediate code

Computer programs are generally translated into instructions for the computer to follow in one of two distinct ways, compilation or interpretation. There is also a possible 'mixed' approach, in which the program is first compiled into an intermediate code made up of simpler instructions that are then executed by a *virtual machine*, see page 177. Once a program has been compiled into intermediate code, it can be run on any computer for which a virtual machine is available. Java is currently the most common programming language using intermediate code. See also *compiler*, page 176, and *interpreter*, page 177.

Low-level language

including: machine-oriented language
Some programming languages are necessarily closely related to the design of the machine; the available instructions reflect the way the machine is built. *Assembly language* and perhaps even *machine code* itself (see page 243) are good examples. Because *high-level languages* (see page 238) generally prevent the user specifying memory locations directly, low-level languages are necessary for programming tasks connected with the running of the computer, particularly where speed is important. For this reason they are described as **machine-oriented languages**. They are not generally good for problem-solving, for which high-level languages are more suitable.

Assembly language

is very closely related to the computer's own machine code. Instead of writing actual machine-code instructions (which would typically need to be entered in binary or hexadecimal), the assembly language programmer is generally able to make use of descriptive names for data stores and mnemonics for instructions. The program is then assembled (by software known as an assembler) into the appropriate machine-code instructions. See also *machine code*, below, and *assembler*, page 175.

Machine code

is the set of all possible instructions made available by the hardware design of a particular processor. These instructions operate on very basic items of data, such as bytes or even single bits. They may be given memorable names in the associated documentation, but can only be understood by the computer when expressed in binary notation. Hence machine code is very difficult to write without mistakes. In practice, machine-code programming is achieved by the programmer writing in *assembly language* (see page 175), which is closely related to machine code.

TYPES OF LANGUAGE

Imperative language

including: procedural language
is one in which the programmer specifies the steps needed to execute the program, such as program statements, declarations and control structures, and the order in which they should be carried out. Most early programming languages were imperative.

Current high-level imperative languages generally have features that enable them to be used as **procedural languages**, in which the program statements can be grouped in self-contained blocks called *procedures* (see page 207) and *functions* (see page 207). These procedures have their own variables, not accessible outside the procedure. The logic of the program is expressed as a series of procedure *calls* (see page 208).

Although a well-written program expressed in a procedural language is generally more comprehensible to the reader, procedural languages are nonetheless imperative in that the responsibility for specifying what steps should be taken, and in what order, falls on the programmer.

Procedural languages and imperative languages were previously seen as distinct.

Object-oriented programming language

is a language that provides the necessary structures to produce object-oriented programs. It enables the programmer to design self-contained objects, which contain both methods (program routines) and the data being processed. A complex system can be built up from these objects. See *object-oriented programming*, page 188.

Declarative language

is one in which the program consists of declarations: statements that specify what properties the result should have. The outcomes are described but not how they are to be achieved, in contrast to an *imperative language* (see page 243). The order of these declarations should not be important. Currently most existing so-called declarative languages rarely achieve these characteristics owing to the difficulty of implementing such a system. See *Prolog*, page 246.

Functional language

is a *declarative language* (see above) where each call produces a value that is returned to the statement being executed at the time the *function* (see page 207) is called. The logic of the program is expressed as one single function *call* (see page 208) that calls other functions in order. These functions in turn may call others directly or call themselves recursively. Consequently, a well-written program in a functional language making good use of recursion has a structure that looks significantly different from that of an *imperative program* (see page 243).

Logic programming language

is a type of *declarative language* (see above) that makes use of logic formulas. It is based on procedures that ideally would be unordered, although this is often not the case, for example *Prolog* (see page 246) or CPL. See Figure C7.1.

Extensible language

is a language that allows additional operations, data structures or types to be defined just as if they were part of the original definition, using the existing language facilities. These can then be incorporated into the language, and used in the same way with

Figure C7.1 Example of use of a logical language

Declared facts like	Philip is male
	William is male
	Elizabeth is female
	Philip is parent of Charles
	Elizabeth is parent of Charles
	Charles is parent of William

Note: all variables are local to the rule in which they occur

Declared rules like	A is child of B **IF** B parent of A
	A is father of B **IF** A is male **AND** A is parent of B
	A is son of B **IF** A is male **AND** A is child of B
	A is daughter of B **IF** A is female **AND** A is child of B
	A is grandparent of B **IF** A is parent of C **AND** C is parent of B
	A is grandchild of B **IF** A is child of C **AND** C is child of B
	A is granddaughter of B **IF** A is female **AND** A is grandchild of B
	Etc., etc.

Now can ask	Is William granddaughter of Elizabeth?
	which X **if** X is grandson of Elizabeth
	which X **if** X is father of Charles
	which X **if** X is grandparent ofWilliam

To speed subsequent deductions, results of these could be added to knowledge base as additional facts (if not already there) by an imperative statement

the same syntax as existing ones. Collections of extensions may be made available to others: see *library routine*, page 174.

List-processing language

manipulates data strings (lists of *data items*, see page 263) and uses linked lists as its primary data structure. It has very few primitive operations, but these are very powerful and use recursion very efficiently. Such languages are used mainly in expert systems and have not generally been used commercially, as they are less comfortable for general-purpose programmers. Examples are *LISP* and *Logo*, see page 246, and Table C7.2, page 241.

MISCELLANEOUS SPECIALISED LANGUAGES

Authoring language

also known as: authoring tool
is a language designed to assist in the preparation of teaching or presentation materials that are to be presented on a computer. These materials may be learning material

for computer-managed learning, web pages or any other situation for which computer presentation is desirable or appropriate.

An authoring language for computer-managed learning allows the author to specify what material will be displayed (this might include the use of sound or video) and what questions are to be asked of the student. Answers to these questions will be listed, together with the action to be taken in response to each one, and the section of the teaching that follows; in this way, remedial lessons can be offered to students who score badly, while students giving correct answers can be directed along a faster route through the material. See also *computer-aided learning*, page 428, and *script*, page 14.

Prolog

including: knowledge base, logic engine
is a high-level programming language. It is a type of logic programming language but procedures are not fully unordered as would be required of a true logic language. The name comes from 'PROgramming with LOGic'. It is used in artificial intelligence and *expert systems* (see page 143).

Programming in Prolog involves building a **knowledge base** by declaring a large number of 'rules' to the system, using mathematical logic notation, and facts, then asking the Prolog system to deduce conclusions from the knowledge base. Prolog sometimes uses imperative statements to add deduced facts to the knowledge base.

The necessary processing is accomplished by a logical inference machine also known as a **logic engine**, emphasising the extensive use of mathematical logic concepts.

Logo

including: turtle graphics, turtle
Is *a functional language* (see page 244) based on list processing and is easily *extensible* (see page 244). It was developed as an educational language for use with young children and encourages children to think in a structured way. It contains graphical operations that are easy to use.

The subset of Logo commands dealing with graphics is called **turtle graphics** because it is used to control the movements of a **turtle**. The turtle can be a small robot with wheels and a pen moving across the floor and drawing or simply a point moving and drawing on the screen.

Another subset of Logo allows the production of music. (See also Section F4 Sound.)

Meta language

including: Backus–Naur Form (BNF), replacement rules
though not a programming language, is often used to describe other languages.

Backus–Naur Form (BNF) is an example. The name comes from its two inventors, although it is sometimes held to be 'Backus Normal Form'. A BNF description is expressed as a series of **replacement rules** that describe how some elements of the language are built up from choices of simpler elements. See Figure C7.2 for an example.

Figure C7.2 Example of Backus–Naur form

Part of a possible definition of the LET assignment statement within the BASIC language:

```
<LET-statement>: : = [LET] <numeric-variable> = <numeric-expression>|
         [LET] <string-variable> = <string-expression>
```

In this example, the vertical bar indicates the presence of alternatives: the 'LET statement' can take either of two forms.

The first form is:

the word LET (which is optional, because it is shown in square brackets),

followed by a numeric variable,

followed by the equals sign '=',

followed by a numeric expression.

Items shown in angle brackets '<'and'>' have definitions elsewhere inthe full language specification.

For example, it is likely that elsewhere you would find the line:

```
<string-variable>: := <numeric-variable>$
```

showing that a string variable obeys the same rules as a numeric variable, but is followed by a dollar sign '$'

Items shown in curly brackets '{' and '}' may occur any number of times, including none.

For example the definition of a numeric variable may be:

```
<numeric-variable>: := <letter> {alphanumeric}
```

showing that the variable name must start with a letter, but that following characters, if any, may be either letters or numbers.

Mark-up languages

including: Standard Generalised Mark-up Language (SGML)
are document description languages used for multimedia documents and not truly programming languages. They are intended to describe the structure of a document, without specifying how it is to be laid out when printed, or displayed on a screen (but see *HTML*, page 247). The document is made up of elements such as text, pictures, sound etc. and their structure is defined by means of *tags* inserted in the document. These tags are quite separate from the elements and might specify, for example, that a particular block of text is a heading, a complete paragraph or the author's name. The interpretation of these tags is not defined in the language, and different users can elect to display these elements in their own ways. The tags are expressed as plain text, so without special codes specific to one particular user, documents defined in a mark-up language are completely portable.

Standard Generalised Mark-up Language (SGML) was the original language, and had no specific reference to computers. Later versions incorporating developments for computer use are HTML, DHTML and XML (see below).

HyperText Mark-up Language (HTML)

including: tag, DHTML, XML
is a mark-up language developed for multimedia documents, such as World Wide Web pages.

Tags in HTML are labels for characterising portions of text. A browser should use the tags to control the display of the text. The tags themselves are never actually displayed. Each tag consists of a name sometimes followed by an optional list of attributes. Tags generally occur in pairs, bracketing elements of the text. Such tags are an instruction about how the text between the tags should be treated. For example glossary indicates that the single word 'glossary' should be emphasised, and this generally results in the browser displaying it in *italic* text. Table C7.3 shows some of the common tags.

As with all mark-up languages, an HTML document is just text and can be transmitted rapidly. Portability is further enhanced by the required behaviour of a browser on encountering an unknown tag, which is simply to ignore it. It is thus possible for a web page to capitalise on features present in later browsers, while still displaying satisfactorily in earlier versions.

In the original specification, the text to be displayed was marked with tags and it was the responsibility of the user's web browser to display the text in an appropriate way. This allowed the user to specify their own preferences. A visually handicapped user might instruct their browser to use a larger or more readable font, for example, and it was unnecessary to consider this in the design of the web page. However, there was understandable pressure from web page designers, asking for more control over the display of their pages. This resulted in the addition of extra tags: bold and italic text is now more commonly specified through explicit <b> and <i> tags, and the ability to specify a particular type face, colour and size of text has been incorporated. This has taken HTML further from the concept of a 'pure' mark-up language, but has provided much greater (but sometimes misused) functionality for web pages. There is now a move back to the original principles of HTML, with control of the layout left to a *stylesheet* (see page 251).

It is possible to build an HTML document by adding the tags to the text using a text editor, but most page design is done using special editors that save the designed page as an HTML file with all tags inserted automatically.

DHTML (Dynamic HTML) is an extended version of HTML that allows more user interaction within the browser. It also allows the user to read from and write to specific database files.

XML (from eXtensible) is a pure mark-up language. It can be used to define the structure of data with existing and user-defined tags. This basic structure can then be interpreted not only by web browsers but by any software. For example, this *Glossary* was converted from the original word processor files into XML, which was then used to generate the typesetting for the book.

Table C7.3 A small selection of common HTML tags

Tag	Example	Result or description
strong: \<strong\>...\</strong\>	the \<strong\>glossary\</strong\> text	the **glossary** text
emphasis: \<em\>...\</em\>	the \<em\>glossary\</em\> text	the *glossary* text
combining style tags	the \<strong\>\<em\>glossary\</em\>\</strong\> text	the ***glossary*** text
image: \<img\>	\<img src="BCSlogo.gif"\>	
anchor: \<a\>...\</a\>	\<a href=page2.html\> Click here to see the next page \</a\>	Produces a link to another page <u>Click here to see the next page</u>
	\<a name=linkname\>Contact details\</a\>	A label within the current page. This label can be used to link directly to this location within the page.
	\<a href=#linkname\> Click here to see the contact details \</a\>	A link to a label within the current page. <u>Click here to see the contact details</u>
paragraph: \<p\>...\</p\>	\<p\>This is the text to be displayed in a paragraph\</p\> \<p\>This is another paragraph\</p\>	This is the text to be displayed in a paragraph This is another paragraph

(Continued)

Table C7.3 *(Continued)*

Tag	Example	Result or description

unordered list: `<ul>...</ul>` ordered list: `<ol>...</ol>` list item: `<li>...</li>`	`<p>The Glossary has four main sections:</p>`
	
	`<ul>`
	
	`<li>How computer systems are used</li>`
	`<li>What computer systems are made of</li>`
	`<li>How computer systems are developed</li>`
	`<li>How computers work</li>`
	
	`</ul>`
	
	`<p>The seasons of the year are:</p>`
	
	`<ol>`
	
	`<li>Spring</li>`
	`<li>Summer</li>`
	`<li>Autumn</li>`
	`<li>Winter</li>`
	
	`</ol>`
		The Glossary has four main sections:
		
		• How computer systems are used
		• What computer systems are made of
		• How computer systems are developed
		• How computers work
		
		The seasons of the year are:
		
		1. Spring
		2. Summer
		3. Autumn
		4. Winter

Stylesheet

including: cascading stylesheets (CSS)
is a definition of the formatting and layout of elements of an HTML document. The stylesheet may be part of the HTML document, or stored as a separate file linked to the document. The use of different stylesheets linked to the same document allows appropriate layout of the same content on, for example, mobile devices, display screens.

Stylesheets encourage consistent design, in that a 'master' stylesheet can be linked to a number of documents or individual documents. Other stylesheets may then override the formatting inherited from the master stylesheet. With this possibility of formatting being defined in different places, potential ambiguities are resolved by the rules for **cascading stylesheets (CSS)**. These rules specify the order in which definitions in one place take precedence over those in another, hence the use of the name 'cascading'.

PART D: DATA

This part is concerned with terms relating to storing data in a way a computer program can access it. They are frequently considered to be associated with computer science, as opposed to the terms in Parts A and B, which are concerned with the needs of computer system users, and Part E, which provides some technical information that might be helpful to both computer users and to students following courses requiring some knowledge of computer systems and peripherals. Part F is concerned with the way software is used.

The range of terms covered in Parts C and D and the depth of treatment of individual terms has been influenced by knowledge of the difficulties encountered by students who are studying courses that involve some computer science, whatever the title of the course.

D1 DATA REPRESENTATION

Related material, particularly about numbers and their representation, can be found in Section D2 Numeric data representation.

The essence of any computer is its ability to store and manipulate data. The data is stored electronically and this section looks at the principles used to interpret the stored data as understandable information.

Within the computer all information is represented as some combinations of physical properties. What these properties mean depends on how we interpret them. Indeed a particular set of these properties could represent a number, a letter, a word, an instruction or a variety of other things. What a particular set of properties is taken to mean depends on the context it is in when interpreted by the computer's central processor.

In a digital computer these properties are made up of individual elements that can have one of two values (often voltages). It is convenient for us to think of this element as a binary digit (a **bit**), which can be written as either 0 or 1. Binary digits can then be grouped to form patterns that are used as **codes**. These codes provide a way of thinking about how the computer works internally but the technology actually used can vary from computer to computer.

The codes allow us to describe how data is stored and manipulated in a way that is common between computer systems. We can also consider the codes as binary numbers, which allow us to use mathematical theory to manipulate the data.

Data representation is about the way in which binary digits are grouped to provide codes, how these are interpreted and how larger groupings, such as arrays, stacks and lists, are used for sets of data.

CONCEPTS

Data

including: information
is information coded and structured for subsequent processing, generally by a computer system. The resulting codes are meaningless until they are placed in the correct context. The subtle difference between data and information is that *information* is in context, data is not.

Character set

including: character, control character, character code, ASCII, American Standard Code for Information Interchange, ISO 8859, Unicode
is the set of symbols that may be represented in a computer at a particular time. These symbols, called **characters**, can be letters, digits, spaces or punctuation marks; the set includes **control characters**. These non-printing characters are used for special purposes. Examples of control characters are:

- end of record and end of file markers in a file;
- carriage return and line feed for a printer;
- begin and end transmission in asynchronous communications; and
- cursor movement on a screen.

Individual characters are represented by a single code number (the **character code**) stored as a binary integer. Any textual data will be stored as a sequence of these codes. When the data is displayed or printed the character code is converted into the appropriate symbol.

There has been a growing convergence among different character sets.

ASCII was devised for use with early telecommunication systems but proved to be ideal for computer systems. It stands for **American Standard Code for Information Interchange**.

The ASCII code uses 7 bits giving 32 control codes and 96 displayable characters (an eighth bit could be used for error checking). See also Section G5. Most modern character sets are extensions of the ASCII code, and provide the possibility for more characters, but letters, digits and common punctuation characters retain the same code numbers. The most noticeable effect of character set variations is that some characters appear to change, for example a '£' may appear as a '$' or as a '#'.

ISO 8859 was a subsequent international standard for computer character sets and had several variations for use in different cultures. The variations were more usually known by their names such as *Latin1 alphabet*, *Latin2 alphabet* and *Greek alphabet*.

Unicode is the standard character set that replaces the need for all the different character sets. It incorporates characters from almost all the world's languages. It is a 16-bit extension of ASCII. See also page 463.

Collating sequence

is the order in which a computer will sort character data. This could be the order in which a particular application sorts data, but it is often the sequence of characters in the order of their character codes. Obviously letters such as A to Z will be in the usual alphabetic order, but various computer systems may differ in whether 'A' comes before 'a' or whether '1' comes before 'A' depending on the codes used in the system. The use of a standard code such as ASCII avoids such differences between computer systems.

STRUCTURES

Data structure

is a group of related data items organised in the computer. A data structure allows a large number of pieces of data to be managed as a single set. Each type of data structure makes it easy for the programmer to find and process the data in particular ways. Each type of structure has its own strengths and weaknesses. Examples of data structures are *arrays, lists, tables* (see page 258), *trees* (see below), *strings* (see *string data,* page 263) and *files* (see page 272).

Tree

including: node, branch, leaf node, terminal node, parent node, child node, root node, binary tree
is a non-linear data structure where the data items can be thought of as occurring at different levels. There are links between items at one level and their descendants at the next. Each data item has data that relates it to its unique parent node. See Figure D1.1.

Figure D1.1 A typical tree structure

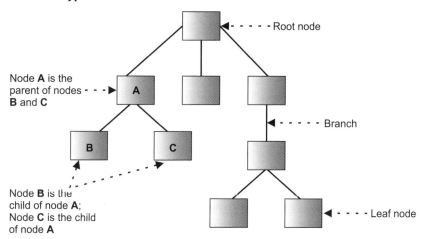

The data items are usually called **nodes** with the links known as **branches**. A node may have any number of descendants but itself may only be the descendant of one other node. This data structure is often encountered in a directory of files, where directory nodes are linked to subdirectories. It is usual in computing to draw a tree diagram 'upside down' with the root at the top, unlike a natural tree.

Data can be added to the tree (by creating a new node) or removed from a tree (by deleting a node). The tree can be traversed using a variety of algorithms but only by following the links between nodes.

Some nodes in a tree have particular characteristics. Of particular importance are leaf nodes, parent nodes and root nodes.

Leaf nodes or **terminal node**s are nodes in a tree without any branches further down the tree. In the conventional way of drawing trees (upside down), the leaves occur at the bottom.

Parent node is the node immediately above a given node, that is, at the next level up. There can only be one parent node for each node, but different nodes, known as **child nodes**, may share the same parent.

Root node is the entry node where we would start before moving around the tree. It is the only node in a tree without a parent node. In the conventional way of drawing trees (upside down) the root occurs at the top. A tree has exactly one root node. If the data suggests that there should be two or more root nodes, the data structure has to be viewed as several trees.

One particular form of tree is the **binary tree** where nodes have at most two branches down the tree. Binary trees are easier to implement on a computer than other forms of tree. Some of the advantages of a binary tree are:

- there is a way of representing all trees as binary trees;

- a fixed amount of space can be reserved for its branches;

- efficient algorithms exist for adding items to the tree and searching it.

Array

including: subscript, list, one-dimensional array, dimension, two-dimensional array, table, array bound, subscripted variable
is a set of data items of the same type grouped together using a single identifier. Each of the data items is addressed by the variable name (*identifier*, see page 217) and a **subscript**, for example in Figure D1.2, NAME(4) is the fourth element of the array NAME. A column of data like this is called a list or a **one-dimensional array**. Many languages have subscripts starting at zero.

Figure D1.2 A one-dimensional array

A one-dimensional array consisting of people's names.
The array has four elements.

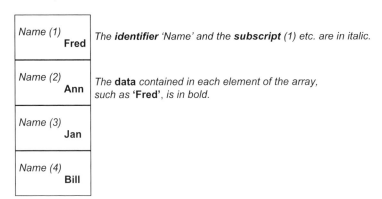

Name (1) **Fred**	The *identifier* 'Name' and the **subscript** (1) etc. are in italic.
Name (2) **Ann**	The **data** contained in each element of the array, such as '**Fred**', is in bold.
Name (3) **Jan**	
Name (4) **Bill**	

Arrays may have many **dimensions**, and have a subscript for each dimension. So in Figure D1.3, Stock(3,2) is an element in the **two-dimensional array** called Stock. On paper two-dimensional arrays are the same as tables (with rows and columns) and are sometimes called **tables** in the computing context.

Figure D1.3 A two-dimensional array

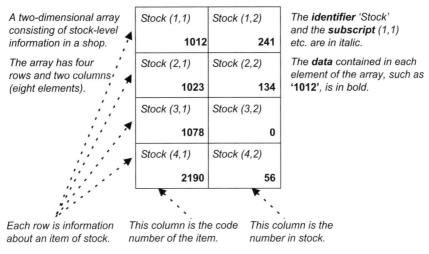

A two-dimensional array consisting of stock-level information in a shop.

The array has four rows and two columns (eight elements).

Stock (1,1)	Stock (1,2)
1012	241
Stock (2,1)	Stock (2,2)
1023	134
Stock (3,1)	Stock (3,2)
1078	0
Stock (4,1)	Stock (4,2)
2190	56

The **identifier** 'Stock' and the **subscript** (1,1) etc. are in italic.

The **data** contained in each element of the array, such as '**1012**', is in bold.

Each row is information about an item of stock.

This column is the code number of the item.

This column is the number in stock.

Figure D1.4 Declaring array dimensions

Two-dimensional array of stock items

One-dimensional array of the results of throwing two dice

In **Pascal**:

```
var stock : array [1..10,1..5]
of real;
```

```
var dice_score : array [2..12]
of integer;
```

In **BASIC**:

```
DIM stock(10,5)
```

```
DIM DICESCORE (12)
```

In **C**:

```
float stock [10] [5]
```

```
int dice_score [12]
```

This example defines an array (of real numbers) that has two dimensions, with upper bounds of 10 'rows' (the first subscript) and 5 'columns' (the second subscript).

This example defines an array (of integers) for a problem using subscripts 2–12. Pascal allows the lower bound to be set at 2, rather than the more normal lower bound of 0 or 1. In many programming languages the subscripts start from zero so a four-statement array will be numbered 0, 1, 2, 3.

259

Before an array can be used in a program, it must be declared (see *declaration*, page 213) and its size defined, so that the computer can allocate a part of memory for the array. Examples of array declarations are given in Figure D1.4. The limits of the array are known as the **array bounds** and it is usual to declare the array by stating its name and giving the maximum values of each dimension.

A *subscripted variable* refers to an individual element of an array, for example Age(20) or Stock(3,2).

Stack

including: last in, first out (LIFO), push, pull, pop
is a list where items are added or deleted from the same end. The operation of a stack is *last in, first out (LIFO)* – the most recent item to arrive is dealt with first.

Push is the term used for adding an item to the stack. *Pull* and *pop* are terms used for taking an item from the stack. Taking an item from the stack makes the next item in the stack available. Items in other positions in the stack cannot be accessed.

Stacks are often represented by an array with a pointer to the top of the stack where the elements are added and removed.

Linked list

is a list where each item contains the data together with a pointer to the next item. There may be an additional pointer to the previous item. This means the items can be accessed in order even if they are not stored in order; they do not have to be stored in adjacent memory locations.

Queue

including: first in, first out (FIFO), circular queue, circular buffer
is a list where any new item is added to one end, and items are deleted from the other. The operation of a queue is *first in, first out (FIFO)*. Items are dealt with in the order they arrive.

Queues are often represented using an array with pointers to the first and last elements of the queue.

A *circular queue* is a queue in which the storage area is fixed and the first item is held in a location that is logically next to the storage location for the last item of the queue. Data items can be thought of as being arranged in a circle; for this reason it is sometimes called a *circular buffer*.

Record

including: record format, logical record, physical record, blocking factor
is the basic unit of data stored in a data file. It is a collection of items, which may be of different data types, all relating to the individual or object the record describes and is treated as a unit for processing. Most data files contain records that have the same types of information but about different individuals or objects.

The contents of a record are described by the **record format**, which specifies the record in terms of its *fields* (see below).

Where it is necessary to distinguish between the content of a record and the computer-stored record, the terms **logical record** and **physical record** are used. Logical record is used to refer to the information held in a record, but a physical record is a *block* (see page 306) of memory in backing store, which can hold one or more logical records.

The number of logical records in each physical record, which will depend on the size of the logical record and the structure of records and blocks on the backing store, is called the **blocking factor**.

Variable-length record

is a record where the number of bits (or characters) is not predetermined but is governed by the amount of data to be stored. This is useful where textual data is to be stored, which would leave a lot of wasted space in *fixed-length records* (see below). However, fixed-length records are more easily processed.

Fixed-length record

also known as: fixed-format record
is a record where the number of bits in a record is decided in advance at the design stage. This length is constant and cannot be changed later. The length of a fixed-length record is often thought of in terms of bytes or characters.

ELEMENTS

End of file (EOF) marker

is a marker written to a file by the operating system immediately after the last record to signal the end of that file to the controlling program. A programmer can use this to process a variable amount of data in a file, processing records until the end of file marker is found. This is similar to using a *rogue terminator* (see page 199).

Field

including: field name
is part of a *record* (see page 260) designed to hold a single data item of a specified type. Most data files contain records that have the same fields of information but about different individuals or objects. Each field is referred to by a **field name**, which identifies the data in the field and makes it possible to generalise about the data being processed.

Key

including: key field, sort key, primary key, key field order, secondary key, composite key
is the field (the **key field**) within a record used to identify the record, for example a bank account number identifies a customer's account. The key can be used for finding the record within a file or as the **sort key** for sorting a file into order.

Most data files will have a ***primary key***, which is unique and used to identify the record. If the records in a data file can be accessed *sequentially* (see *sequential access*, page 273) the records will be accessed in ***key field order***, which is the order they will be in when they have been sorted using the key field.

Data files may also have ***secondary keys***, which enable the file to be accessed in a different order. ***Composite keys***, made up of more than one field, can be used to sort a file. The use of composite keys is shown in Figure D1.6.

Figure D1.5 Fields and records in a data file

A **data file** *holding details of club membership.*

Each **record** *would contain* **fields** *of a member's data:*

       Name, initials, date of birth and membership number.

The **field names:**

       Name, Initials, Date_of_Birth and Membership_Number

identify the data present, rather than being the actual data, which may be:

       Smith, F, 12/3/78, 458923

Each **record** *would have the name, initials, date of birth and membership number of a different member.*

Figure D1.6 Key fields in a data file

In the example (Figure D1.5) of a data file holding details of club membership containing fields for:

       Name, Initials, Date_Of_Birth and Membership_Number

the Membership_Number *could be the primary key field because it is unique and identifies who the record is about.*

Name *could be a* secondary key.

Date_Of_Birth *or* Initials *could not be* **key** *fields because without the other fields they are out of context (and the data is unidentifiable and meaningless).*

Date_Of_Birth *could be a* **sort key** *because the resulting list would be in order of age, which is useful.*

Name *and* Initials *(i.e.* SmithF*) could be a* **composite key***. If the file is sorted using this as a sort key, then all the* Smiths *would be together, in alphabetical order according to initial.*

Data type

including: variable type, field type, user-defined data type, alphanumeric data, character data, string data, Boolean data, logical data, sample data, sound data, video data, video clip, date data
is a formal description of the kind of data being stored or manipulated within a program or system, for example alphabetic data, numeric data or logical data.

Variable type in a high-level language describes the kind of data held by a *variable* (see page 214).

Field type describes the kind of data stored as a *field* (see page 261) within a data file.

The specification of data types is important because:

- it provides a limited validation of data;
- different operations can be performed on different data types;
- memory can be efficiently allocated to store data.

Different programming languages provide different data, variable and field types. Many allow programmers to specify their own data types; these are called **user-defined data types** and are often combinations of existing data types.

Some systems provide a wide range of data or field types, such as date, sample (sound recordings) and video (moving pictures). These are particularly useful in database systems.

Data, variable and field types can be specified for any data item that has an identifiable structure. Some of the more important ones are detailed below:

Alphanumeric data is a general term used for textual data, which may include letters, digits and, sometimes, punctuation. It includes both character data type and string data type.

Character data is a single character represented by the codes from the character set in use on the computer. See also *character*, page 256.

String data is textual data in the form of a list of characters, for example words and punctuation. String data is made up of character data and will usually vary in length.

Boolean data or **logical data** can only have one of two values, true or false (see *truth value*, page 106). This makes it easy to use the values of Boolean variables to control the flow of a program. See also Section E8 Truth tables and logic gates.

Sample data (digitally recorded **sound data**) and **video data** (a **video clip**) are large complex data structures containing all the information needed to enable a suitable subroutine to play a sound sample or display a video clip.

Date data is in a form recognised as representing a date, for example 1.2.09 or 1st February 2009. Date data must represent a valid date, for example 11/12/09 is allowed, but 31st April 2009 is not allowed because April only has 30 days.

Numeric data can have a variety of types (see *numeric data type*, page 270).

D2 NUMERIC DATA REPRESENTATION

This section defines terms associated with some of the methods used to store numbers in ways that can be efficiently processed. Other related material can be found in Section D1 Data representation.

Much of the data stored in a computer are numbers of some kind. Numbers create special problems for the computer scientist because they vary in type and size in an unpredictable way.

A number, such as '123', could be treated as the three separate **characters** '1' '2' '3', but if it is necessary to store its **value**, 'one hundred and twenty three', then there are several of ways of doing this. Storing numbers as values, rather than as characters, has the advantage that it is easier to perform arithmetic efficiently.

A number could be very large or very small, positive or negative, a whole number or a fraction. Whatever it is, it must be converted to a binary pattern for storage and manipulation in a computer. For a given number of bits there is a finite number of patterns available to represent number values and this places limits on the numbers that can be stored. Table D2.1 shows the number of patterns available for different numbers of bits.

Table D2.1 Number of patterns provided by different numbers of bits

---

1 bit	Example: 1	2 patterns (0 and 1)
2 bits	Example: 11	4 patterns (00, 01, 10 and 11)
3 bits	Example: 101	8 patterns (000, 001, ..., 111)
4 bits	Example: 1101	16 patterns (0000, 0001, ..., 1111)
7 bits	Example: 1101100	128 patterns
8 bits	Example: 11011001	256 patterns
...	...	...
16 bits	...	65,536 patterns
...	...	...
32 bits	...	4,294,967,296 patterns
...	...	...

The way numbers are stored involves a compromise between the **range** of values needed and the **accuracy** with which these values can be represented.

For a limited range of whole numbers, each number can be represented exactly using one of the available code combinations. As the required range of numbers increases, eventually there will not be enough codes for each code to represent a single value. A longer word length (more binary digits) could be used to extend the range of values, but there will always be a limit at some value, and using a very long word length all the time would mean that the computer would be slower and could only run smaller programs.

To store an even larger range of numbers with the same set of codes, two or more numbers close to each other will have to use the same code, which could introduce errors into the results of calculations. Similarly, if provision is made for negative numbers, the largest value that can be stored will be halved, since one of the binary digits is used to indicate the sign.

Even larger numbers require different methods of representation, which may also introduce errors into the computed results because similar numbers will share the same codes. To represent very large numbers and fractions, **floating-point representation** is used. This enables a wide range of numbers to be represented to a known accuracy. Figure D2.1 illustrates the range of numbers that can be represented in different forms.

Figure D2.1 Number ranges for different number forms

Number lines (not to scale) showing the range of numbers that can be used in different number forms

*The range of numbers that can be used in **two's complement integer** form:*

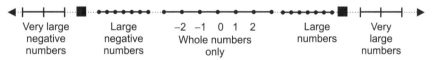

*The range of numbers that can be used in **single-precision floating-point** form:*

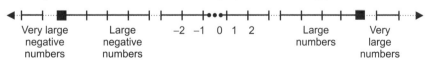

*The range of numbers that can be used in **double-precision floating-point** form:*

In any representation, numbers can be stored only to a limited predetermined accuracy – the number of significant figures.
*In **floating-point form**, numbers that are very close to zero cannot be represented accurately – shown by the gaps between the dots •. Also there are limits to the range for large numbers, both positive and negative – shown by ⊢—⊣ ■.*
Zero is a special case and has unique representation (all noughts) in floating-point form.

An additional constraint is that the computer has to perform arithmetic with the result-ant codes; in particular it has to be able to add and subtract them. The methods used to represent values have to be related to the way the computer does arithmetic, in particular the way it deals with negative numbers.

A programmer normally has control of the types of representation used. A program can be optimised to work as fast as possible, to handle numbers with great accuracy or to handle a wide range of numbers. Some compromise is normally essential since these properties are often mutually exclusive.

Binary notation

is the number system using base two and the digits 0 and 1. It is a convenient way of representing numbers in an electronic computer. Most computers do arithmetic using binary numbers and other representations need converting into binary form before the computer can do anything with them.
For example: 123 (denary) is 1 111 011 (binary). See *denary notation*, (see below).

Denary notation

is the familiar number system using base ten and the digits 0 to 9. It is often incorrectly referred to as decimal notation.

Integer

is any whole number, whether positive or negative.

Real number

is any number represented with a fractional part. In most high-level languages, real indicates that *floating-point representation* (see below) is to be used when the number is stored or manipulated. This implies that the number may contain a fractional part and that it is processed to a limited number of significant figures.

Fixed-point representation

is the form of representation in which numbers are expressed by a set of digits with the decimal (or binary) point in its correct position. During operations in the computer the position of the decimal (or binary) point is generally maintained by instructions in the program. The size of fixed-point numbers is limited by the construction of the computer, but operations are generally very fast and preferred for most commercial data processing work.

Floating-point representation

including: mantissa, exponent
is a form of representation in which numbers are expressed as a binary or decimal fractional value, called the **mantissa**, which is non-zero, together with an integer **exponent**. The use of floating-point representation increases the range of numbers that

can be represented, although the number of significant figures remains constant for any given system. Generally, the advantage of the extra range available when working in floating-point representation is gained at the expense of processing time and precision. Floating-point numbers are often called real numbers in a computing context, although this meaning is different from the strict mathematical use of the term real number. See Figure D2.2.

Figure D2.2 Fixed-point and floating-point representation

	Fixed point	Sign	Mantissa	Exponent	Floating point	Equivalent to
Denary	142.687	+	.142687	+3		0.142687×10^{3}
	−0.0034128	−	.34128	−2		-0.34128×10^{-2}
Binary	−101.011	−	.101011	+11		$-0.101011_{2} \times 2^{3}$
	+0.0010111	+	.10111	−10		$0.10111_{2} \times 2^{-2}$

Negative numbers

including: sign bit, sign and magnitude, sign and modulus, complementation, one's complement, two's complement
are represented within the computer by binary patterns that enable the computer to do arithmetic easily. Generally one bit, called the **sign bit**, is used to indicate the sign of the number, usually 0 for positive and 1 for negative. Common methods of representing negative numbers are:

Sign and magnitude (or **sign and modulus**) is a method of representing numbers by allocating one bit of a binary word, usually the most significant bit, to represent the sign of a number whose magnitude is held in the remaining bits of the word. For example: in the 16 bit number: **1000101010101000** the 1 at the left-hand end is the sign bit, the remaining 15 bits are the magnitude (or modulus) of the number.

Complementation is a method of representing positive and negative numbers. This system requires numbers to be represented by a fixed number of bits. There are two forms of complementation, one's complement and two's complement, which are illustrated below. Two's complement is preferred because subtraction can be performed by adding the two's complement of the number to be subtracted.

43 (denary) is represented as an 8-bit binary number by **00101011**.

One's complement is formed by changing each 1 bit to a 0 and changing each 0 bit to a 1.

The one's complement of **00101011** (+43) is **11010100** and this complement, **11010100** could be used to represent −43.

However, more often the two's complement is used.

Two's complement is one greater than the corresponding one's complement.

The two's complement of **00101011** (+43) is **11010101** (11010100 + 1) and this complement is normally used to represent −43.

Binary coded decimal (BCD)

is a coding system in which each decimal digit is represented by a group of four binary digits. This is sometimes useful because it maintains the relationship between the place values in decimal and the values stored in the computer. It is not efficient for the computer to store and manipulate numbers in this form but it may have advantages in some applications.

Figure D2.3 Denary to BCD conversion

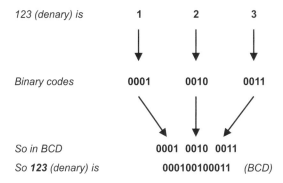

Octal notation

is the number system using base 8 and the digits 0–7. It has similar advantages to *hexadecimal* (see below) in that it is related to the binary pattern (each octal digit represents three bits). Most people use hexadecimal in preference to octal. See Figure D2.4.

Hexadecimal notation

also known as: hex
is the number system using base 16 and the digits 0–9 and the letters A–F. It is often used in computing because long binary patterns can be written as short hexadecimal numbers without losing the relationship between the value and the individual bits in the pattern, with each group of four bits being represented by one hexadecimal digit. See Figure D2.5.

Figure D2.4 Binary to octal conversion

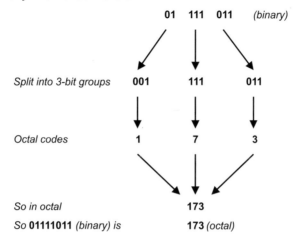

01 111 011   *(binary)*

Split into 3-bit groups   001   111   011

Octal codes   1   7   3

So in octal   173
So **01111011** *(binary)* is   173 *(octal)*

*Both these numbers are equivalent to **123** (denary)*

Figure D2.5 Binary to hexadecimal conversion

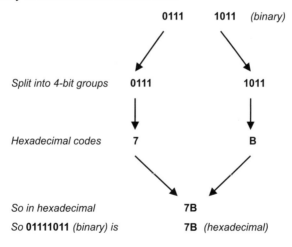

0111   1011   *(binary)*

Split into 4-bit groups   0111   1011

Hexadecimal codes   7   B

So in hexadecimal   **7B**
So **01111011** *(binary)* is   **7B** *(hexadecimal)*

*Both these numbers are equivalent to **123** (denary)*

Normalise

is to change a number in floating-point form into standard floating-point representation format. Using a standard format for floating-point representation has some advantages, such as:

- avoiding the problem of having two different binary codes meaning the same thing;

- the form chosen is usually that which provides maximum precision;

- multiplication is performed more accurately.

Numeric data type

including: numeric variable type, numeric field type, integer type, int type, real type, float type, double precision, single precision, complex type
is a formal description of the kind of numeric data being stored or manipulated within a program or system, for example *integers*, *real numbers* (see page 266), and complex numbers.

Numeric variable type or **numeric field type** specify the kind of numeric data held by a *variable* (see page 214) in a high-level language or as *fields* (see page 261) in a file.

In many cases the same numerical value can be stored using any of the representations available; the one that is chosen by the programmer will be the most appropriate to the task being programmed. Some of the more important numeric data types are detailed below:

Integer type data are whole numbers, either positive or negative. Internally the computer will usually store integer type data as binary integers in *two's complement form* (see page 268). Integer type data is sometimes called **int type**.

Real type data are numbers that include a fractional part. Internally the computer will usually store real type data using *floating-point representation* (see page 266). It is sometimes called **float type**.

Double precision type data provides a more accurate representation than the usual **single precision** type data, by using twice the number of bits to store and manipulate the data. Double precision is usually applied to real type data.

Complex type data are complex numbers. Some programming languages allow complex type data, which provides for the direct manipulation of complex numbers.

D3   MANAGING DATA FILES

Related topics can be found in Section F1 Word processing and text manipulation, Section B4 Commercial data processing, Section F2 Spreadsheets, Section B3 Data handling and information retrieval, Section E3 Memory, Section D1 Data representation and Section D2 Numeric data representation.

Computer users tend to keep their programs separate from the data they operate on. The data is usually held as one or more **files** on backing storage, and the systems software encourages the user to believe that the file is held here (for example, on a disk) all the time. In fact, when a program wishes to use the data in a file, it is necessary for the portion of the file being worked on to be copied into primary storage in order to work on individual items of data. The systems software is responsible for copying between backing and primary storage, ensuring that the correct portion is readily available, without explicit action by the user. Because of this automatic management, it is necessary for users to access files in a formal way.

If the file is a new one, it must first be **created**, and this might include specifying how large the file will become, and how it will be organised. Before any use of an existing file, it is necessary to **open** the file, when a section will be copied to primary storage, and other programs will be notified that the file is in use. Any changes will be made to the copy, and when access is requested to a part of the file not currently in primary storage, the systems software is responsible for making the changes to the permanent version, and loading a fresh copy of the required portion. Networks of any kind complicate the work of the systems software and the user may need 'permissions to access the data'.

When access to the file is no longer needed, it must be **closed** so that any remaining changes are written back to the permanent version, and other programs can be notified that the file is no longer in use.

A file may be **deleted** from backing store, but it is usual for the systems software simply to mark the file in some way, so that the space it occupies may be used for other files, rather than physically erase the contents.

FILES

File structure

including: serial file, sequential file, random file, address-generating, hashing algorithm, random access file

is the way in which data is physically stored in a file. The file structure describes the order in which the data is stored, how the data is split into individual elements and how the data is stored as binary codes. In a database system the file structure defines what data a record contains and details of individual fields used.

Any complex system must allow for the data to be retrieved efficiently. This can be done using the *key* (see page 261), which is data that allows any record to be identified and located. The choice of physical file structure and the *file access method* (page 273) have a big impact on the speed and efficiency of any system using data files.

Common file structures are:

Serial file – one in which the data is physically stored without a specific order other than the order in which it was added to the file. To retrieve any particular record, it is necessary to read through every preceding record. If the record does not exist in the file, this will not become apparent until you read to the end of the file. New records can only be added at the end of the file. Deleted records will leave a gap that cannot be reused, unless the file is completely recreated. Serial files are mostly used with linear storage devices, such as tape drives.

Sequential file – a serial file in which the data is physically stored in order, usually in the order of the data in a key field. For example, in a student record system this could be in alphabetic order (of the surname) or in numerical order (of reference number). This allows more efficient processing than a serial file. When searching a file, if a record does not exist this will become apparent as soon as the appropriate value of the key is passed. However, new records can only be added if the file is recreated. Similarly, records deleted will leave a gap, unless the file is completely recreated. Sequential files can be combined with index files to allow random access using *indexed sequential access method (ISAM)*, see page 274.

Random file – is one in which the physical location of the record is derived from the data in the key field. Unlike most file structures, there is no concept of storing data in a physical linear order; hence the data may appear to be randomly scattered. Usually, the file uses a dedicated area of a storage device such as a disk, and may not even appear as a file to the operating system. The algorithm for deriving the location from the key is known as an **address-generating** or **hashing algorithm** (see *hashing*, page 274). This structure allows particular records to be accessed directly, without reading other unrelated records.

Random access file – is a file where the records are stored as a serial file, but which can be directly accessed like a random file. This may be done by using the position of the data in the file as its 'address'. Random access files have the simplicity of simple sequential files as well as giving some of the benefits of the random file. See also *file access*, page 273.

Table D3.1 summarises the suitability of these structures for various access methods.

Table D3.1 Suitability of file access methods

File structure	Access method		
	Serial access	Sequential access	Direct access
Serial	Yes	No	No
Sequential	Yes	Yes	No
Sequential (indexed)	Yes	Yes	Yes (using indexes)
Random	No	No	Yes (using hashing)
Random access	No	No	Yes (using hashing or indexes)
Notes	Not suitable for large quantities	Particularly suited to searches with a **high hit rate**, as in batch processing	Particularly suited to searches with a **low hit rate**, as in real-time systems, interactive systems and transaction processing

File access

including: serial access, sequential access, direct access, random access, indexed access, index sequential access method (ISAM)
describes the method used to locate and retrieve records in a file. The way in which a file is to be accessed when in use influences the choice of *file structure*, as does the information the systems software needs in order to allow for efficient reading and writing. See *file structure*, page 272.

Although file access methods relate to the physical file structure, each file structure can often be accessed in different ways, and possibly alternative ways for reading and for writing the data. Table D3.1 shows how file access is related to the file structure and that the more complex file structures can be accessed more flexibly.

Serial access is where the records are read, one at a time, from the physical start of the file, in the order in which they are stored. Items may vary in length, provided there is some marker to signal the end of one item and the start of the next.

Sequential access is where the records are read, one at a time in key value order, from the logical start of the file. Hence items are processed in a known, and therefore predictable, order making large amounts of data easier to process. For example if we are updating many customer records and the changes are in key field order, we can work through the customer file once, without backtracking. This means *serial access* to a *sequential file* will also be *sequential access*. Similarly, because the records in a *serial file* are in an order, perhaps the order they were acquired, *serial access* has sometimes been referred to as *sequential access*. Usually *sequential access* is used with a *sequential file* but *sequential access* can also be achieved if the file structure is indexed (see *ISAM*, below) or uses a *linked list* (see page 260).

Direct access is where any record can be retrieved immediately, provided its position in the file is known. This often means that items must have a known length, so that software can calculate where in the file the required item is located, see also *fixed-length record*, page 261. Direct access is sometimes called **random access** because any record can be located at random in the same relatively fast time. This is similar to *random-access memory*, page 298.

Indexed access uses additional data files that contain information about the location of each record. In a simple system the index file may be a sequential file only containing the keyword and the location of the record on the disk. This makes the index file small and easy to search. Using multiple indexes or storing the index as a binary tree can improve performance.

Index sequential access methods (ISAM) use *index files* containing indexes to the records in a sequential file. This allows both sequential and indexed approaches to be used. For example, to search an index sequential file of surnames for the name 'Smith', an index is first consulted to discover the first item beginning with 'S', after which the file is searched sequentially. For this to work both the data file and the index file must be in key value order, in this case alphabetic order.

Record number

is a unique number that identifies the position of a record in a data file. This means that record number 001 identifies the first physical position and the data in that position. The concept of a record number is not used in some file structures such as *random files* (see page 272) and in some *relational database systems* (see page 97).

Many data files can be processed serially by working through the file, one record at a time; in this situation, the record number identifies the position of the record currently being processed. A record number may serve as a *pointer* (see page 277). See also *file access*, page 273.

Hashing

including: address-generating algorithm, hash table, collision, overflow data, overflow area is the process of calculating a numeric value from one or more data items. While this value obviously depends on the value of the data items, it need not depend on the meaning attached to them, simply producing a number that is used within the computer.

The **address-generating algorithm** is the mathematical formula used to convert the value of the data into the whole number used for a hash table or random file.

A **hash table** is a data structure where the calculated value is used to mark the position in the table where the data item should be stored, enabling it to be accessed directly, rather than forcing a sequential search.

A **collision** occurs when the hashing process gives two different data items the same value. This suggests they should be stored in the same place in a hash table or random file, which must not be allowed to happen; there are techniques to deal with the resulting *overflow data*, see page 275.

Overflow data cannot be stored in its proper place because other data is already at the same location, which would result in a collision. Techniques to deal with this problem include using an overflow area or using the next available location, possibly with some sort of indicator that overflow has occurred.

An *overflow area* is an area of storage in a random file reserved for overflow data. Data that cannot be stored in the correct location due to a *collision* (see page 275) is stored here. Later when other data is deleted it may be possible to move it from the overflow area to its correct location.

Hashing is also used to produce a *hash total*, which is a *verification method*, see page 110.

Data file

including: archive file, backup file, journal file, reference file, master file, transaction file, grandfather-father-son files, index file, temporary file, temp file
is a *file* (see page 272) that usually contains just the data that the computer is storing and processing. Other data such as program defaults, set-up information or report layouts are stored in more specialised files. Usually a data file just holds one type of data, such as payroll information. Many data files have a special purpose, particularly in complex data-processing operations. Some important types of data file are:

Archive file is one containing data no longer in use, but held for historical purposes, perhaps for auditors. It is often stored away from the computer system, in a secure location. See *archive*, page 111.

Backup file is a copy of a current file kept as a security measure in case the original is corrupted in any way. As with an *archive file* (see above), it is often kept in a secure location away from the computer system.

Journal file is a record of changes made to a database system. This may be kept as part of the *audit trail* (see page 111) or may be kept as a *transaction file* (see below) that can be used to *restore* the database in the event of it becoming corrupted. See page 281.

Reference file is a special type of *master file* (see below) that is not updated during the job being processed. It contains fixed data that does not change. When changes are necessary a separate program is used.

Master file is the principal source of data for an application. It holds data that is mostly static but which can be added to or amended by updating as necessary during processing. In a traditional commercial batch-processing application, such as a payroll, the master file (of all employees) is updated by reference to a *transaction file* (see below) of hours worked in the current month, leave, sickness, promotions etc.

Transaction file contains new data to be added to a database or *master file* (see above), usually as part of a *batch processing system* (see page 17). All the data in the transaction file will be processed as one operation, making the process very efficient. A *journal file* (see above) contains data that has been added to a database and is sometimes also called a transaction file. Transaction files are often retained as part of the system's *backup procedures*, see page 115.

Grandfather-father-son files are the three most recent versions of a file that is periodically updated, for example the *master file* (see page 275) in a batch-processing application such as a payroll. The most recent, the '**son**' file, is used for the next run of the program; if an error occurs that corrupts this copy of the master file, the '**father**' version is still available, and can be used with an archive copy of the *transaction file* (see page 275) from the previous run, to recreate the damaged 'son' version. The '**grandfather**' version provides an additional level of security.

Index file is a file used to access a large data file quickly. It contains key field data from the file that the index is for. The key data is in a format that can be searched quickly and the attached addresses are used to access the data.

Temporary or *temp file* is used to store files during processing and is usually deleted automatically at the end of the processing.

OPERATIONS

File operations

including: read, write, update, insert, append, overwrite
are those activities that can be performed on an existing data file.

Reading is the operation of taking a copy of a data item from a file into the computer's main memory.

Writing is the operation of saving any changes to a file from the computer's main memory.

Updating is altering an existing data item already written in the file.

Inserting is adding a new data item to an existing file. This implies moving all later items to make space.

Appending is adding a new item at the end of an existing file.

Overwriting is the erasing of a data item by writing another in its place.

File locking

including: read-only access, record locking, field locking
is used to prevent the contents of a data file being changed if the file involved is already being used by a different user or process.

When a data file is first accessed the operating system (or database management system) marks the file as locked so that when a different user (or process) tries to use the same data it is not allowed to do so until any changes have been made and the file is unlocked.

In multi-user systems problems can arise if more than one user is allowed to change a file at any one time. This can lead to the data being changed by one user without another user being aware of it. If the second user then saves the data, the first user's change is lost. Changes to the data could be lost if two or more users are accessing the same data at the same time.

File locking can be inconvenient in large systems and more sophisticated methods are available such as:

Read-only access that allows the data from the locked file to be viewed and used, but not changed.

Record locking that only prevents access by others to the record being updated; other records can be processed normally.

Field locking that prevents access by others to the specific field, while allowing access to the rest of the data.

Pointer

is the address or reference of a data element that allows it to be retrieved without further searching.

For example, a database which stores information about students may use pointers to identify students in a particular class. It may use one pointer to locate the first student and further pointers between the students. In this way, to find the students in a class, the pointers allow the next student in the class to be accessed without searching other parts of the database. Pointers allow fast access to data because little searching is required. When used on data stored in the computer's memory the pointer is usually the address of the data in the memory. However, in a database system the pointer may be the *primary key* (see page 262) or the reference number of the related record.

Merge

is to combine two or more ordered data structures, such as files, into a single structure in the same order. For example two lists of names, already in alphabetical order, can be merged into one list of names that is also in alphabetical order.

The order could be alphabetical or numerical but if two data files are merged the order is usually that of the *primary key*, see page 262 and Figures D3.1 and D3.2.

Sorting

including: sorting algorithms, bubble sort, selection sort, merge sort, quick sort, timsort
is arranging data items in a specified order (usually alphabetical, numerical or date order). When the data items are themselves structured – a record in a file, for example – one particular part of the structure must be specified as the item to be used in determining the ordering: this item is known as the *key* (see page 261). In a file of names and addresses, for example, the 'surname' might be used as the key. See Figure D3.3.

Sorting algorithms are the processes implemented in a computer program to arrange the data in order. There are over 40 sorting algorithms in common use each of which has its own disadvantages:

- it may be slow to sort large amounts of data;
- it may use large amounts of memory compared with the data being sorted;
- it may take a long time to sort data in unfavourable situations.

Figure D3.1 An example of two data sets being merged using 'Name' as the key field

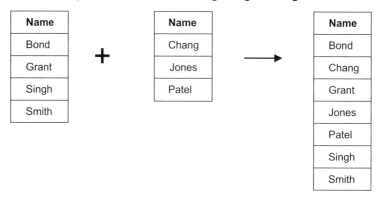

Figure D3.2 An example of two data sets being merged using 'ID' as the key field

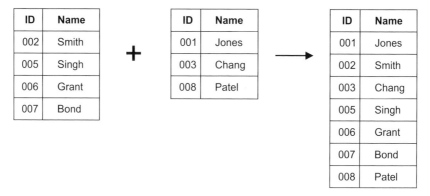

Bubble sort is a simple algorithm popular with inexperienced programmers. It is inefficient when sorting large amounts of data as the time taken is related to the square of the number of items. If 10 items take 1 ms then 100 items will take 100 ms (this is 10 times the number of items and so the time will be 10^2 or 100 times longer). It works by swapping adjacent data items until they are in order. The name is derived from the effect of data items 'bubbling up' through the data until their correct position is reached.

Selection sort is a conceptually simple algorithm popular with inexperienced programmers. It is inefficient when sorting large amounts of data as the time taken is related to the square of the number of items. If 10 items take 1 ms then 100 items will take 100 ms (this is 10 times the number of items and so the time will be 10^2 or 100 times longer). It works by taking each data item in turn, searching the rest of the list for larger items and swapping them over when found.

Figure D3.3 Two examples of a data set being sorted, one using 'ID' and the other 'Surname' as the key fields respectively

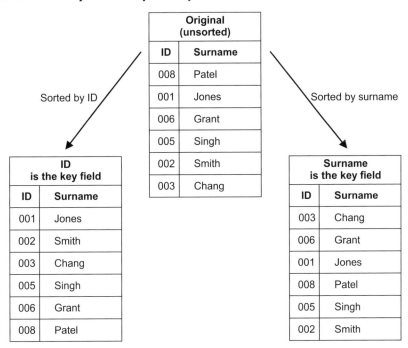

Merge sort is a relatively simple algorithm popular with more experienced programmers. It is more efficient when sorting large amounts of data as the increase in time taken is related to the logarithm of the number of items. It does, however, use considerable memory. It works by merging groups of the data that are already known to be in order. This is done with a recursive algorithm that splits the data into pairs of groups, repeated until each group is single item, and then repeatedly merges each pair of groups until a single sorted list is achieved. It is particularly suitable for sorting large data sets where the data is stored in backing store, such as on disk.

Quick sort is a simple recursive algorithm, but it is more difficult to understand how it works and so how to program it. It is popular when efficient sorting is required. It is less consistent than a merge sort but uses less memory. It works by partitioning the data into two groups where the values in one group are higher (and the other group are lower) than a specified value. The partitioning process is repeated on each group. This is done with a recursive algorithm that partitions the data into pairs of groups, repeated until each group is single item, and then repeatedly joins each pair of groups until a single sorted list is achieved.

Timsort is an optimised version of the merge sort. It provides a good balance between speed, consistency and memory used, particularly when used with data generated in real life. It works by identifying groups of data already in order and then merging them. It was named after its inventor, Tim Peters.

279

Search

including: hit, hit rate, serial search, linear search, binary search
is examining a file to see if a given data item occurs in it. Efficient methods are important in searching as searching a large amount of data requires considerable computing power. This may involve *sorting* the data (see page 277) first, which allows subsequent searches to use efficient techniques.

A *hit* is the successful location of an item.

The *hit rate* is the success rate. It is the number of items found divided by the total number of items and is usually expressed as a percentage. If a process has a high hit rate (perhaps over 10 per cent) it will be more efficient to process the whole file. If a process has a low hit rate (perhaps under 1 per cent) it will be more efficient to use a search technique, such as *indexing* (see page 371) or *binary search* (see below).

A *serial* or *linear search* involves examining each entry in turn in the file until the item is found or the end of the file is reached. Unless the file is in some useful order a serial search has to be used. (See Figure D3.4.) The average number of tries to find a single item is half the number of records, that is, 500 tries for a 1000-record file.

A *binary search* is a particularly efficient search method. It only works if records in the file are in sequence. A binary search involves accessing the middle record in the file and determining whether the target record has been found or, if not, is before or after in the sequence. This process is repeated on the part of the file where the target record is expected, until it is found. The maximum number of tries to find a single item is the base 2 logarithm of the number of records, that is, 10 tries for a 1000-record file or three tries for the eight-record example (see Figure D3.4). Obviously 10 tries will be much quicker than the 500 tries average for the *serial search*.

Figure D3.4 Comparing the two methods of searching for the key 'Singh'

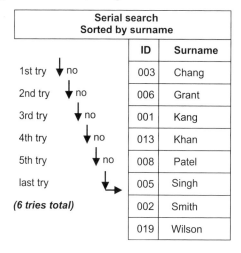

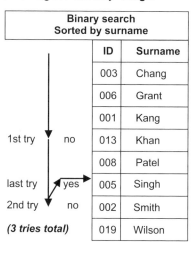

GENERAL

Corruption

is the introduction of errors into data or programs during storage or copying. It is usually due to physical causes, such as electrical *interference* (see page 353) or faulty equipment.

Data compression

including: LZW algorithm, ZIP files, zipping
is reducing the space occupied by a large file, usually for storage on backing store or for transferring it over a network.

There are many different methods, suited to different types of data. For example data compression is essential for the efficient management of digital images and video, both of which consist of a large amount of digital data, and are described in *image compression*, page 389.

For compressing other forms of data it is usual to use the LZW algorithm to produce ZIP files:

The ***LZW algorithm*** (devised by the mathematicians Lempel, Ziv and Welch) is considered to be the most efficient general method of data compression and most systems now use it.

ZIP files are produced by using the LZW algorithm to compress data files and are the most common form of storing data in a compressed form.

Zipping the data is the process of compressing data files.

As a simple example of compression consider the first paragraph of the introduction to this section on page 271. It contains 743 characters, including spaces. It can be reduced in size, without losing any of the information it contains, by replacing certain common pairs of letters by a single character. We have illustrated this by using numbers. For example, there are 18 occurrences of the pair 'th'. If these are replaced by '0', 18 characters have been saved. Making the changes listed in Figure D3.5, the introduction is reduced to 634 characters, a saving of 109 characters or about 15 per cent. The file must be re-expanded before it can be used, of course, but space has been saved in storage.

Download

including: upload
is the transfer of data from one computer to another. This is usually from a larger computer to a smaller one, for example from a mainframe to a personal computer, or across a network such as the internet to the local computer. Generally, the term is used when the user who starts the process is operating the computer that will eventually receive the file.

Figure D3.5 A simple example of data compression

Comput9 us92te6 to keep 0eir program2separ73from 03d7a 0ey op973on. 03d7a i2usually held82on3or mol file2 o4backi5 storage,86 03system2softwal encourage203us9 to believ307 03fil3i2held hel (for example, o4a disk)8ll 03time. I4fact, whe4a program wishe2to us303d7a i4a file, it i2necessary for 03portio4of 03fil3bei5 worked o4to b3copied into primary storag3i4ord9 to work o4i6ividual item2of d7a. 03system2softwa1 i21sponsibl3for copyi5 betwee4backi586 primary storage, ensur5 07 03cor1ct portio4i21adily8vailable, wi0out explicit8ctio4by 03us9. Becaus3of 0i2autom7ic management, it i2necessary for us92to8cces2file2i4a formal way.

Replacements:

0 = th	1 = re	2 = s'N'	3 = e'N'	4 = n'N'
5 = ng	6 = nd	7 = at	8 = 'N'a	9 = er

(a space is represented by 'N')

Upload is usually when the user is sending the data to another computer or site.

Raw data

is data as input to a computer, before any *validation* (see page 109) or processing.

Overflow

including: numeric overflow, stack overflow, underflow
is a general term describing what happens when something becomes too large to be processed satisfactorily. For example, the result of a numeric calculation may become too large to be stored in the space reserved for numbers (**numeric overflow**); or a data structure, such as a stack, may have space reserved for just 100 entries, so that attempting to add a 101st would cause **stack overflow**. **Underflow** is also possible, in the case of a number too small (close to zero) to be represented in the computer, or an attempt to remove an item from an empty stack. Overflow can also occur when adding a record to a random file if the location is already in use.

Rounding

including: rounding error
is the approximation of a numeric data item by its nearest equivalent, to a given number of significant figures or decimal places. For example, 1.36 rounded to one decimal place is 1.4. **Rounding error** is the error introduced by rounding (+0.04 in the example). See also *truncation*, page 283.

Truncation

including: truncation error

is the approximation of a numeric data item by ignoring all information beyond a given number of significant figures or decimal places. For example, 1.36 truncated to one decimal place is 1.3. **Truncation error** is the error introduced by truncation (–0.06 in the example). This use of the term 'error' comes from mathematics and is important in situations where numbers are represented in a fixed-length format but should not be confused with other uses of the term. See also *error*, page 230, *floating-point representation*, page 266, and *rounding*, page 282.

PART E: HARDWARE

Computer systems can be assembled out of a variety of different pieces of equipment in a whole variety of different arrangements. This part of the *Glossary* defines terms that will be encountered when considering how computer systems are arranged, organised and connected to other computer systems. Terms related to the uses of computers are in Parts A and B, and terms concerned with the internal workings of computers are in Parts C and D. Part F is concerned with the way software is used.

E1 TYPES OF COMPUTER

This section includes those terms that are descriptive of computers in general.

A digital computer is an automatic, programmable, data processor. Every part of this definition is crucial to our understanding of what the modern computer is, and how it works.

Automatic means simply that it operates without human intervention, except where this is expressly preplanned and provided for. This feature alone distinguishes the computer from the simple pocket calculator, where each computation results from a manual key press.

Programmable means that the instructions to be followed automatically are held (as a 'program') within the store of the computer. If a repetitive calculation (a 'loop') is necessary, the same instructions can be used and reused. The instructions are usually held in the same storage area as that used for data – computer programs and the data they operate on can comfortably coexist in the same sort of storage.

Digital means that the computer operates with quantities that take only distinct values from a known range: often these are binary quantities that take only two values, which represent the digits 0 and 1. The power of digital data is that sequences of 0s and 1s can represent a wide range of types of data, including pictures, music, text and others. Notice that, because programs and data can occupy the same storage in the computer, program instructions are also expressed digitally. Although digital processing is now almost universal, some computers do not work this way – see **analog computer**, page 288.

Finally, the last two words, **data processor**, simply express what a computer does – it uses digital data, and produces results.

Computer generations

including: first-generation computers, EDSAC, EDVAC, ENIAC, DEUCE, Pegasus, LEO (Lyons Electronic Office), UNIVAC I, second-generation computer, Atlas, third-generation computer, ICL 1900, IBM 360, fourth-generation computer, fifth-generation computer
are a convenient way of distinguishing major advances in computer technology. The first three generations have well-accepted meanings, but the later generations tend to be used by manufacturers to stress the more modern features of a particular machine; the generation terminology appears to be falling into disuse.

First-generation computers were the earliest designs. They used valves, mercury delay lines, electrostatic memories and had very limited storage. Important first-generation computers include the experimental *EDSAC*, *EDVAC* and *ENIAC* (which lacked stored-program facilities, and would now fail our definition of computer) and the production scientific computers *DEUCE* and *Pegasus*. Commercial machines were *LEO (Lyons Electronic Office)* and *UNIVAC I*. These machines were all large, typically filling one or more rooms, and consumed large amounts of power.

Second-generation computers arrived when the transistor replaced the valve as the basic component. They were consequently much more reliable, and consumed less power. They were cheaper, but still out of reach for most businesses and certainly for individuals. One of the most significant machines was *Atlas*.

Third-generation computers saw the transistor replaced by the *integrated circuit* (the 'silicon chip'), see page 338. Again they were cheaper, and consumed less power and became even more reliable. One consequence of new design methods was the ability to produce whole families of computers that were similar but of different computing power – the *ICL 1900* series, or the *IBM 360* family, for example.

Fourth-generation computers are those commonly encountered today. There is no single technological advance that distinguishes fourth-generation computers from the third-generation, except possibly the much greater use of *large-scale integration* (see page 338) of components on silicon chips, which resulted in increasing similarity of machine design. A dramatic fall in the cost of internal memory, and increases in the speed and capacity of external storage, led to new applications and new methods of programming. In addition there was a growing realisation that standardisation of software, particularly operating systems, was necessary.

Fifth-generation computers are a vision of a totally different way of designing and using computer systems. It involves both novel computer architectures and new types of software, and the vision has been achieved in some respects. It focuses on virtual reality, expert systems and natural language interfaces that can interact with people.

Analog computer

including: hybrid computer
is a different design of computer from the digital computers we normally use. Instead of operating on digital data, these use continuously variable quantities. For example, the electrical current may represent the value of the data, which will vary continuously as a smooth change rather than in discrete jumps. In theory every possible change can be represented no matter how small. It is also possible to design mechanical analog computers.

This term is now mainly of historic interest. Inevitably, some computers, known as *hybrid computers*, used both analog and digital technology in combination.

Digital computers

including: computing power, Macintosh®, iMac®, personal computer, PC, micro, desktop computer, tower, mini-tower, portable computer, laptop computer, notebook computer, smartphone, tablets, hand-held, minicomputer, mainframe computer, supercomputer
are computers that operate with digital data. These are quantities that take only two values, such as 'off' or 'on', which are represented by the digits 0 and 1. More complex data is represented by combining binary digits into binary numbers; see also Section D1 Data representation and Section D2 Numeric data representation.

Originally, a 'computer' was something that filled a room, needed air-conditioning and several operators to run it. Rapid technological advances allowed computers with the same power to become available in much smaller packages, leading to a range of computers of different sizes and capabilities. **Computing power** is a measure of the speed at which the computer works and the complexity of the operations performed. Newer computers tend to be smaller (and faster) than those they replace. See also *embedded systems*, page 4. Names are needed to distinguish each new type of computer.

A significant development of the late 1970s was the introduction of a type of computer small enough and cheap enough to be bought by individuals. Apple® led the way commercially with their range of computers that offered the first convenient *graphical user interface* (see page 417), the **Macintosh®** through to the **iMac®**. IBM introduced the **personal computer** (or **PC**). A general name was needed for these types of small computer. The following names are all relative to one another, and are often ill-defined. Most personal computers and Macintosh® computers now are more powerful than the earlier computers, whose descendants are now known as mainframes.

Recently the introduction of mobile computing devices such as **smartphones** and **tablet** computers (see page 290) have seen the development of miniaturisation to the extent that hand-held devices have high capacity and power. This has enabled them to become all-in-one devices with the ability to record audio and video, take photos, access the internet and use *apps*, see page 89.

Micro became the general name, with 'PC' the name for computers based on the original IBM design. These PCs were also known as IBM compatibles. The various types of PC could run the same software without needing any changes (but see also *software version*, page 44). The term used most often currently is PC.

Desktop computer is used at a desk as a tool for the individual user. It is a conventional micro with a full-sized screen and keyboard. It needs a mains power supply so cannot be described as easily portable. The box containing the central processor, disk drives and other storage usually provides the support for the monitor; however, the box may be in the shape of a **tower** designed to stand on the floor by a desk or be small enough to stand on the desk beside the monitor, when it is called a **mini-tower**.

Many large organisations now use *thin-client* terminals rather than PCs (see page 135).

As computers have become smaller, lighter and more powerful, **portable computers** have been developed. Most portable computers include facilities to transfer data to a larger machine or network. These include the following:

- **Laptop computer** runs off battery power as well as mains electricity. It is normally between 2 kg and 3 kg in weight, and its *footprint* (see page 291) is about the size of an A4 sheet of paper so it can be carried in a briefcase. It is suited for use while travelling or at business meetings. Currently, users expect communications capability, significant storage, and a DVD writer. Many of them can be connected to a full-sized monitor. They are also called **notebook computers**.

- **Smartphones** are pocket-sized devices that are mobile phones as well as mobile computers with internet connectivity. They are a development of the mobile phone and most solely interact with the user through a touch-screen interface. A lot of the features of earlier mobile devices are incorporated into these devices.

- **Tablet PCs** are larger hand-held devices, usually with a touch screen only, that runs with a mobile operating system and uses application software known as *apps* (see page 123), which are downloaded onto the device. It is rapidly becoming a major platform for internet browsing.

Minicomputer is a larger, more powerful computer, usually accessed from several *terminals* (see page 139). It is small and inexpensive enough to be bought by small- and medium-sized organisations. Current applications include internet communication and managing checkouts at supermarkets. Such machines may be used as *servers* (see page 137) on a network. They are now often considered to be small *mainframes*.

Mainframe computer is the term for the large computer usually accessed from many (sometimes several thousand) terminals. It is used mainly for large-scale data processing in businesses, such as managing central databases.

Supercomputer is a very large computer that works very fast indeed. It is likely to have many processors working in parallel to achieve this. Data is processed simultaneously (in parallel processors) as well as sequentially to complete tasks very quickly. Examples include computers used for weather forecasting and testing aircraft design.

Stand-alone computer

is a computer that is not connected to others by a network and cannot share devices such as data storage or printers.

Front-end processor (FEP)

is a computer dedicated to managing communications devices or other computers linked to a more powerful computer system, generally a *mainframe* (see page 186). The front-end processor receives messages and commands from the communications devices, and organises these before passing them on to the larger computer for processing.

Multiprocessor system

is a computer system with several *processors* (see page 324). These will work cooperatively, handling specific tasks (managing the screen display, doing arithmetic computation, handling peripherals) or simply sharing out the processing to enable parts of a task to proceed simultaneously (in parallel). See also *parallel processing*, page 328.

Quantum computers

are based on the properties of subatomic particles (quantum mechanics). These are at a theoretical stage of development. If their potential is achieved they are likely to run billions of times faster than *supercomputers* currently do (see page 290).

Word processor

is a computer dedicated to, or primarily for, word processing. Some have displays that are the proportions of conventional paper sizes; some offer black text on a white, or coloured, background; most provide an extended keyboard with function keys for the software provided with the computer. Nearly all these facilities are now available as standard on general-purpose computers.

Original equipment manufacturer (OEM)

including: badging, proprietary
is a firm that makes basic computer hardware for other manufacturers to build into their products. For example, a manufacturer assembles a washing machine using a microprocessor from an OEM as a control device, or a computer manufacturer fits another manufacturer's disk drive mechanisms into their computer. Many components of computer systems are made by only a small number of manufacturers, and are then built into systems that are sold by other manufacturers under their own brand name: this practice is known as ***badging***. Software or hardware may be marketed and sold under a name that is patented or is a registered trademark, which is known as a ***proprietary*** name.

Footprint

is the amount of space (area) taken up by a peripheral or computer on a desk.

E2 INPUT

Other related terms may be found in Section F4 (for sound), Section E6 and Section E7 (for communications), Section F3 (for graphics), Section B5 (for control and monitoring) and Section B4 (commercial data processing) for automated input applications.

A computer operates on data (including instructions). The data, the input, must be entered into the computer. There are many devices that could be used for the purpose of entering data, called **input devices**.

Input devices are one type of the many peripherals that can be attached to a computer system to do particular jobs and which are frequently necessary for the effective use of a computer system. There is a range of devices and any computer system is unlikely to have all possible types provided. This section is not exhaustive and some input peripherals have been covered in other sections. For example, **sound**, **communications**, **monitoring** and **control** each have their own input peripherals and details will be found in the sections listed above.

There are various means, requiring hardware devices and software techniques, to deal with the different ways in which the input is presented to the computer system. Input devices, which may be manual or automatic, deliver the data in a format that is suitable for processing by the computer system. The data may also be transferred into one computer system from another, for example over a network (including the internet) or from CD-ROM, particularly for large volumes of data.

For **manual** devices, the data items are provided by the user's action, such as typing at a keyboard, moving a mouse or speaking into a microphone. The device converts the input to **machine-readable** form before it can be processed by the computer. Further conversion may be carried out by the software within the computer. The most familiar input devices are the **keyboard**, by which data is entered, together with the **mouse**, or its alternatives the **trackerball** or **trackpad**. Personal digital assistants (PDAs) have built-in input devices that allow direct input and recognition of handwriting.

Automated input devices read data items that are already encoded and machine readable, and transfer them directly to the computer for processing without further user action. This is used, for example, for data already stored magnetically on a credit card or a machine-readable passport. An important, but often overlooked, input is printed matter read into a computer using a **scanner**.

MANUAL INPUT

Keyboard

including: qwerty keyboard, numeric keypad, function key, embedded keyboard
is the typical typewriter-like input device used with all general-purpose computers. The number of keys on the keyboard will not be the same for all computer keyboards nor is the arrangement necessarily the same, because it will vary according to the country or application where it is used.

Part of the keyboard is likely to be arranged in the same way as a traditional typewriter; this is called a **qwerty keyboard** (so called because of the order of the first row of letter keys).

Sometimes the numeric keys are repeated as a separate block called a **numeric keypad**. This aids rapid one-handed data entry.

In addition to the keys for letters, numbers, punctuation marks and Enter (or Return), a typical keyboard will have special keys that, when pressed, change the effect of other keys on the keyboard. This includes ESC (escape), CTRL (control), SHIFT and ALT and some **function keys**. What these keys do will depend on the software, rather than the hardware, being used. For example pressing F1 may call up a *help system* (see page 426).

It is sometimes possible for the user to assign part of the keyboard for special purposes. This part of the keyboard is called an **embedded keyboard**. For example, keyboards with a restricted number of keys, such as on laptop computers, allow a group of the keys to be assigned the role of a numeric keypad if the user wishes.

Mouse

including: mouse mat, mouse button, mouse event, scroll wheel
is an input device, similar in shape and size to a dormouse, communicating with the computer either by a thin cable connection or by wireless. Moving the mouse (by hand) in contact with a special flat surface, called a **mouse mat**, causes a rolling ball on the under side of the mouse, or an optical sensor, to detect motion. This movement is echoed on the display screen by movements of a pointer or cursor.

A mouse has one, or more, finger-operated press switches, called (mouse) **buttons**. When a mouse button is pressed or released it causes a 'click' and passes a signal to the computer. These are sometimes called **mouse events**. (See also *event*, page 192.) What effect such events have will depend upon where the pointer is on the screen and what software is being used. Mouse operations, such as *clicking* (see page 419), dragging (see *drag*, page 422) and combinations of these with the use of keys on the keyboard, provide a wide range of possible options at any moment. Some mouses have an additional control called a **scroll wheel**, which makes dragging and scrolling easier to control.

Alternatives to a mouse are a *trackerball* or a *trackpad* (see page 294).

Trackerball

also known as: trackball
including: trackpad, trackpoint
is an input device that is used to do the same actions as a *mouse* (see page 293). It is a ball, set into a cup, which can be made to roll in any direction by using a finger or the palm of a hand, depending on the size of the ball. The movements of the ball are echoed on the screen by a pointer, and finger-operated switches work in the same way as mouse *buttons* (see page 293). Trackerballs can be used on *laptop computers* (see page 290), being easier to use in a confined space than a mouse. An alternative to a trackerball is a **trackpad**, where movements of a finger over a sensitive plate are used to control the movements of the screen pointer. A **trackpoint** is a small extra 'button' on the keyboard that works like a *joystick* and responds to a finger movement to control the movement of the screen pointer.

Touch-sensitive device

including: touchscreen, touch-sensitive keyboard, stylus
is a device that responds to touch to enable the user to input data or instructions.

Touchscreens are used on many *tablets* and *smartphones* (see page 290). Input is by touching the screen with finger(s) or a *stylus*. An on-screen keyboard can be used for textual input. (See *handwriting recognition*, below.)

A **touch-sensitive keyboard** is a keyboard on which the 'keys' are areas on a sensitive surface. These keyboards are generally used in special situations, for example where there is a risk of dirt or liquids getting into a conventional keyboard. They are seen on checkout tills and in self-service restaurants. Overlays are put on the keyboard to indicate the areas and their meaning, and software interprets these for the computer.

A **stylus** is a device shaped like a pencil used for drawing on a touchscreen or *graphics tablet* (see page 393). The movement of the stylus is detected by the screen or tablet and its software in one of a variety of ways, for example through the use of a wire matrix in the pad. In some specialist applications the angular movement of a mechanical arm supporting the stylus is detected. A stylus may be pressure sensitive, producing a darker or more intensely coloured line if pressed firmly.

Pressure controls

including: pressure pad, pressure switch, single switch devices
is the form of sensor **pads** or **switches**, operated by pressure or touch, that are used as input devices for some applications. They can be used in conjunction with special software to enable people with physical disabilities to select items displayed on a screen by touching (or pressing) the pad when the item needed is highlighted. They are often known as **single switch devices**. See also *touch-sensitive keyboard*, above, and *graphics tablet*, page 393.

Handwriting recognition

is the analysis of handwritten input, comparing the result with samples already stored in the computer and turning it into characters that can be processed by the computer.

In simpler systems the user has to write in discrete characters. Although some software can recognise cursive (joined-up) writing, this needs greater processing power and the system has to be 'trained' to recognise an individual's handwriting.

Interactive whiteboard

is a large version of a computer display combined with the facilities of a *touchscreen* (see page 294). The image is displayed either by rear projection or front projection, although large LCD screens are an expensive alternative. As the user writes on this board, it is scanned by sensors, either behind the screen or along its edge, and the image is fed to the computer.

Speech recognition

including: speech recognition software
is analysing spoken words recorded through a microphone and comparing them with those known to the system. **Speech recognition software** enables data or instructions to be spoken to the computer, for use by software such as a word-processing package. Specialist vocabularies are available with additional words for particular types of user, such as accountants or pathologists. However, the differences between the same words spoken by different people still make this an unreliable process and the software has to be 'trained' to work with each user. For accurate recognition words need to be spoken separately and consistently, but some software can accept continuous speech.

AUTOMATED INPUT

Machine readable

describes data or instructions that can be entered into a computer without the need for any preparation. This data may be stored magnetically, for instance on a credit card or travel ticket, or printed on paper that is also readable by humans. See also *magnetic ink character recognition (MICR)* (see page 113), *document reader* (see page 114) and *optical character recognition (OCR)* (see page 114).

Automated reader

also known as: card reader
including: magnetic stripe, card encoder, swipe card, smart card
can read or scan data already stored in electronic form on cards such as credit cards, travel tickets or car park passes. The data may be written on a **magnetic stripe** on the card by a (magnetic) **card encoder**. Such cards, which are swiped through a slot in the card reader, are known as **swipe cards**. The cards are easily read but contain only small amounts of data. See also *PIN* (page 162).

More complex readers will read data stored on, and send data to, a **smart card**, a plastic card with a microprocessor sealed inside it. A smart card is more versatile than a magnetic stripe card; in particular it can:

- hold more information, which can be altered as required;

- encrypt the data, making it difficult for unauthorised users to understand it (see *encryption*, page 163);

- ensure that a user is authorised to perform a particular action by the use of various security checks.

Readers can also be used to read *personal identification devices (PID)*, see page 162, giving secure entry to restricted areas.

Scanner

including: image scanner, flat-bed scanner, sheet-feed scanner, hand-held scanner, bar code reader, bar code scanner
is a device that systematically traverses a page or object with a beam of light in order to sense and retrieve an image that may then be stored in a computer. There are several techniques and devices to deal with the variety of types of input so that the computer can recognise, interpret and use the data.

An ***image scanner*** is an input device that scans a document (text and/or graphics) and sends to the computer an image of the input in a form that a graphics package can use, normally a *bit map* (see page 306). Either a beam of light moves over the drawing or text or the paper moves through the scanner past the stationary light. A detector senses the reflected light and separates out the colours and intensities. See also *optical character recognition*, page 114.

In a ***flat-bed scanner***, the object to be scanned is placed face downwards on a flat surface (usually glass) and a light source and sensors move backwards and forwards across it.

In a ***sheet-feed scanner***, the paper passes over the read head. Some flat-bed scanners have a sheet-feeder attachment that places the document, page by page, on the glass platen where it is scanned by the moving read head.

A user moves a ***hand-held scanner*** over the object to be scanned.

A ***bar code reader or bar code scanner*** is an input device used to read information in *bar code* form (see page 112). Sometimes the reader is built into equipment such as a supermarket checkout terminal, where it is usually referred to as a scanner. This form of reader shines laser light beams onto the object being scanned and interprets the reflected patterns of the bar code.

E3 MEMORY

Memory is the part of a computer system that stores the data for use by the processors. This data is made up of program files and data files for use by the programs. Generally there are three categories of memory each defined by the purpose it serves:

- The holding of programs and data that the processor needs immediately – for this reason it is sometimes known as **immediate-access memory**.

- The holding of programs and data that may be needed sometime later – often called **backing store**.

- In order to gain access to documents, data, etc. wherever the user may be, there is **the cloud** as backing store (see page 299).

Most processor operations involve the movement of data around the immediate-access memory, so it is necessary to read from and to write to immediate-access memory very quickly. Backing store is usually only accessed by the processor in order to load the data so it can have comparatively slower reading and writing speeds. Generally, immediate-access memory is at least 1000 times faster than backing store. In order to keep the speed of the immediate-access store as high as possible it is physically located on the processor circuit board, whereas backing store can be in separate units connected to the processor by cables (e.g. by a USB cable or network connection).

Memory and storage have meanings that overlap and are often used as interchangeable words; but memory suggests data is immediately available, whereas storage suggests that data has to be retrieved. Sometimes memory is described as **primary**, for the immediate-access memory; **secondary**, for the principal backing store; and **auxiliary**, for other forms of backing store. A variety of other names are used for immediate-access memory, such as immediate-access store (IAS), main memory, memory and store, and for backing store, such as backup memory, peripheral memory, offline storage.

Throughout the development of computers there has been a continual search for ways of improving memory technology. The search has been for reliable, compact storage devices with low energy consumption. Whenever a suitable new device has been developed, ways of cheap mass production have been found.

Because of the different requirements for the two functions of memory, it is usual for completely different kinds of technology to be used in a particular computer system. For immediate-access memory, most present-day computers use some form of random-access memory integrated circuits, in which very large amounts of data can be stored in a single plastic encapsulated chip. For backing store there is some form of magnetic storage (such as disks or tapes) and also optical storage (such as CDs or DVDs).

Immediate-access memory is sometimes in two parts. One part, called **cache memory**, is made up of a small capacity, but exceedingly fast, memory and is located next to the processor. The other part is much larger, and a copy of some of its contents is put into the cache memory in readiness for instant use. The choice of size for the main memory of a computer is partly determined by the addressing methods used and the cost of memory components. It is usual for computers to be sold with the potential for later memory expansion.

Backing store consists of the medium (the material on which the data is stored) and any associated mechanisms. Most computers use magnetic backing store (tapes or disks), while some use integrated circuit semiconductor memory. Optical systems are increasingly being used. As far as the user is concerned, the medium may be removable, for example tapes and optical disks; or fixed, for example hard disks. The advantage of using removable media is that an expensive mechanism can be used for a variety of purposes with cheap media. Fixed disks provide faster access and greater capacity than removable disks and are used to store programs and data that are frequently needed. Most computer systems now have both fixed and removable disks. A large computer system will have fixed disks, removable disks, tape storage and optical storage. A personal computer will have at least a hard fixed disk and an optical disk unit.

Memory may be **volatile** or **permanent**. Volatile memory loses its data when there is no power supply to it, whereas permanent memory does not require power. All magnetic and optical media provide permanent memory, as do some forms of integrated circuit memory. However, the most widely used form of integrated circuit memory for immediate-access store is volatile; this means that, when the computer is switched on, programs and data have to be loaded from backing store. If power is cut off, for some reason, then all data in memory will be lost.

Memory is often described by the type of **access** that is possible. For example, all the storage locations in immediate-access memory can be directly accessed and the access time for all locations is the same; this is described as **random-access memory**. In contrast, the data stored on a tape can only be reached by going through the tape, in sequence, until the right place is found; this is described as **serial-access memory**. Storage on a disk is in concentric rings and is a collection of small sequential lengths of storage. Since disk storage can be so quickly accessed, it is generally thought of as direct (random) access storage.

Some memory is only able to be read (known as **read-only memory**) and may take one of two possible forms:

- Once the data has been written to the memory it is fixed and unalterable by any means – the data is often written at the time of manufacture of the device it is in.

- The data may only be altered by the use of special facilities (e.g. by a program or by hardware) – such memory chips are known as **programmable memory** chips and their uses include storing programs for controlling devices (e.g. traffic lights and lifts) and in computer games consoles. When a computer is switched on it loads a program from such a group of chips (called the *BIOS*, page 171), this allows for the BIOS to be upgraded later if necessary. The process of upgrading the data on such chips is often referred to as a flash upgrade.

GENERAL CONCEPTS

Storage

also known as: memory
is a general term covering all units of computer equipment used to store data (and programs).

Memory

also known as: store
including: (store) location, (store) address, main store, immediate-access store (IAS), primary store, (memory) cell
The memory, or store, is the part of a computer system where data and instructions are held for use by the central processor and where the central processor puts results it generates. The computer store is made up of a large number of identifiable units, called **(store) locations**. Each store location has a unique label, called a **(store) address**, which is recognisable and used by the central processor. Those store locations that can be addressed directly by the central processor are called the **main store**, **immediate-access store (IAS)** or **primary store**. A store location, sometimes called a **(memory) cell**, is capable of holding a single item of data, a *word* or *byte* (see page 14).

Backing store

also known as: secondary store, mass storage
including: magnetic disk storage, optical disk storage, magneto-optical storage, the cloud
is a means of storing large amounts of data outside the *immediate-access store* (see above). A computer system will have at least one form of backing store. Most backing store uses magnetic storage, but increasing use is being made of optical storage systems. Backing store is sometimes referred to as *secondary store* or *mass storage*.

Magnetic disk storage is backing store in which flat rotatable circular plates, coated with a magnetic material, are used for storing digital data. The data is written to and read from a set of concentric circular *tracks* (see *magnetic disk*, page 300).

Optical disk storage is backing store that uses plastic discs on which the data is stored as patterns on the surface. One method uses hollows etched into the surface of the disk for prerecorded data in the form of *CD-ROMs* (see page 303). Other methods provide read/write optical storage.

Magneto-optical storage is backing store that uses plastic discs on which data is stored by a combination of optical and magnetic methods.

The cloud used as backing store makes access and storage available wherever the user may be (see page 88).

Volatile memory

including: non-volatile memory, permanent memory
is a form of storage that holds data only while power is supplied. This is in contrast to **non-volatile memory**, which keeps its contents even when the system is switched off. All currently used forms of magnetic storage and optical disk storage are non-volatile, but most other forms of storage are volatile. **Permanent memory** retains its contents regardless of power supply and cannot be erased or altered; many forms of read-only memory (ROM) are permanent.

DISK

Magnetic disk

also known as: computer disk, disk
including: hard disk, platter, disk pack, track (disk), cylinder
is a circular plate, usually made of plastic or thin rigid metal, coated with a layer of magnetic material on which data can be stored by magnetically setting the arrangement of the magnetic material. This is done by electromagnetic *read/write heads* (see page 301).

Hard disk is a rigid disk, when it is also known as a **platter**.

Disk pack is where a disk drive has multiple disks (platters) – these are generally rigid, hard disks on a common spindle with separate read/write heads for each disk.

The general layout of recording surfaces on a disk and on a multi-surface disk pack is shown in Figure E3.1. Data is stored on disks in concentric rings, called **tracks**. In a disk pack, a set of tracks one above the other, for example the tenth track on each disk, is called a **cylinder**. It is normal to store data that needs to be kept together on a cylinder rather than on one disk, because the read/write heads will not need to move to access the data.

Figure E3.1 Tracks on a disk and a cylinder

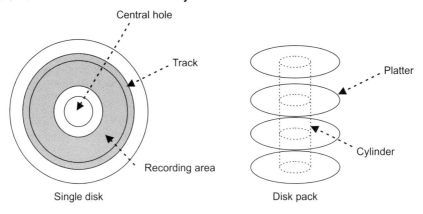

Magnetic disk drive

including: hard disk drive
is the unit made up of the mechanism that rotates the disks between the *read/write heads* (see below) and the mechanism that controls the heads. Most disk drives have one set of read/write heads for each surface that have to be moved to the required track.

Hard disk drives use rigid magnetic disk(s) enclosed in a sealed container. This has the advantage of allowing high recording density because the recording heads can be very close to the magnetic material on the disk.

Read/write head

including: disk access time, seek time, latency, head crash, park
is the set of electromagnets and necessary circuitry used to magnetise the magnetic material used for storage or to read from it. Most disk units have the set of heads on an arm, which moves them from track to track, but fixed head disk units have a set of heads for each track, which greatly reduces the time taken to access data on the disk. Double-sided disks require a set of heads for each side. The time taken to get data from a disk, the **disk access time**, includes the time taken to move the heads to the correct track, called the **seek time**, and the time taken for the disk to rotate to the correct part of the track, sometimes called **latency**. However, some people use latency to mean the total waiting time.

Head crash is when the read/write heads hit the surface of a disk. This can cause serious damage to the mechanisms and loss of data. To avoid this happening with personal computers, for example when a machine is moved, the read/write heads are often automatically put in a safe position (**parked**) whenever they are not being used to access the disk. Following the proper procedures of closing all files before ending a session of work will ensure that the disk is properly parked. Some early personal computers required the user to give the command for parking the disk.

Disk array

including: RAID (redundant array of inexpensive disks)
is a set of disk units used as if they are a single mass storage device. By using two disks to hold the same data, a disk drive fault will be unlikely to have any effect on the operation of the whole system. By writing some of the data to each of a number of disks, storage and retrieval of data can be speeded up. This method of organising backing store for large computer systems is known as **RAID**, which stands for **redundant array of inexpensive** (or **independent**) **disks**. RAID systems provide a low-cost method of ensuring that losses of data are nearly impossible.

Disk format

including: sector, disk formatting, disk verification
is the arrangement and organisation of the *tracks* (see Figure E3.1) on a disk.

Sector is where each track is divided into a number of equal-length blocks, which are known as sectors. A sector is the smallest addressable portion of a track and is the smallest unit of data that is written to or read from a disk. Normally each sector on each track holds the same amount of data, even though outer tracks are longer than inner tracks, so the *density of data* depends upon the distance of the track from the centre of the disk. Some disk systems use variable speed disks, which then have different amounts of data on each track.

Disk formatting is the initial preparation of a blank (unformatted) disk for subsequent writing and reading. This is achieved by adding control information such as track and sector numbering. When this has been done then the disk is known as a format-ted disk. Reformatting a disk that contains data will erase all the data on it.

Disk verification is the checking of a formatted disk to ensure that all the tracks and sectors are fit for recording data. This includes checking that any data on the disk is readable.

Solid-state drive

Also known as: SSD
is a collection of memory chips that is controlled by its own software to make the collec-tion of chips act like a disk drive. Solid-state drives are replacing hard disks in some computers.

Features of solid-state drives (compared with hard disk drives) are:

- faster random access, due to not having to move a read/write head;
- faster start-up, because no spin-up of the disk is necessary;
- no noise, because a fan is not required;
- no defragmenting is required;
- power requirements are less;
- capacity is limited – current capacities of a hard disk drive are much greater.

The main difference between a solid-state drive and a *USB memory stick* (see page 304) is that the former is intended to be used in place of a hard-disk drive, whereas the latter is used as a portable storage unit for computer files.

Optical storage

including: WORM (write-once, read-many), CD-ROM (compact disc read-only memory), CD-R (compact disc-recordable), CD-RW (compact disc-read/write), DVD (digital versatile/video disc), BD (Blu-ray disc)
uses laser technology to etch the surface of a storage medium to form minute patterns that represent the data. The scattering effect on a narrow laser beam is used to read the data, which may be digital or analog. The storage medium can take any of several

physical forms and various data formats. The data may include programs as well as sound, graphics or text data. Optical storage with a computer capable of manipulating, storing and outputting high quality sound and graphics is a multimedia system. See *multimedia*, page 4.

Table E3.1 lists the various formats of optical storage disks currently in use.

Table E3.1 Optical storage

Format of disk	Description	Notes
CD-ROM (compact disc read-only memory)	Manufactured with the data preset at manufacture (pressed).	Used for audio CDs and data CDs.
CD-R (compact disc-recordable)	Uses dye technology to enable the writing of data to the disk.	Once written to the disk acts as a CD-ROM.
CD-RW (compact disc-read/write)	Uses a technology that not only allows the writing of data to the disk, but also allows previously written data to be erased/overwritten with new data.	Sometimes called a read/write CD.
DVD (digital versatile disc, formerly digital video disc)	In essence a large capacity CD coupled with a faster data transfer rate; this allows for video to be stored and replayed. It is available in the same recordable and rewritable formats as CDs.	Used for video (having replaced video-tape in the home). Due to their large capacity DVDs are also used for data storage.
BD (Blu-ray disc)	A very high capacity 'DVD-like' disk that uses blue laser light to read/write the data. It was developed because HD television requires much greater amounts of data to be stored compared with standard television. It is available in the same recordable and rewritable formats as CDs.	A Blu-ray disc can store 25 Gb on a layer. A disk can be multilayered; dual-layer disks can store 50 Gb (approximately 9 hours of HD television).

WORM (write-once, read-many) is an optical disk system that allows the user to write data on the next available portion of the disk. A portion of the disk can have data written on it only once, but all the data can be read as often as required. Some WORM disks allow the overwriting of data so as to spoil it, effectively erasing it, but not regaining the storage space. (This should not to be confused with *worm* as a virus, see page 166.)

MISCELLANEOUS FORMS OF MEMORY

Portable storage device

including: flash drive, pen drive, memory stick, USB stick
is a form of portable backing store that is easily connected/disconnected to a computer.

Flash drive, also known as **pen drive, memory stick** or **USB stick**, is a mostly robust device, small enough to be carried in a pocket. It consists of a form of *semiconductor memory* (see below) often known as flash memory. When connected, a PC will treat it as an additional installed disk drive. It usually has a USB interface, see *expansion slot*, page 335. They are available in a range of capacities.

Memory card

including: Secure Digital (SD), Memory Stick (MS)
is a small portable storage device for use in various electronic devices like digital cameras (both still and video), games consoles, mobile phones etc. There have been several types of memory card over the years, none of which are interchangeable. Currently the main ones are **Secure Digital (SD)** and Sony's **Memory Stick (MS)**. They are obtainable in various capacities and SD cards have differing classes depending upon use – usually because of the differing speed of access.

Most computers nowadays have the appropriate interface to various memory cards to be used, thus allowing the transfer of images/video to the computer for possible editing or longer term storage.

Semiconductor memory

also known as: integrated circuit memory
including: MOS, CMOS
is a form of memory that uses integrated circuit semiconductor chips. The storage capacity of this form of memory is very high, the time taken to read a data item is very short and the access is direct. There are a number of different forms of semiconductor storage; the more common ones use **MOS** (metal oxide semiconductor) or **CMOS** (complementary MOS) technology. The advantage of CMOS types is that they require little power to retain their contents; powered by small batteries they can be used as non-volatile memory while the computer is switched off (see *volatile memory*, page 300). Most current computer designs use semiconductor memory for immediate-access storage.

RAM (random access memory)

including: static RAM, dynamic RAM (DRAM), refreshed
is memory that has the same access time for all locations. Each location holds one *word* or *byte* (see page 11) and is directly addressable. RAM may be either **static**, which holds its memory so long as there is a power supply, or **dynamic**, which has to be **refreshed** by reading and rewriting the contents very frequently (about every 2 milliseconds). Dynamic RAM (**DRAM**) is more widely used than static RAM because it needs less power. Both dynamic and static RAM are *volatile* (see *volatile memory*, page 300). See also *semiconductor memory*, page 304.

RAM disk

also known as: silicon disk
is a part of main memory that is addressed as if it were a very fast random access disk. It behaves as an extremely fast backing store for the user but is usually volatile and has to be loaded from backing store. It is normally an area of main memory reserved for this use.

ROM (read-only memory)

including: PROM (programmable ROM), EPROM (erasable PROM), EAROM (electrically alterable ROM), EEPROM (electrically erasable PROM), flash PROM, cartridge
is memory from which the contents may be read but cannot be written to by the computer system. Read-only memory is used for both data and programs. There are optical ROM systems (see *CD-ROM*, page 303, and semiconductor (integrated circuit) ROM systems (see *semiconductor memory*, page 304).

The term **ROM** is frequently used to mean the (integrated circuit) read-only memory used to hold programs and associated data for building into computers. Software in ROM is fixed during manufacture, but there are other ways of putting programs and data into ROM.

PROM (programmable ROM) is a type of ROM that is manufactured as an empty storage array and is later permanently programmed by the user.

EPROM (erasable PROM) is a type of PROM whose data can be erased by a special process (e.g. by exposure to ultraviolet radiation) so new data can be written as if it were a new PROM.

EAROM (electrically alterable ROM) and **EEPROM (electrically erasable PROM)**, sometimes called flash PROM, are other similar types of read-only memory.

Some small computers and games computers use software on (integrated circuit) ROM, which is packaged in plug-in modules called **cartridges**. This is a convenient way of preventing the software from being copied.

Cache memory

also known as: cache
including: disk caching
is a part of the main store, between the central processor and the rest of the main store. It has extremely fast access, so sections of a program and its associated data

Figure E3.2 Cache memory

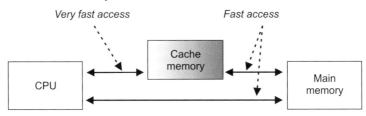

are copied there to take advantage of its short fetch cycle (see *fetch-execute cycle*, page 326). The use of cache memory can greatly reduce processing time.

A way of speeding up the transfer of large amounts of data from disks is to use ***disk caching***, that is, using a section of memory for holding data that has been read from disk storage. See also *buffering*, page 329.

GENERAL

Block

including: bucket
is the name for the smallest unit of data that is transferred between backing store and main store in one operation. In large computer systems, a ***bucket*** defines a unit of storage in random-access memory. A bucket will contain a (variable) number of blocks. Access to the data is by reference to the bucket it is in.

Memory map

including: bit map, disk map, file allocation table (FAT)
describes the way storage is organised in a computer. For example, sections of memory may be allocated to the screen display, program code or variables.

A ***bit map*** is a pattern of bits describing the organisation of data. It may provide an index into a section of memory or, more directly, each bit may hold one item of data such as the state of each individual pixel in a graphics package.

The memory map for disk storage is called a ***disk map***. It describes how the information held on the disk is organised. It is kept on the same hard disk and may be held as a bit map. Details of where files are stored in secondary memory are kept in a ***file allocation table (FAT)***, which is a file also kept in the secondary memory. See also *directory*, page 423.

Write protection

including: request verification
is the prevention of unintentionally overwriting data on backing store and may be implemented by software or hardware methods.

Software methods include:

- double checking a request (*request verification*) to overwrite or delete a file;
- checking the characteristics of a file to see if it is protected;
- asking for passwords before overwriting or deleting any data.

Hardware methods include:

- the moving of a slider to cover a slot on a disk to protect it physically from being written to, a method used for SD memory cards;
- the altering of a switch on some hard drives will electronically prevent/allow the writing to the disk, depending upon the state of the switch.

E4 OUTPUT

Other terms and concepts relating to output are to be found in Section F1 (for elements of print), Section F4 (for sound), Section B7, Section E6 and Section E7 (for communications) and Section B5 (for control).

We give instructions and data to computers. The computer uses the instructions as computer programs to process the data to produce results, which are known as **output**. The results may be of various forms, sound, text and diagrams, data for external storage, messages to control equipment or to send or receive emails and access the internet. They may be dynamic images, visible on a computer screen, or static, such as those produced by a **printer**.

The **output devices** attached to the computer system make the output usable. The two output devices that are used most often, particularly by PC users, are display devices, that is, **monitors**, and **printers**. Specialised output devices are not necessarily provided as part of the computer system.

Vision enables us to see objects in great detail and colour. Information and graphics in colour are more interesting, remembered longer and can contain more detail than the same material in **monochrome**, that is, shades of two colours – often black and white. For example, the software and user interface used to produce a word-processed document normally benefits from a colour display. The output from a printer may be in colour or monochrome. For business use where **multipart stationery** is still prevalent or high volume or speed is required, monochrome printers are common.

Monitors give out light, so work according to the rules of transmitted light. White light transmitted from a light source may be split into coloured light of a spectrum of different wavelengths. The human eye has receptors for the three primary (primary additive) colours red (R), green (G) and blue (B) and perceives other colours as mixtures of varying amounts of light selected from these primary colours. The brain interprets the colours at both ends of the visible spectrum as a combination of red and blue giving the effect of a colour wheel.

If a page printed in colour is illuminated by white light, some light is reflected and some absorbed by the coloured pigments (inks), and the eye perceives the combination of primary colours, which is reflected, not absorbed. Combining different proportions of the three secondary (primary subtractive) colours, cyan (C – light blue), magenta (M – a deep red), and yellow (Y) gives the various shades. Mixing two secondary (primary subtractive) colours creates a pigment that absorbs two primary colours, leaving the eye to see the remaining primary (primary additive) colour.

Not all the light is reflected, as some is absorbed by the pigment, so the printed image is less bright than that from the monitor. It is no simple matter to ensure that the colours displayed on your monitor will be matched by the output of your printer. Furthermore, human sensitivity to colour varies so that no two people are likely to see a given colour or combination of colours in exactly the same way.

Images displayed by the most common types of monitors and printers are made up of patterns of dots. It is possible to produce any character or shape simply by arranging for the dots to go in the right places. This method can be used for producing a piece of computer graphics (for example a picture or a design) as well as for printing text. For example, the letter 'h' can be crudely formed by a simple pattern of dots, as shown in Figure E4.1. The quality of the output from both monitors and printers depends on the **resolution**, that is, the numbers of dots per inch. By using a matrix with many more squares, it is possible to improve the shape of the letter. If the dots are very small and close together, the quality of display or printing can be very fine.

Figure E4.1 A character formed by a pattern of dots

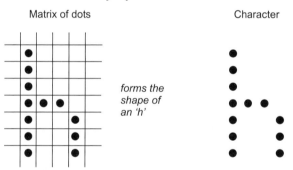

The **pixel** is the smallest element of the display for programming purposes, made up of a number of dots forming a rectangular pattern. Coloured display screens are made up of pixels, which consist of the three primary colours of white light.

In the past, most monitors used the **cathode ray tube**. However, laptop computers have always required high-performance, lightweight, thin screens, and these are now available as monitors. This has been achieved by major enhancements to **liquid crystal** technology, which is also used in pocket calculators.

The electronics that pass the information from the computer to the screen are generally specific to the type of screen device. These electronics have to be installed by fitting a specific interface board, called a **display adapter** (or **graphics card**) into the computer. For example, an SVGA display (a common display standard) consists of an SVGA screen device and a matching SVGA display adapter in the computer.

Printers are connected to a computer for the sole purpose of transferring the information from the computer to paper or other media, such as transparencies for overhead projectors. The version printed out is often referred to as **hard copy**. There are many types of printer varying in quality, cost and purpose.

Types of printers in common use are **inkjet printers** and **laser printers**. There are also specialist printers, such as **plotters**, **thermal wax printers** and **dye sublimation printers**. The quality of printing will depend on the type and quality of the paper as well as the resolution. In colour printing, one must also consider both the range of distinct colours the printer can produce (**colour palette**) and the software that controls the printing process (**colour management**).

In summary, deciding upon an output device is not easy as all monitors and printers today can display almost anything that your computer can produce. Often the use of the output will determine the type of device. Probably cost, speed, quality of display and choice of output (colour or monochrome) are the main areas to focus upon.

COLOUR

Palette

also known as: colour palette
including: dithering
is the range of distinct colours that a computer system can produce. No computer system will be able to produce every possible shade of colour and the palette is the total set of shades available. Most computers have a palette of sixteen million colours, which is a large number to work with so the user can select their own palette of colours suitable for the task. The user may be allowed to change this selection.

In some situations the user is unable to use the full range of colours and only has a smaller palette. Each of these colours can be chosen from the full range. Examples include art work for display on the internet (which has a standard palette) and desktop publishing work, which is restricted to the coloured inks to be used by the printer.

Dithering is reproducing a particular colour that is not in the palette by using a pattern of dots of a limited number of colours. This is used when the output device cannot reproduce a particular colour. For example true orange may be produced by a pattern of dots of red and yellow, see Figure E4.2.

Colour mixing is often software controlled. See *colour management*, page 311.

Colour model

including: spot colour, RGB model, RGB colour model, CMYK model, hue saturation value, greyscale model
is the way that separate colours are defined. Any colour can be defined using three values, but the different colour models do this differently. Each model is suitable for a particular application.

Figure E4.2 Dithering

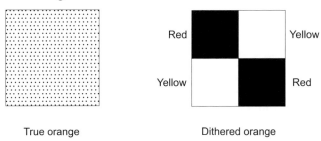

True orange   Dithered orange

The range of colours each model represents may be different and when an image is converted from one model to another the colours will be changed to the nearest available colour. Sometimes an additional colour, known as a **spot colour**, is needed to produce exact colour matching.

The usual models are:

RGB model or **RGB colour model**, defines the different amounts of red, green, and blue, which are the primary colours, and is ideal for use in display screens.

CMYK model also known as: CYMK or YMCK, defines the different amounts of cyan, magenta and yellow, which are the secondary colours. An extra value, the key (K) colour black is added because imperfections in printing make it difficult to make black from CMY. It is ideal for producing work to be printed.

Hue saturation value defines the hue (the different colours), the saturation (the luminosity or strength of colour) and value (the darkness). This is ideal for defining colours in, for example, photographic work.

Greyscale model defines the range of shades of grey from white to black that is used for reproducing monochrome images. A colour model can be mapped onto a greyscale model. Two different colours of the same luminosity may look the same as they have the same greyscale value.

Colour management

including: colour management system (CMS), Pantone
is the software process that controls the colours displayed by a monitor or printed by managing the transfer of colour data between devices. The flow of data is shown in Figure E4.3.

The management of the transfer of colour data associated with different devices such as screens, scanners, CD-ROM readers and printers is handled by software known as a **colour management system,** or **CMS**. The CMS may be included in the operating system or provided and installed separately. It works by comparing the colours for a device with independent colour standards, and translating the colours for different devices so that they appear similar. When they cannot be exactly matched, for example the differences between a screen using the RGB system and a printer using the CMYK system, the CMS will select the nearest match.

Pantone is a *proprietary system* (see page 291) in which numbers are allocated to colours for exact colour matching. The Pantone numbers may be held in a *look-up table* (see page 194).

Figure E4.3 Data flow in a colour management system

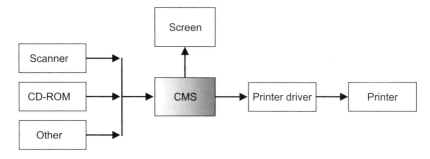

Colour separation

is the process needed for preparing colour data for (full colour) commercial printing. For example, if a photograph is to be printed commercially, the printer is supplied with four files each containing the data for one colour, using the *CMYK model* (see page 311). Each file is a monochrome image, showing the intensity of the particular colour.

In order to print in colour, a coloured image has to be separated into its component colours. This is part of the process of preparing the data for a colour printer.

QUALITY

Resolution

including: low resolution, high resolution, screen resolution, dot pitch, dots per inch (dpi), low-resolution graphics, printer resolution
is the term for the clarity of text and graphics as they appear on a monitor screen or printed on paper. **Low-resolution** images have coarse dots, and a 'grainy' appearance with jagged diagonal lines and curves. **High-resolution** images have many small dots closer together and produce clearer images with diagonal straight lines and curves both appearing smoother and less jagged. See also *raster graphics* (page 315) and *vector graphics* (page 316).

Screen resolution is usually quoted as the number of *pixels* (see page 315) in a row by the number of rows of pixels (horizontal × vertical), and the **dot pitch**, which is the distance between the centres of two dots on the screen. Values of between 0.28 mm and 0.38 mm for the dot pitch are considered acceptable; this is between 100 and 70 **dots per inch (dpi)**.

Low-resolution graphics is generally applied to graphical display units where simple pictures can be built up by plotting large blocks of colour or by using special graphics characters. It was used for *teletext* images.

Printer resolution is measured in dots per inch, or **dpi**. The smaller the dots making up the printing and the closer they are together, the clearer the image will be. Laser and inkjet printers normally have a resolution of at least 300 dpi for normal use, while high resolution of 2400 dpi is used by commercial printers.

Print quality

including: correspondence quality, letter quality, draft quality, condensed type
is a description of how well formed the characters are when printed. The descriptions relate to printers for use in business when only simple text printing is required. Desktop computers usually have the flexibility of printing the text as a graphical image, allowing for a wide variety of fonts, font sizes and effects.

The descriptions of characters are expressed in terms of the standards expected of printed output for different purposes:

Correspondence quality also known as **letter quality**, is similar to the quality of a traditional typewriter, or of an inkjet or laser printer.

Draft quality is an option on some printers; the characters are not well shaped, but can be printed quickly.

Condensed type is produced by some printers, which can reduce the width of a character, so that more text can be fitted on a line.

See also *photo printer*, page 397.

Font

including: scalable, printer fonts, screen fonts, printer drivers, font cartridges, proportional spacing, monospace font, pitch
is the set of printing or display characters in a particular type, style and size. Printer fonts may be produced by the same software as screen fonts and appear identical on the screen and in printed output. Such fonts are **scalable**, that is, they can be enlarged or reduced without changing their shape. See also *font*, page 373, *PostScript®*, page 322, and *point*, page 373.

Printer fonts are stored within the printer itself and therefore available for draft printing or faster printing in other circumstances.

Screen fonts are the way text of a particular style is displayed on the screen. Ideally these will appear the same as the printer fonts, but for technical reasons they may be displayed differently. See also *WYSIWYG*, page 19.

The font options, which can be selected by the user, may be stored in the computer and accessed through **printer drivers,** which are part of the systems software that formats data for printing. See Section B12 Systems software. Alternatively fonts may be stored in read-only memory (ROM) **font cartridges** installed in the printer.

Proportional spacing is a way of printing text so that the spaces between letters and between words look the same. The letter 'i' is narrower than the letter 'm' and without proportional spacing there would be more white space around the letter 'i'. The software adjusts the space between letters.

Not all fonts support proportional spacing. When using a **monospace font**, the **pitch** is the number of characters in an inch, which varies for different fonts, and is used mainly in commercial printing.

DISPLAY

Display screen

also known as: screen, monitor, visual display unit (VDU)
including: LCD, liquid crystal diode, E Ink, LED, light-emitting diode
is an electronic visual display for computers. Originally, most display screens used *cathode ray tube (CRT)* technology (see below), which was then the universal technology behind the domestic television set. At the time of writing the commonest device is a flat-screen using **LCD** (**liquid crystal display**) technology (see page 316).

With the advent of ebook readers, another technology, **E ink** (electrophoretic ink) that uses no power to maintain a static display is growing in popularity – not only for ebooks, but also for mobile phones and watches. Currently expensive, but expected to become the dominant display technology are **LED** (**light-emitting diode**) displays (see page 316).

Cathode Ray Tube

also known as: CRT
is a glass tube used to form the screen in a monitor or television set. The cathode ray tube is a large bulb with a flattened end, and the viewer sees only this flatter end. The inside of the flat end is coated with phosphor, and a beam of electrons is directed at it to make the end glow with patterns of dots. The electronics of the system controls the beam of electrons and the number and nature of the excitation of these dots determines the quality of the picture that the user sees.

Screen refresh

also known as: refresh
including: refresh rate
is to replace the image currently displayed on the screen by a new image, either because the image fades or because the data displayed has changed, but is not reflected in the display.

The screen picture needs to be able to change quickly, to display anything from just simple text to a fast-moving graphics image. This ability to change is achieved because the picture is redrawn many times a second even if it is not actually changing.

The **refresh rate** is the number of times the image is redisplayed per second. A low refresh rate tends to produce flicker. An SVGA monitor has a refresh rate of 72 scans per second. See also *video adapter* (page 315).

Frame

is used to describe a contained set of data treated as a single unit and which may change over time. Examples are a response frame for the input of data in a screen input data capture system, or a web page.

In electronics, a frame is one complete screen picture. In a standard television set this consists of 625 separate lines. A new frame is transmitted every one twenty-fifth of a second as two interlaced fields. The first field is the odd-numbered lines and the second is the even-numbered lines. (See *screen refresh*, page 314.)

Raster graphics

is a method of producing an image on a display screen. The image is drawn as horizontal lines of dots, repeated for each line of the screen. The bit map is encoded as a one-dimensional stream of bits, formed by each line of the display in order.

Each pixel in the image may consist of several dots depending on the resolution of the image and the *resolution* of the monitor, see page 312. In general, any line that is neither vertical nor horizontal will have a jagged appearance. If very high quality screen display of line drawings is required, then *vector graphics* (see page 316) is the appropriate system.

Pixel

including: pixel graphics
is a single dot of an image. It is usually rectangular or square and is the smallest element that can be displayed. Each pixel will be a single colour intensity and saturation. Pixel is a contraction of 'picture-element'.

Pixel graphics is a method of constructing a picture consisting of a rectangular array of dots. Each dot may be any of the colours available to the computer but it is not possible for a dot to be split into smaller pieces. This means that it is impossible to have detail smaller than the size of the pixels.

Video adapter

also known as: display adapter, graphics adapter, video card, video adapter card
is the circuitry that generates the signals needed for a video output device to display computer data. The data may be text only or text and graphics. The circuits are contained on a circuit board, which is installed in the computer with output via a cable to the display unit (the monitor).

A number of manufacturers have developed adapters with different screen proportions such as a page-shaped screen for use in the newspaper industry. Computers that are not IBM-compatible PCs frequently use their own video adapters with different standards.

315

Video RAM (VRAM)

is a separate high-speed memory into which the processor writes the screen data, which is then read to the screen for display. This avoids the use of any main memory to hold screen data.

Vector graphics

is a screen display method in which each line of a drawing is produced on the screen individually. A line can be drawn in any direction (although there is a minimum width of a line) and so the display is a more accurate presentation of the picture with no jagged edges. The resolution of vector graphics screens is usually very high. Vector graphics is an expensive technique to implement with the result that most displays use *raster graphics* (see page 315). See also *vector graphics* (page 393).

Liquid crystal display (LCD)

including: backlit screens
is a display technique that uses the phenomenon that certain liquids alter their ability to reflect or transmit light if a voltage is applied to them. Originally used for pocket calculators, it is now common for computer screens.

In its basic form, a liquid crystal display consists of a thin layer, a film, of fluid sandwiched between two sheets of glass or plastic. Complex wiring is used to apply voltages to different small areas of the film of liquid. The applied voltage alters the ability of the liquid to reflect or transmit light. Thus a pixel display is built up of light and dark dots of varying intensity. One way of producing colour is to have three layers of different types of liquid, with different colour characteristics, where each layer has its own associated wiring. Some systems rely on reflected light and cannot be used in poor lighting conditions.

Backlit screens, where the liquid films transmit light from a light source behind the screen, give a more easily viewed display than reflective systems.

Light-emitting diode (LED)

is a display that uses the property of some semiconductor diodes to emit light when a voltage is applied to them. Their power consumption is negligible and they give off no heat. They are commonly used as indicator lights on devices such as disk drives. They are also useful for monitoring the logic state of lines in control applications.

PAL (Phase Alternating Line)

is the UK standard method of encoding colour information in a television signal. The computer must contain a PAL encoder for colour if a domestic television set is used as a display device via the ordinary aerial socket.

PRINTING

Printer

including: monochrome printer, colour printer, print head, dot matrix printer, inkjet printer, laser printer
is an output device producing characters or graphics on paper. **Monochrome printers** use a single ink colour, normally black on white paper. **Colour printers** use coloured inks to produce the coloured image, as well as black ink. There are many methods of printing and of organising the operation of a printer, for example some printers use a moving **print head**, which travels backwards and forwards across the paper carrying the printing mechanism.

Dot matrix printers are relatively cheap, but the quality of printing may be poor. Most domestic printers today are **inkjet printers**, which produce print quality rivalling that produced by a laser printer (but not as quickly). The advantages of **laser printers** are their speed and high quality of printing. They are generally used in offices as they are robust and the printed image is waterproof. Colour laser printers are still relatively expensive. Some printers require special media. For a summary of information about the commoner printers see Table E4.1. See also *print buffer*, page 329.

Impact printer

is a printer that creates marks on the paper by striking an inked ribbon (or carbon paper) against the paper. The object that strikes the ribbon may be the shape of a complete character or may form a pattern of dots, which combine to reproduce a character or to produce a graphic image.

Character printer

including: daisy wheel printer, golf ball printer
is an impact printer that prints single characters one at a time. A moving print head holds the mechanical part, a wheel (**daisy wheel**) or ball (**golf ball**), on which the set of characters are arranged, and can travel from side to side across the paper. The character is lined up with the striking position and then struck against a ribbon onto the paper. A change of font is achieved by replacing the mechanical part. Character printers were based on the typewriter and are rarely used today.

Dot matrix printer

also known as: pin printer
is a printer that forms characters or graphics images out of ink dots in a rectangular matrix of printing positions. A print head moves in straight lines across the paper. Inside the print head is a vertical line of pins each of which can print a dot on the paper. The dots are printed by pins striking a ribbon against the paper. By making a particular set of the pins hit the paper at the right moment it is possible to print a pattern of dots that looks like any character that is wanted.

Table E4.1 Printers

	Character printers	Matrix printers	Page printers
Types of printer	line printers (barrel, chain), golf ball, daisy wheel	pin dot matrix printers, inkjet printers	laser printers
Where in use	Obsolescent technology but some line printers are still in use in large-scale data processing contexts	Replacement for typewriter-style printers; generally compact machines; wide range of speeds and quality	Have almost completely replaced the older line printers for large volume printing. Sizes range from desktop to very large, floor standing machines
Application range	Obsolescent	From personal printers to network printers on small networks and specialised such as ATM-printing devices	Personal printers to large-scale data processing
Printing method	Impact on a ribbon or carbon paper is used to form the characters Characters are printed as complete characters in a single action	Uses pins (impact or thermal) or inkjet to print the image Text and images made up of dots in a matrix pattern (similar to a screen image)	Uses photocopier principles Prints a complete page at a time
Mechanism	Line printers use a print hammer for each print position to strike the paper and ribbon/carbon paper against embossed type on barrels or chain loops when the right character is in position Daisy wheel and golf ball printers print a character and then move to the next print position and have easily changeable fonts	Print mechanisms move backwards and forwards over the paper, which advances after each pass by the print mechanism Print quality is determined by the number of pins or ink bubble size and the minimum size of head and paper movements	Image of the page is 'written' by lasers onto a special drum as an electrostatic charge: the drum attracts toner particles, which are transferred to the page and heated to set the image

(Continued)

Table E4.1 (*Continued*)

	Character printers	Matrix printers	Page printers
Text/graphics	text only	text and graphics	text and graphics
Quality	line printers – poor daisy wheel, golf ball – very good	print quality depends on the resolution (dots per inch)	capable of very high resolution (dots per inch)
Fonts	usually only a single (limited) font available at a time	wide range of fonts available through software	wide range of fonts available through software
Line spacing	restricted line spacing (often only full lines)	flexible line spacing	can print anywhere on the page print area (possibly excluding margins)
Print area	unlimited page length, fixed maximum width	unlimited page length, fixed maximum width	fixed maximum page length and width

These printers are reliable, cheap and can make multiple (carbon) copies at the same time because the impact can produce an image on several layers of *multipart stationery* (see page 322). They will work with almost any quality of paper, and are generally able to print on either continuous paper or single sheets. They are surprisingly prevalent to this day, often in industrial environments where they are used for packing lists or invoices despite newer printing technology. The quality of print is not as good as from other printers.

Thermal printer

uses wires arranged like the pins of a *dot matrix printer* (see page 317), which are heated to form dots on heat-sensitive paper. Thermal printers are very quiet, light, fast and portable but do not produce high quality printing and the printing fades in time. Thermal printers are often used for supermarket till rolls, parking tickets etc.

Inkjet printer

also known as: bubble jet printer
including: ink cartridge, print cartridge, photo-quality printer
is one that uses small bubbles of quick-drying ink to produce the printing. The ink is held in small replaceable containers, called **ink cartridges** or **print cartridges**. The printed image is created by forcing droplets of ink from the cartridge through fine holes onto the paper, forming the characters by patterns of dots. It can print text or graphics. Almost all inkjet printers print in colour, using separate cartridges for cyan, magenta, yellow and black and sometimes variants such as 'light cyan' (see *CMYK model*, page 311).

Current inkjet printers are capable of extremely high-resolution printing and are the **photo-quality printer** of choice for most individuals; the use of special media, such as glossy photographic paper, produces results acceptably close to traditional film developing and printing. Only professional photo printing services have any need for higher quality printing.

Some models can print on large sizes of paper; others can print designs onto suitable CDs or DVDs, using a special carrier tray. A wide variety of media such as special films that can be transferred to T-shirts or plates and mugs has increased the versatility of this type of printer.

Laser printer

is a page printer that uses a laser beam to 'write' the image to be printed onto a light-sensitive drum. The drum then uses electrostatics (as in a photocopier) to attract toner, a fine plastic powder, to coat the image on the drum. Paper is pressed against the drum transferring the toner to the paper. The paper is then heated to melt the toner onto the paper. This is using technology called xerography.

A monochrome laser printer will use black powder. In a colour laser printer, each colour is printed separately, for each of the three secondary colours cyan, magenta, yellow, and black (see *CMYK model*, page 311).

Thermal wax printer

including: dye sublimation printer
is a printer that works by melting coloured wax dyes onto special paper from a wax-coated roll. **Dye sublimation printers** work in a similar way but with slight differences in the print head and formulation of the dye. They are used for high quality realistic colour reproduction. Both types are expensive.

Graph plotter

also known as: plotter
including: flat-bed plotter, digital plotter, XY plotter, incremental plotter
draws lines on paper by moving a pen in a holder relative to the paper on which the drawing is being made. In some designs the paper is on a roller and both the pen and the roller move. In others, known as **flat-bed plotters**, the paper is fixed on a flat surface, and all the movements are made by the pen.

Colour is achieved by changing the pens. Graph plotters are used by architects and engineers for *computer-aided design* (see page 427) because they are very accurate.

Digital plotters receive digital input specifying the coordinates of the points to be plotted, together with information about how the next point to be plotted is joined to the current point.

XY plotters create the drawing by plotting data at points defined by their *x*- and *y*-coordinates. They are used by architects and engineers for *computer-aided design* (see page 427) because they are very accurate.

An **incremental plotter** receives input data specifying increments to its current position, rather than data specifying coordinates.

Paper feed mechanism

including: line feed, page feed, friction feed, tractor feed, pin feed
is the means of making the paper move through the printing process. Many printers require **line feed**, that is, the paper is moved after a line (or sometimes half a line) has been printed. Laser printers eject one page at a time, **page feed**.

Friction feed is a mechanism for advancing paper by gripping it between rollers.

Tractor feed, also known as **pin feed**, is a mechanism for advancing paper by the use of perforations down the side of the paper and a toothed wheel (a sprocket).

Printout

also known as: hard copy
is computer output printed on paper.

Continuous stationery

including: fan-fold paper, bursting, multipart stationery, decollate
is printer paper that is perforated to make pages and folded in alternate directions at each set of perforations to form a stack of **fan-fold paper**. **Bursting** is the separating of continuous stationery into individual sheets by tearing the paper along the perforations; it may be handled mechanically or by humans. Continuous stationery sometimes has a tear-off margin on both sides with holes for a tractor feed mechanism to use. It can be a series of pre-printed forms. In a similar manner, business card blanks can be printed on pre-perforated cards that are subsequently burst by hand.

For some applications it may consist of several sheets together, either with carbon paper in between or made of pressure-sensitive paper (termed **multipart stationery**) so that several copies are printed at the same time using an impact printer. To **decollate** is to separate the sheets of each page of multipart stationery. See also *pre-printed stationery*, below.

Pre-printed stationery

has certain fixed information already printed on each sheet so that the computer can fill in the gaps. This increases the speed of printing and improves the presentation. The paper may be cut sheets or continuous stationery. Common examples are letter headings, customer accounts for gas and electricity, and computer-printed cheques.

Page description language

including: PostScript®
is a *high-level computer language* (see page 238) used to pass instructions to printers for setting up the data to be printed.

PostScript® is a page description language used by some laser printers for complex graphics and desktop publishing. The computer will code its printout requirements, for example the size, direction and style of a piece of text or the format for a diagram. These will then be interpreted by the PostScript® translator into the corresponding image of dots ready for printing. The PostScript® translator is held as software in a processor in the printer. PostScript® is the basis for the *Portable Document Format (PDF)*, see Table A2.1 page 12.

E5 MACHINE ARCHITECTURE

Other related terms can be found in Section E3 Memory and Section E7 Communications technology.

The structure of a computer, or more properly the **central processing unit (CPU)**, and how the particular components are related to each other is called machine architecture. The working of the computer can still be considered in terms of binary patterns and codes. The physical characteristics of the central processor affect the way the computer is used and also determine the speed, power, cost and suitability of the computer for a particular application.

The choice of integrated circuits and other components can determine how fast the computer will operate. This is important when selecting a computer for a particular application. For example, an important part of the specification of a personal computer is its **microprocessor** (such as a 'Core 2', 'Athlon' or 'Atom'), since this tells the purchaser something about the complexity of the programs it will run. Other parts of the central processor can affect a computer's performance for particular jobs, for example a **floating-point unit** will make a computer much faster at solving scientific problems, but may be of little value in an office context.

An important factor in the design of the central processor is the selection of the binary patterns used internally. For example, the number of bits used as an address affects the maximum size of the main memory and the number of bits used to store a number affects very large and very small numbers.

Ways exist of getting round these issues, but always at the expense of performance and at a price. Various techniques may be employed within the hardware of the central processor to enhance performance, but further development of a type or series of computers will be limited by these technical factors and the initial design decisions.

Most users are only affected by the computer's architecture when faced with the practicalities of using a personal computer, and in particular when connecting peripherals. All peripherals are connected to a computer through an **interface**, but each type of computer may have to be fitted with slightly different interfaces depending on the computer's internal design. Some peripherals require their own dedicated interface, but other peripherals may be connected using a general purpose interface, allowing several peripherals (of a suitable type) to be linked to one computer interface.

Most personal computers provide several general purpose interfaces integrated into the computer design. Other interfaces need to be fitted inside the computer case.

All the components inside a computer are connected together by a **bus**. Any peripherals have to be connected to this bus. **Interface boards** plug into special sockets connected to the bus. The electronics on this interface board need to be tailored to fit the electrical connections used by that particular computer's bus. So each design of bus requires its own particular interface boards. The degree to which a microcomputer can be expanded depends on the physical space available in its case, which limits the size of the interface board, and the number of sockets available; these are normally called **slots**. The power rating of the power supply unit (PSU) must not be exceeded.

Each peripheral is provided with an interface and is connected, generally through a cable although wireless interfaces can be used, to the equivalent type of interface on the computer. For the computer and the peripheral to communicate with each other, the interface in the peripheral and the interface in the computer need to be of the same type.

Some peripherals use a **bus interface**. Several peripherals attached to the same bus can share one computer interface, making it easy to use many different peripherals and change peripherals as needed. The computer can identify each peripheral by an address, which is set when the peripheral is first installed.

There is a range of electronic components that perform specific functions within the computer system. Some of these components, such as the *clock*, simply provide the controlling electronics needed by a computer, while others allow a particular type of computer to be designed for a specific role.

Many of these components are integrated circuits and are designed to a standard size, which makes them easy to incorporate into computer designs. The development of standardised components means that they can be mass-produced rather than being individually constructed. This has the advantage that components are much cheaper and that it becomes economic to design a variety of computers with particular characteristics.

Although computer systems are usually viewed conceptually as a 'black box', it is useful to appreciate the functions of some of the individual components.

THE PROCESSOR

Central processing unit (CPU)

also known as: central processor, processor
is the main part of the computer, consisting of the registers, arithmetic logic unit and control unit. See *control unit* and *register* (page 326), and *arithmetic logic unit*, page 330. Usually the central processing unit includes the main memory (see *immediate-access store*, page 299). It is sometimes called the **central processor** or **processor**. Many computers have more than one processor.

A special form of central processing unit is the *microprocessor* (see page 325), which is used in microcomputers and small computerised devices, for example the control circuits of washing machines or mobile phones.

Microprocessor

including: Complex Instruction Set Computer (CISC), Reduced Instruction Set Computer (RISC), transputer, multicore
is an *integrated circuit*, see page 338, where the components of the *central processing unit* (see page 324), excluding the main memory, are combined as a single unit. Microprocessors are manufactured in large numbers for use in microcomputers and small computerised devices. The general user has to obtain software specific to the type of processor. Software cannot usually be used on different types of processor.

There are now many approaches to the design of microprocessors that optimise them for particular uses. These include:

Complex Instruction Set Computer (CISC) is a design that produces a complicated and expensive integrated circuit capable of performing a large variety of complex operations. This is the traditional approach to microprocessor design. Integrated circuits made to these designs can perform complex operations very efficiently with a small number of machine instructions. The complexity of the circuitry makes them relatively slow to perform each machine instruction, expensive to produce and have high power consumption. They are usually used for general purpose computers.

Reduced Instruction Set Computer (RISC) is a design that produces a simple, cheap integrated circuit with a basic range of machine instructions. Integrated circuits made to these designs are fast and rely on speed to perform complex operations by using several machine instructions. It can be customised cheaply for specific applications and is particularly suited to specialised applications that require fast but limited processing or have environmental considerations such as low power consumption. Typical applications include laser printers, MP3 players, personal organisers, mobile phones and most games consoles.

Transputer is a specific microprocessor that, unlike other microprocessors, includes the *main memory* (see page 299) as well as the other components of the CPU, hence its nickname 'computer on a chip'. Combining processor and store in the same chip makes it very easy to build parallel processing arrays containing many processors. Transputers are no longer manufactured but it has significance as an alternative approach to microprocessor design.

Multicore is the development of CISC architecture with several sets of CPU components in one microprocessor. A two-core processor has effectively two separate CPUs in one chip. This makes faster microprocessors possible at lower clock speeds. However, a two-core processor is not as fast as a single processor running at twice the speed as some tasks cannot be shared equally between the cores, reducing efficiency.

Instruction set

is the complete collection of instructions that are used by a particular type of central processor. These are the instructions available for use in machine-code or assembly-language programs for that computer. The instruction set is part of the design of a central processor or microprocessor and so the machine code of different types of computer are rarely compatible. See also *machine-code instruction*, page 195.

Control unit

including: fetch-execute cycle, instruction cycle, instruction decoder, fetch phase, execute phase
is the part of the central processor that manages the execution of instructions. A characteristic of all computers is the ability to follow a set of instructions automatically. The control unit fetches each instruction in sequence, decodes and synchronises it before executing it by sending control signals to other parts of the computer. This is known as the **fetch-execute cycle**. See *also program counter*, below.

The fetch-execute cycle is the complete process of retrieving an instruction from store, decoding it and carrying it out. This is also called the **instruction cycle**. Part of the control unit is the **instruction decoder**, which decodes the machine-code instructions during the fetch-execute cycle and determines what actions to take next. The cycle consists of two phases, the **fetch phase** where the instruction is copied into the control unit and decoded, followed by the **execute phase** in which the instruction is obeyed.

Register

including: program counter, instruction address register (IAR), next instruction register, sequence control register (SCR), address register, memory address register (MAR), memory buffer register (MBR), memory data register (MDR)
is a location, normally used for a specific purpose, where data or control information is temporarily stored. Some registers are used in the different parts of the *fetch-execute cycle* (see above) while others may be available for use by the program being executed. Registers usually are much faster to access than the immediate-access store, since they have to be accessed so often.

The various registers include the following:

Program counter in the control unit that contains the address of the next machine-code instruction to be executed. **Instruction address register (IAR)**, **next instruction register** and **sequence control register (SCR)** are alternative names for the program counter.

Address register in the control unit that holds the address part (see *address field*, page 195) of the instruction being executed.

Memory address register (MAR) in the central processor stores the address of the memory location currently in use. In the fetch phase this would be the address of the instruction being loaded and in the execute phase the address of the data being used. The memory unit has access to the MAR and switches the address selection circuitry to access the appropriate location.

Memory buffer register (MBR) in the central processor stores the data being transferred to and from the immediate-access store. It acts as a *buffer* (see page 329) allowing the central processor and memory unit to act independently without being affected by minor differences in operation. A data item will be copied to the MBR ready for use at the next clock pulse, when it can be either used by the central processor or stored in main memory.

Memory data register (MDR) is another name for the memory buffer register.

MEMORY

Address calculation

including: direct addressing, indirect addressing, vector, immediate addressing, indexed addressing, index register, address modification
is working out which *memory location* (see page 190) is to be accessed by a machine-code instruction. Part of a machine-code instruction is called the *address field* (see page 195), which contains data about which memory location the instruction is to use. There are a number of alternative methods for determining the address of the memory location, such as:

Direct addressing uses the data in the address field without alteration. This is the simplest method of addressing and also the most common.

Indirect addressing uses the address field to hold the address of a location that contains the required address. The action of a program can easily be changed by altering the data in the location pointed to by the instruction. The location holding the real address is known as a **vector**. One use of a vector is to provide access to library routines. Program control is passed to the address in the vector. The locations of the vectors are defined for other programmers to use. Routines can be changed without all the programs using them also being changed. This is because the address of the vector remains the same, but its contents can be altered to point to the new start address for the routine. See also *vectoring*, page 334.

Immediate addressing uses the data in the address field, not as an address, but as a constant that is needed by the program. An example is a routine counting up to 10, which may have the constant '10' supplied in the address field of an instruction. Although the address field cannot hold numbers as large as those that can be stored as data in a memory location, because space has to be left for the *operation code field* (see page 195), this is a particularly convenient method of loading constants into the accumulator.

Indexed addressing modifies the address (either a direct or an indirect address) in the address field by the addition of a number held in a special-purpose register, called an **index register**, before the address is used. Index registers are quickly and easily altered providing an efficient way of accessing a range of memory locations, such as in an array.

Address modification is changing the address field of a machine-code instruction as the program is running, so that each time the instruction is executed it can refer to a different memory location.

Memory management

including: memory management unit (MMU), bank switching, virtual memory, paging, page, page turn, page fault, thrashing, direct memory access (DMA)
is organising the flexible use of the computer's main memory, the *immediate-access store* (see page 299). This can be done by the **memory management unit (MMU)**, often a single integrated circuit in a microcomputer, which allows the addresses used by the *central processing unit* (see page 324) to be stored at a different physical location. The memory

management unit automatically converts the logical address provided by the central processor into the physical address in memory.

This allows programs in a multi-user or multi-tasking computer system apparently to use the same memory locations. The memory management unit places them in different physical parts of the immediate-access store. Four memory management techniques that can be used are bank switching, virtual memory, paging and direct memory access.

Bank switching is used for overcoming the limitations of computers that can only address a limited amount of immediate-access storage. Several 'banks' of storage are provided, each one occupying the same place in the computer's memory map. Only one bank may be active at any one time, and the required one is selected as needed by the software.

Virtual memory is used when sufficient immediate-access store is not available. Part of a disk drive is allocated to be used as if it were main memory. When accessing these memory locations the software has to copy the contents of the relevant disk block into a reserved area of main memory, having first copied its existing contents back onto disk. This is very slow and the software will attempt to use the immediate-access store if possible.

Paging is the organisation of memory into fixed size units, called **pages** (for example, a page of 32 kb). The immediate-access store is organised as a number of physical pages. The logical pages used by the central processing unit can be assigned, by the memory management unit, to any page in physical memory. A form of *virtual memory* (see above) can be used with less frequently used pages being stored on disk, but when required they are reloaded into the immediate-access store as a complete page.

Page turn is the movement of a page to or from backing store. The movement of pages is counted in page turns, which are sometimes confusingly called **page faults**. Monitoring the rate of page turns can lead to improved efficiency by indicating where unnecessary movement is taking place. Rapid uploading and downloading of pages is known as **thrashing** and can be recognised by a very high rate of disk access. In extreme cases something close to a *deadlock* (see page 234) may occur, because tasks cannot continue for any effective time before being interrupted, while new pages are loaded.

Direct memory access (DMA) is the use of part of the immediate-access store independently from the operating system or the memory management unit. This is usually used in the design of games for use on microcomputers, where the screen display is accessed directly allowing a faster and more complex display.

GENERAL CONCEPTS

Parallel processing

is the simultaneous use of several processors to perform a single job. A job may be split into a number of tasks each of which may be processed by any available processor.

Bus

including: address bus, data bus
is a common physical pathway shared by signals to and from several components of a computer. For example, all input and output devices would be connected to the I/O (input/output) bus. In practice each bus has two parts, an **address bus**, which carries identification about where the data is being sent, and a **data bus**, which carries the actual information. The principle of a bus is that the same wires go to each component in turn. The components watch the address bus until an address that they recognise, by using an address decoder, is present. When this occurs they take action, either retrieving the data from the data bus or placing new data on the bus for the central processor.

Buffer

including: buffering, single buffering, double buffering, print buffer
is an area of computer memory allocated to transferring data between the computer and a peripheral, for example a printer buffer. Sometimes a buffer is used between components within the computer (see *memory buffer register*, page 326). Using a buffer provides a barrier between devices with different working speeds or data organisation.

It is much more efficient to send or receive data as a *block* (see page 306) of many words or bytes. Magnetic disks and tapes require data to be read or written in such a way that a block of data is moved in a single operation. The computer and the peripheral have to be capable of sending or receiving a whole block of data at high speed when required.

Buffering manages the block transfer of data. An area of memory is allocated as the buffer, and when information is to be transferred, it is stored in the buffer until an entire block is complete. This block is then sent, leaving the area it occupied free for assembling the next block of data. When a block is received into a buffer, the data is processed before the next block is requested and transferred.

Single buffering is where one device has to wait for the block to be received before using the data (and the other device has to wait while it is processed). This is inefficient and slow.

Double buffering is an improved method where two areas of memory are allocated, and as one buffer is emptied the other can be filled up. This reduces the time a device has to stop while waiting for the data transfer.

Print buffer is an example of a buffer where an area of computer memory stores data to be printed until the printer is ready to print it. It enables a program to continue operating without waiting for each character to be printed, as it can send its data to the buffer. The buffer is normally managed by the operating system. When a printer, which works much slower than a computer, is ready to print the next data, it can signal this by means of an *interrupt* (see page 331) to the operating system. The operating system will remove the data from the buffer and send it to the printer.

Some peripherals may communicate with single bytes of data, for example keyboard input or musical sounds. The buffer for these peripherals may be organised as a *circular queue* (see page 260) enabling data to be added or removed as required.

Cycle

including: cycle time, processor cycle time, machine cycle time, millions of instructions per second (MIPS)
is the sequence of actions to perform a particular hardware operation, which is either repeated continuously or performed whenever it is required. In many cases the time taken for an operation is constant and is known as the **cycle time**. Cycle time is useful when calculating the speed of a particular computer task.

The **processor cycle time** or **machine cycle time** is the cycle time for one *fetch-execute cycle* (see page 326) and is governed by the speed of access to the immediate-access store. Processor cycle time gives a rough guide to the speed of a computer, although other factors, such as word length, are also important. Processing speed is sometimes expressed in **millions of instructions per second (MIPS)**, which is also only a rough guide, and is normally based on the average number of machine-code instructions executed.

Arithmetic logic unit (ALU)

including: arithmetic unit, accumulator, arithmetic register
is the part of the central processing unit where data is processed and manipulated. It is also called the **arithmetic unit**. The processing and manipulation of data normally consists of arithmetic operations or logical comparisons allowing a program to take decisions.

Most operations involve the **accumulator**, a special storage register within the arithmetic logic unit. It is used to hold the data currently being processed by the central processor. Any data to be processed is temporarily stored in the accumulator, the results ending up in the accumulator before being stored in the memory unit.

Most computer calculations are based on addition methods and so the 'accumulator' is where the computer does its 'additions'. A computer performs subtraction by two's complement addition and multiplication by combining addition with shifts for column alignment. See also *two's complement*, page 268, and *shift*, page 331.

The ALU usually includes **arithmetic registers** (see *register*, page 326), which are special store locations used to hold operands and results temporarily during calculation.

Micro-code

also known as: microcode
including: micro-program, micro-instruction
is the specialised code that controls the logic operations of a microprocessor when implementing machine-code instructions. Typically, it is part of the physical design of the processor and cannot be changed.

The machine-code instructions are executed by calling small programs held elsewhere in the computer. To the user a micro-code instruction behaves like a machine-code instruction but the control unit implements it by passing control to the micro-code routine. The micro-code is stored within the central processor for speed of access. Micro-code enables the instruction set of a computer to be expanded without the addition of hardware components, but it will be slower than a machine-code instruction.

Each micro-code routine is a **micro-program** consisting of a sequence of **micro-instructions**, typically defining a machine-code instruction.

Interrupt

including: timer
is a signal, generated by a source such as an input or output device or a systems software routine, which causes a break in the execution of the current routine. Control passes to another routine in such a way that the original routine can be resumed after the interrupt.

This enables peripherals to operate independently, indicating to the operating system, with an interrupt, when they need to communicate with the central processor. An example is a keyboard, which only sends data to the central processor when a key is pressed. The central processor continues with other tasks until, on receiving an interrupt, it polls (see *polling*, page 334) the various peripherals to establish the reason for the interrupt. If the interrupt is from the keyboard, the central processor collects the data, the code for the key that has been pressed, and stores it in the keyboard *buffer* (see page 329) before continuing. Timing circuits, called **timers**, are also used to generate interrupts at fixed intervals, for example to refresh the screen display.

Shift

including: shift register, arithmetic shift, logical shift, cyclic shift, rotation
is an operation that moves the bits held in a register, called the **shift register**, either to the left or to the right.

There are three different types of shift: arithmetic shift, logical shift and cyclic shift (also called a rotation). They are distinguished by what happens to the bits that are shifted out of the register at one end and what is moved in to fill the vacant space at the other end.

Arithmetic shift (see Figure E5.1) to the right causes a bit at the right-hand end of the register to be lost at each shift, and a copy of the sign bit is moved in at the left-hand end. This operation preserves the sign of a number and has the effect of dividing a binary number by two at each shift, regardless of the representation system or whether the number is negative or positive. The division will be inaccurate because of the truncation caused by the loss of a digit at each shift.

Arithmetic shift to the left causes the bit at the left-hand end of the register, the sign bit, to be lost at each shift. A zero bit is moved in at the right-hand end. If the bit to be moved into the sign bit position is different from the one that was there before the shift, an overflow flag is set.

Figure E5.1 Arithmetic shifts

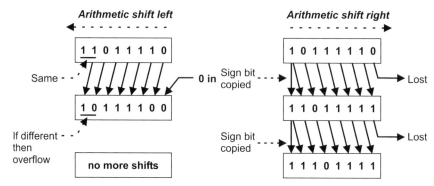

The use of two's complement representation ensures that shifting left gives correct results for multiplication by two until an overflow is flagged, because the number is too large to be represented in this size of register. See also *two's complement*, page 268.

Logical shift (see Figure E5.2) is where the bits shifted from the end of the register are lost, and zeros are shifted in at the opposite end. It is called a logical shift because it is suitable for *logical operations* (see page 194) rather than for arithmetic.

Cyclic shift or *rotation* (see Figure E5.3) is where the bits shifted out at one end of the register are re-inserted at the opposite end.

Pipelining

is the concurrent decoding of two or more machine instructions. While part of one instruction (for example, an address field) is being decoded, another part of a second instruction (for example, an operation code) may also be decoded, as a means of increasing the speed of execution of a program.

Figure E5.2 Logical shifts

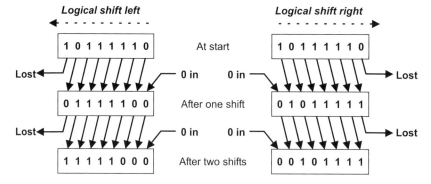

Figure E5.3 Cyclic shifts

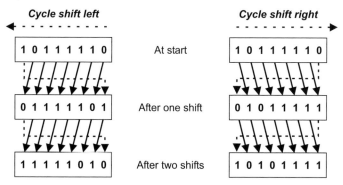

Wait state

is an interval built into some *machine-code instructions* (see page 195), to enable other parts of the computer to complete their actions before the processor moves on to the next instruction. For example, because the processor runs much faster than the RAM, it has to wait for some memory operations to be completed.

Masking

is an operation that selects certain of the bits in a register for subsequent processing. Usually, another register of equal length holds a bit pattern called a mask with each bit set to 1 where a corresponding bit is to be selected and 0 otherwise. For example, if a 16-bit register holds a machine-code instruction divided as follows:

OPERATION CODE							ADDRESS								
1	0	0	0	1	0	1	0	0	1	1	0	1	0	1	1

the operation code can be selected by constructing the following mask:

1	1	1	1	1	1	1	0	0	0	0	0	0	0	0	0

Using the *AND operation* (see page 106) gives a result of:

1	0	0	0	1	0	1	0	0	0	0	0	0	0	0	0

If necessary, the result can then be shifted (see *shift*, page 331) to the right by nine bit places to put the operation code at the right-hand end of the register.

The idea of using a mask in this way is so fundamental that the same words are used to describe similar selections at a much higher level, such as in using a *Data Manipulation Language* (see page 105).

Polling

is the sequential checking of a range of possibilities to identify which should be dealt with next. This allows the operating system to manage a range of choices, such as determining what has caused an *interrupt* (see page 331) or which terminal in a multi-user system is waiting for processing. Usually a message is sent to each routine in turn and the routine has to respond positively to claim the attention of the operating system. The routines are polled one after another so that each routine can claim (if required) its full share of the processor.

Vectoring

is the technique for passing control in a computer program through an intermediate address or vector. For example, on detecting an interrupt, instead of the computer passing control directly to a service routine, it may first jump to a location that in turn hands control to the routine. By altering the contents of this intermediate location, alternative service routines may be introduced without affecting programs that have already been written for that system.

Von Neumann architecture

also known as: Von Neumann concept or machine, stored program concept
is the name given to traditional computer architecture that forms the basis of most digital computer systems. A single control unit manages program control following a linear sequence of 'fetch-decode-execute-output'.

John von Neumann (1903–57), who was a member of a team working on first-generation computers, is credited with the idea that programs and data were indistinguishable, and hence could be stored in the same memory unit. In early computers, programs and data were stored in separate memories and the process of entering or altering programs was very tedious. Treating programs as just one form of data made changing programs easier and opened the way for compilers, whose input was text and whose output was a program in binary code.

Von Neumann is also credited with the introduction of the flowchart and with the concept of 'assertion boxes'. These say *what should be true* before or after a step in a program as opposed to *what should be done* at that point in the program.

INTERFACES

Motherboard

including: mainboard, daughterboard, carrier board
is the printed circuit board (PCB) that holds the principal components in a microcomputer system. The motherboard contains at least the main bus. The other components, such as the microprocessor and clock chips, will be either plugged into the motherboard or soldered to it. The motherboard is also known as the ***mainboard***.

Some components may be mounted on their own printed circuit board, called a **daughterboard**, which will be plugged into the motherboard Components attached using daughterboards can easily be replaced or upgraded and are not limited by the sockets or circuitry provided by the motherboard. Daughterboards are sometimes called **carrier boards**.

Expansion slot

including: slot, expansion card, card, memory module
is a socket that is provided in a computer to allow additional components, such as more sophisticated sound cards and network interfaces, to be added to the computer later. These sockets are also called simply **slots.** The more slots that are provided, the greater the number of extra components that can be added.

Expansion cards (or **cards**) can be added to these expansion slots. These expansion cards are usually *interface boards* (see below) but can also provide extra facilities such as better sound or a TV receiver. Similarly many computers have slots for **memory modules**, which allow the computer's main memory to be increased, slots for *flash memory cards* (see page 304) to provide additional removable storage, and extra bays for additional disk drives. These cards or modules have to be compatible with the slots they are going to use and usually have a unique design of connector to ensure they only fit the appropriate socket.

Interface

including: interface card, interface board
is the hardware and associated software needed for communication between processors and peripheral devices, to compensate for the difference in their operating characteristics (e.g. speeds, voltage and power levels, codes etc.). A number of internationally accepted standard interfaces (and their associated protocols) have been defined. A number of common interfaces are described in Table E5.1.

Interface cards (or **interface boards**) are interfaces provided for computers with the necessary electronics mounted on a small printed circuit board (PCB). These electronics are needed for a microcomputer to communicate with a peripheral device (or another computer). Appropriate interface cards can easily be plugged into the *expansion slots* (see above) of a desktop computer.

PHYSICAL COMPONENTS

Clock

including: clock rate
is the electronic unit that synchronises related components by generating pulses at a constant rate. Clock pulses are used to trigger components to take their next step, so keeping all components in time with each other. The **clock rate** is the frequency at which the clock generates pulses. The higher the clock rate, the faster the computer may work. One limiting factor for machine speed is the manufactured tolerance of the slowest component.

Table E5.1 Common interfaces

Common names	Technical standards	Notes	Usually
USB (Universal Serial Bus)	USB 1.1, USB 2.0, USB 3.0	Uses compact plugs and is designed for ease of use. USB can be configured for almost any purpose and is included in most modern computers. USB 2.0 is fast enough for transmitting video data.	Built-in
FireWire®, i-link, FireWire® 800	IEEE 1394	Uses compact plugs and is designed for ease of use in transmitting video data. USB 2.0 has replaced it for most purposes but FireWire® 800 is a faster version used in professional video processing.	Expansion card
Keyboard, mouse	PS/2	Used on older computers to connect the keyboard and mouse. Now being replaced by USB.	Built-in
SCSI (Small Computer System Interface)	SCSI-1, SCSI-2, SCSI-3	Designed for reliable high speed transfer of data. It is now mainly used in file servers as a very reliable and fast interface for hard disks and tape drives. USB has replaced it as a general purpose high-speed interface.	Expansion card
Serial Attached SCSI	SAS	Designed for reliable high-speed transfer of data. SAS is designed to provide a very reliable and fast interface for the new generation of hard disks and tape drives. It is mainly used in file servers.	Expansion card
IDE (integrated drive electronics), PATA (Parallel ATA)		Used to control and interface disk drives on desktop computers. Now being replaced by SATA.	Built-in

(Continued)

Table E5.1 (*Continued*)

Common names	Technical standards	Notes	Usually
SATA (Serial ATA)		Used to control and interface disk drives on desktop computers. Replacing the older IDE/PATA interfaces.	Built-in
Parallel port	Centronics, IEEE 1284	Originally the standard interface used for connecting to printers. Now replaced by USB.	Built-in
Serial port, com port	V24, RS432, RS232	Originally the standard interface used for connecting to most peripherals. It is reliable over distances of several meters although not fast enough for bulk data transfer. Now replaced by USB for desktop computers but still used in industry where its reliability and wide range of established applications are important.	Built-in
PCI (Peripheral Component Interface), PCI express		The standard interfaces used for connecting expansion boards to a desktop computer. It allows another interface (such as USB or sound card) to be purchased as an add-on card that is plugged into the PCI connectors (slots) inside the computer case.	Built-in to take expansion cards
Modem	V92/V44 (latest)	The standard interface for connecting to a telephone line for dial-up (non-broadband) access. Uses an RJ11 connector. See page 340.	Either built-in or expansion card
LAN	Ethernet, IEEE 802	The standard interface for connecting to a local area network. Uses an RJ45 connector.	Either built-in or expansion card
MIDI (Musical Instrument Digital Interface)		The standard interface for connecting electronic musical instruments to a computer allowing the notes to be recorded and played back. See page 411.	Expansion card or USB
PCMCIA (Personal Computer Memory Card International Association) card	PCCard, Carcbus, Expresscard 2.0	The standard interfaces used for connecting expansion boards to a laptop computer. It allows another interface (such as a network adapter) to be purchased as an add-on card, the size of a credit card, which is plugged into a PCMCIA slot in the laptop case. Now replaced by USB.	Built-in to take expansion cards

Real-time clock

is an electronic unit that maintains the time of day in a special register that may be accessed by suitable instructions in a computer program. It is powered by internal batteries, and continues to function even when the computer is switched off. For example, the computer can use this time information to label files with the time and date they were created, or to trigger timed events such as collecting a weather satellite broadcast.

Hard-wired logic

is a function permanently built into the circuitry. Often this is an integrated circuit designed to control the function. Such functions are immediately available when switched on and cannot be altered by the user. This ensures that the device will always be in the same initial state when switched on.

Integrated circuit (IC)

including: chip, very large-scale integration (VLSI)
is a solid-state electronic component in which all the elements (such as transistors and capacitors) are formed within a very thin slice of silicon. The popular name for an integrated circuit is a '(silicon) **chip**'.

Very large-scale integration (VLSI) is a manufacturing technology used to produce the integrated circuits of very high density used in computers. These can have several billion components (transistors, diodes etc.) representing up to a billion circuits (decoders, flip-flops etc.) combined as a single integrated circuit. These circuits are made from *logic elements*, see below. See also *bistable*, below.

The older technologies of small-scale integration (SSI), medium-scale integration (MSI) and large-scale integration (LSI) are now obsolete.

Logic element

including: logic circuit
is a *gate* (see page 356) or combination of gates needed to perform a logical function as part of the circuitry of a computer. It may be a single *AND gate* (see page 360) or a more complex component. Hardware system designers can produce complex circuits using logic elements as modules in the construction of their designs.

A **logic circuit** is designed to perform a more complex function, perhaps specific to the system being built, producing a required set of outputs from a given set of inputs.

Bistable

including: flip-flop
is a device that has two stable states. Since each state is stable the device effectively forms a memory that can differentiate between two pieces of data. Whatever the technology, which could be electronic, magnetic, liquid or pneumatic, the two states are used to represent the binary digits 0 and 1. This means that mathematical manipulation can be performed on data held in binary form.

The bistable in the integrated circuits used for the main memory of computers is a **flip-flop**, a logic circuit designed to store a single data bit. The receipt of an electrical pulse by the flip-flop will reverse its state, and a series of pulses causes it to flip successively between the two stable states.

Latency

including: propagation delay, access time
is the time delay before a component in the computer responds to an instruction, for example the time between data being requested from a memory device and the time when the answer is returned.

Even a single logic gate has a latency (or **propagation delay**), which will be very small (a fraction of a microsecond) but, with a large number of gates involved, these delays can be significant. The computer cannot work any faster than the limit imposed by latency.

A special case of latency is **access time**, which is the time delay in retrieving data stored either in main memory or on backing store. Access time is relevant when deciding which backing store should be used in any particular context to produce an acceptably fast computer system.

Programmable logic array (PLA)

also known as: uncommitted logic array (ULA)
is an array of standard logic gates, in which each element is identical, manufactured on a single LSI (large-scale integration) chip. The logic circuits required for a particular application are created by 'burning out' unwanted connections.

DIP switch

is one of a set of small slide-operated switches mounted together in a bank (Figure E5.4). These are used to set options on hardware, such as printers. For example, they may control what language alphabet to use or the size of font. (DIP stands for dual in-line package.)

Figure E5.4 DIP switches

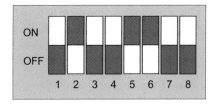

Jumper

is a detachable flexible-wire connection between suitable socket points on a circuit board. Sometimes a rigid version may be found on printers and other peripherals, possibly arranged in banks like *DIP switches* (see above), for which they are an alternative.

E6 COMMUNICATION COMPONENTS

This section is concerned with terms used in describing the transmission of data between computers within a network. Other related terms may be found in Section B7 Networking or Section E7 Communications technology.

Communications and control require that data is passed rapidly and accurately between parts of a system. The origins of present-day communication systems are the electric telegraph in which signals were sent as electric pulses, the telephone in which sound is passed as a varying electric current, and radio in which the signals are sent as electro-magnetic radiation.

Modern communications systems are highly reliable, accurate and affordable. From the earliest days of computers until the late 1980s it was necessary to install special quality telephone lines between linked computers. Now it is possible to use standard voice quality lines for connecting computers and remote devices. This is partly due to the use of digital signal systems and partly due to the use of more reliable materials and devices for the transmission of signals in the public communications systems. The installation of digital telephone exchanges in many parts of the world, and the use of radio links where cables are not available, mean that it is impossible for a user to know whether a link between two telephones or two computers is by cables or via some terrestrial or satellite radio link. Where public communication links are not available, private links are installed.

The materials for connecting computers are wires of some form, fibre optic cables, radio links or infrared radiation. Each has its advantages and its disadvantages. If wires or optic cables are used, then the individual locations of equipment may be restricted to sites served by the cables; if infrared links are used then receivers and transmitters have to be in sight of each other; if radio is used then privacy may not be easily achieved. At present, nearly all local area networks are linked by some form of wire cable. Where these connect into the wider world, they require some device to make the connections to the outside world. These connecting devices arrange for the signals to be sent in an appropriate form, at the correct speed and with the necessary destination information attached. The computer user determines the content and destination of the messages but the linking devices determine the way in which the messages are sent and often the route.

Modem (MOdulator-DEModulator)

is a data communications device for sending and receiving data between computers over telephone circuits. It converts the digital signals from the computer into audio tones for transmission over ordinary voice quality telephone lines and converts

340

incoming audio signals into digital signals for the computer. It is normally plugged directly into a standard telephone socket.

Terminal adapter

is an interface that is plugged into a microcomputer to link into an *ISDN (Integrated Services Digital Network)* (see page 350).

Private branch exchange (PBX)

including: private automatic branch exchange (PABX)
is a private telephone exchange. It provides the interface between a group of telephone extensions and the public network lines. There is usually a facility that allows any extension to dial any other extension directly and to dial into the public network using only a simple connect code and the outside number. Normally, external callers only get the operator unless they know the direct dial number for an individual extension.

A digital ***private automatic branch exchange (PABX)*** can control and interconnect a mix of telephones, fax machines, teletext devices and computers all operating at different bit rates.

Multiplexor

also known as: multiplexer
including: time division multiplexor (TDM), time slice, statistical multiplexor, intelligent time division multiplexor, frequency-division multiplexor (FDM)

Figure E6.1 Multiplexors connecting remote workstations to a computer
All connections are two way.

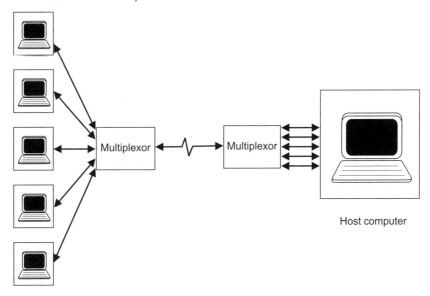

Host computer

is a device that receives data from several independent sources for transmission along a single route to a single destination. A two-way communication multiplexor must be able to separate signals for each of the destinations. The demultiplexor could be a *front-end processor* (see page 290).

A *time division multiplexor (TDM)* transmits the signals from two or more sources in successive short time intervals, called *time slices*. Each source gets the same duration of time interval. Where the multiplexor time allocation is proportional to the activity of each source, it is called a *statistical multiplexor*, or an *intelligent time division multiplexor*.

A *frequency-division multiplexor (FDM)* uses the available route link to transmit the data from the different sources at the same time. This is achieved by dividing the available channel *bandwidth* (see page 349) into a number of narrow bands, each of which is used for a separate transmission but at a slower speed.

Wireless communication

including: infrared communication, microwave transmission, satellite
covers a whole range of possible methods of data transmission, which can be used for linking computers within networks or for links within computer systems.

Infrared communication uses the same systems as domestic remote control of televisions. Examples of its use include the control of robotic devices and remote keyboards. It is necessary for there to be direct unobstructed line of sight between the transmitter and the receiver. Strong sunlight will interfere with infrared signals.

Microwave transmission is used as a method of communication within public telephone services. Many organisations use private installations to transmit data between key sites. Unlike the cellular phone systems that are broadcast systems, microwave transmissions use highly directional transmitters and receivers with dish aerials.

Satellite links are used for international communications by many providers of public telephone services. Unlike satellite broadcast systems, these links use highly directional, narrow beam, two-way transmissions. A single channel is capable of simultaneously carrying a very large number of separate transmissions.

Wire connector

including: copper cable, coaxial cable, twisted pair (TP), unshielded twisted pair (UTP)
is a standard form of wire cable used to provide the connections in a network.

Copper cables are commonly used as connectors for local area networks, since they are readily available and have suitable electrical characteristics. Various types of copper cable are used, including:

Coaxial cable, which is made to a variety of specifications, is the same kind of cable that is used for connecting a television aerial to a television set. It has two conductors. One is a wire down the centre of the cable, which may be a single strand, insulated from the second, which is made up of many strands braided around the insulation for the inner wire. See Figure E6.2.

Figure E6.2 Section of coaxial cable

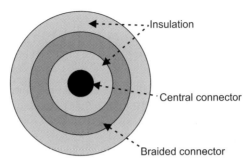

Twisted pair (TP) cable is commonly used for data transmission. In its simplest form it is a pair of insulated copper wires twisted together surrounded by a copper braid and external insulation. Some cables are made up of a number of twisted pairs surrounded by an overall (earthed) braid screen. In another form, stranded copper wires are twisted together in pairs with an earth wire. These pairs may be grouped to form a single multi-connector cable. These cables all have different specifications and, used in the correct situation, provide minimum interference data transmission.

Unshielded twisted pair (UTP) is similar to the twisted pair cables described above, but have no earthed shield. In suitable circumstances they can be used for data transmission.

Fibre optic cable

also known as: optical fibre
is a very fine glass strand that allows rapid transmission of data, using modulated light beams. It is usual to put many strands together in a single cable, each one capable of carrying one or more data signals. Fibre optic cable provides interference-free, secure data transmission and, unlike metal wires, is not subject to corrosion.

Signal level

including: signal amplifier, signal booster
is the measure of the strength of a communications signal. In the same way that sound and light become weaker with distance, electrical signals passing down a wire become weaker as they travel along the wire. For this reason **signal amplifiers** or **boosters** are built into communications networks at appropriate intervals. These increase the signal level before passing the signal on to the next part of the network.

Signal converter

including: digital signal, analog signal, analog-to-digital (A-to-D or A/D) converter, digitising, digital-to-analog (D-to-A or D/A) converter
is a device that converts serial signals from one form to another. Signals may be **digital**, consisting of discrete bit patterns, or **analog**, consisting of a continuously variable voltage. Both analog and digital signals are used to represent data. Some devices

343

generate analog signals or need to be supplied with data in analog form, while others generate or have to be supplied with data in digital form.

An *analog-to-digital (A-to-D) converter* converts analog signals into digital signals for subsequent processing. This conversion is sometimes called *digitising*. For example, the analog output from a microphone has to be digitised before it can be stored or processed by a computer.

A *digital-to-analog (D-to-A) converter* converts serial digital signals into analog signals. For example, the digital data for a computer display has to be converted into analog signals if it is to be used as input to a television (unless the television is configured to receive digital signals).

Handshake

is the exchange of signals between devices to establish their readiness to send or receive data, for example the transmission of data from a computer to a printer. Handshaking is one of a number of methods of ensuring that both the sender and receiver are ready before transmission begins.

Data transmission rate

including: bits per second (bps), bytes per second (Bps), characters per second (cps), baud rate
is the numerical measure of the speed at which signals are transmitted over (wired or wireless) data links. *Bits per second (bps), bytes per second (Bps)* and *characters per second (cps)* are largely self-explanatory.

It is important to realise that because of the presence of control data signals, such as start, stop, and check bits and because of techniques such as *data compression* (see page 281), there is no simple direct relationship between these measures. See also *data transmission*, page 346.

The *baud rate* is an earlier measure now largely confined to telecoms engineering.

Transducer

is an electronic component that converts one form of energy to another. For example, a thermistor converts a temperature into electrical energy with a varying voltage, a photocell converts brightness of illumination into a voltage. The term is generally applied to devices that produce electricity rather than those that convert electricity into another form of energy.

Sampler

also known as: digital sampler
is an electronic circuit that takes samples of an electronic signal at intervals and stores them for future processing. In particular, they are used to take frequent measurements of analog signals for converting an analog signal into a digital signal, when it is known as a *digital sampler*.

E7 COMMUNICATION TECHNOLOGY

This section is concerned with the principles involved in achieving communication between computer systems, and the conventions that determine how such systems communicate with each other. Related terms can be found in Section B7 Networking and Section E6 Communications components.

Ways of communicating data between distant places using electrical energy have been in use for over 100 years. The telegraph was the first. Very quickly, machines replaced people and automatic communications became typical. Telephones, teleprinters, radio and television were all well developed before computers were combined with them to produce the range of global communications that is now available.

Global communications require that there are the same standards for the equipment used in all the countries of the world. Some of these standards have been set by those countries that initially developed the systems, but most have been worked out and agreed by international bodies, sometimes with the direct authority of the United Nations. Each industrial country has a national organisation that sets standards for all kinds of products. These organisations have been setting standards, and revising them, throughout the last 100 years. Thus there are international standards defined by ISO (the International Organization for Standardization) and by ITU (International Telecommunications Union), formerly the CCITT (Comité Consultatif International Téléphonique et Télégraphique) of the United Nations, and other standards of a national origin are accepted through organisations like the General Agreement on Tariffs and Trade (GATT).

The specification of standards is a complex and expensive process. The implications of a particular choice can be very far-reaching, both for the industries that make products to those standards, and for the consumers of those products. As far as the consumer is concerned, the acceptance of a single manufacturer's standards for some device or system can have limiting effects, particularly when there is severe competition for sales of the product. However, in a situation of rapid technical development, the consumer is likely to benefit from clearly defined standards, which help to ensure some measure of compatibility between hardware and software originating from different sources. The most important areas of standards definition for the computer and information technology industries are those of input/output specifications and external communications.

TRANSMISSION

Data transmission

including: duplex, full duplex, half duplex, simplex, synchronous transmission, asynchronous transmission, start bit, stop bit, parallel data transmission, serial data transmission, echo
is the passing of data from one device to another. This may be between parts of a computer system or between computers in a network.

Data transmission may have a number of distinct characteristics:

- It may be synchronous or asynchronous.

- It may be serial or parallel.

- It may be in both directions at the same time, called **duplex** or **full duplex**; in only one direction at a time, called **half duplex**; or in one direction only, called **simplex**.

- Checks may be made on the accuracy of transmission (*parity checks*, see page 111, or by using *echo* processes).

Synchronous transmission is a method of transmitting data between two devices in which all the data transfers are timed to coincide with a clock pulse. Within a computer the timing is provided by the computer's clock. Between computers, the clock in one computer acts as the master clock for the system.

Asynchronous transmission is a method of data transmission, in which a character is sent as soon as it becomes available rather than waiting for a synchronisation signal or a clock pulse. A **start bit** marks the beginning of a character and one or two **stop bits** mark the end of a character.

Parallel data transmission sends the bits for a character simultaneously along separated data lines. This means that an 8-bit code will require a minimum of nine *channels* (see page 18) for parallel transmission (eight data and at least one ground, return channel).

Serial data transmission sends the bits for a character one after another along the same data line. This means that serial transmission requires only two wires (a data line and the ground, return line), although more may be provided.

Echo is a feature of data transmission in which the data received is returned to the point of origin for comparison with the original data in order to check it.

Signal routing

including: circuit switching, message switching, message queuing
is the choice of route for a particular message through a network. In *ring* (see page 130) and *star networks* (see page 131) there is little choice of route. More complex network topologies provide many possible routes for any message. If the direct connection between two nodes is unavailable, perhaps because of some fault or because the connection is busy, then the intelligence in the *routers* (see page 139) at the nodes sends the message forward in a direction that is available. Since the time for a message to

travel between nodes is often nearly the same regardless of the distance apart, this is more efficient than waiting for the direct link to become available. For example, it is possible that a message from London to Manchester may be routed via a satellite to Los Angeles and then on to Manchester. The computer in London that sent the message and the computer in Manchester have no control over the route used, nor has the computer in Los Angeles through which it may have passed. The next part of the message may go by some completely different route.

Circuit switching is a method of communication in which a path is set up from sender to receiver immediately before the start of transmission and kept open until the transmission is completed. After the transmission is completed, all parts of the path are released and can be used for other transmissions. See also *packet switching*, below.

Message switching is a method of batching, organising and storing sections of data, so that they can be transmitted economically in a network; it is usually applicable to networks with many computers. Each section of a message is sent from node to node with each node responsible for the choice of route for the next part of the journey. This requires that the nodes are intelligent. A message will be accepted at a node and, if necessary, stored until it can be transmitted onwards. Finally, all the sections of the data are assembled, in the correct order, at their destination.

Message queuing is a method of passing messages in a network in which a host computer stores a message for a terminal until it is ready to receive the message. This is a system appropriate to *star networks* (see page 131).

Packet switching system (PSS)

including: packet, datagram, IP datagram
is a method of sending data over a *wide area network* (see page 129). Packet switching networks are available for general use in most countries.

A **packet** is a group of bits, made up of control signals, error control bits, coded information and the destination address for the data. In a given situation the size of a packet may be fixed. These packets of information are sometimes called **datagrams**. An **IP datagram** is the basic unit of information that is transferred under TCP/IP.

Since each packet occupies a channel for only a short time, this arrangement is a very efficient use of the system. Error checking should ensure that errors are detected, and that appropriate recovery procedures are automatically started. If there is an error, it will only be in a small part of the data, and this can be retransmitted quickly. See also *TCP/IP*, page 138.

Message fragmentation

is the breaking down of *IP datagrams* (see above) into smaller units so that they can be passed to, or through, a particular processor. See also *maximum transmission unit*, page 348.

Maximum transmission unit (MTU)

is the largest unit of data that can be transferred by a particular communications system. See also *message fragmentation*, page 347.

PROTOCOLS

Open system

including: Open Systems Interconnection (OSI), ISO 7
is a set of protocols allowing computers of different origins to be linked together. The standards relating to open systems are called **Open Systems Interconnection (OSI).**

ISO 7 is the seven-layer design for the OSI protocols established by the International Organization for Standardization (ISO). It enables manufacturers to design equipment and software for a particular layer. These systems will interconnect with equipment designed for the layer above and the layer below. A brief summary of some of the aspects covered by ISO 7 is given in Table E7.1.

The relationships between the levels of TCP/IP (Transmission Control Protocol/Internet Protocol) network protocol 'family' and ISO 7 are shown in very simple form in Table E7.2. See also *TCP/IP*, page 138.

Table E7.1 Seven-layer network organisation model (ISO 7)

Level	Level name	Some functions specified within the level descriptions
Level 7	Applications	specific applications, for example data transfer, messaging, distributed databases; operating system functions and end-user interface
Level 6	Presentation	data transformation, syntax adjustments and formatting for output devices; data encryption and compression
Level 5	Session	establishes and maintains session dialogues; synchronises data exchange; provides access control and protection of higher levels from low-level functions
Level 4	Transport	establishes and maintains communications between users; levels out the data flow; provides greater flow control than the Data Link layer
Level 3	Network	routing/addressing between open systems; preventing packets from getting lost when crossing networks; multiplexing and physical network access
Level 2	Data Link	error-free connections to networks; error recognition and correction; creating and synchronising data blocks
Level 1	Physical	how bit sequences are to be sent; there is no error correction

Table E7.2 Relationship between OSI and TCP/IP protocols

OSI	TCP/IP
Application	FTP
Presentation	TELNET
Session	SMTP
Transport	TCP
Network	IP
Data Link	Ethernet
Physical	

Key:
OSI: Open Systems Interconnection
TCP/IP: Transmission Control Protocol/Internet Protocol
FTP: File Transfer Protocol
TELNET: TELetype NETwork
SMTP: Simple Mail Transfer Protocol

Bandwidth

including: broadband, narrow band
is a measure of the capacity of a *communications channel* (see page 18). It is the range of frequencies that a channel can handle. Bandwidth may be given as a frequency (range), such as 3 kHz, or as a transmission rate in bits per second (bps), such as 63 kbps. Transmission rate is often referred to as *line speed* (see page 350). For example, channels might be described as having line speeds of 56k or 64k, meaning 56 kbps or 64 kbps.

Broadband is used to describe a transmission channel having a bandwidth in excess of 3 kHz. But for practical network applications it probably needs to exceed 300 MHz.

Narrow band is used to describe bandwidths less than the smallest recognised broadband bandwidth. The term is frequently used to mean fractions of a broadband, since a broadband channel is often divided into a number of narrow band channels.

Communications protocol

including: ZMODEM, kermit, X.25, X.400, V.22bis, V.32bis, V.34, Automatic Repeat Request (ARQ), Transmission Control Protocol (TCP), Microcom Network Protocol (MNP)
is a standard set of rules used to ensure the proper transfer of data between devices. Protocols exist that specify the format of the data, and the signals to start, control and end the transfer. Many current protocols have been specified by the United Nations communications committee, the ITU (International Telecommunications Union), formerly the CCITT (Comité Consultatif International Téléphonique et Télégraphique). See also *ITU*, page 79, *internet protocol*, page 76, and *Open Systems Interconnection (OSI)*, page 348.

ZMODEM is a file transfer protocol for networks in general, but principally on the internet.

Kermit is an early file transfer protocol for networks in general, which is simple to implement and is still often used.

X.25 is the ITU standard for public *packet switching system (PSS) networks* (see page 347).

X.400 is the ITU standard for *email* (see page 86).

V.22bis is the ITU standard for 2400 bps modems.

V.32bis is the ITU standard for 14,400 bps modems.

V.34 is the ITU standard for 28,800 bps modems, formerly called V-fast.

Automatic Repeat Request (ARQ) is an error control protocol used by some modems.

Transmission Control Protocol (TCP) is a data transmission protocol defined for high-speed communications within networks.

Microcom Network Protocol (MNP) is a set of protocols for error correction and data compression.

Integrated Services Digital Network (ISDN)

is an ITU definition for (global) digital data communications. Its purpose is to ensure that people, computers and other devices can communicate over standardised connection facilities. The criteria include the setting of standards in such a way that users will have access through a limited set of multi-purpose interfaces. This really amounts to the establishment of worldwide digital communications for speech, and other data, with the simplicity of access that current telephone dialling systems provide. ISDN has definitions for the data transmission speeds, or capacities, of channels and the number of channels in each service.

Line speed

including: high-speed links
is the measure of the data capacity of a communications link.

High-speed links are available to provide the opportunities to take advantage of the information available on large networked systems. Transmission capabilities need to be fast enough to handle the large data flows involved. Among the more common transmission capabilities are:

DS0	(Digital Signal Level 0)	64 kbps
DS1	(Digital Signal Level 1) or T1	1.544 Mbps, that is, 24 DS0s
DS3	(Digital Signal Level 3) or T3	44.736 Mbps, that is, 28 T1s
FT1	(Fractional T1)	uses less than 24 DS0s, which is less than 1.536 Mbps

Frame

including: header, trailer
is a block of data together with its relevant header and trailer. The **header** contains data about the destination and route for the subsequent data, and the **trailer** indicates the end of the data.

SIGNALS

Signal

including: carrier signal, carrier wave
is electrical or electromagnetic energy transmitted from one point in a circuit to another along the *channels* (see page 18) connecting them. A signal can carry data of either analog or digital origin. A basic **carrier signal** consists of a constant-frequency electro-magnetic wave. This wave, the **carrier wave**, is modified by combining it with a represen-tation of the data in a way that can be reversed to extract the data after transmission. This process is called *modulation* (see below).

Noise

including: signal-to-noise ratio
is electrical disturbance affecting the transmission of intended signals. The existence of noise generally has the same effect on the accurate transmission of signals that people experience when listening to a person talking in a room with other people who are also talking. This is the basic origin of the term. When the noise level is too high, effective transmission ceases. The comparison of the strength of the signal with the level of noise is called the **signal-to-noise ratio**.

Modulation

including: amplitude modulation (AM), frequency modulation (FM), phase modulation, pulse code modulation (PCM), demodulation
is the process of introducing variations into the shape (the waveform) of a *carrier wave* (see *signal*, above). The modulation is used to superimpose data onto the carrier wave.

Figure E7.1 Unmodulated carrier wave

There are three forms of modulation used for the transmission of digital data, amplitude modulation, frequency modulation and phase modulation.

Amplitude modulation (AM), in which the amplitude, that is the height, of the carrier wave is used to represent 0 and 1. The simplest form of amplitude modulation is to switch the carrier wave on for a 1 and off for a 0.

Figure E7.2 Modulation by switching the wave off

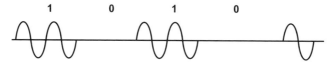

Other forms involve increasing above a chosen height and decreasing below a chosen height to represent 1 and 0.

Figure E7.3 Modulation by changing the amplitude

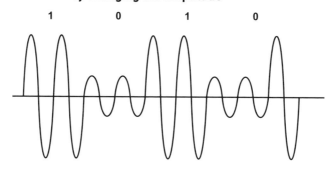

Frequency modulation (FM) combines two different frequencies with the carrier wave to produce a waveform that is made up of high and low frequency parts. This is a very common form of modulation for lower speeds of transmission.

Figure E7.4 Modulation by changing the frequency

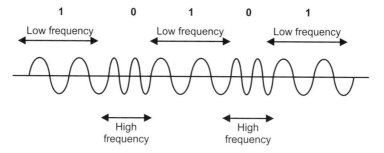

Phase modulation combines the carrier wave with an identical wave that is out of phase with it. Two-phase modulation combines two waveforms to provide patterns that are used to represent 0 and 1, shown in Figure E7.5. Four-phase modulation combines four waveforms to provide patterns that are used to represent 00, 01, 10 and 11. Four-phase modulation transmits two data bits for each element of the wave, and thus sends data at twice the bit rate of two-phase modulation. Eight-phase modulation provides for three bits (000 to 111) for each wave pattern and sends data at three times the bit rate of two-phase modulation.

Figure E7.5 Phase modulation

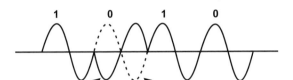

Carrier wave and a wave 180° out of phase

Pulse code modulation (PCM) is a method of sampling analog signals to produce an acceptable digital signal that contains sufficient data to allow an acceptable analog reproduction of the original signal. It requires three stages: sampling, quantisation and encoding. It was developed for sound transmission and is principally used for voice transmission.

Demodulation is the extraction of the modulating data from the modulated carrier wave signal. The circuits to do this are similar to those used in radio receivers to convert the received signals into sound signals.

Interference

including: electromagnetic interference (EMI), radio frequency interference (RFI)
is the introduction of unwanted variations into a transmitted signal. These variations may be caused by faulty design of communications equipment or by external energy sources. Interference can sometimes occur inside a computer system, but more usually affects external communications. At any place there is a large variety of electromagnetic signals, many of which are unintentionally generated by equipment such as electric motors. These signals may be picked up by wire conductors carrying electronic communications and become part of the signal that reaches the receiver. In addition there is an increasingly high density of intentionally transmitted signals (for example, from portable phones), which may cause interference on equipment for which these signals are not intended.

Electromagnetic interference (EMI) is the general term for interference caused by electromagnetic radiation at any frequency, whether continuous or intermittent.

Radio frequency interference (RFI) is interference that is generated at typical radio frequencies, in the range 10 kHz to over 100 GHz. Radio frequencies are at the lower end of the electromagnetic frequency spectrum and are more prone to interference than the higher frequency radiations such as infrared and light.

Collision detection

including: Carrier Sense Multiple Access/Collision Detection (CSMA/CD)
is a method of managing data traffic on a *local area network* (see page 129). Individual computers are responsible for waiting for the network to be free before sending a message. If two messages are sent at the same time, a collision occurs. It is detected and the messages have to be retransmitted when the network is free.

The network interface in each computer is watching all the messages being sent over the network and waits if it detects a message being transmitted. When no traffic is detected by the computer, any message awaiting transmission can then be sent. As it is likely that several computers are waiting to transmit messages and that they will do so at the same time, message corruption will result. The network interfaces detect this corruption (or collision) and are designed to wait for a short time before trying again. This staggers the load on the network.

Carrier Sense Multiple Access/Collision Detection (CSMA/CD) is a protocol for implementing this process on Ethernet local area networks. See also *token ring network*, page 131.

ACK (acknowledge) signal

is a signal sent back to the sender to confirm that a message has been received by the next point in the communications link. It normally contains the sequence number from the header of the message. See *sequence number*, below, and *header*, page 351.

Sequence number

including: initial sequence number (ISN)
is a number attached to each part of a multi-part message to ensure that after transmission the message is assembled in the correct order.

Initial sequence number (ISN) is the first number used in a particular TCP connection (see *communications protocol*, page 349).

Public telephone operator (PTO)

is any provider of a publicly available telephone service such as BT, cable companies and mobile telephone companies.

Public switched telephone network (PSTN)

is the traditional analog telephone network. It is being replaced by digital services, which are elements of *ISDN* (see page 350).

Very small aperture terminal (VSAT)

is a satellite communication system using dishes less than 3 m in diameter. It is primarily for down-linking (receiving satellite transmissions), but it can be used for up-linking (transmission to satellites).

High definition television (HDTV)

is a form of television transmission that provides a picture of much clearer quality than previous standards. HDTV transmission requires much greater bandwidth but data compression techniques are possible. For the decompression of picture data, considerable computer processing power is needed in HDTV receivers. See also *high definition digital video format (HDV)*, page 399.

E8 TRUTH TABLES AND LOGIC GATES

Binary logic (also known as Boolean algebra) is important in computing because the truth values, true and false, can be represented as the binary digits 1 and 0. All integrated circuits are designed using Boolean logic. They respond to the binary patterns they receive, and produce the required outputs as binary patterns. Binary logic influences not only the design of hardware, but also the design of algorithms and programming languages, for example the way a test such as 'If the month is February and if it is a leap year' is programmed in a high-level language.

BINARY LOGIC

Boolean algebra

also known as: binary logic
including: George Boole, Boolean values
is a set of rules for manipulating *truth values* (see page 106) according to *truth tables*, see below, and is named after the mathematician **George Boole** (1815–64). Boolean algebra is important in computing because the truth values (or **Boolean values**) in Boolean algebra, true and false, can be represented as the binary digits 1 and 0.

In digital electronics, different voltages usually represent these values. Digital integrated circuits are designed using Boolean logic. Integrated circuits respond to the binary patterns they receive and produce their outputs as binary patterns.

Binary logic also influences the design of algorithms and programming languages. The rules for combining conditional tests in statements using *logical operators* (see page 106) such as 'IF a payment is overdue AND no reminder has been sent THEN send reminder' in a high-level language involve Boolean algebra.

Truth table

is a notation used in Boolean algebra for defining the output of a logic gate or logic circuit for all possible combinations of inputs. Examples can be found in the *logic gates*, page 359.

Gate

is an electronic device to control the flow of signals. The output of a gate will depend on the input signal(s) and the type of gate. The components of a computer system can all be seen as combinations of a number of gates, each with a number of possible inputs and a single output. For details of gates, see *logic gates*, page 359.

Logical equivalence

exists when two logic circuits have the same output(s) for given inputs. Two equivalent circuits will do the same thing even though their designs are different. One result of this is that it is possible to construct all logic circuits using only NAND gates or only NOR gates. This is very useful because it allows the use of a single form of component for a variety of purposes. See also *programmable logic array*, page 339.

Karnaugh map

is a method of displaying and manipulating the relationships between Boolean operations. Karnaugh maps are mainly used to reduce logic expressions to their simplest form. They make use of the fact that all logic can be expressed as the 'AND' of 'ORs' or the 'OR' of 'ANDs'.

Figure E8.1 Karnaugh map

Input (A)	Input (B)	Input (C)	Output (P)
1	1	1	1
1	1	0	1
1	0	1	0
1	0	0	0
0	1	1	0
0	1	0	1
0	0	1	0
0	0	0	1

	$\bar{A}.\bar{B}$	$\bar{A}.B$	$A.B$	$A.\bar{B}$
$\bar{C}$	1	1	1	0
C	0	0	1	0

$\bar{A}.\bar{B}.\bar{C} + \bar{A}.B.\bar{C} = \bar{A}.\bar{C}$ $A.B.\bar{C} + A.B.C = A.B$

The shaded areas represent 1 (or true). These are combined in suitable pairs to make the simplified form.

Hence, $A.B.\bar{C} + \bar{A}.B.\bar{C} + \bar{A}.\bar{B}.\bar{C} + A.B.C = \bar{A}.\bar{C} + A.B$

In the three-input logic table, the rows for which the output is 1 represent the logic expression $A.B.C + A.B.C + A.B.C$.

The Karaugh map contains those elements for which the output is 1.

Logic symbol

is a symbol used to represent a logical operation. In addition to circles with words in them, there are standard symbols that are conventionally used to denote logic operations. These symbols are shown in *logic gates*, page 359.

Venn diagram

is a way of representing the relationships between sets in diagrammatic form. There is a close connection between set operations and logic operations. For example, in Figure E8.2(a) the shaded area represents the set operation corresponding to 'XOR'. When the rules for manipulating Venn diagrams are known, it can be seen that this diagram also establishes the logical equivalence

A XOR B = (A OR B) AND NOT (A AND B).

Figures E8.2(b) and (c) illustrate the same relationships between the two sets.

Figure E8.2 Venn diagrams

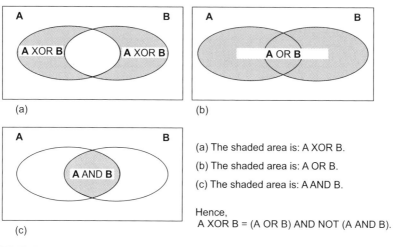

(a) The shaded area is: A XOR B.

(b) The shaded area is: A OR B.

(c) The shaded area is: A AND B.

Hence,
A XOR B = (A OR B) AND NOT (A AND B).

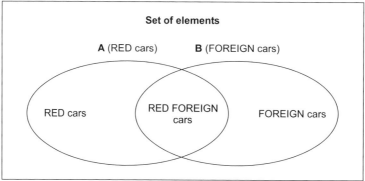

GATES

Logic gates

are the components used in making logic circuits. Each gate has one or more inputs and produces a single output that depends upon the input(s).

Some important simple logic gates are described below.

For each, the following information is given:

- The name of the gate.
- A brief description of its function.
- How it may be written (there are several notations in common use).
- Its truth table (showing how the output changes with different inputs).
- How it may be represented in diagrams (there are several methods, some using different shaped boxes for different gates).

NOT gate

including: inverse, inverter
The output of a NOT gate is the ***inverse*** of its input. If the input is TRUE then the output is FALSE and if the input is FALSE then the output is TRUE.

NOT gates have only one input and one output.

A NOT gate is also known as an ***inverter***.

It may be written as: $\qquad\qquad\qquad$ P = NOT A

Other notations express this as: $\qquad\qquad$ $\overline{A}$ or $\neg$ A

Figure E8.3 NOT gate

Input (A)	Output (P)
0	1
1	0

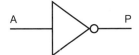

OR gate

The output of an OR gate is TRUE if any input is TRUE, otherwise the output is FALSE. OR gates have two or more inputs and one output.

It may be written as: P = A OR B

In other notations as: P = A + B or P = A ∨ B

Figure E8.4 OR gate

Input (A)	Input (B)	Output (P)
0	0	0
0	1	1
1	0	1
1	1	1

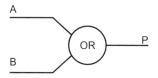

AND gate

The output of an AND gate is TRUE if all inputs are TRUE, otherwise the output is FALSE. AND gates have two or more inputs and one output.

It may be written as: P = A AND B

In other notations as: P = A.B or P = A ∧ B

Figure E8.5 AND gate

Input (A)	Input (B)	Output (P)
0	0	0
0	1	0
1	0	0
1	1	1

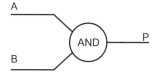
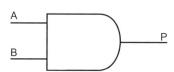

NOR gate

The output of a NOR gate is TRUE only if all inputs are FALSE, otherwise the output is FALSE.

NOR gates have two or more inputs and one output. They are important because all logic circuits can be constructed from NOR gates alone.

It may be written as: P = A NOR B

In other notations as: P = NOT (A + B) or P = $\overline{A + B}$

It is equivalent to: P = NOT(A OR B)

Figure E8.6 NOR gate

Input (A)	Input (B)	Output (P)
0	0	1
0	1	0
1	0	0
1	1	0

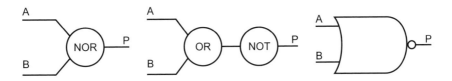

NAND gate

The output of a NAND gate is FALSE only if all inputs are TRUE, otherwise the output is TRUE.

NAND gates have two or more inputs and one output. They are important because all logic circuits can be constructed from NAND gates alone.

It may be written as: P = A NAND B

In other notations as: P = NOT (A.B) or P = $\overline{A.B}$

It is equivalent to: P = NOT (A AND B)

Figure E8.7 NAND gate

Input (A)	Input (B)	Output (P)
0	0	1
0	1	1
1	0	1
1	1	0

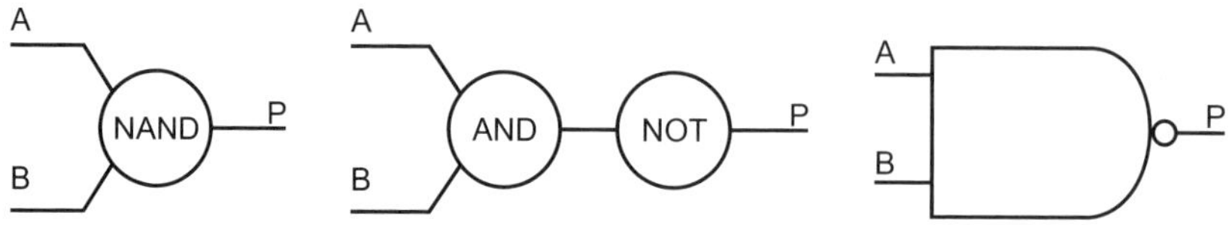

XOR (Exclusive-OR) gate

also known as: EOR gate, NEQ gate, non-equivalence gate
The output of an Exclusive-OR gate is TRUE if the two inputs are different, the output is FALSE if the inputs are alike.

XOR gates have only two inputs and one output.

The Exclusive-OR gate is also known as **EOR gate** or **NEQ (Non-EQuivalence)** gate.

It may be written as: P = A XOR B or P = A EOR B

In other notations as: P = A NEQ B or P = A ⊕ B

Figure E8.8 XOR or NEQ gate

Input (A)	Input (B)	Output (P)
0	0	0
0	1	1
1	0	1
1	1	0

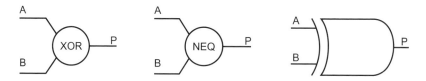

XNOR (Exclusive-NOR) gate

also known as: EQ gate, equivalence gate
The output of an Exclusive-NOR gate is TRUE if the two inputs are the same, the output is FALSE if the inputs are different.

XNOR gates have only two inputs and one output.

The Exclusive-NOR gate is also known as **EQ (EQuivalence)** gate.

It is written as: $\qquad$ P = A XNOR B or P = A EQ B

In other notations as: $\qquad$ $P = \overline{A \oplus B}$

Figure E8.9 XNOR or EQ gate

Input (A)	Input (B)	Output (P)
0	0	1
0	1	0
1	0	0
1	1	1

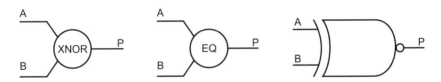

PART F: EFFECTIVE USE OF COMPUTER APPLICATIONS

This section contains terms that might be met by any computer user working with application software in any of the areas covered. The sections in Part B are concerned with more general issues involved with various areas of computer use. Some sections contain terms that might have been placed in other parts, but they have been kept with other related terms for completeness. Some terms have references to terms in other parts that will provide readers with pointers to other associated terms and concepts.

F1 WORD PROCESSING AND TEXT MANIPULATION

For details of printing and display devices used in word- and document-processing applications, see Section E4 Output.

Computers are routinely used for creating and manipulating text. This is probably the one application that most people use. The software that carries out such tasks has evolved over the years.

The first application of this type was **text editing**. The text editor was a (relatively) simple program that allowed the user to input text and subsequently make changes to it. There were usually facilities for searching the text, and for printing it out, but the first text editors were very limited in function.

The next development was the **word processor**. The principal innovation here was that the user was given control over the layout of the document – not only a choice of font and size, but also settings such as margins and line spacing. As word processors became more powerful, features were added to allow for the inclusion of diagrams and other illustrations, and to import data from other applications such as spreadsheets and databases. The table feature was added, both for the display of numerical data and for increased control over layout of the page. Components of the content, such as chapters, sections and footnotes, could be numbered automatically. In large documents, indexes could be compiled, and cross-references generated. This allows for sophisticated **document processing**.

There are other specialist software applications in this area – for example **page makeup** or **desktop publishing** software that focuses on the tasks necessary to prepare a document for professional printing; and **web editors** that prepare web pages.

SOFTWARE

Text editor

is software for creating and amending text. The first text editors were designed for the preparation of the source text of programs and for editing text files. Nowadays, they can also be used for the preparation of HTML *web pages* (see page 80) or unformatted email messages.

Word processor

is software that enables the production, editing and formatting of letters, memos and documents. The term was also used for a dedicated computer system (with keyboard, file storage and printer) that had no other function.

Figure F1.1 A word processor (top) and a desktop publishing package (bottom)

A word processor offers better facilities for creating and editing documents that are substantially continuous text, whereas a desktop publishing package is better for making up documents from different elements such as text, graphics, decorative borders and so forth.

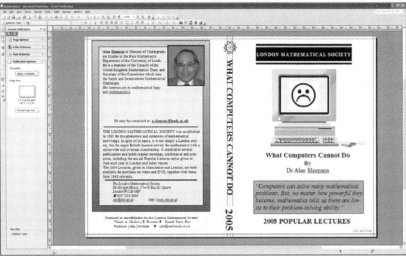

Desktop publishing

also known as: DTP
including: page makeup, page layout
is the use of a powerful word processor, or a specialised application, to prepare a document for printing. Generally, DTP software adds to the capabilities of word

processors by allowing the precise placing, orientation and alignment of text and illustrations on the page. Text can be made to flow from one area into another, and automatic links such as 'continued on p94' may be added.

When one person is using a DTP package on a stand-alone PC, it is not immediately obvious that **two** processes are involved. This is most clearly seen, for example, in the production of a newspaper on a publisher's network:

Page makeup is the process of assembling the content of the document from different sources – such as pictures, text, advertisements – and compiling appropriate indexes and numbering schemes.

Page layout is the process of adjusting the precise relationship between the elements on the made-up pages, such as distributing the white space appropriately.

While output from a DTP package can be printed on an 'ordinary' computer printer, these packages usually allow the preparation of files for sending to a commercial printer – for example, separate files for the different coloured inks used.

Web editor

is designed for the production of web pages. Text *tags* (see page 248) are used to manage the layout and formatting of web pages. While such pages can easily be created in a basic text editor, web editors are generally enhanced and allow the user to work as if they were using a DTP package with the tags being inserted behind the scenes. See Figure F1.2.

Figure F1.2 Web editor
The user has selected a mode in which the upper panel shows the HTML code that is being created while the lower panel is edited; many users will ignore the HTML completely unless it is absolutely necessary.

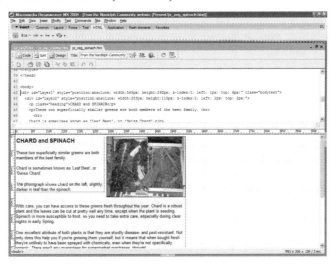

T$_E$X

including: L^{A}T$_E$X, METAFONT

is a specialised text-processing system devised by the American mathematician and computer scientist Donald Knuth. It allows much greater control over the display of mathematical and scientific formulas than do conventional word processors and is often used by academic authors submitting technical manuscripts to journal or book publishers. It is often printed as T$_E$X in recognition of this control. The power of T$_E$X makes it daunting for beginners, and a number of alternative user interfaces, such as *LATEX*, have been designed – these offer facilities for the production of a number of common types of scientific document without the user needing to write pure T$_E$X. As well as the text-processing features of these languages, there is an associated typeface definition system called METAFONT.

T$_E$X is commonly pronounced to sound like 'teck'.

PROCESSES

Editing

is the alteration of existing text, either to correct it or to add new material or to delete part of what is there.

Find

also known as: text search
including: replace
is to locate the position of one or more occurrences of a specified string of characters in a document. Usually it is also possible to *replace* the found text by a second specified string. This process is not without pitfalls – for example, a careless attempt to change every occurrence of 'disc' to 'disk' may also produce 'diskount' and 'diskover'.

Document checking

including: change tracking, annotations, spell checking, grammar checking, dictionary, thesaurus
is to use one of the many tools that are available to assist in checking and improving a document, particularly where a number of different authors are working on it.

Change tracking allows readers to examine alterations that have been made or suggested by other authors, and to accept or refuse these alterations.

Annotations are comments attached to specific places in a document that can be viewed while the document is being edited, but do not generally appear in the final printed version.

Spell checking makes use of a *dictionary* (see page 371) to suggest where words may have been wrongly spelled. Often, close matches will be displayed for the user to select the correct word. Although most applications contain a provided dictionary, there is usually a facility to allow an individual user to create a separate personal dictionary, which is then referred to if a particular word entered by that user is not found in the provided dictionary. See Figure F1.3.

Grammar checking uses a set of rules to identify where the grammar in a document may not match the chosen style and to suggest alternative grammatical structures.

A *dictionary* is a list of words that are recognised by particular software such as a word processor. Unlike a conventional dictionary, a computer dictionary is not concerned with meanings.

A *thesaurus* gives words with similar meaning to a given word. An author's style may be improved through access to a thesaurus while editing: the user selects a word in the text, and is offered a range of words with similar or related meanings.

Figure F1.3 Checking a document

This is how part of the above definition appeared as it was being typed in an earlier draft. The grammar checker has underlined 'including' on line 2, and 'is' on line 4, because it believes they should have initial capital letters. In line 4, there is no space between 'one' and 'of'; this is flagged as a spelling error. Finally, in the definition of 'change tracking', the grammar checker suggests that the underlined phrase should be amended so that it is not passive – a style suggestion that the author chose to ignore.

> **Document·checking¶**
>
> *including·: change·tracking,·annotations,·dictionary,·thesaurus,·spellchecking,· grammar·checking¶*
>
> is·to·use·oneof·the·many·tools·which·are·available·to·assist·in·checking·and·improving· a·document,·particularly·where·a·number·of·different·authors·are·working·on·it.¶
>
> ***Change·tracking***·allows·readers·to·examine·alterations·that·have·been·made·or· suggested·by·other·authors,·and·to·accept·or·refuse·these·alterations.¶

Cross-referencing

is inserting directions from one part of a document to another. For example: '*see page 11*' or '*Chapter 5 discusses this in detail*'. Many document processors make this process automatic, and the page or chapter numbers in the above examples will change as necessary when the document is edited.

Indexing

including: table of contents

is the creation of a list of words (ideas or names) used in a document, together with the pages on which they appear. This process is now largely automatic in modern document processors. The author either provides a list of words that should appear in the index, or marks particular sections of the text as being appropriate. The software scans the document for any occurrences of the words, records the page numbers and formats this to create the index; changes to the document will be automatically reflected in the index, which generally appears at the end of a document.

Where a document is structured into chapters or sections, it is also possible to create a *table of contents* that generally appears at the front of the document.

Preview

also known as: print preview
is a display of a full page, taking account of paper size, margins and so forth. While most modern document processors give a very close representation on the screen of how the document will look when printed, it is common to offer the facility to preview the output separately. This allows the user to see how complex elements will be positioned and printed, for example to check that a spreadsheet will fit on a page. See also *WYSIWYG*, page 19.

Mailmerge

is the combining of a single document (for example a letter) and a data file (often a list of people's names and addresses), see *flat file* page 95, so that a different version of the document is created for each different *record* (see page 260). The process involves setting up a document with *fields* (see page 261) marked within it. When the output is generated, data is read from the file and inserted at the marked positions completing the merge.

More complex merges can include the results of calculations on the data. A typical example would be 'how many days are left before your antivirus subscription is due'.

Figure F1.4 Mailmerge
The top illustration shows a form letter, written using codes such as <<PostCode>> to mark places where data will be placed. This letter is then 'merged' with a data source (a spreadsheet or database of names and addresses) to generate automatically the letters shown below.

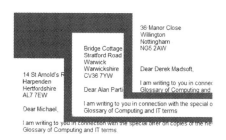

ELEMENTS OF PRINT

Typeface

including: weight
is the basic design of a character in text – what it looks like. In practice, a typeface is a set of characters of similar design, but which may occur in different **weights,** such as a 'heavy' or a 'light' version. See *font*, below and page 313.

Font

including: serif font, sans serif font, decorative font, proportional font, monospaced font, miscellaneous font
is a particular combination of *typeface* (see above), font size and *emphasis* (such as *bold*, *italic*, see page 374). There are many thousands of different fonts available, and electronic versions of these can be added to those already provided with word-processing software. Fonts can be classified in a number of ways:

Serif fonts are those like the typeface of characters in this paragraph, where the ends of the strokes forming the letters are finished with a small cross-bar or serif. Generally, readers feel that serif faces are more traditional, and are more comfortable for sustained reading.

Sans serif fonts are those like the characters in the typeface of this paragraph. There are no serifs, and one consequence of this is that the text appears to be a different size (this paragraph and the preceding one are both set in the same type size). Generally, readers feel that sans serif faces have a more modern feel, but that it is tiring to read for any length of time. The printed book version of this *Glossary* is set using DIN Next LT Pro.

Decorative fonts *are designed for headings or display work*

Proportional fonts are those, like the characters in the present paragraph, where wider letters such as 'w' or 'm' are given more space than 'i' or 'j'. This increases read-ability, but makes it difficult to align columns of information.

Monospaced fonts such as the one used for this paragraph, allocate the same space to every character. Note how each character in the cur-rent line falls exactly beneath the one in the line above.

Miscellaneous fonts are those where the 'characters' are designed for adding simple graph-ics or decoration to text: ☞ ❶ ❷ ❀ are examples from the Dingbats font.

Font size

including: point, pica, em, en
is a measure of the height of the characters. It is usual to give the height of a character such as 'L or 'K' that rises the full height of the line. Height is measured in the traditional units of **points** (1 pt = 1/72 inch) or **picas** (1 pc = 1/6 inch = 12 pt).

Because the proportion of the character is part of the design of the *typeface* (see above), it is unnecessary to specify the width separately. But some elements of layout, such as the width of a space or a dash, require a width measurement. In these cases, the width is specified as a number of **ems** or **ens** – the width of the letters 'm' or 'n' in that typeface respectively. Some fonts may appear unsatisfactory at some sizes and alterna-tive designs may be provided.

Case

including: upper case, lower case, small capitals, sentence case, title case
is the appearance of a character in a typeface. The name derives from the days of hand setting of metal type in printing works. The typesetter would have all the characters available in the font laid out in two trays ('cases'), one above the other. The capital letters were in the upper case, the rest of the letters in the lower case. The most common cases are:

UPPER CASE (capital letters);

Lower case (like most of this text).

In word processing there are these extensions to case:

SMALL CAPITALS are the same as regular UPPER CASE LETTERS, but in a slightly smaller font size. Setting text in **SMALL CAPITALS** is usually an option in a Word processor, as regular UPPER CASE LETTERS generally look over-sized when it is necessary to use them in a line of lower case text;

Sentence case where only the first letter of the sentence is in upper case;

Title Case Where Every Initial Letter Is A Capital.

Emphasis

including: bold, italic, bold italic, slanting, upright, underline, strike-through
is an additional property of the text character. The commonest examples are **bold** or *italic* text, used alone or in combination as ***bold italic***. See Figure F1.5.

Figure F1.5 Italic fonts

This example (using the Garamond typeface) demonstrates that italic is not simply slanting text. All the italic letters are specially designed; the most striking differences are in the 'h' and the 'a'. Also, despite being the same font size, the italic version is more condensed than the upright version – largely because of the kerning *(see page 375).*

Mathematics

Mathematics

Other devices used in making the meaning of text clearer are ***underlined*** text and ~~strike through text~~. The latter indicates a deletion, while making it possible to see what has been deleted.

Superscript

including: subscript
is a character that is set in a smaller type size ^{above} the line. Similarly, a ***subscript*** is set $_{below}$ the line. This is useful in displaying mathematical expressions: x^2; chemical formulas: H_2O; or footnote markers.

Leading

including: tight, loose
is the vertical space between lines of type. It was originally achieved through the insertion of strips of lead or other metal between the rows of characters and hence is pronounced to rhyme with 'wedding' rather than 'weeding'. Generally, the space allowed is about 20 per cent of the type size. Hence in a paragraph of 10pt text, an extra 2pt leading will be allowed. This is sometimes described as 10/12pt.

Paragraphs can be set without any leading at all, as this one is. Text that is displayed like this is said to be set *tight*, although this generally makes it harder to read as the eye may stray from one line to another.

Similarly, paragraphs can be set *loose* to provide more space between the lines; this is more useful, as it can allow room for corrections or insertions in a draft document.

Kerning

is the adjustment of space between adjacent letters to provide a more attractive layout. While the design of the typeface has considered the appropriate amount of space to allow following each character, some common pairs such as 'W' followed by 'A' can be improved by setting the letters closer together. This is usually done automatically but some authors may wish to change the design.

W A compared with WA

Kerning is closer on italic characters than upright ones: see Figure F1.5.

LAYOUT

Space

including: white space, river, soft space, hard space, non-breaking space
is simply the absence of printing. Designers of documents need to pay attention to the use of space as well as to the layout of text. The designer of the printed book version of this *Glossary* has used space in the layout to make it easy to identify where new definitions start, for example.

Many people are surprised that there are so many types of space:

White space is the overall name for any space on the page, whether part of the layout or within a single line. It can arise in many ways: as a character entered with the space bar on the keyboard; from the insertion of a non-printing character such as a *tab* (see page 376); automatically when software justifies a line; or from layout decisions made about spacing before and after paragraphs. Sometimes the white space will give the unintentional appearance of one or more white lines running down through a block of text – white space like this is called a *river*.

Soft space is one entered by the user, most often to separate words. A soft space may be removed automatically, for example where the word processor wishes to insert a *line break* (see below) at that point. Or it may be increased in size, for example where a word processor is inserting extra space in order to fully justify text (see *justification*, page 378)

Hard space is intentional space that the user has explicitly keyed. Hard spaces will remain as part of the text, even when it is reformatted, say at a *line break* (see below). A hard space has a fixed length and will not be expanded.

Non-breaking space is the type of space that occurs between words that should not be allowed to appear on separate lines (such as that in 'Henry IV'). Most document processors allow the user to type a special combination of keys to insert such a character, which will print as a space but will not be allowed as a place to break a line.

Page break

including: line break, word wrap
is the place where a page of printed text ends and a new page begins. Word processors normally break pages automatically at the end of the last complete line that will fit on the page, or where the user has inserted an explicit page break. See also *widow*, page 378. A **line break** is the place where a line of printed text ends and a new line begins. Word processors normally break lines automatically between words or where the user has entered an explicit line break character.

Word wrap is a facility available in many packages to break lines automatically between words. When the text on the line reaches beyond the right-hand margin, the whole of the word is transferred to the beginning of the next line.

Header

including: footer
is one or more lines of text that appears at the top of every page in a document; the corresponding lines at the bottom of the page are known as the **footer.** Headers and footers can be quite sophisticated areas, and may include the current section title and page number, both of which can be automatically updated when the document is edited.

Rule

is simply any straight line on a document. It may be vertical to separate columns or horizontal to separate sections of text.

Tabs

including: tab stop, left-aligned tab, centred tab, right-aligned tab, decimal tab
are non-printing characters that may be inserted into text, and that cause the next character to appear a predetermined distance (known as the **tab stop**) from the left-hand margin. Tab stops can be set by the author, but generally word processors have a default set of tab stops, say every five centimetres across the page.

It is common for the header or footer of a document to be laid out using different sorts of tab. See Figure F1.6 and Figure F1.7.

Figure F1.6 Tab stops

The use of tabs allows data to be laid out in table form. As this example shows, particularly in the last line where the decimal points do not fall below those in the line above, good layout may require more than simply continuing typing from a predetermined position.

Compensation	£500	£1000	£2500
100g	£3.85	£4.30	£5.20
500g	£4.25	£4.70	£5.60
1kg	£5.35	£5.80	£6.70
2kg	£6.95	£7.40	£8.30
10kg	£19.00	£19.45	£20.35

Figure F1.7 Use of tabs

This is the footer from an early version of this glossary section. Tabs are displayed as small arrows, and in the ruler above the text you can see the tab stops: a centred tab between 7 and 8 cm, and a right-aligned tab between 14 and 15 cm.

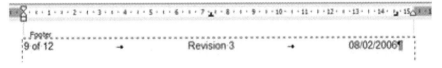

Most word processors offer different types of tab:

Left-aligned tab is the sort described above; typing will continue from the tab stop.

Centred tab causes the new text to be centred about the tab stop; while text is being added, the text will adjust itself so that it remains centred.

Right-aligned tab causes typing to finish at the tab stop; while text is being added, characters will shift back into empty space to keep the alignment.

Decimal tab will align any decimal point in a number with the tab stop; this is appropriate for columns of numbers or sums of money.

Table

is a rectangular display area of rows and columns that can be used to present data, or simply to lay out text in a controlled way. Although *tabs* (see page 376) can be used in much the same way, tables are more versatile, as borders and shading can be used to make the data stand out. See Figure F1.8.

Figure F1.8 Use of tables

Compensation	£500	£1000	£2500
100g	£3.85	£4.30	£5.20
500g	£4.25	£4.70	£5.60
1kg	£5.35	£5.80	£6.70
2kg	£6.95	£7.40	£8.30
10kg	£19.00	£19.45	£20.35

Justification

including: left justification, right justification, full justification, centred text
is the arrangement of text so that it aligns with the margins of the document. This may occur on the screen or on a printer. See Figure F1.9.

Figure F1.9 Justification of text

This paragraph of text is **left justified**. That is, all lines begin at the left-hand margin. No extra space has been added, so the right-hand margin will appear ragged. Most normal text is left justified.

This paragraph is **right justified**. Now all the lines end at the right-hand margin, and as a consequence it is the left-hand margin that appears ragged. This sort of justification is almost never used for ordinary text, but can be helpful in displays or captions and in tables.

This paragraph is **fully justified**. That is, extra space has been inserted automatically so that both margins are straight. You should notice that the second line of the paragraph is much tighter (has less added space) than those on either side of it. Full justification is less noticeable when the span of text is wide, but nonetheless it is most commonly encountered in newspaper columns. This book text is fully justified.

This final paragraph is **centred text**. This style is most frequently used in captions beneath illustrations or tables.

Widow

including: orphan
is a single line at the start of a paragraph or table that is followed immediately by a page break, with the remainder of the text out of sight on a fresh page. Similarly, an **orphan** is a single line falling on a new page, with all preceding lines on the previous page.

Widows and orphans are generally to be avoided, and most word processors can automatically adjust page breaks so that no single line appears by itself.

STYLES

Gutter

is extra horizontal space allowed in a document, at the edge of a page that will be bound, to compensate for the difficulty of reading text that goes too close to the binding.

Footnote

including: endnote
is an explanatory comment or reference placed outside the main body of the text, at the foot of the page that contains the reference to it. **Endnotes** are similar to footnotes but are placed at the end of the chapters or sections where there are too many to be placed at the foot of individual pages. The reader's attention is drawn to the footnote (or endnote) by a reference mark (usually an asterisk *).

Style

including: character styles, paragraph styles, linked styles
is a collection of formatting and layout characteristics that may be applied to the text in a document. Figure F1.10, on page 380, shows the existing styles in one document, and suggests the variety of elements that can be specified. Usually, a word processor will be supplied with a number of built-in styles, but the user is free to define new styles or to modify existing ones. Once a style has been defined and named it can be applied to any section of text in a single operation.

Styles are sometimes classified as **character styles** that define characteristics of the text (size, colour, typeface and so on) or **paragraph styles** that specify spacing, indentation and so on.

Linked styles are a common device to simplify the production of a consistent document. After the use of one style (say for a section heading), moving on to a new paragraph automatically applies an appropriate style for the next material – body text, perhaps.

Stylesheet

including: cascading stylesheets
is a collection of *styles* (see above) defining the layout and appearance of a document. Users, particularly those working in a large organisation, can link new documents to existing stylesheets, and in this way ensure that there is a corporate style – all letters, memos, forms and reports will have the same 'feel'.

---

* This is the footnote attached to the reference mark (the asterisk) in the main body of the text. If the document is reformatted, the software ensures that the footnote always appears on the same page as the reference mark.

It is possible to link more than one stylesheet to a single document. This may simply add more styles to those originally available, but is also useful in the creation of a series of **cascading stylesheets**, each of which modifies earlier ones. For example, a basic stylesheet for a business might define the typeface to be used for all documents, while later stylesheets might define the exact fonts to be used in headings, quotations, notes and so forth. Here, the styles actually used in the document inherit definitions from the basic sheet (such as the typeface), but modify (or overrule) definitions such as the font size where these are explicitly redefined. See also *stylesheet*, page 251 in Section C7.

Figure F1.10 Style definition dialogue box
The description section shows the characteristics that have been specified for the style named 'Heading 2'. This style combines character properties (that the font is Arial bold, 14pt) and paragraph properties (space before and after, tinted background).

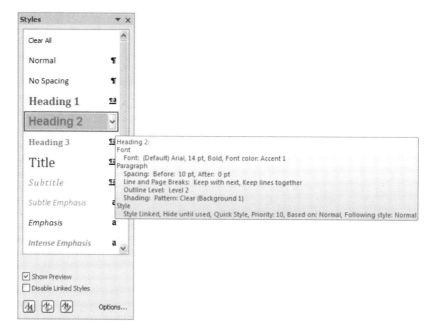

Template

is an 'empty' document that may be used as the starting point for the creation of a new document. Although a template may have no text, it will be attached to a *stylesheet* (see page 379) so that the user can begin adding text to a document that has already been designed and laid out.

In fact, a template *may* contain text: A template for a letter may contain a company logo and return address, for example. These elements will therefore be automatically inserted whenever a new document based on the template is created.

Body text

is the basic style of the text in a document. The majority of text in most documents will be body text.

F2 SPREADSHEETS

Before personal computers were readily available, accountancy and bookkeeping were often made easier by the use of large sheets of paper ruled into a grid of rows and columns – spreadsheets. Columns could be totalled, and a number in one box used in a calculation to give a value in another. This activity was a natural one for a computer application, and this type of software has developed in power ever since.

Figure F2.1 A typical spreadsheet

	C6		$f(x)$ Σ =	23.28					
	A	B	C	D	E	F	G	H
1								
2	miles	kilometres	litres	gallons	trip (miles)	trip (km)	L/100 km	mpg
3	0	0						
4	328	525	29.12	6.41	328	525	5.55	51
5	708	1133	28.81	6.34	380	608	4.74	60
6	985	1576	23.28	5.12	277	443	5.25	54
7	1384	2214	31.17	6.86	399	638	4.88	58
8	1691	2706	25.41	5.59	307	491	5.17	55
9	2017	3227	27.52	6.06	326	522	5.28	54
10	2363	3781	26.29	5.79	346	554	4.75	60
11	2698	4317	27.29	6.01	335	536	5.09	56
12	3024	4838	29.70	6.54	326	522	5.69	50
13	3354	5366	25.34	5.58	330	528	4.8	59
14	3687	5899	25.72	5.66	333	533	4.83	59
15	3985	6376	24.26	5.34	298	477	5.09	56
16	4322	6915	27.23	5.99	337	539	5.05	56
17	4595	7352	24.00	5.28	273	437	5.49	52
18	4932	7891	27.43	6.04	337	539	5.09	56
19	5223	8357	25.31	5.57	291	466	5.44	52
20	5502	8803	24.22	5.33	279	446	5.43	52
21	5794	9270	25.29	5.57	292	467	5.41	52
22	6152	9843	27.26	6.00	358	573	4.76	60
23	6459	10334	26.48	5.83	307	491	5.39	53
24	6836	10938	30.12	6.63	377	603	4.99	57
25	7212	11539	28.70	6.32	376	602	4.77	60
26	7568	12109	32.89	7.24	356	570	5.77	49
27	7945	12712	27.28	6.00	377	603	4.52	63

Figure F2.1 shows a typical computer spreadsheet package in use. The screen is dominated by the cells making up the sheet, which are referred to by their row and column – the selected cell, highlighted by a black outline, is cell C6 as you can check by the row and column labels along the edges of the spreadsheet, or in the box at the top left above the worksheet.

Other features of this display will be discussed in this section, but even the most casual of examinations shows that the cells contain information of different types. The cells in row 2, for example contain only text. These 'labels' identify the contents of the columns they head and suggest – correctly – that this is a spreadsheet created by a motorist who is interested in monitoring the performance of his or her car. Elsewhere, you can see whole numbers (columns A and B, for example) and numbers with decimal parts (columns C and D). The designer of the spreadsheet has also been able to format the entries – text headings in bold, for example, and a vertical line between columns G and H to separate the performance figures to the right from the individual entries to the left. Some cells have been given a tinted background; how this improves usability is described below.

There are also important differences between the cells that are not apparent simply by inspecting the display. For example, compare the two cases in Figure F2.2.

Figure F2.2 Cell contents

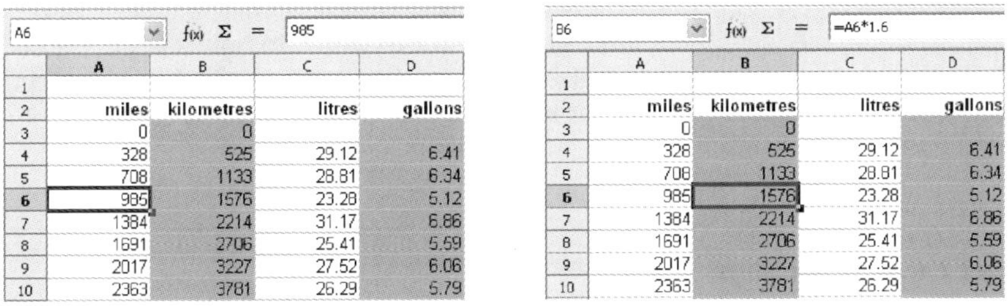

A6 | f(x) Σ = | 985

	A	B	C	D
1				
2	miles	kilometres	litres	gallons
3	0	0		
4	328	525	29.12	6.41
5	708	1133	28.81	6.34
6	985	1576	23.28	5.12
7	1384	2214	31.17	6.86
8	1691	2706	25.41	5.59
9	2017	3227	27.52	6.06
10	2363	3781	26.29	5.79

B6 | f(x) Σ = | =A6*1.6

	A	B	C	D
1				
2	miles	kilometres	litres	gallons
3	0	0		
4	328	525	29.12	6.41
5	708	1133	28.81	6.34
6	985	1576	23.28	5.12
7	1384	2214	31.17	6.86
8	1691	2706	25.41	5.59
9	2017	3227	27.52	6.06
10	2363	3781	26.29	5.79

On the left, the selected cell is A6, which contains the number 985. This is confirmed in the space above the column labels (A, B, C, ...). In fact, this number was entered into cell A6 by the user, to record the mileage reading when the car was filled up. Cell B6 appears to hold the same information in kilometres, but this was not keyed in. As the illustration on the right shows, cell B6 actually contains `=A6*1.6`. These are the instructions (a formula) that convert miles to kilometres; although the cell contains the formula, it is the result '1576' that is displayed in the body of the sheet. When the user of the spreadsheet enters a new mileage figure into a blank cell in column A, the corresponding reading in kilometres appears automatically in column B. In fact in this spreadsheet only two numbers in each row are directly entered by the user – the mileage and the number of litres of fuel added. Everything else in the sheet is calculated automatically. The designer of the spreadsheet has emphasised this by adding a tinted background to the cells that will be calculated automatically – the user should enter values only in the untinted cells.

Although it is not really appropriate in our example spreadsheet, some of the power of a computer spreadsheet comes from the ability to ask 'what if?' questions. The consequences of entries being slightly different can easily be explored when a large amount of data can be calculated rapidly and automatically from one or two direct entries. Figure F2.3 is a simple example.

Figure F2.3 'What if?'

	A	B	C	D
1				
2	€	rate	£	
3	1	0.69	0.69	
4	5		3.45	
5	10		6.90	
6	25		17.25	
7	50		34.50	
8	100		69.00	
9				

	A	B	C	D
1				
2	€	rate	£	
3	1	0.72	0.72	
4	5		3.60	
5	10		7.20	
6	25		18.00	
7	50		36.00	
8	100		72.00	
9				

The spreadsheet on the left shows the equivalent of some amounts of money in euros when converted into pounds and pence at an exchange rate of €1 = £0.69. To see what would happen if the rate changed to 0.72, it is only necessary to alter the value in B3, as shown in the spreadsheet on the right.

As well as simply manipulating arrays of numbers, spreadsheets can also be used in other ways. Where the information is suitably structured, a spreadsheet can be used as a simple database (see Section B3, page 93), for example to hold a list of names and addresses. And, as shown in Figure F2.4, spreadsheet software offers graphing and charting options for displaying the numerical information in a number of more readily understandable forms.

Figure F2.4 Chart options

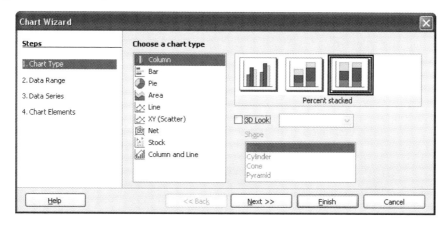

Spreadsheet

is an applications package often used to process and display financial or statistical information. It takes its name from the way data is arranged on the screen in rows and columns, as in the traditional layout of numbers in account books. The user can specify that data items displayed in particular positions are to be dependent on entries in other positions, and are to be recalculated automatically when these entries change. For example, the effects of changes to one data item on totals, subtotals, and other calculations such as 'profits' and 'VAT' can be explored. See Figure F2.1 and the introduction to this chapter for further examples.

Cell

including: address, column, row, block, range
is one of the grid of boxes on a spreadsheet in which a single entry can be placed. The single entry can be a number, text or a formula. It is usually referred to by its **address** in the spreadsheet using the **column** and **row** labels. The column label refers to a vertical group of cells and the row label refers to a horizontal group of cells (see Figure F2.2). A rectangular grouping of the cells is usually called a **block** and is identified by giving the **range** of addresses from the upper-left cell to the lower-right cell of the rectangle, for example B2:D6 would have three columns (B to D) of five rows (2 to 6). See Figure F2.5.

Figure F2.5 A cell block

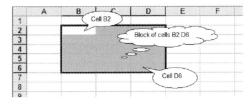

Formula

is the way a calculation is represented in a cell, using mathematical operations and references to other cells. The formula is entered into a cell, but the display shows the current result of the calculation, which may change as the values in other cells change.

For example, in Figure F2.1, to calculate the trip mileage shown in cell E6 as '257', it is necessary to use the formula:

```
= A6 - A5
```

That is, to subtract the previous mileage figure (708 in cell A5) from the current figure (965 in cell A6).

Function

is a 'ready-made' formula provided by the spreadsheet application. It has usually been set up to represent a formula that is commonly used or is too complex to enter repeatedly. Examples of functions include:

=SUM( ) to calculate the sum (i.e. the total) of a row or a column or a block of cells. For example, =SUM(A1:A10) adds up all the numbers from cells A1 to A10.

=MEAN ( ) to calculate the average (mean) of a row or a column or a block of cells. For example, =MEAN (B2:D6) finds the average of the numbers in the block B2 to D6.

=IF ( ) sets the value of the cell containing the formula to different values, depending on the contents of other cells. For example, =IF(A1>5,1,0) will put a '1' in the current cell if the contents of cell A5 are greater than 5, and a '0' if not.

=NOW ( ) puts the current date and time into the cell containing the formula. Of course, this will be updated whenever the spreadsheet is recalculated. This function has no arguments, so although the brackets are necessary, nothing is put between them.

Recalculation

including: automatic recalculation, manual recalculation
is the updating of the cells that may be changed because of the last input of data. When new data is entered into a spreadsheet cell, this affects the results of any formulas that refer to that cell.

There are two sorts of recalculation:

Automatic recalculation is the normal method and is done after each and every entry in the spreadsheet.

Manual recalculation is where the user decides when it should be done and presses a particular set of keys to have the whole spreadsheet recalculated. This can be efficient in a large or complex spreadsheet by postponing the recalculation until all new data items have been entered.

Replication

including: relative reference, absolute reference
is the process of copying a formula from one cell to another. As a formula usually involves references to cells, this process requires care.

Figure F2.6 shows the spreadsheet of Figure F2.3 after the user has chosen to display formulas rather than values. The values in columns A and B appear just as they did before, because these are values entered directly and not calculated by formulas. But the formulas in column C are all slightly different.

Figure F2.6 Replication

	A	B	C
1			
2	€	rate	£
3	1	0.69	=A3*B$3
4	5		=A4*B$3
5	10		=A5*B$3
6	25		=A6*B$3
7	50		=A7*B$3
8	100		=A8*B$3
9			

The one in cell C3 was the original formula entered by the designer of the spreadsheet. It multiplies the value in A3 by the value in B3, but the designer has referred to these cells in different ways.

A **relative reference** is one like the cell reference A3 in the formula in cell C3. No special markers are added to the reference, and when this formula is copied into the cells below it, you can see the A3 changing to A4, A5 and so on, depending on the row it is in. This is a common situation: the values in column C are obtained by multiplying the corresponding value in column A by the exchange rate.

An **absolute reference** is used in the same formula to refer to the exchange rate in cell B3. Here a $ is placed before the 3. This indicates that when copying this part of the formula the 3 should never change – it will always refer to cell B3, whichever row it is copied to.

Because of this care in planning the formula, the designer could copy the formula from cell C3 and paste it into cells C4:C8 in one step, rather than having to type the different formulas into each cell individually.

Goal seeking

is a common technique in using spreadsheets, especially for 'what if?' type problems. For example, the currency converter spreadsheet in Figure F2.3 changes euros into pounds. To convert in the opposite direction, from pounds to euros, it would be simple enough to write another spreadsheet, but it would also be possible to answer the question 'How many euros are equivalent to £100?' by systematically trying a range of euro values in column A to find the one that converts into £100 in column C. Here, you would be seeking the 'goal' of £100. More powerful spreadsheets make this process automatic; the user specifies the goal, and the spreadsheet automatically increments the values used in the formula until the goal is reached.

Pivot table

is a facility offered by many spreadsheet and database management packages for working with data items that can be classified in several ways, and where it is required to display the same data in a number of different views.

For example a single shop might record sales month by month in a number of categories – groceries, sweets, newspapers etc. This might be displayed as the spreadsheet in Figure F2.7.

However, if this were not just a single shop, but a chain of similar shops, it would be desirable to examine the data across **all** the shops. Figure F2.8 shows just two possible analyses: grocery sales month by month, and comparative shop performance for one particular month.

The name arises because the data in this simple example is 'three dimensional' – that is, every number has three attributes: its shop, its category and its month. You could imagine it as a solid figure made up by stacking spreadsheets similar to that in Figure F2.7 one

Figure F2.7 Spreadsheet for a single shop

	A	B	C	D	E	F	G	H
1	*SHOP 1*							
2		Jan	Feb	Mar	Apr	May		
3	Grocery	£4,284	£3,987	£4,615	£4,117	£3,869		£20,872
4	Sweets	£847	£1,012	£973	£1,142	£982		£4,956
5	Newspapers	£550	£587	£543	£598	£603		£2,881
6	Magazines	£1,549	£1,479	£1,568	£1,601	£1,541		£7,738
7	Fruit	£804	£819	£978	£1,055	£1,203		£4,859
8								
9		£8,034	£7,884	£8,677	£8,513	£8,198		£41,306
10								

behind the other, one for each shop. To display the required views of the data, as in Figure F2.8, you can imagine that the solid shape is pivoted so that correct attributes are facing the viewer.

Figure F2.8 Two views of data from several shops

On the left, the sales month by month for each shop are displayed for the 'grocery' category; there will be a similar sheet for each category. On the right, sales for each shop and category are displayed for January; there will be similar sheets for each month. Pivot tables allow this data to be displayed without creating fresh spreadsheets and copying the data.

F3 GRAPHICS, DESIGN AND DIGITAL IMAGING

Other related terms may be found in Section E2 Input.

Computers are very well suited to producing and editing digital images, pictures and other graphics. These images may be created entirely within the computer (using a **painting** or **drawing** package) or they may be loaded into the computer from an increasing number of suitable electronic devices – digital camera, image scanner or video camera.

There is much more data in a picture than in other forms of data such as a text document. A typical still picture may use 5 Mb of storage or more, and a four-minute uncompressed HD video sequence as much as 30 Gb. Storing and processing such images have always been possible on larger computers, but are now possible on PCs as adequate storage media and processor speeds are available. Many people now regularly use digital cameras and download the images to improve, retouch or edit them on the computer before sharing them with friends by email, CD, DVD or the web.

Other packages use graphics as part of the design process for books and other printed matter – adding illustrations or decorative borders. In some cases, a photograph (or even 'live-action' video) can be 'retouched' electronically, to add, remove or recolour some elements of the picture. Most TV or film graphics are nowadays generated purely electronically.

In other applications, such as **computer-aided design (CAD)** – see Section F6 – the processing power of the computer is used for calculation, as well as for the pure drawing.

The use of the **internet** – see Section B2 – has made the technical details of graphics (especially **image compression**, see below) particularly important. Website designers must make appropriate choices of format in order to reduce the time taken to download a web page, without compromising quality.

IMAGE DATA FORMATS

Image compression

including: compress, redundancy, lossless, lossy, JPEG, MPEG, delta compression
is to reduce the size of an image data file, i.e. **compress** it, so that it may be stored more economically or transmitted faster. This is particularly important where video sequences are played on a screen or recorded onto video tape, as a failure to transmit the data at a steady (high) speed will cause the images to distort. There are many

storage and compression schemes for graphical data, optimised for different characteristics of images. Some common ones are listed in Table F3.1.

Redundancy is repeated data describing the same element of an image. A common
technique in compressions schemes is the identification of redundancy. For
example, in an image with a solid background colour, it can be more efficient to
store the information that the next 500 pixels are all the same, rather than repeating
the pixel data 500 times.

Lossless compression schemes are those that allow the original images to be recreated; others are **lossy** and generally involve a loss of resolution in parts of the image
where experience shows that it will be least noticed.

The **JPEG** format (defined by the Joint Photographic Experts Group) is used for still
images, and works by identifying areas of the image that are similar – an arrangement of pixels that is repeated elsewhere in the image, perhaps after a scaling or a
rotation. It is more efficient to store information about these similarities than it is to
repeat the data.

The **MPEG** formats (defined by the Motion Picture Experts Group) are used for moving
images, such as video, and work by a method known as **delta compression**. In order
to cope with the high demands of TV standard pictures (25 separate frames transmitted every second in the UK), a full picture is sent only occasionally (typically 5 times a
second); between these frames, information concerning only changes to the image is
transmitted. This uses much less data, particularly where the picture is relatively static,
as with a title or caption. See also *data compression*, page 281.

Render

including: wire frame, texture, light sources
is to prepare a complete, full-resolution version of an image that previously only existed
in a draft form. Many image manipulation programs and video editing systems offer
the user an inferior version of the image while it is being worked on, which must be
rendered before it appears in its final form. For example, a 3D drawing package may
represent solid objects in **wire frame** form, showing only the outlines. When the user
is satisfied with the arrangement of the objects, the image will be rendered to incorporate surface texture, illumination and shadows. Similarly, a complex transition applied
to a video sequence, such as a 'page turn' to introduce a new image, will be ignored
or presented at low resolution until the user is satisfied with the timing, after which it
must be rendered before it can be viewed as intended. Video rendering for even modest
sequences can take an appreciable length of time, possibly several hours.

Texture can usually be added to images of solid objects when rendering, giving the surface the appearance of being created from a 'real' material such as stone or wood.

Light sources can also be specified when rendering. The position and colour of the lights
illuminating an object will affect where reflections and shadows fall in the finished
image.

Table F3.1 Image compression formats

Type	File Extensions	Lossless?	Type	Comments
Windows® bitmap (PC)	bmp	Yes	Still image bitmap	Uncompressed data; one of the standard formats
Tagged Image File Format	tif, tiff	Yes	Still image bitmap	Compressed data, one of the standard formats
Graphics Inter-change Format	gif	Yes	Still image bitmap	Good for images with large areas of solid colour. As 8 bits are used, only 256 distinct colours can be represented. A simple 'animated' version is available, suited to web graphics
Portable Network Graphics	png	Yes	Still image bitmap	Good for images with large areas of solid colour. PNG uses 24 bits and can represent millions of distinct colours
Joint Photographic Experts Group	jpeg, jpg, jpe	No	Still image	Good for photographic images
Vector	wmf, dxf	Yes	Still image vector	dxf is the industry standard CAD format
QuickTime®	mov	See comments	Video	Although storage as a .mov file is lossless, the data being stored is probably already held using lossy compression
Audio-video interleaved	avi	See comments	Video	Although storage as an .avi file is lossless, the data being stored is probably already held using lossy compression
MPEG-1	mpg	No	Video	Suited to small, low-resolution sequences on CD
MPEG-2	m2v, mpg, mp2	No	Video	Suited to full-screen high-resolution sequences on DVD
Digital video (DV)	avi	See comments	Video	DV data is already compressed in the camera This format does not compress further
Windows® Media Player	wmv	No	Video	Proprietary format for Microsoft®'s Windows® Media Player. The accompanying audio, if any, is stored in .wma format
RAW	many, specific to camera manufacturers	Yes, see comments	Still image data	RAW format is the unprocessed data seen by a digital camera sensor; it is essentially the digital equivalent of a film negative

Colour correction

including: white balance, colour channel, alpha channel
is to adjust the colour information in an image. This may be done for effect or to correct an error when the image was captured. Cameras see colours in a different way to humans. For example, sunlight is generally bluer than indoor lighting, which is redder. When viewing a scene, the human brain compensates for this, and we are generally unaware of the effect. In 'ordinary' photography, corrections are made when the photograph is printed. Digital devices can compensate, provided they know which colour in the scene is intended to be white. This can be done automatically (but may be fooled by, for example, a very red sunset) or manually, by pointing the camera at a white object and making the camera perform a ***white balance.***

When a scene has been captured incorrectly (the camera has been told it's indoors when the scene is lit by sunlight), it is possible to adjust the colours after the picture has been downloaded into a computer. Often, separate controls to manipulate red, green and blue separately are provided; these are known as the ***colour channels,*** and are similar in principle to methods of printing where each colour is applied separately. See also *colour model*, page 310. A further channel, known as the ***alpha channel*** is sometimes provided, which allows the user to specify which areas of the picture are to be transparent and allow a background image to show through.

Streaming video

including: streaming audio
is a technique used to allow moving video to be displayed on a website, without an excessive delay while a (potentially massive) data file is downloaded. The opening seconds of the video must be downloaded before playback can begin, to provide a buffer. The player software starts to play this video to the user and keeps the buffer filled by downloading the next images while the first are playing. If transmission delays over the internet cause the buffer to become dangerously low, the quality of the new images is reduced to allow more of them to be transmitted, in order to catch up. One characteristic of this method of delivery is that once playback is completed, the user has no permanent copy of the video on their computer. This can be an advantage, for example where a film company wishes to show extracts from a popular film, but not allow these extracts to remain in other hands.

Similar ***streaming audio*** techniques can be used for sound files.

GRAPHIC DESIGN APPLICATIONS

Computer graphics

is the use of the computer to display pictorial information. This can be as simple as a line drawing or chart, or as complicated as an animated sequence of pictures. The output might be shown on the computer screen, printed out as hard copy or transferred directly to videotape.

Vector graphics

including: line art, 'drawing on the fly'
is a method of creating images where the instructions for drawing certain basic shapes, such as lines, rectangles, circles and so forth, are stored, rather than the picture itself. These basic shapes, or 'objects', can easily be moved around the drawing, or laid on top of other objects; because of the way they are constructed, they do not interfere with one another, and can be thought of as existing in separate 'layers'; text in drawings would be stored as shapes – each letter a separate object.

Most **line art** of this sort tends to have only a few elements, so there is a considerable advantage in that less storage is needed, as compared with *bitmapped graphics* (see page 394). As the image is created each time from the instructions (**'drawing on the fly'**), rather than simply copied from storage, scaling the picture up or down in size does not alter the resolution.

Figure F3.1 Vector graphics at two scalings

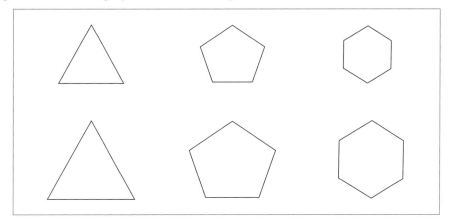

Graphics tablet

also known as: graphics pad
including: stylus
is a device used to input drawings into a computer, mimicking the use of a pen or a paintbrush. The user draws with a stylus on a flat pad or tablet (sometimes called a **graphics pad**), either copying a drawing or working freehand. See Figure F3.2.

Stylus is the generic name for devices used for drawing on a graphics tablet. The movement of the stylus is detected by the tablet and its software in one of a variety of ways, for example through the use of a wire matrix in the pad or by sensing the angular movement of an arm supporting the stylus. A stylus may be pressure sensitive, producing a darker or more intensely coloured line if pressed firmly. The position of the stylus on the tablet is input to the computer and used to position a cursor on the screen. Subsequent movement causes a drawing on the screen that matches the movements on the tablet. These devices are generally preferred to a mouse for computer drafting packages.

Figure F3.2 A graphics tablet and stylus

The stylus is being used on the tablet as a paintbrush to create the shape seen on the screen.

Bitmapped graphics

is a method of creating images where a picture is held as a *bit map* (see page 306) – where the state of each individual *pixel* (see page 315) is stored. Text in such a picture would also be stored in the same bit map. Such drawings require a lot of storage space, because even 'blank' portions of the picture contribute to the size. They can also appear jagged when scaled up or down in size. However, for freehand drawings, and graduated areas of tone, bitmapped graphics are better than *vector graphics* (see page 393).

Figure F3.3 A typical bitmapped graphic

Photo editing

including: layers, image enhancement
is the process of altering a digital photographic image, either for effect or to correct errors in the original. Typically, photo editing software will allow the cropping and resizing of images, *colour correction* (see page 392), a variety of distortions (for example to create 'buttons' for websites), and the ability to add text or freehand drawing elements to the image (for example, to produce a labelled diagram). In addition, such packages usually convert images from one still image format or resolution to another (see Table F3.1).

Figure F3.4 Examples of photo editing

In the original picture (1) the giraffe is too far away. The picture is cropped (2) to make a more pleasing composition. This has then been scaled up to make it a more appropriate size (3). This image in turn can be either flipped (4) or (rather pointlessly) skewed (5) or rotated (6). As well as changes to the size and shape of the image, the image itself could be modified in a number of ways, see Figure F3.5.

Figure F3.5 An example of image enhancement

The original picture at top left was taken with a simple point-and-shoot digital camera. The bright window has confused the exposure, and the flash was not triggered. As a result, the man is in silhouette. Below the picture is a display of the brightness levels in the picture – predominantly at the darker (left) end with a single bright spike at the right. These levels cannot be changed, but their brightness in a print can be adjusted by dragging the middle pointer below the histogram. Moving this to the left leaves the blacks and whites untouched, but adjusts the mid-tones, resulting in the acceptable photograph at the top right.

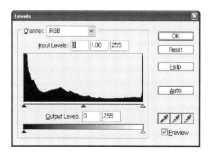 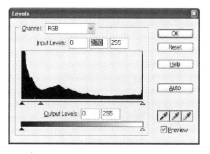

Such packages usually allow an image to be seen as a number of separate **layers** each of which can be moved separately and edited without affecting other layers. In this way, a part of one image can be superimposed on another, and edited to blend in seamlessly.

Specialist *image enhancement* software can take low quality images (perhaps taken under poor lighting) and improve the picture by removing *noise* (see page 397) and strengthening outlines. Such techniques are now commonly used with images sent back from space probes.

Integrated graphics package

including: painting package, drawing package
is one that incorporates both *vector* and *bitmapped graphics* (see page 394). At one time, it was common to use separate software to create and manipulate different types of graphics, stored on separate layers. **Painting packages** worked exclusively with bitmapped graphics, **drawing packages** with vector graphics. It is now more usual to find both methods available in a single software package, particularly in *photo-editing* packages (see page 394).

Integrated packages will handle text separately from graphics, in separate layers, using the font definitions installed on the computer, and allowing the text to remain completely editable (as in a word processor) until the user wishes to export the combined image in a graphics format.

Clip art

while computer graphics software allows users to draw their own illustrations, many publishers offer professionally drawn pictures that can be edited to suit an individual user's needs. These are available on disk or for download over the internet. They are popularly known as 'clip art' because of the way in which they are 'clipped' out of the file and 'pasted' into a drawing.

Figure F3.6 Typical clip art

DIGITAL STILL IMAGING

Digital camera

is a stills camera that produces a digital image file of the scene photographed. This colour image may be printed directly from the camera or may be downloaded to a computer for storage or further manipulation (see *photo editing* page 394). Most digital cameras also record video.

Noise

is unwanted data in a digital picture; it often appears as random dots or patterning across the image. It is most often seen in images gathered by cameras operating in very low light, such as surveillance cameras.

See also *noise*, page 351 in Section E7 Communications technology.

Photo printer

is a printer of sufficiently high quality and resolution to print acceptable photographs. While photographs may be printed on plain paper using a colour inkjet or laser printer, the increasing popularity of digital stills photography has resulted in the introduction of affordable specialised printers that produce better quality results through the use of glossy photographic quality paper and through software designed to optimise the printing of photographs. Such printers often accept images directly from a camera or removable *storage* device (see below), without the need for connection to a computer. Sometimes, the printer will finish the process by cropping the print to a standard size. See also *printers*, page 317.

Digital camera storage

including: memory stick, compact flash card, xD card, smartmedia
generally consists of a small removable solid-state device that can be plugged into a special reader for input to a computer, or directly into a printer to produce a paper copy without the use of a computer. Most digital cameras (and also some video cameras that have a still photograph capability) use removable storage. For long-term storage these images need to be transferred to a more reliable form of memory, such as DVD. There are several proprietary makes, incompatible with each other, including the **memory stick**, the **compact flash card, xD card** and **smartmedia.** See also *memory card*, page 304 in Section E3.

DIGITAL VIDEO

Digital video camera

also known as: camcorder
is a movie camera that records digital images onto video tape, a small DVD, memory card or built-in hard disk. Many video cameras can also record still photographs. As the resolution needed for an acceptable moving image (72 dots per inch) is much less than for an acceptable still photograph (at least 300 dpi), this facility is unlikely to replace the dedicated digital stills camera.

Computer animation

including: in-betweening, tweening, key frame, morphing
is the creation of apparent movement through the presentation of a sequence of slightly different still pictures. The screen display of a computer is redrawn every 1/25th of a second, at least, whether it has changed or not, because of the television technology used in many display devices. With a fast computer, it is possible to generate a new picture in this time, so that an impression of movement can be created, in the same way as a cinema film creates the illusion of movement from still pictures. Computer animation packages are now routinely used in the television and film industry, particularly where they can mix 'live action' with computer-generated images.

In-betweening (or **tweening**) is the process of creating intermediate images for use in computer animation. Images of an object that is moving or changing will be defined at intervals, perhaps several seconds apart; these are known as **key frames**. Software is then used to interpolate the movements of points of the image and draw the larger number of intermediate frames needed for convincing animation.

Morphing is the use of *in-betweening* to change one image into another, typically to make one person appear to become another.

Video capture card

also known as: video digitiser
is a specialised analogue-to-digital converter that reads video signals from a video tape or video camera, digitises them, and stores them in a computer. The most recent video cameras record their data digitally, and strictly speaking a capture card is unnecessary. However, many users continue to use a capture card because other functions (such as *colour correction*, see page 392, or special effects) are packaged on the card.

Codec

is short for coder/decoder. It is the component that processes a video signal for storage and subsequent processing in a computer, and may be implemented as software or hardware. While all codecs perform the same function, they are not equivalent; in order to recreate the video signal for playback to a TV set or video recorder, the coded data must be decoded by the same codec that was used originally. It is an important component of a *video capture card*, see above.

Digital Video format (DV)

including: miniDV, DVCam
is the most widely accepted format for standard definition digital video tape recording. Because the images are held and transmitted digitally, there is no deterioration of the picture when sequences are loaded into a computer, edited and rerecorded to tape. For this reason, the standard has become popular with both amateurs and professionals. The representation of the digital data is standard on all equipment, but there are two sizes of tape cassette; that most commonly encountered is **miniDV**, which is slightly smaller than an audiocassette. Professionally, most recording is done using **DVCam**, which uses identical cassettes and data format, but spaces the data more widely on the tape to provide greater security from interference between adjacent tracks. Although a digital format, the DV system uses hardware *image compression* (see page 389) in the camera to produce data that is only 20 per cent of the size originally captured.

High definition (HD) digital video format

including: AVCHD, HDV, DVCProHD, AVCIntra, XDCAM, RED, interlace, progressive scan
is the latest development in video formats. Whereas the resolution of *DV* (see above) is 720 × 576 pixels (in the UK), HD extends this to 1920 × 1080. Such higher resolution requires 'HD-ready' televisions for display. As well as increased resolution, HD allows a greater contrast range in reproducing subtle shades of colour and is more like film.

As high definition video is recorded digitally and is increasingly stored on memory cards or hard disks, it is less imperative for manufacturers to conform to a common standard, and there is an increasing number of formats. These include: **AVCHD, HDV** (a tape-based format that uses the same cassettes as DV), **DVCProHD** and **AVCIntra** (both specific to Panasonic), **XDCAM** (Sony) and **RED**.

Together with increased resolution comes a choice of display mechanisms:

Interlaced video is the method that has traditionally been necessary to prevent annoying flickering of a broadcast television picture. The lines making up a TV frame are transmitted in two batches (fields), the odd numbered lines followed by the even numbered ones. The brain merges these images into a single picture. HDV interlaced video is described as 1920 × 1080i or simply 1080i.

Progressive scan video has become possible as processing speeds have increased. Here the lines making up the picture are simply transmitted in order; this is the normal method of computer display. HDV progressive scan video is described as 1920 × 1080p or simply 1080p.

Video editing system

including: offline editing, online editing, real-time editing
is a software package that allows the user to capture video material through a *capture card* (see page 399) and organise it on the hard disk of the computer. Individual sequences may be trimmed to length and placed next to one another to assemble a final video programme. Transitions between sequences (a dissolve from one to the other, or an animated 'page turn', for example) can be added, as can effects such as increasing the contrast of the picture or adding reverberation to the sound track. Titles may be created and added to the sequence, possibly by superimposing them over live action. Still images can be imported in a variety of formats and moved around the screen. Sequences may be speeded up or slowed down. Music and commentary may be added, either replacing the original sound or mixed with it through the use of sound-editing facilities in the package. When this creative work is complete, the finished sequence may be played back and recorded to videotape or DVD.

The video data remains in its original position on the hard disk, and the instructions for compiling it into a finished sequence are stored as a series of references to the original files. Among other advantages, this allows a sequence to be reused without the need to create an additional (space consuming) copy. Usually, these instructions can be saved independently of the video data, allowing the editor to delete the data, but retain a copy of the instructions that can be used to recreate the sequence in the future by reloading the data.

Some terms have a very different meaning when applied to video editing by computer than that suggested by a more general computing context. Most edited video is only a small selection from the larger amount originally recorded. Where storage is an important consideration, it may be impossible to hold all the original material at the required resolution.

Offline editing is a method of working where all the material is loaded, but at a very high degree of *compression* (see page 389); it is unacceptable for the finished sequence, but adequate for the user to make decisions. When the sequence is complete, careful note is taken of the material actually used. The low-grade working data is then deleted, freeing up the space in the computer.

Online editing, where only the material actually needed is loaded, at the best possible quality. Most video editing systems allow this process to be automated.

Real-time editing has a similar meaning to that in *real-time system* (see page 17). Editing systems that are powerful enough to create effects and transitions without the need to *render* them (see page 390) are said to do so in real time.

Figure F3.7 Typical semi-professional video-editing system

Running along the bottom of the display (which uses two monitors) is the timeline, with trimmed video and audio tracks in place, with transitions marked between them. At the left above are the clips available to the editor – some shown as thumbnails in the 'floating' window that has been opened, the remainder filed in 'bins' or folders. To the right are displayed the current pictures from a clip to the left, and from the completed programme to the right – in each case, the 'safe areas' for TV display are shown. Also visible are the palette of editing tools and an audio-level meter. Most of the windows have tabs allowing the user to 'call forward' other windows that are currently hidden.

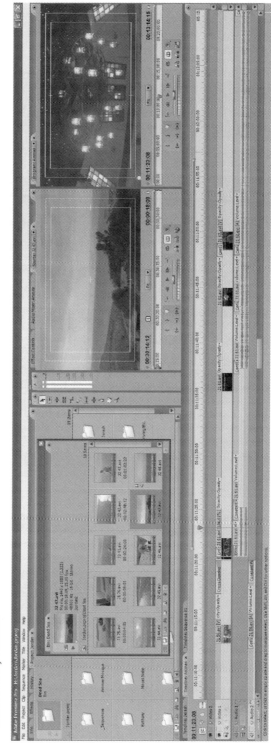

F4 SOUND

Other related terms, especially those concerned with modulation, can be found in Section E7 Communications technology.

Electronic recording and reproduction of natural sound has been available for many decades, through the use of tape recorders or gramophones. Similarly, the ability to generate natural sounds electronically – sound synthesis – was developed long before computers. What is relatively recent is the ability to process sound on computer equipment that is affordable by the consumer.

Sound is produced by the continuous vibration of air. This means that it has analog properties. The electrical output from a microphone consists of a continuously fluctuating voltage and has to be converted into a digital form if it is to be stored on any digital device (for example, compact disc or digital audio tape) or if it is to be manipulated in a computer. The conversion of analog signals to digital is achieved by **sound sampling**, a process in which special hardware measures the level of sound many times a second (typically up to 50,000) and records this as numerical data. The reverse process of turning digital sound data into audible sound is accomplished by using the data to determine the level of, for example, voltage applied to a loudspeaker or headphone.

Specialised sound equipment, such as mixing desks in a recording studio, use digital data in the same way as a computer, and hence contain microprocessors and storage devices such as hard disks.

Most personal computers are now supplied with a simple microphone for recording sound and a CD player for playing sound files. There is also at least a simple loudspeaker, and possibly a more sophisticated stereo sound system for replaying sound.

While the most common applications of sound in computers are simple recording and playback, it is also possible to edit sounds using a suitable software package. This can involve simply removing unwanted portions of a recording, but may also be used to alter the characteristics of the sound – adding echo or reverberation, for example, or removing hiss or crackle from older recordings. It is also possible to generate sounds purely by creating the digital data; the noises made by a computer when a key is pressed or an error message appears are just such 'artificial' sounds.

Any electronic music device that is controlled by a keyboard similar to a piano is called a (music) **keyboard**. The keys, which are arranged like the black and white keys on a piano, are frequently supplemented by switches, sliders or other ways of setting and changing the electronic signals produced by the device.

In order to fully understand what computers can do with sound, it is necessary to be aware of the nature and characteristics of sound, entirely separate from computing. The medium that carries sound (most usually air, but sound can also travel through, for example, water) vibrates, and there are technical terms used to measure this vibration.

CHARACTERISTICS OF SOUND

Waveform

is a representation of the vibrations that cause sound. A complex waveform is shown in Figure F4.1. This is the waveform corresponding to a real sound, and it is hard to see any regularity in it. Figure F4.2, later in this section, shows a simpler waveform (a single note) and how the terms explained below may be interpreted.

Figure F4.1 A waveform (the opening of a Strauss waltz)

Frequency

also known as: pitch
including: hertz (Hz), cps, kilohertz (kHz), wavelength
is the number of complete cycles made in one second. It is measured in **hertz** (**Hz**), after the German physicist, Heinrich Hertz. One hertz is equal to one cycle per second (**cps**). To avoid the use of large numbers, audible frequencies are also quoted in **kilohertz** (**kHz**); 1 KHz = 1000 Hz. The higher the frequency, the higher the sound heard by the listener. For example, the lowest note on a piano has a frequency of 27.5 Hz, while the highest is 4186 Hz.

An alternative measure of the same characteristic is the **wavelength**. This is the distance between places where the vibration is in the same place. Higher frequencies correspond to lower wavelengths. See Figure F4.2.

Amplitude

including: volume
is the maximum amount that the vibrating particles move. It is basically the **volume** of the sound: the higher the amplitude, the louder the sound heard. See Figure F4.2.

Figure F4.2 Characteristics of a (sound) wave

Two pure waveforms showing the same note. Wavelength and amplitude are marked, and are the same in each case. However, the lower note starts earlier in time, and hence there is a phase difference between the waveforms.

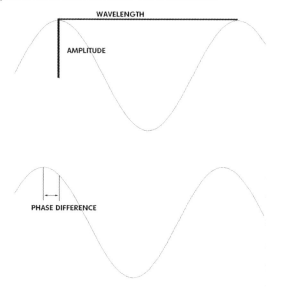

Phase

is the amount of a complete cycle that has elapsed. It is measured in degrees – 360° is one complete cycle. We do not *hear* the phase of a sound, but it is important when sounds become out of phase. See *stereophonic sound*, below.

Harmonics

including: timbre
It is possible to generate a 'pure' note electronically, or with a tuning fork, but the situation is considerably more complicated with a real musical instrument. Here, whenever a note is sounded, there will be other, higher, notes present, called harmonics. Exactly which harmonics, and how loud they are, will depend on the instrument, and it is the particular blend of harmonics that gives an instrument its characteristic sound or **timbre**. Figure F4.3 and Figure F4.4 explain this process.

Stereophonic sound

also known as: stereo
including: stereo image, monophonic, mono, A&B, M&S
We hear sounds through our ears. Because these are on opposite sides of the head, sound takes different amounts of time to reach each ear. The human brain uses this time difference to create a three-dimensional picture of where sound sources are positioned in relation to each other (sometimes called a **stereo image**). A single microphone cannot sense this three-dimensionality, and records the sound as a **monophonic** (**mono**) signal.

Figure F4.3 Harmonics and timbre (1)

The basic note being played on a violin (left) and on a clarinet (right) is shown at the top of each picture. Because violin strings are fixed at each end, the waveform is a closed loop. With the clarinet, which has an open mouth, the waveform is different. As well as these basic notes, a number of higher frequency notes sound at the same time. These are added together to give the timbre of each instrument, as shown in Figure F4.4.

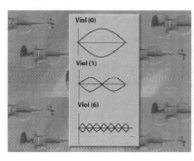
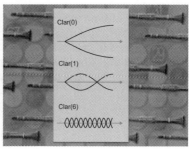

Figure F4.4 Harmonics and timbre (2)

Three stages in the addition of the harmonics from Figure F4.3. The pure note at the top is modified in strikingly different ways. Although both instruments are sounding the same note, the resulting waveform is very different.

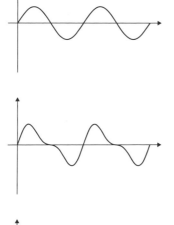
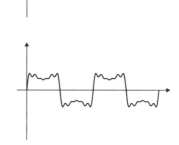

In pursuit of realism, modern recordings and broadcasts use two microphones a small distance apart, and play the sound back through a pair of speakers.

For simplicity of recording and processing, stereo signals are usually separated as left channel and right channel, sometimes called **A&B** signals. For transmission, particularly radio or television broadcasts, an improved method is possible. Two signals are sent, but these are a combined signal formed by adding left and right together (A+B) and a 'stereo difference' signal formed by subtracting one signal from the other (A–B). The difference signal would make poor listening by itself, as the B signal largely cancels out the A signal.However, the combined signal is just a (louder) version of what a mono microphone would have heard; a receiver such as a portable radio without stereo facilities can simply play this signal without further processing. A stereo hi-fi can use the difference signal to recreate the left and right channels before they are sent to separate loudspeakers or headphones. This system, transmitting a mono signal and a stereo difference signal is known as **M&S** stereo.

The *phase* (see page 404) of a signal is important in stereo. While we cannot hear the phase in a sound, if the left and right channels of a stereo system are not perfectly in phase, one will tend to cancel out the other.

SOUND PROCESSING

Envelope

including: ADSR (attack, decay, sustain, release)
is a shape that is used to describe the changes in volume (amplitude) or pitch (frequency) of a note as it changes with time. The form of a sound envelope is normally used in *sound*

Figure F4.5 Stereophonic sound
This is the same music as in Figure F4.1, but recorded as a left (top) and a right (bottom) channel. Although the waveforms are very similar, because the microphones are hearing the sound from the same source, there are differences. For example, the peak of sound in the centre of this fragment is louder (has greater amplitude) in the right channel than the left. The instrument that produced this sound was positioned to the right of the recording microphones and will sound as if it was positioned to the listener's right.

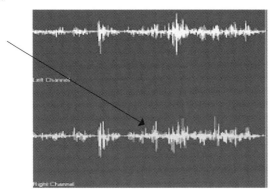

synthesis (see page 408). One commonly used way of describing a volume envelope is known as **ADSR**, short for attack, decay, sustain and release. See Figure F4.6 and Figure F4.7.

Figure F4.6 Volume envelope

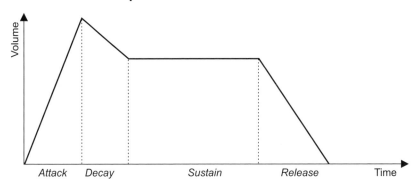

Figure F4.7 Two pitch envelopes

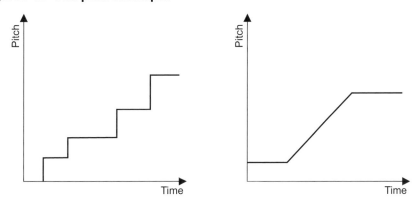

Attack is the rate at which an envelope rises to its initial peak before starting to decay. For example, percussive sounds (piano or drums) have a high attack rate for their volume (amplitude).

Decay is the rate at which an envelope falls from its initial peak to a steady (sustain) level.

Sustain is the level at which an envelope remains while a key is still pressed after the initial attack and decay stages.

Release is the rate at which an envelope fades away from its sustain level when the key is released.

Frequency modification

also known as: frequency shifting
If a sound recording is played back faster than the speed it was recorded at, the frequency increases – voices sound like high-pitched squeaks. Using a computer to digitally process the sound by manipulating the sampled data allows the frequency to be adjusted so that a speeded-up recording sounds natural, but faster. It is even possible, within limits, to correct tuning errors.

SMPTE codes

are an agreed set of standards that make it possible to synchronise sound and video signals. SMPTE is an acronym for the (US) Society of Motion Picture and TV Engineers.

Sound sampling

including: sampling rate, sampling resolution
is the process of receiving analog sound signals from a microphone (or other sound source) and analysing them in order to store them as digital data. By performing this analysis very quickly and very frequently, a faithful digital representation of the sound can be stored.

The quality of sound produced using sound sampling depends upon the sampling rate and the sampling resolution; the higher each of these is, the more faithful the sample, but the larger the amount of data storage required. It is not always necessary to strive for the highest quality: a telephone uses the equivalent of a very low sampling rate because it is the message that is important, not the quality of the speaker's voice. It is simply perverse to attempt to listen to music on your telephone handset, however hard the manufacturers try to persuade us that this is a good thing.

Sampling rate is the frequency with which samples are taken. For theoretical reasons, to do with capturing not just the basic sound but also its higher frequency *harmonics* (see page 404), the sampling frequency needs to be at least twice the highest audible frequency in the sound being sampled. For music, this indicates values around 40–50 kHz (40,000–50,000 samples per second). See Figure F4.9.

Sampling resolution is the number of bits used for storage of each sample value; CD quality sound uses 16 bits, but acceptable sound for use on the internet or through a computer speaker may be achieved from only 8 bits.

Sound synthesis

also known as: sound generation
including: frequency modulation (FM), phase distortion (PD), linear arithmetic (LA), additive synthesis
is the use of electronic devices for creating sound, sometimes called *sound generation*. The final, audible, sounds will be generated using analog techniques, but digital methods may be used to generate the sound prior to this final stage. With care, electronically generated sound can create notes that are like those produced by a variety of musical instruments.

Figure F4.8 Sampling

The curve is part of a sound waveform. At regular intervals (the sampling rate), the amplitude of the waveformis recorded. When these samples are played back, it is the angular waveform that the listener hears. The effect of this is shown in Figure F4.9.

Figure F4.9 The effect of sampling rates

The upper waveform has been sampled at twice the sampling rate of the middle waveform. As a result, the small high-frequency variation about three-quarters of the way through has been captured, while it is completely missed at the lower rate. The bottom illustration superimposes the two samples to show the difference.
Source: Key Stage 3 National Strategy Communication: sound and video. DFES 0011/2003. HMSO

In creating sound from scratch (that is, not using sound that has already been sampled), it is common to start from pure waveforms and modify these to mimic the characteristics of 'ordinary' sound. The most commonly used methods are:

Frequency modulation (FM) in which the frequency of a waveform is continuously altered to carry sound information.

Phase distortion (PD) in which the phase of a waveform is continuously modified.

Linear arithmetic (LA) in which sampled sounds are used as well as pure tones at the start of the process. Arithmetic operations are then carried out on the values of the bit patterns representing the sounds. (See *sound sampling*, page 408.)

Additive synthesis is a software method in which the user selects a mixture of harmonics and the computer calculates the values for the waveform at very small successive time intervals. In all cases the digital values for the sound are turned into sound signals by a *digital-to-analog converter* (see page 344). Different methods of creating sounds produce different qualities of sound.

Sound formats

including: lossless, lossy

A number of standard formats have been adopted for the storage and interchange of digital sound data; some of the more common of these are listed in Table F4.1. Generally, different formats are incompatible with one another. Some formats are **lossless**, in that they preserve all the information in the original sample; others are **lossy** and involve some degradation of the signal.

Table F4.1 Audio storage and compression schemes

Type	File Extensions	Comments
Windows® waveform	wav	A sampled lossless format, with selectable sampling rate
Audio Interchange File Format	aif, aiff	Sampled lossless format, with selectable sampling rate
Real Media	rm	Sampled format, used for *streaming audio* (see page 411)
Motion Picture Experts Group	mp3	A compressed, lossy format that is efficient. Usually used for downloading audio files over the internet. Selectable compression rate
Windows® media	wma	A compressed, lossy format with selectable compression rate
Musical Instrument Digital Interface (MIDI)	midi	A format for interchange only, not for storage. The sound itself is generated from samples already stored in the sound hardware, and the MIDI file consists simply of instructions on how to play these samples.

Note that the video file formats in Table F3.1 page 391 generally have their own associated audio formats, which are not shown in Table F4.1.

Streaming audio

is a technique used to allow audio to be played on a website without an excessive delay while a large data file is downloaded. The opening seconds of the sound must be downloaded before playback can begin, to provide a buffer. The player software starts to play this sound to the user and keeps the buffer filled by downloading the next sound while the first is playing. If transmission delays over the internet cause the buffer to become dangerously low, the quality of the new sound is reduced to allow more of it to be transmitted, in order to catch up. One characteristic of this method of delivery is that once playback is completed, the user has no permanent copy of the audio on their computer. This can be an advantage, for example where a record company wishes to promote music from a popular record, but not allow these extracts to remain in other hands.

Table F4.2 The effect of sampling and format on file sizes

Method	File Size	
wav sampled at 44.1 kHz	3.10 Mb =	3,100,000 b
wav at 22.05 kHz	1.54 Mb =	1,540,000 b
wav at 12.025 kHz	854 kb =	854,000 b
wav at 6 kHz	432 kb =	432,000 b
mp3	303 kb =	303,000 b
MIDI	2 kb =	2,000 b

One piece of music, encoded by different methods, results in the different file sizes shown.
Source: Adapted from Key Stage 3 National Strategy Communication: sound and video. DFES 0011/2003. HMSO

Similar *streaming video* (see page 392) techniques can be used for moving image files.

DEVICES

MIDI (Musical Instrument Digital Interface)

including: MIDI channel, MIDI standard, MIDI code
A musical instrument digital interface, MIDI (frequently, but incorrectly, referred to as a MIDI interface) is a particular form of serial interface (see *interface* and *interface card*, page 335) built into or added to the parts of an electronic music system. The interface allows electronic music data to be passed in both directions between parts of the system. The links between parts of the system are called **MIDI channels**. The form of the interface and the structure of the data are defined by the **MIDI standard**, which was agreed between the major manufacturers of electronic musical instruments in 1983. The standard defines the codes (**MIDI codes**) to be used for musical data; for example the pitch of a note and its volume. These codes allow music data to be passed between

devices from different manufacturers in the same way that ASCII codes (see *character set*, page 256) allow alphanumeric data to be passed between different computers.

Music synthesiser

including: synthesiser, analog synthesiser, digital synthesiser, multi-timbral synthesiser, polyphony

is an electronic device for creating sounds. It is often just called a **synthesiser**. The sounds may be generated electronically using either analog or digital techniques (see *sound generator*, below). Most synthesisers have a piano-style keyboard and need to be connected to an amplifier with loudspeakers for the sounds they produce to be heard.

- **Analog synthesisers** are usually intended to be used as musical instruments to be played, and most do not generally have the ability to store the sounds they create.

- **Digital synthesisers** generally incorporate some form of digital storage and frequently have a built-in store of ready-made sounds. Digital synthesisers generally offer a much greater variety of sounds and a wider range of manipulation options than analog synthesisers. For example, a **multi-timbral synthesiser** can play two or more different sounds at the same time, or produce a number of different notes at the same time (**polyphony**), or a combination of both of these capabilities in the same synthesiser.

Sound controller

including: musical instrument controller, audio controller

is a hardware device that controls sounds generated by a sound source. Controllers usually do not produce sounds themselves, though they may be made to look like (and be used like) musical instruments, for example a piano keyboard or a guitar. These are called **musical instrument controllers**. Some controllers use joysticks, sliders or wheels. These may be built into other controllers or attached to a musical instrument. Control of sounds is usually achieved by using MIDI codes (see *MIDI*, page 411). There are also **audio controllers**, which can generate (MIDI) control signals from audio sounds. With an audio controller looking like a microphone, a user can sing into it while 'playing' a synthesised sound from a connected sound generator, and thus control the sound produced.

Sound generator

also known as: sound source

is a digital device capable of producing sounds as part of an electronic music system. A range of such devices exists, which create sounds similar to those produced by particular musical instruments, such as drum machines, electric guitars or electronic organs. A *music synthesiser* (see above) is an example of a sound generator; it has a piano-type keyboard that is used to play it, but most sound generators have no direct means of being played as if they were musical instruments. Some have a collection of pre-defined sounds and some have synthesising capabilities. The sounds may be accessed via *MIDI* (see page 411), to be used as input to a sequencer or a music controller, or the device may be attached to a computer as a dedicated peripheral.

Figure F4.10 A typical computer sound-processing package

A stereo waveform is shown being edited in the larger window. The menu choices show that reverberation or echo may be added, that a fade in or out can be applied, or the stereo image adjusted. Note the options to shift the phase of the recording (see stereophonic sound, page 404) and to modify the frequency.

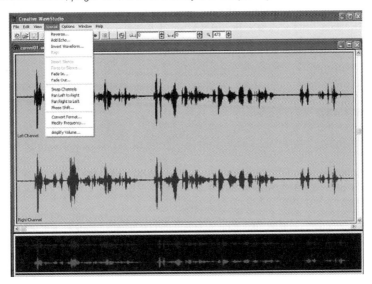

Sound processor

is the general term for electronic sound equipment that can take a sound as an input, modify the signal and output the new sound. The processing may use either analog or digital techniques, but the use of digital methods is now more common. Most sound processors have a particular function, for example echo units, reverberation units, graphic equalisers, noise reduction units. All of these work in *real-time* (see *sequencer*, page 414). Sound-processing software on a suitable computer can do the same things that individual sound-processing items achieve. Thus a computer may be used as a general-purpose sound processor.

Sound mixer

also known as: mixing desk
including: channel, music channel
is an electronic device for combining sound signals. It is commonly found in recording studios where it is used to balance the loudness of sounds from a number of sources, and to add effects through use of built-in *sound processors* (see above). An operator (also often known as a sound mixer, in which case the hardware may be known as a **mixing desk**) selects how input signals are to be combined to form one or more output signals, and adjusts the levels of individual sources and combinations. The independent input and output signals are known as **channels** or **music channels**.

Sequencer

including: real-time entry, step-time entry
is a digital device that can store a set of representations of notes, rhythms and other musical data for replaying at a later time. It may also include facilities for editing or for producing repeating patterns. Sequencers may range from the very simple, capable of storing only a small number of notes or a single chord, to the complex, capable of simultaneously handling many independent musical parts. Sequencers are often built into synthesisers (see *music synthesiser*, page 412) and drum machines or other electronic music devices. One example of the use of a sequencer is to play a piece of stored music at different speeds without the distortion of pitch, which happens if the speed of a tape recorder is varied. Another is to change the sound of a series of notes previously entered, rather like changing the colours of parts of a computer-generated picture with a graphics program.

Music parts can be entered into a sequencer in one of two ways, real-time or step-time:

Real-time entry has the musical information provided by playing the notes with the correct relative time intervals. They need not be the actual intervals since the sequencer can modify the speed (tempo).

Step-time entry has the time interval between each note defined by the person entering the musical information.

Computer-based music system

including: digital sound system
is an arrangement of electronic music devices and a computer linked together so that music and other sounds, such as speech and singing, can be captured, stored, manipulated, generated or reproduced. These systems will probably contain both digital and analog components. Where only digital-processing components are used, they are referred to as **digital sound systems**.

Music workstation

is a collection of connected music-generating and sound-manipulating equipment. A typical arrangement will include a keyboard, a synthesiser and a sequencer. They are increasingly likely to include a computer with appropriate software. See *computer-based music system*, above.

F5 USER INTERFACE AND DOCUMENTATION

For more details of terms met when using the internet see Sections B1 and B2.

Software writers try to make their products attractive to the user as well as being effective and easy to use. Much time and effort is spent on designing ways in which the user interacts with the computer and the software. Most software users are more concerned with what a package can do than with how it works. They expect to be able to see and understand what the software can do, they want to be able to communicate their instructions easily and have quick and understandable responses from their computer. This requires a consistent approach to design and use of features such as logos, icons, menus, pointer types, swipe actions and mouse clicks.

As the scope of computer applications has increased and the number of computer users has also increased, a variety of ways have evolved for communication between the user and the computer; this is called the **user interface** or **user environment**. There are fashions in user interface design, just as there are in car or clothes design, but what is important is that the interface should achieve its objectives as efficiently as possible.

All user interface designs are limited by the capabilities of machines and people. Each design seeks to make the most of the strengths and avoid the weaknesses of computer equipment and its users. Aspects of computer hardware (for example processing speed, memory capacity, input and output devices) restrict what software can achieve. Speech is the most common form of communication between people and speech recognition systems for communication from people to computers are now available for personal computers. Communication through text is limited by the speed at which people can read text presented on a screen and the time taken to type accurately on a keyboard. Most software designers have chosen graphical ways of presenting the activities or concepts available for selection at any time: **icons** (small pictures with an easily understood meaning) are widely used since graphical information should be independent of the user's language and can be used wherever the meaning of the icon is understood and not offensive. All user interface designs are compromises between what it is desirable to provide and what it is possible to achieve. All of this applies to the design of web pages and websites.

The combination of those parts of the hardware and software of a system with which the user interacts makes up the user interface. User interfaces are described in a variety of ways, with names highlighting their main features; for example **touch screen interface**, **graphical user interface (GUI)**, **menu selection interface**, **windows environment**, **forms dialogue**. There is no single kind of user environment that suits all applications or all users; the choice of an appropriate user interface depends on the amount of information to be presented or elicited, the experience of the users and their familiarity with the particular software.

Since taste and personal preference largely determine people's reactions to different user environments, there will always be scope for variety in their design. For those people who spend a long time working at a computer it is very important that the user interface they experience makes a positive contribution to their efficiency. It is increasingly common for the user to be able to adapt (**customise**) the facilities provided by the system to fit the situation in which the system is used. The usability and efficiency of software can also affect the health and safety of users.

Additional arrangements can be made where there is a special user environment, such as where provision has to be made for people with disabilities. These might include the provision of customised input and/or output devices, such as touch-sensitive keyboards, and the appropriate additional software.

When a software package or piece of hardware is purchased, instructions on how to set up and use the software or the device will be needed. The instructions, known as **user documentation**, might be printed, but are frequently seen on the screen when the software or driver has been installed. Increasingly the interface is through the browser.

INTERFACES

Human–computer interaction (HCI)

is the behaviour of people when engaging with computers and the computer's response back to the person. The behaviour is affected by the design of the *user interface*, see below.

User interface (UI)

also known as: human computer interface, man–machine interface (MMI), user environment
is part of a computer program that allows a user to communicate and control either the complete computer system or an application program. A user interface is usually supplied with a computer system and tools are provided to enable application programmers to make the user interface to their programs work in a similar way. See also *operating system*, page 9.

Other terms for this are **human computer interface, man–machine interface (MMI)** and **user environment**. Any of these terms is likely to be used in discussions of how people and computer systems interact and the ease of use of a system.

One way of classifying interfaces is by the style of communication they provide. Some are purely textual while others rely on a graphical presentation or audio communication.

Common types of user interface are described below.

Graphical user interface (GUI)

replaces some or all of the words with icons that indicate what action is required. It usually relies on a *pointer device*, see page 419, or *gesture recognition*, see page 420. The most common GUI is the *WIMP interface*, see page 420.

Touch screen interface

is a graphical user interface that uses a touch sensitive screen as the *pointer device*, see page 419. Managing computer devices such as tablet computers and smartphones, where a pointer device such as a mouse would be inconvenient and the screen size might be limited, is very efficient with this interface.

Command line interface

including: command sequence
is a form of user interface in which the user types commands for the computer to carry out. The command is usually restricted to a single line of text, which might consist of any sequence of acceptable commands. The user has to know the conventions of the *command line interpreter* (see page 178). This form of interface can be efficient in the hands of experienced users, but can be very frustrating for those who do not know the right commands to use.

Command line interfaces are widely used in control systems, network management and program development systems where precise complex commands are needed. More complex application programs might also include simple command line interfaces to enable them to be automated using a *script language*, see page 14. See also *wildcard*, page 424.

A **command sequence** combines the commands into a *script*, or *macro*, which can make this a convenient way of getting the computer to perform a sequence of actions. See also *macro*, page 14.

Menu selection interface

including: menu bar, action bar, pull-down menu, drop-down menu, pop-up menu, short cut menu
is where the computer displays a list of options from which the user must make a choice, usually by selecting it with a pointer device, for example a mouse, or by typing the code displayed near the option.

A **menu bar** or **action bar** is a line of titles for menus across the screen (usually at the top, but sometimes at the bottom). These are the menus that the user can choose at that point. The choice is usually displayed as a *pull-down menu*.

Pull-down menu (also known as **drop-down menu**) is a menu that appears on requesl after its title has been selected from the menu bar. It gets its name because it usu-ally appears immediately below the menu title.

Pop-up menu (also known as **short cut menu**) is a menu that appears on the screen wher-ever a user happens to have positioned the cursor.

417

Conversational interface

is a form of user interface in which the computer and the user appear to be holding a conversation or dialogue, using the screen for output and the keyboard for input. The user might be seeking information from the computer, but the computer might need to ask its own questions before it is able to provide the answer to the question originally asked. Figure F5.1 shows an example that could be a dialogue about a request to print a file, and gives an indication of the kind of communication that might be experienced.

Figure F5.1 Conversational dialogue screen

PROMPT (computer)	RESPONSE (user)
~ ~ ~	~ ~ ~
~ ~ ~	~ ~ ~
Name of file to print?	MYTEXT.TXT
Print all 10 pages	No
Which pages?	1 to 3 and 10
Print pages 1-3, 10: correct? (Y or N)	yes
How many copies:	3:
~ ~ ~	~ ~ ~

Each line will appear one after another

Interactive computing

including: conversational mode
is a mode of operation in which a user and a computer system are in two-way communication throughout the period of use. In practice, most personal computer applications are interactive, whereas some applications on terminals attached to large central computer systems, for example in supermarket branches, are still run in batch mode with data and command instructions supplied through the terminal. See also *batch processing*, page 17.

When a terminal user on a network appears to be in continuous communication with the central computer, getting replies almost immediately, it is described as **conversational mode**.

Forms dialogue interface

including: response field
is a user interface in which the computer outputs separate *prompts* (see page 424) and response fields for a number of inputs.

Response field is a place in a dialogue screen (Figure F5.2) where users might type their responses, in any order as if filling in a form. There might be automatic movement of the cursor, depicting the entry point, from response field to response field. The process is similar to filling in a form on paper and allows the entries to be changed at any stage until the 'execution' key or button is pressed.

Figure F5.2 Forms dialogue screen

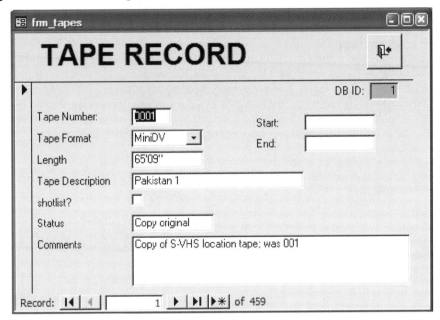

INTERFACE CONCEPTS

Pointer device

is a method used to indicate a position on a screen. It enables different actions to be selected by pointing at different icons, menus or labels. Pointer devices include:

- *Mouse*;
- *Tracker ball*;
- Dedicated keys on the keyboard, usually the *arrow* or *cursor keys*;
- *Stylus* or a finger used with a *touch screen*;
- Voice input.

Most pointer devices incorporate buttons that can be pressed, or clicked, to indicate an action. If a touch screen is used, then an action can be indicated by tapping the screen and other actions indicated by swiping the screen with fingers.

Gesture recognition

occurs when the computer detects physical movement by the user and interprets it as a command to be executed. Commonly gesture recognition is used with a *touch screen* (the gestures acting as a *pointer device*, see page 419), where tapping and swiping in different ways can be interpreted as different commands. Gestures can also be detected by a camera that can identify a hand waving in different ways or even eye movement.

Gesture recognition can be considered as a *user interface* (see page 416), but it actually provides the input to a user interface similar to other *input devices*, see page 6.

WIMP environment

also known as: Windows Icons Menus Pointers environment
including: window, icon, menu, pointer, cursor, desktop
is a method of accessing a computer making minimum use of the keyboard by using a mouse (or similar device) to move a pointer over *icons* or text *menus* displayed on the screen. For example, selecting an icon might open a window and start a task.

Window is an area opened on a screen displaying the activity of a program. There can be several windows on the screen at any one time. They can be moved or removed completely (restoring the original information on the screen).

Icon is a small picture or symbol, with an easily understood meaning, displayed on the screen as a method of offering a choice of activity. A pointer is moved to select an icon using, for example, a *mouse*. Icons can be independent of the user's language, provided the symbols are generally recognised and not offensive.

Menu is a range of options offered to a computer user so that a choice can be made. A menu might simply be a screen display that lists a number of choices. A user is expected to press an appropriate key or click a mouse button to select one of them; one of the choices offered is likely to be another menu, known as a *submenu*. Sometimes a special panel appears when a choice has to be made. This hides part of the screen, but the screen is restored to its original state after the choice has been made.

Pointer is an icon (often in the form of an arrow) on the screen. It moves around the screen in response to the movements of a *pointer device*, see page 419, such as a *mouse*.

Cursor is the screen symbol, known as the *caret*, that indicates where on the screen the next action will begin. It usually shows where text will be entered next.

Desktop is the combination of windows and icons displayed on a screen.

Graphical user interface elements

also known as: window furniture, user interface controls, widget
including: label, text box, list box, button, screen button, radio button, check box, slider, tab, toolbar
are the individual components of a window in a graphic interface. The different functions required within a graphic interface window have been categorised and standard *objects* are provided within the design system. This makes it much more efficient to design applications and ensures a degree of standardisation in design. The common elements are:

Label is text displayed on the screen. It can be changed by the program, but not by the user.

Text box is a box in which the user can enter information. The data is not processed until a button is clicked to indicate input is complete.

List box is a text box that has a drop-down menu enabling the user to select a suitable value.

Button, or **screen button** is an icon, which could be a word on a suitable background, that when clicked by the mouse causes the program to take some action.

Radio button is one of a group of small buttons (usually round), only one of which is selected at any one time, and when another radio button is clicked the original button is deselected.

Check box is a small button, usually square, that when selected displays a cross or a tick.

Slider is a bar that can be dragged to input a numeric value.

Tab is a label, see above, usually in a group at the top of a set of sub-windows. They allows a user to select different sub-windows.

Toolbar is a group of buttons displayed in a panel. A user can click these to perform a variety of actions or select choices.

Figure F5.3 Graphical user interface elements: a) label, b) text box, c) list box, d) button, e) radio button, f) check box, g) slider, h) tab, i) toolbar.

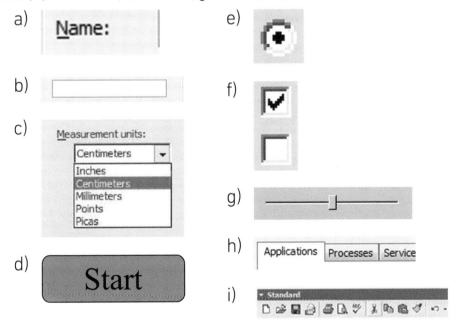

Dialogue box

is a window that appears when information about a choice is needed or when options have to be selected. For example, choosing PRINT from a FILE menu might cause a dialogue box to appear, requiring answers to such questions as which pages to print, number of copies etc. See Figure F5.4. Normally, a dialogue box will offer the chance to cancel the request as well as the option to proceed. Dialogue boxes are intended to make it easy to obtain the necessary information quickly.

Figure F5.4 Dialogue box

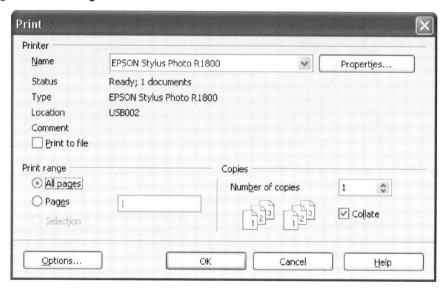

Focus

indicates where the next command in a graphical interface takes effect. The icon is changed to show it has focus. This could be a text box that changes colour to show where typed in data will go, or a button that changes colour to show it is about to be selected.

Drag

including: drag-and-drop editing
is the use of a mouse (or other similar device) to move an area of a screen display, which might be text or some part of a graphic display, from one location to another. Moving things around in this way is sometimes referred to as ***drag-and-drop editing***, which might also be used to copy, as well as move, part of a screen display.

Directory

also known as: folder
including: subdirectory, directory file, root directory
is a group of files or a group of files and **subdirectories**. A subdirectory is a directory within a directory, its contents might be files or other subdirectories or both. A directory is held, in the form of a list of file and subdirectory names (the **directory file**), on the backing store to which it refers; stored with it will be information needed for files to be retrieved from the backing store. Directories are usually represented in a tree structure, where the **root directory** is the entry point to the tree, as shown in Figure F5.5. See also *tree*, page 257, *organising data*, page 10 and *folder*, page 11.

Figure F5.5 Directory tree

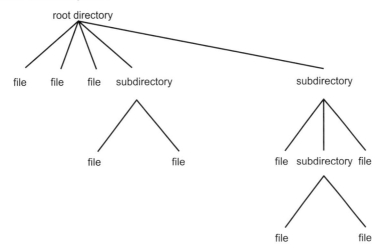

Error message

is a message to a user indicating that something has gone wrong; it might include instructions on what action is needed. Well-designed applications packages will include comprehensive error-detection routines and helpful error messages. These routines will detect errors resulting from user mistakes, such as entering invalid data, letting the printer run out of paper or failing to put the correct disk into a DVD drive, as well as errors occurring in the system itself.

Hot key

also known as: quick key, short cut key, keyboard short cut
is a function key or a key combination (frequently combining *control* or *alt* with other keys) that causes an action (such as calling up a menu, or running another program) related to whatever the user is doing.

Prompt

is a character or message displayed on a screen to indicate that the user is expected to do something, usually to input data into the system. Sometimes a visual prompt is emphasised by a sound.

Profile

is a file that holds data on how the system is to be presented for an individual user each time they log on. These customised interfaces are often available on network operating systems and online services.

Screen saver

is software that removes the image from the display, either as a security measure or to reduce the risk of damage to the interior surface of the display screen. If the screen display is not changed for a long period of time, the coating of the screen can become damaged.

User friendly

describes a system, either hardware or software, that is kind to its users. Since the user interface largely determines what a user experiences, it is the software system that is generally being described. However, some aspects of hardware, such as the feel of a keyboard, can improve or spoil user friendliness.

User transparent

including: transparency
describes actions by a computer system, hardware or software, that are not apparent to the user. Nearly all hardware actions, for example autosave, other than those affecting the screen, are transparent, and most operating system actions take place without the user being aware of them. Well-designed user interfaces aim to achieve high levels of **transparency**.

Wildcard

is a symbol used in some commands or search instructions to stand for a range of characters. They are a very useful tool when using a *command line interface*, see page 417, when programming using a script language or even when searching for a file on a personal computer. Often the symbol ? is used to stand for any single character and the character * is usually used to stand for any group of characters. For example:

- `copy picture?` – copies all files named 'picture' followed by one character – e.g. picture1, picture2, pictureX, ...

- `copy picture*` – copies all files that start with 'picture' – e.g. picture, picture2, pictureX123, ...

- `scale image?? 4` – in a program, scales all images referred to as 'image' and followed by 2 characters by 4 – e.g. image00, image21, image X1, ...

Wizard

also known as: assistant
is a feature of some applications packages that helps users to perform a task. By asking the user some questions, a wizard gives help in making best use of the available facilities. For example, a table wizard might help to create tables by offering a number of possible types, or a letter wizard might show how you could set out a letter for a particular situation.

DOCUMENTATION

User documentation

gives the user any information necessary for the successful running of a piece of software or hardware. This does not generally include many technical details, which will usually be found in *maintenance documentation* (see page 36).

Software documentation

is documentation received when a computer software package is bought, whether it is a computer game, a spreadsheet or a programming language etc. This might be anything from an instruction leaflet to a series of manuals. This 'documentation' is designed to introduce the package and to tell the user how to use the software to its best advantage. It might be totally in printed form or more likely it might be seen on the screen when running the package. There might also be files in digital form on the accompanying media or online. These might be referred to as an electronic manual or e-manual. The latest technical information might be provided as a small file called *Readme* or *Help*, see page 426.

Typical software documentation includes:

- an overview of the package describing what it is capable of doing in fairly broad terms;
- sample screen displays and printouts to show the users what to expect;
- how to install the software (to make the software available on the user's system);
- how to configure the software (where the user has a choice of options on how the software is to work and what hardware will be used, such as the type of printer);
- how to make hardware adjustments that might be needed – these might be described for the user to do or might require the help of a dealer;
- a tutorial designed to familiarise the user with the simple aspects of the system;
- a reference section explaining how each function works;
- an index to the documentation, which helps the user to find how to do specific tasks and to find more detailed explanations of error messages.

Some of these operations might refer to hardware documentation. For example, reference might be needed to printer documentation.

Hardware documentation

contains the instructions on how to use the hardware. Usually a physical connection will need to be made between items of equipment, for example between a monitor and computer. This will specify details of the connecting leads and where they are to be connected.

More technical detail is usually available (at extra cost) from the manufacturer or a third party.

Typical hardware documentation includes:

- an overview of the product describing what it is capable of doing in fairly broad terms;
- how to connect the product;
- how to install the related software (usually including *drivers*, see page 9) to configure and manage the product;
- diagrams and sample screen displays to show users what to expect;
- how to configure the product;
- how to make hardware adjustments that might be needed;
- a troubleshooting section;
- an index to the documentation.

Help system

including: context sensitive help
is a means of providing helpful messages to guide a user when using a software package. It will give indications of how to answer prompts from the software and how to perform relevant operations.

Context sensitive help is when the help given relates specifically to what the user appears to be currently doing, rather than more general information.

README file

is a file that is provided on the installation medium with the software. It is often called **readme.txt** or something similar. It contains the latest details of using or loading the software that haven't been included in the supplied documentation.

F6   SPECIALISED COMPUTER APPLICATIONS

Other specialised applications can be found in Section F3 Graphics, design and digital imaging and in Section F4 Sound.

Most information technology (IT) involves the use of the computer as a general-purpose tool capable of solving a variety of problems. However, some tasks are quite difficult to do with the standard IT tools of word processor, spreadsheet or database. Some of these tasks could be done manually but with the development of suitable computer software can often be done much more easily using the processing power available in a computer system. The market for these specialised applications is obviously smaller than for general software but the savings in time and money are sufficiently great, particularly in large organisations, to make it worthwhile for software producers to develop them.

Most specialised computer applications are expensive but are developed for complicated tasks that have to be repeated many times. To do this they incorporate functions to load the data, edit it and usually to save it for future use. This is common to most applications whilst the actual processing will be different.

This section describes some of the more important specialised applications that have been developed.

Accounting package

also known as: finance package
records the use of money in a company or other organisation. A modern organisation is dependent on the accurate recording of financial information, which includes money received (from sales), money paid out (to buy goods or services), wages paid to employees, taxes paid and money transferred between departments within the organisation. Accounting packages can record this information accurately, allowing better use of resources and preventing misuse. Accurate accounting is also required by law to enable taxes to be collected fairly.

Any accounting package will maintain a database of financial transactions and provide spreadsheet-like facilities for financial planning.

Computer-aided design (CAD)

also known as: computer-aided draughting
is the use of a computer system to produce drawings as part of the design of some construction project; this might be the layout of components on a printed circuit board,

the civil engineering design of a motorway, or the layout of furniture positions in an office or a home – to give just three common examples. Most modern CAD packages also use the design data as the basis for calculations – for example, of costs, mechanical stresses, quantities of materials needed etc. With the information available from the design stage, it is possible in many cases for the computer system to control the manufacturing process as well. See also *computer-assisted manufacturing*, below.

Computer-assisted manufacturing (CAM)

including: CAD/CAM
is the use of a computer system to control the production in a factory, including the supply of components, planning daily production and controlling the machinery involved.

Computer-assisted manufacturing is usually combined with a *computer-aided design (CAD)* (see page 427) system and is often known as **CAD/CAM**. In a CAD/CAM system the designs are transferred electronically between the design system and the manufacturing system. This allows the machinery to be programmed automatically by the computer-assisted manufacturing system. The combined system becomes an integrated process in which the manufacturing is controlled automatically. This is important in the development of new products and allows minor improvements in the design to be implemented without stopping production.

Computer-aided learning (CAL)

including: computer-based training (CBT), computer-managed instruction (CMI), computer-managed learning (CML), integrated learning system (ILS)
is the use of a computer to provide instructional information to a student, to pose questions and to react to the student's response.

Computer-based training (CBT) is the use of a computer as an instructional system in a training environment. The approach is the same as CAL but the learning area is confined to a well-defined training objective.

Computer-managed instruction (CMI) is the use of a computer to manage a student's progress through a course of instruction. The student's performance is recorded by the computer and new modules of instruction are defined or delivered as determined by the curriculum. A computer-managed instruction system may or may not contain CAL material.

Computer-managed learning (CML) is the use of a computer in a similar fashion to computer-managed instruction, but with additional emphasis on providing help, which depends upon the responses given by the student. Some computer-managed learning systems can build up a detailed learning profile for each student. This profile can be used for both reporting and directing the studies of an individual student.

Integrated learning system (ILS) is a computer system that combines providing the student with instructional material with monitoring the student's success and speed. This enables the computer to adjust the material presented to the student and provide analyses for the tutor.

Virtual learning environment (VLE)

also known as: managed learning environment (MLE), learning platform
is a software system designed to support teaching and learning. For the student it provides course material to download, often over the internet, and allows for collaborative work. For the tutor, as well as tools to accept and store students' work, it offers assessment often by multiple choice methods, record keeping, and communication such as feedback to the students. Tutors and students will have different levels of access.

Cryptography

including: secret message, cipher
is the science of creating and sending **secret messages**, or **ciphers**. When communicating by code, it is usual for everyone to use the same coding method, but to have some personal and secret key that is used by the method in a way that makes the message remain hidden, even if the method is known. Modern cryptographical methods involve complex mathematical calculations to encrypt and decrypt the message. This is usually done by a computer. See also *encryption*, page 163.

Cryptanalysis

including: code breaking
is the analysis of encrypted messages to reveal the original information. This is often known as **code breaking**. Nowadays, this requires many mathematical calculations and is almost always done by computer. Captured cipher messages are analysed to see if patterns emerge that will indicate the method of coding, after which further analysis may indicate the precise cipher key used in the enciphering. In some ways the *cipher key* acts as a password to the information. See also *encryption*, page 163.

Geographical information system (GIS)

including: global positioning system (GPS), satellite navigation, satnav
stores complex geographical data and presents it as various types of maps. Since the data is stored separately from the map but linked to it, the GIS can easily produce scale maps to the user's requirements and plot the particular data the user is interested in. This enables the maps to be clearer and relationships between particular types of data explored easily.

It is often used in conjunction with the **global positioning system (GPS)**, which by measuring the signals from satellites in space can determine a position to within a few metres, anywhere in the world. These signals are used by **satellite navigation** systems guiding ships and aircraft as well as enabling maps to be constructed that are very accurate (essential for use in geographical information systems). They are also used for route finding in **satnav** devices in cars and by hikers.

Management information systems (MIS)

including: decision support system (DSS)
provide understandable amounts of management-level information that individual users might require – such as summaries from larger collections of data. When data is

collected it usually consists of large quantities of simple information and needs further processing before it is usable. This type of processed information may typically be used by managers as an aid to monitoring budgets, assessing sales targets or making business decisions.

Decision support systems (DSS) are refined *management information systems* where the emphasis is on providing senior management with key information for strategic decision making. Such systems use sophisticated analysis techniques and may include *expert systems* (see page 143).

Mathematical applications

including: number cruncher
allow the power of the computer to be used to solve mathematical problems. The computer can carry out the required arithmetic much faster and draw the results on the screen. This allows tedious problems to be solved much more quickly than by a human being. Examples include the solving of differential equations and geometrical construction. These applications that rely on the computer being able to do large amounts of simple arithmetic very fast are often referred to as **number crunchers**.

Statistical applications

allow the computer to process large amounts of data to find patterns and determine its accuracy. This requires a lot of simple and repetitive arithmetic, which used to be very time-consuming to do manually. The computer enables data to be processed quickly and accurately.

Accurate statistics are an important part of many tasks, allowing complex data to be analysed and forecasts made from it. An example would be the analysis of sales by a marketing department before and after a sales promotion.

Scientific measurement and analysis

collects data from *sensors* (see page 119) and uses or stores it for later analysis. The sensors allow the computer to collect data that otherwise would have been collected by hand. The computer can collect a large number of readings reliably. The data can then be analysed without having to be re-entered into the computer. The analysis can involve statistical calculations or simply the production of graphs to illustrate how the experiment proceeded. See also *telemetry*, page 120.

Music composition software

allows a composer to record their ideas using the computer. The music can be entered using either the normal keyboard or a music keyboard connected using a *MIDI* (see page 411). The composition can be played directly using the computer's sound system and changes made immediately. The output can be, for example, a printout in a traditional musical notation or in electronic form (such as MIDI code allowing it to be played on any MIDI musical system).

Presentation package

is used to produce multimedia presentations and displays. It allows the construction of a series of pages that can include sound and video clips as well as text and graphics. These pages can be linked together and displayed easily using a single key press or mouse click. The presentation can also be displayed automatically with a new page being displayed after a given time. Presentations are usually displayed on a large monitor, which the whole audience can see, or projected on to a large screen by the computer.

Speech synthesis

including: speech synthesiser, voice synthesiser, phoneme
is the production of sounds resembling human speech by electronic methods. **A speech synthesiser** (or **voice synthesiser**) achieves this either by the use of software or by using standard sound-generating hardware. An example of a speech synthesiser is a talking word processor. The sound is produced either by selecting an appropriate sound from a collection of stored sounds or by breaking down the input data into its individual speech components, which are output in sequence. These speech components are known as **phonemes**. For example, the vowel sound in 'meet' and in 'meat' are the same phoneme.

Health Informatics

including: bio-informatics, medical informatics
is the application of computing to support the delivery of health care, diagnosis and promotion of health. The design of the interface is important as the accuracy and security of data and privacy of patient's details is of prime concern. Special applications in health informatics cover a wide range of topics including:

- control of equipment and display of results from scanning to digital hearing aids, robotic aids and keyhole surgery;

- simulations of events such as pandemics and how they can be contained;

- **Bio-informatics**, which deals with biological information about all organisms some of which is relevant to health and healthcare, such as such as DNA sequencing and organ matching;

- **Medical informatics** is that part of health informatics concerned with the narrower domain of medicine.

PART G: REFERENCE

One characteristic of modern life, and particularly any form of technological activity, is the use of abbreviations, acronyms and other 'jargon' by those who are involved in any specialised activity. This use of words, terms and acronyms when writing for or talking to others involved in the same activity can be a way of economically passing information between like-minded people, but, on the other hand, it can also be a barrier to understanding for those who do not know the meanings of the strange new words. Computer users have always made great use of a vocabulary containing many abbreviations and acronyms. Over time this vocabulary has changed as new ideas are developed and old ones are no longer appropriate.

No list would ever be complete or up to date, but in Section G1 there is an extensive list of acronyms and abbreviations whose use is either commonplace throughout most computing activities or is specific to a particular aspect of computing. The list is alphabetic and includes many terms that are treated in the main body of the *Glossary*; for these terms the appropriate page references are given. For terms that have no page reference, the only information provided is the expansion of the acronym and, for some, an indication (in brackets) of the context in which they might be met.

G1 ACRONYMS AND ABBREVIATIONS

Where a page number is given, it indicates where additional information can be found. Brackets are used to indicate the context in which the acronym or abbreviation may be met.

ACC	accumulator	330
ACIA	asynchronous communications interface adapter	
ACK	acknowledgement signal	354
ACM	Association for Computing Machinery	
A-to-D	analog-to-digital	344
A/D	analog-to-digital	344
ADC	analog-to-digital converter	
ADC/MPS	analog-to-digital/microprocessor system	
ADSL	asymmetric digital subscriber line	75
ADSR	attack, decay, sustain, release (sound)	406
AES	Advanced Encryption Standard	164
AFIPS	American Federation of Information Processing Societies	
AI	artificial intelligence	142
ALCOL	ALGOrithmic Language	239
ALU	arithmetic logic unit	330
AM	amplitude modulation (communications)	352
ANSI	American National Standards Institute	
API	application program interface	42
APL	A Programming Language	239
APT	automatically programmed tools (machine tool language)	
AQL	acceptable quality level	
ARP	address resolution protocol	
ARPAnet	Advanced Research Projects Agency Network	

ARQ	Automatic Repeat Request	350
ARU	audio response unit	
ASCII	American Standard Code for Information Interchange	256
ASIC	application specific integrated circuit	
ASR	automatic send-receive	
AT	advanced technology (bus)	
ATM	asynchronous transfer mode	
ATM	automatic teller machine	115
AUP	acceptable use policy	
BA	bus available	
BABT	British Approvals Board for Telecommunications	
BASIC	Beginners All-purpose Symbolic Instruction Code	241
BBC	British Broadcasting Corporation	
BBS	bulletin board system	66
BCC	blind carbon copy	87
BCC	block check character	
BCD	binary coded decimal	268
BCS	BCS, The Chartered Institute for IT (formerly the British Computer Society)	
BD	Blu-ray	303
BDOS	basic disk operating system	
BEAB	British Electrical Appliances Board	
BEL	bell (buzzer) (ASCII character)	464
BiMOS	bipolar-MOS	
BIND	Berkeley internet name domain (software)	
BIOS	basic input output system	171
bit	binary digit	11
BNF	Backus–Naur form	246
bpi	bits per inch	
bpp	bits per pixel	
bps	bits per second	344
Bps	bytes per second	344
BS	back space (ASCII character)	464
BSI	British Standards Institution	
BTW	by the way	

CAD	computer-aided design/computer-aided draughting	427
CAD/CAM	computer-aided design and manufacture	428
CAI	computer-assisted instruction	
CAL	computer-aided learning	428
CAM	computer-assisted manufacturing	428
CAN	cancel (ASCII character)	465
CASE	computer-aided software engineering	47
CBT	computer-based training	428
CC	courtesy (or carbon) copy	87
CCA	Central Computing Agency	
CCD	charge-coupled device	
CCITT	Comité Consultatif International Téléphonique et Télégraphique	79
CCP	console command processor	
CCR	condition code register	
CCTA	Central Computing and Telecommunications Agency	
CD	compact disc	303
CD-I	compact disc interactive	
CD-R	compact disc-recordable	303
CD-ROM	compact disc read-only memory	303
CD-RW	compact disc read / write	303
CDI	collector diffusion isolator	
CEG	Computer Education Group (historical)	
CEPIS	Confederation of European Professional Informatics Societies	
CGA	colour graphics adapter	
CIR	current instruction register	
CISC	Complex Instruction Set Computer	325
CIX	commercial internet exchange	
CMI	computer-managed instruction	428
CML	computer-managed learning	428
CMOS	complementary metal oxide semiconductor	304
CMS	colour management system	311
CMYK	cyan, magenta, yellow, key (black)	311
CNC	computer numeric control	119

COBOL	COmmon Business Oriented Language	239
COM	computer output on microfilm	
COMAL	COMmon Algorithmic Language	
CPE	central processing element	
CP gate	comparator-gate (XOR)	362
CP/M	control program for microcomputers	
CPM	control program monitor	
CPM	Critical Path Method	38
cps	characters per second	344
cps	cycles per second	403
CPU	central processing unit	324
CR	carriage return (ASCII character)	464
CR/LF	carriage return/line feed	
CRC	cyclic redundancy check	111
CROM	control ROM	
CRT	cathode ray tube	314
CSCD	carrier sense collision detection	354
CSCW	computer supported cooperative work	
CSMA/CD	Carrier Sense Multiple Access/Collision Detection	354
CSS	cascading style sheets	251
CSV	comma separated variable (file)	457
CTRL or Ctrl	control (ASCII character)	
CTS	clear to send	
CUG	closed user group	
CYMK	cyan, yellow, magenta, key (black)	311
D-to-A	digital-to-analog	344
DAC	data acquisition and control	
DAC	digital-to-analog converter	344
DAT	digital audio tape	
DBA	database administrator	150
DBMS	database management system	94
DBS	direct broadcast by satellite	
DCD	data carrier detect (communications)	

DCE	data communications equipment	
DCS	telephone data carrier system	
DD	double density	
DDE	direct data entry	
DDL	data description language	
DDN	Defense Data Network	
DDoS	distributed denial of service	92
DEL	delete (ASCII character)	
DES	Data Encryption Standard	164
DFD	data flow diagram	49
DHTML	Dynamic HyperText Mark-up Language	248
DIB	data input bus	
DIL	dual in-line	339
dil	dual in-line	339
DIN	Deutsches Institut für Normung	
DIP	dual in-line package	339
DLE	data link escape (ASCII character)	464
dll	dynamic link library	13
DLT	digital linear technology	
DMA	direct memory access	328
DML	Data Manipulation Language	105
DNS	domain name system	78
DoD	Department of Defense (US)	
DOS	disk operating system	172
DoS	denial of service	92
DP	data processing	
dpi	dots per inch	312
DRAM	dynamic random access memory	305
DSA	digital signature algorithm	
DSL	digital subscriber line	75
DSR	data set ready	
DSS	decision support system	429
DSW	device status word	
DTE	data terminal equipment	

DTL	diode-transistor logic	
DTP	desktop publishing	368
DTR	data terminal ready	
DV	digital video	399
DVD	digital versatile disc or digital video disc	303
EA	extended addressing	
EAN	European Article Number	112
EAROM	electrically alterable read-only memory	305
EB disk	electronic book disk	
EBCDIC	extended binary coded decimal interchange code	
EBR	electron beam recording	
ECD	electrochromeric display	
ECL	emitter-coupled logic	
ECMA	European Computer Manufacturers Association	220
EDP	electronic data processing	
EDS	exchangeable disk storage	
EEPROM	electrically erasable PROM	305
EFT	electronic funds transfer	115
EFTPOS	electronic funds transfer at point of sale	114
EGA	enhanced graphics adapter	
E ink	electrophoretic ink	314
EIA	Electrical Industries Association (USA)	
EISA	extended industry standard architecture	
EM	end of message (ASCII character)	
EM	end-of-medium character (ASCII character)	465
email	electronic mail	86
EMI	electromagnetic interference	353
ENQ	enquiry (ASCII character)	
EOF	end of file	261
EOM	end-of-message	
EOR	exclusive-OR	362
EOT	end of transmission (ASCII character)	464
EPOS	electronic point-of-sale	
EPROM	erasable programmable read-only memory	305

EPS	encapsulated PostScript®	
EQ	equal	
EQ	Equivalence	363
ESC	escape (ASCII character)	465
ESDI	enhanced systems drive interface	
ETB	end of text block (ASCII character)	465
ETX	end of text (= end of last block) (ASCII character)	464
EULA	end-user licence agreement	167
FAM	fast-access memory	
FAQ	frequently asked question	66
FAST	Federation Against Software Theft	
FAT	file allocation table	306
FAX	facsimile	
FD	floppy disk	
FDD	floppy disk drive	
FDDI	fibre distributed data interface	
FDM	frequency-division multiplexor (communications)	342
FEP	front-end processor	290
FET	field-effect transistor	
FETMOS	field-effect transistor metal oxide semiconductor	
FF	form feed (ASCII character)	464
FFT	fast Fourier transform	
FIFO	first in, first out	260
FM	frequency modulation (sound, communications)	409, 352
FORTRAN	FORmula TRANslation	241
FPA	floating-point accelerator	
FPU	floating-point unit	
FROM	fusible ROM	
FS	file separator (ASCII character)	465
FSK	frequency shift keying	
FSM	frequency shift modulation	
FTP	File Transfer Protocol	89
G	giga	454
GATT	General Agreement on Tariffs and Trade	345

GB	gigabyte	11
GDU	graphical display unit	313
GIF	graphics interchange format	
GIGO	garbage in garbage out	
GIS	geographical information system	429
GND	ground (connection)	
GPIB	general-purpose interface bus	
GPR	general-purpose register	
GPS	global positioning system	429
GS	group separator (ASCII character)	465
GUI	graphical user interface	417
HCI	human–computer interaction/interface	416
HD	high-density or hard disk	300
HDD	high-density disk	
HDD	hard disk drive	301
HDTV	high definition television	355
HDV	high definition video format	399
hex	hexadecimal	268
HMOS	high-performance metal oxide semiconductor	
HRG	high resolution graphics	312
HT	horizontal tabulation (ASCII character)	464
HTML	HyperText Mark-up Language	248
HTTP	HyperText Transfer Protocol	76
Hz	Hertz	403
I/O	input/output	6
IAB	Internet Architecture Board	79
IAM	immediate-access memory	297
IAR	instruction address register	326
IAS	immediate-access store	299
IC	integrated circuit	338
ICMP	internet control message protocol	
ICT	information and communications technology	3
ID	identification	162
IDE	integrated development environment	40

IDE	integrated (or intelligent) device electronics	336
IDS	intrusion detection system	161
IEE	Institution of Electrical Engineers (UK) (historical)	
IEEE	Institute of Electronic and Electrical Engineers (USA)	
IET	Institution of Engineering and Technology	
IFIP	International Federation for Information Processing	
IGFET	insulated gate field-effect transistor	
IIL	integrated injection logic	
IKBS	intelligent knowledge-based system	143
ILS	integrated learning system	428
ILS	international language support	
IMHO	in my humble opinion	
IO	input/output	
IOP	input/output processor	
IORQ	input/output request line	
IP	internet protocol or internetworking protocol	76
IPL	initial program loader	
IR	index register	327
IR	infrared	342
IR	instruction register	
IRC	internet relay chat	
IS	information systems	
ISA	industry-standard architecture	
ISAM	index sequential access method	274
ISBN	International Standard Book Number	112
ISD	international subscriber dialing	
ISDN	Integrated Services Digital Network	350
ISM	industry structure model (British Computer Society)	
ISM	information systems manager	
ISN	initial sequence number	354
ISO	International Organization for Standardization	345
ISP	internet service provider	74
ISR	interrupt service routine	
IT	information technology	3

MCA	micro channel architecture	
MDA	monochrome display adapter	
MDR	memory data register	326
MHS	message-handling system	
MICR	Magnetic Ink Character Recognition	113
MIDI	musical instrument digital interface	411
MIME	Multi-purpose Internet Mail Extensions	87
MIPS	millions of instructions per second	330
MIS	management information system	429
MLE	managed learning environment	429
MMI	man–machine interface/interaction	416
MMU	memory management unit	327
MNP	Microcom Network Protocol	350
modem	modulator/demodulator	340
MOS	machine operating system	
MOS	metal oxide semiconductor	304
MOSFET	metal-oxide semiconductor field-effect transistor	
MPEG	Motion Picture Experts Group	390
MPS	microprocessor system	
MPU	microprocessor unit	
MPX	multiplex	
MREQ	memory request	
ms	millisecond	
MS	Memory Stick	304
MS-DOS®	Microsoft® Disk Operating System	174
MSB	most significant bit	
MSD	most significant digit	
MSI	medium-scale integration	338
MTBF	mean time between failures	
MTF	mean time to failure	
MTU	maximum transmission unit	348
MUG	multi-user game	
MUX	multiplexor	341
n	nano	454

NAK	negative acknowledgement (ASCII character)	464
NAND	Not AND	361
NEQ	Not Equivalent	362
NFS	network file system	
NLQ	near letter quality	
NMI	non-maskable interrupt	
NMOS	n-channel metal-oxide semiconductor	
NOR	Not OR	361
ns	nanosecond	
NSFNET	National Science Foundation Network (USA)	
NTSC	National Television System Committee (USA)	
NUL	null (do nothing) (ASCII character)	
OCR	Optical Character Recognition	114
OEM	original equipment manufacturer	291
OLE	object linking and embedding	17
OLR	offline reader	
OMR	optical mark recognition	112
OOD	object-oriented design	46
OOL	object-oriented language	
OOP	object-oriented program(ming)	188
OS	operating system	9
OSI	Open Systems Interconnection	348
OV	overflow	282
p	pico	454
PABX	private automatic branch exchange	341
PAL	Phase Alternating Line	316
PBX	private branch exchange	341
PC	personal computer (IBM-PC compatible)	289
PC	program counter	
PC-DOS	personal computer disk operating system	
PCB	printed circuit board	334
PCI	peripheral component interconnect	
PCI	programmable communications interface	
PCM	pulse code modulation	353

QBE	Query By Example	105
QD	quad density (disks)	
QIC	quarter-inch cartridge (historical)	
QR	quick response (code)	112
QWERTY	conventional typewriter keyboard	293
R/W	read/write	
RAD	Rapid Application Development	33
RAID	redundant array of independent (or inexpensive) disks	301
RAM	random access memory	305
RD	read	
RDBMS	relational database management system	97
RDP	remote desktop protocol	133
REM	remark(s)	
REN	ringer equivalent number	
RF	radio frequency	
RFC	request for comment	
RFI	radio frequency interference	354
RFID	radio frequency identification device	112
RGB	red green blue	311
RI	ring in	
RISC	Reduced Instruction Set Computer	325
RJE	remote job entry	181
ROM	read-only memory	305
RPG	report program generator	240
RS	record separator (ASCII character)	465
RSA	Rivest, Shamir, Adleman (algorithm)	165
RSS	Really Simple Syndication	85
RTF	rich text format (file)	
RTL	resistor-transistor logic	
RTS	request to send	
SAR	store address register	
SBC	single-board computer	
SCR	sequence control register	326
SCSI	Small Computer Systems Interface	

SD	Secure Digital	304
SDK	software development kit	
SDR	store data register	
SDSL	symmetric digital subscriber line	75
SET	Secure Electronic Transaction	160
SFIAplus	Skills Framework for the Information Age plus	148
SGML	Standard Generalised Markup Language	247
SHF	super high frequency	
SI	shift in (ASCII character)	464
SIC	silicon integrated circuit	
SID	standard interchangeable data (file)	
SIMM	single in-line memory module	
SIMS	Schools Information Management System	
Simula	SIMULAtion Language	240
SIO	serial input/output (controller)	
SLIP	serial line internet protocol	
SLSI	super large-scale integration	
SMPTE	Society of Motion Picture and TV Engineers	408
SMTP	Simple Mail Transport Protocol	87
SNOBOL	StriNg Oriented SymBolic Language	240
SO	shift out (ASCII character)	464
SOH	start of header (ASCII character)	464
SOS	silicon on sapphire	
SP	stack pointer	
SQA	software quality assurance	
SQL	Structured Query Language	105
SSADM	Structured Systems Analysis and Design Methodology	33
SSD	solid-state drive	302
SSI	small-scale integration	338
SSL	Secure Socket Layer	160
STD	subscriber trunk dialling	
STX	start of text (ASCII character)	464
SUB	substitute (ASCII character)	465
SVGA	super video graphics array	309

449

SWR	status word register	
SYLK	symbolic link	
SYN	synchronisation character (ASCII character)	465
sysop	system operator	
TCP	Transmission Control Protocol	350
TCP/IP	Transmission Control Protocol/Internet Protocol	138
TDM	time-division multiplexor (communications)	342
TEMP	temporary	
TLA	three-letter acronym	
TP	tele-processing	18
TP	transaction processing	17
TP	twisted pair	343
TPA	transient program area	
TPI	tracks per inch	
TRL	transistor-resistor logic	
TSV	tab separated variables (file)	12
TTL	transistor-transistor logic	
TTP	trusted third party	159
UART	universal asynchronous receiver/transmitter	
UCE	unsolicited commercial email	
UDP/IP	user datagram protocol/internet protocol	
UHF	ultra high frequency	
UJT	uni-junction transistor	
ULA	uncommitted logic array	339
UML	unified modelling language	56
UPC	Universal Product Code	112
UPS	uninterruptible power supply	
URI	Uniform Resource Identifier	78
URL	Uniform Resource Locator	78
US	unit separator (ASCII character)	465
USART	universal synchronous/asynchronous receiver/transmitter	
USB	Universal Serial Bus	304
USRT	universal synchronous receiver/transmitter	
UTP	unshielded twisted pair	343

UUCP	UNIX® to UNIX® copy protocol	
UV	ultraviolet	
VAN	value added network	137
VANS	Value Added Network Service	137
VDG	video display generator	
VDT	video display terminal	
VDU	visual display unit	314
VESA	Video Electronics Standards Association	
VGA	video graphics array	
VHF	very high frequency	
VLAN	virtual local area network	140
VLE	virtual learning environment	429
VLSI	very large-scale integration	338
VM	virtual memory	328
VMOS	vertical-current-flow metal oxide semiconductor	
VoIP	voice over internet protocol	90
VPN	virtual private networking	133
VR	virtual reality	120
VRAM	video random access memory	316
VRAM	volatile read-only memory	
VRML	virtual reality mark-up language	
VRR	vertical refresh rate	
VSAT	very small aperture terminal	355
VT	vertical tabulation (ASCII character)	464
W3C	World Wide Web Consortium	79
WAIS	wide area information service	
WAN	wide area network	129
WAP	wireless application protocol	
WIMP	Windows Icons Menus Pointers	420
WMA	windows, media, audio	
WORM	write-once, read-many	304
WP	word processing	367
WR	write	
WS	working store	

G2 UNITS

Prefixes for metric multiples

In scientific notation prefixes are used to absorb some of the powers that might otherwise occur. Thus instead of 1,000,000 metres we say 1 Mm.

Each prefix is 1000 times the last so that they represent powers of 1000.

Thus a kilometre is 1000 metres and a mega-metre is 1000 km.

Binary multiples also have prefixes and these are spaced with factors of 2^{10} or 1024.

The use of the metric prefixes above (**kilo**, **mega** etc.) in computing has often caused confusion. It was convenient to use these metric prefixes as *binary prefixes* as well, leaving the reader to work out what was meant from the context. For example, as a *metric* prefix, **kilo** is defined as 1000 (derived from 10^3), whereas the *binary* prefix **kilo** is defined as 1024 (derived from 2^{10}). This means that 5k could be 5000 or 5120, depending on the context.

For most purposes, the differences are too small to be important, but because *they are different* confusion has been caused. When using these prefixes in computing, it is important to recognise the context.

Generally, prefixes are used as *metric* prefixes, so for example a 2 kHz speed is simply 2000 Hz.

If units of data (such as bytes) are involved, then the prefixes are usually used as *binary* prefixes, so for example a 2 kB memory is usually 2048 bytes rather than 2000. It is important to be aware of this potential ambiguity.

An attempt has been made to clarify the issue by introducing new abbreviations for *binary prefixes*, which are **kibi**, **mebi** etc. These are unambiguously binary prefixes. An increasing number of professionals are using these prefixes, but most still use the old prefixes (**kilo**, **mega** etc.) in the binary context.

Prefix	Symbol	Powers of 10	Meaning	Decimal
yocto	y	−24	one million million million-millionth	
zepto	z	−21	one thousand million million million-millionth	
atto	a	−18	one million million-millionth	
femto	f	−15	one thousand million million-millionth	
pico	p	−12	one million-millionth	0.000 000 000 001
nano	n	−9	one thousand-millionth	0.000 000 001
micro	µ	−6	one millionth	0.000 001
milli	m	−3	one thousandth	0.001
		1	one	1
kilo	k	3	one thousand	1 000
mega	M	6	one million	1 000 000
giga	G	9	one thousand million	1 000 000 000
tera	T	12	one million million	1 000 000 000 000
peta	P	15	one thousand million million	1 000 000 000 000 000
exa	E	18	one million million million	1 000 000 000 000 000 000
zetta	Z	21	And so on...	
yotta	Y	24	And so on...	

Prefixes for binary multiples

Prefix	Symbol	Powers of 2	Meaning		Derivation	
kibi	ki	10	kilobinary	1024^1	kilo	1000^1
mebi	Mi	20	megabinary	1024^2	mega	1000^2
gibi	Gi	30	gigabinary	1024^3	giga	1000^3
tebi	Ti	40	terabinary	1024^4	tera	1000^4
pebi	Pi	50	petabinary	1024^5	peta	1000^5
exbi	Ei	60	exabinary	1024^6	exa	1000^6

Examples and comparisons

one kibibit	1 kibit = 1024 bit
one kilobit	1 kbit = 1000 bit
one mebibyte	1 MiB = 1 048 576 bytes
one megabyte	1 MB = 1 000 000 bytes
one gibibyte	1 GiB = 1 073 741 824 bytes
one gigabyte	1 GB = 1 000 000 000 bytes

G3 FILENAMES AND FILENAME EXTENSIONS

Each computer-stored file needs to have a unique name (a **filename**), in order that it can be saved, located or retrieved by the computer's file management system.

Different operating systems treat files in different ways. Consequently, filenames associated with different operating systems may have different structures or be displayed differently. It is common for the filename to be represented by an icon instead of the text. Nevertheless, most operating systems associated with personal computers have similar filename conventions where, generally, full filenames such as glossary.doc consist of two parts separated by a dot (.).

The first part is chosen by the person who creates the file and is the name by which the file is recognised. The second part – usually known as the **filename extension** – is determined according to a set of rules (illustrated below) and enables the computer system to determine what action it may need to take in order to enable the file to be processed.

To be valid, filenames must not include certain characters that have specific roles in the command expressions of the operating system (such as * ? " \ / < > : | ~). There may also be a restriction on the length of the filename.

The following is a selection of the more commonly used filename extensions that may typically be seen in directory listings.

Filename extensions designating files used in the set-up configuration of a computer system or denoting files with specific links to operational aspects of the system:

.bat	batch file	file containing several commands that are operated on in sequence
.cfg	configuration file	file containing information on the way in which the computer is set up
.com	command file	small program that launches executable programs or system commands
.dll	dynamic link library file	application extension file
.drv	driver file	program file that sets communication parameters for printers, monitors etc.

.exe	executable file	file that calls a specific program
.fnt	font file	file containing the specification of a particular type font
.ini	initialisation file	file containing reference data relating to the first running of a program
.sys	system file	file containing instructions controlling aspects of the operating system

Filename extensions that usually identify files as being of a particular type:

.asp, .aspx	Active Server Pages	web page code
.avi	digital video file	audio-video interleaved format
.bak, .bup	a backup file	copy of an original file, sometimes written by the system, when the original is changed and the changed version is saved by the user using the original filename
.bmk	a bookmark file	
.bmp	a bitmap file	used to store characters or graphics for displaying data as a series of pixels
.cab	cabinet file	Microsoft® compressed format, combining several files in one
.clp	a clipboard file	temporary file used to store data for later use in the same computer session
.csv	comma-separated variables	text file copy of a data file
.dat	a data file	
.dxf	still image vector file	industry standard computer-aided design file
.epub	ebook file	open standard ebook format
.gif	graphics interchange format file	developed to compress and store graphics image data
.hlp	a help file	

457

.htm, .html	HTML	web page
.jpeg, .jpg, .jpe		a graphics file standard compression format developed for photographic images, from Joint Photographic Experts Group
.log	a log file	
.mobi	ebook file	Amazon Kindle proprietary ebook format
.mpg, .mv2, .mp2, .mp3, .mp4	audio and video files	various audio and video formats defined by the Moving Picture Experts Group
.old	an archive file	created by 'install' programs to preserve previous versions of system files
.ovr	an overlay file	file that can be displayed superimposed over another file
.pat	a pattern file	
.php	script filr	used on web pages
.png	a graphics file	compressed file containing graphics
.rtf	a Rich Text Format file	word-processed file that saves formatting as text – used in file transfer
.scr	a screen file	format for many screen savers
.tif, .tiff	a graphics file	compressed file containing graphics
.tmp	a temporary file	file used by some programs to store data while waiting further instructions
.tsv	tab-separated variables	text file copy of a data file
.txt	a text file	unformatted (ASCII) file that can be opened in any word processor or text editor
.vob	video object	video files on a DVD
.wav	a 'wave' format file	sound file

| .xml | mark-up file | extensible markup language |
| .$$$ | a temporary file | used within a program and normally discarded by that program when no longer required |

Filename extensions that usually identify files as belonging to, and associate the files with, particular application programs:

.bas	BASIC program file	
.cdr	CorelDraw file	drawing package application file
.doc, .docx	document file	word processor application file
.mdb	Microsoft® Access® file	database application file
.mov	video file	QuickTime® video format file
.odt, .ods, .odb, .odp	Open Office documents	word processor, spreadsheet, database and presentation respectively
.pdf	portable document format	Adobe® Acrobat® file
.pm	Pagemaker file	desktop publishing application file
.ppt, .pptx	PowerPoint® file	presentation file
.psd	Photoshop® file	Adobe® Photoshop® internal format
.pub	Publisher file	Microsoft® Publisher file
.rm	audio-video file	Real Player
.wbk	back-up file	Word backup document
.wma	audio file	Windows® Media Player
.wmf	MetaFile	clipart file
.wmv	video file	Windows® Media Player
.xls	Excel® file	Microsoft® spreadsheet file
.zip	compressed data file	Winzip compression utility

G4 GEOGRAPHICAL DOMAIN EXTENSIONS

The following is a list of country codes often seen in email or website addresses. These are added to (or even re-allocated) from time to time. A complete up-to-date listing of country codes can be found on the Internet Society website: www.isoc.org

am	Armenia
aq	Antarctica
ar	Argentina
at	Austria
au	Australia
be	Belgium
bg	Bulgaria
br	Brazil
ca	Canada
ch	Switzerland
cl	Chile
cn	China
co	Colombia
cz	Czech Republic
de	Germany
dk	Denmark
dz	Algeria
ee	Estonia
eg	Egypt
es	Spain
fi	Finland
fr	France
gb	Great Britain (alternative to UK)

gr	Greece
hk	Hong Kong
hr	Croatia
hu	Hungary
id	Indonesia
ie	Ireland
il	Israel
in	India
is	Iceland
it	Italy
jp	Japan
kr	South Korea
li	Liechtenstein
lt	Lithuania
lu	Luxembourg
lv	Latvia
ma	Morocco
mx	Mexico
my	Malaysia
nl	The Netherlands
no	Norway
nz	New Zealand
pe	Peru
pk	Pakistan
pl	Poland
pt	Portugal
ro	Romania
ru	Russia
se	Sweden
sg	Singapore
si	Slovenia
sk	Slovakia
th	Thailand

tr	Turkey
tv	Tuvalu (but widely rented to TV companies)
tw	Taiwan
ua	Ukraine
uk	UK
us	USA, relatively little-used
ve	Venezuela
za	South Africa

See also electronic mail, page 86.

G5 ASCII CODE

The 8-bit ASCII codes following only cover the unaccented characters of English.

Unicode is the standard 16-bit extension of ASCII that allows characters from all the world's alphabets. See www.unicode.org

Decimal value	ASCII character	Usage	Decimal value	ASCII character	Usage	Decimal value	ASCII character	Usage
0	NULL	Fill Character	43	+		86	V	
1	SOH	Start of Header	44	,	Comma	87	W	
2	STX	Start of Text	45	-	Hyphen	88	X	
3	ETX	CTRL-C	46	.		89	Y	
4	EOT	End of Transmission	47	/		90	Z	
5	ENQ	Enquiry	48	0		91	[	
6	ACK	Acknowledge	49	1		92	\	Backslash
7	BEL	BELL	50	2		93	]	
8	BS	Backspace	51	3		94		
9	HT	Horizontal Tab	52	4		95	_	
10	LF	Line Feed	53	5		96	`	Grave accent
11	VT	Vertical Tab	54	6		97	a	
12	FF	FormFeed	55	7		98	b	
13	CR	Carriage Return	56	8		99	c	
14	SO	Shift Out	57	9		100	d	
15	SI	CTRL-O	58	:		101	e	
16	DLE	Data Link Escape	59	;		102	f	
17	DCI	Device Control 1	60	<		103	g	
18	DC2	Device Control 2	61	=		104	h	
19	DC3	Device Control 3	62	>		105	i	
20	DC4	Device Control 4	63	?		106	j	
21	NAK	CTRL-U	64	@		107	k	

Decimal value	ASCII character	Usage	Decimal value	ASCII character	Usage	Decimal value	ASCII character	Usage
22	SYN	Synchronous Idle	65	A		108	l	
23	ETB	End of Transmission Block	66	B		109	m	
24	CAN	Cancel	67	C		110	n	
25	EM	End of Medium	68	D		111	o	
26	SUB	CTRL-Z	69	E		112	p	
27	ESC	Escape	70	F		113	q	
28	FS	File Separator	71	G		114	r	
29	GS	Group Separator	72	H		115	s	
30	RS	Record Separator	73	I		116	t	
31	US	Unit Separator	74	J		117	u	
32	SP	Space	75	K		118	v	
33	!		76	L		119	w	
34	"		77	M		120	x	
35	#	Hash	78	N		121	y	
36	$		79	O		122	z	
37	%		80	P		123	{	
38	&		81	Q		124	|	Vertical line
39	'	Apostrophe	82	R		125	}	
40	(		83	S		126	~	Tilde
41	)		84	T		127	DEL	Rubout
42	*		85	U				

INDEX

data preparation 109

data privacy 157

data processing (DP) 108

data processor 5, 287

data protection 156–157

Data Protection Act 1998 155, 157–158

data representation 255–331
    numeric data 332–263

data retrieval 94

data security 156–165

data structure 257

data subject 157

data terminator 199

data transmission 346

data transmission rate 344

data type 263
    numeric 270
    user-defined 263

data warehouse 107

data-processing manager 150

database 93
    distributed 95
    hierarchical 95, 96
    object-oriented 96–97
    relational 97

database administrator (DBA) 150

database management system (DBMS) 93, 94, 95

database manager 150

database server 135

datagrams 347

date data 198, 263

daughterboard 335

DBA (database administrator) 150

DBMS (database management system) 93, 94, 95

DDL (data description language) 97

DDoS (distributed denial of service) 92

deadlock 234

deadly embrace 234

debit card 115

debugger 229

debugging 229

debugging tools 229

decay 407

decimal tab 377

deciphering 164

decision box 222

decision support specialist 150

decision support system (DSS) 430

decision symbol 222

decision table 220, 221

declaration 213

declarative language 244

decoding 164

decollate 322

decommissioning 41

decomposition 26

decorative font 373

decryption 164

decryption key 164

deep web 64, 91

default 16–17

default option 16, 193–194

default value 16

defrag 183

defragmentation 183

deinstall 20

delta compression 390

demodulation 353

denary notation 266

denial of service (DoS) 92

dependencies 40

derived class 189

DES (Data Encryption Standard) 164

design
    modular 45
    object-oriented 46
    systems 34

design methodology 33

desktop 420

desktop computer 289

desktop publishing (DTP) 368–369

destructor 189

DEUCE 288

developer 149
    website 150

development cycle
    software 32–33
    system 32

developmental testing 42–43

device 6

DFD (data flow diagram) 49–50

DHTML (dynamic HTML) 248

diagnostic aids 229

diagnostic program 229

dial-up connection 75

dialogue box 422

dictionary 371

differential backup 116

digital 287

digital camera 397

digital camera storage 398

digital certificate 159–160

digital computer 289–290

digital divide 22

digital literacy (DL) 22

digital plotter 321

digital sampler 344

digital sensor 120

digital signal 343

digital signature 159

digital sound system 414

digital still imaging 397–401

digital subscriber line (DSL) 75

digital synthesiser 412

digital versatile disc (DVD) 303

digital video 398–401

digital video camera 398

digital video disc (DVD) 303

Digital Video (DV) format 399

digital-to-analog (D-to-A) converter 344

digitising 344

dimension 259

dip switch 339

direct access 274

direct addressing 327

direct changeover 35

direct memory access (DMA) 328

directive 218

directory 11, 423
    data 95
    root 423

directory file 423

disassembler 178

discussion forum 66

disinfection 166

disk 300
    compact disc 303
    computer 300
    digital versatile disc 303
    hard 300
    installation 168–169
    key 169